Management of Pastoral Development in the Third World

A WILEY SERIES ON
PUBLIC ADMINISTRATION IN DEVELOPING
COUNTRIES

MANAGEMENT OF PASTORAL DEVELOPMENT IN THE THIRD
WORLD
By Stephen Sandford: Overseas Development Institute

LOCAL GOVERNMENT IN THE THIRD WORLD
The Experience of Tropical Africa
edited by P. Mawhood: University of Birmingham

FINANCING REGIONAL GOVERNMENT
International Practices and their Relevance to the Third World
By K. J. Davey: University of Birmingham

Management of Pastoral Development in the Third World

Stephen Sandford

*Published in association with the
Overseas Development Institute, London*

JOHN WILEY & SONS

Chichester · New York · Brisbane · Toronto · Singapore

Library of Congress Cataloging in Publication Data:

Sandford, Stephen.
   Management of pastoral development in the third world.

   (Public administration in developing countries)
   'Published in association with the Overseas Development Institute, London.'
   Includes index.
   1. Underdeveloped areas — Range management.
   2. Underdeveloped areas — Livestock. 3. Rural development. I. Title. II. Series.
SF85.43.S26 1982   333.74'15'091724   82-17323

ISBN 0 471 90085 0 (U.S.)

British Library Cataloguing in Publication Data:

Sandford, Stephen
   Management of pastoral development in the third world.
   — (Public administration in developing countries)
   1.   Underdeveloped areas — Agriculture
   — Economic aspects — Management
   I. Title. II. Series.
   338.1'09172'4   HD1417

ISBN 0 471 90085 0

Phototypeset by Input Typesetting Ltd., London
Printed by Pitman Press Ltd., Bath

*To
Pippa*

Contents

Preface

I am indebted to several hundred people who, through discussion and their writings, have contributed to the ideas and information set out in this book. Clearly I cannot mention them all by name, but I take this opportunity of expressing my thanks particularly to the 600 members of ODI's Pastoral Network who have, through friendship, encouragement, and direct assistance, made the completion of the work possible. In almost all cases I have given details of the sources of my information. In a very few glaring instances I have not, sometimes not even mentioning the country concerned because to do so would cause embarrassment and compromise my source to an unjustifiable degree. Nevertheless, even though anonymous, the cases seem sufficiently interesting to deserve description although readers will have to rely solely on my integrity for evidence that they are genuine.

A few people have contributed to an outstanding degree. Berhanu Wakwaya and Robert Wood, as heads of the Ethiopian Government's Livestock and Meat Board (LMB) in Addis Ababa and the Overseas Development Institute (ODI) in London respectively, gave me the opportunity to study pastoral development and unstinting support while I did so. The British Government, through its Ministry of Overseas Development (later Overseas Development Administration), provided financial support over a long period. The Leverhulme Trust Fund provided a generous grant between 1979 and 1981.

My brother, Dick Sandford, Brian Hartley, and Gudrun Dahl have opened my eyes to how fascinating is the study of pastoralism. Gudrun Dahl and Guy Hunter have done more than others to try to teach me how to understand pastoral societies and the management and organization of agricultural development respectively. My colleagues in the Project Office of LMB and the Agricultural Administration Unit at ODI have been generous in their encouragement, assistance, support, and tolerance. R. M. Edelston, Bill Ferguson, Brendan Halpin, Guy Hunter, Ian Lane, Allan Low, Alec McCallum, Clare Oxby, Denys Rollinson, and Dick Sandford have given their time to reading and commenting on substantial sections of the book. Margaret Cornell has struggled hard to bring clarity into the original text. Valerie Campling and Christine Palmer typed the final version with great speed and accuracy. Christine Palmer has provided much other support in publication. To all of them I am immensely grateful. No one but I bears any responsibility for the remaining follies and faults. My involvement with pastoral development for over a decade would not have been possible without the love, support, and understanding of my wife, Pippa Sandford, to whom this book is dedicated.

STEPHEN SANDFORD

Chapter one
The physical and analytic framework

PASTORALISTS AND THEIR ENVIRONMENT

Pastoralists are people who derive most of their income or sustenance from keeping domestic livestock in conditions where most of the feed that their livestock eat is natural forage rather than cultivated fodders and pastures. In most cases, also, pastoralists devote the bulk of their own, and their families', working time and energy to looking after their livestock rather than to other economic activities. This study is concerned with those pastoralists who live at least part of each year in arid and semi-arid areas where rainfall is too low to permit profitable rain-fed crop farming under current economic and technical conditions. Pastoral *areas* are areas used by pastoralists and *pastoralism* is the term used to describe their way of life and their economic and land-use systems. The term *pastoral situation* is used in this book to denote a particular conjunction of pastoral people and land at a particular period of time. The tribe A in country P at time X represent one situation, the same tribe in the same country at a different time Y another. The tribe A in another country R at time X represent yet a third pastoral situation.

The term 'pastoralists', when defined in this way, will, of course, include absentee shareholders in commercial ranches who may spend all their time in the rich cities of the world, as well as those who keep pigs, ducks, and reindeer under the conditions stated. But, although the definition of the term is very wide, this study is mainly about the pastoral societies in the Third World countries of Asia and Africa whose main forms of livestock are sheep, goats, cattle, and camels. The definition is left wide, for too restrictive a definition leads to unprofitable semantic quibbles which prevent useful lessons being learnt from the experiences of groups who fall outside the definition. Some definitional difficulties remain in the case of people inhabiting the areas on the physical boundaries between pastoral and cultivating regions, who practise both cultivation and extensive keeping of livestock, and whose relative emphasis on these two activities changes from season to season and year to year in response to climatic and other conditions. These difficulties arise not only in deciding how these people should be classified in occupational statistics but also where the appropriate development of their cultivating activities might lead to measures at variance with the development of their pastoral ones. A further definitional difficulty arises over whether a study of pastoral development should also include a concern for finding and improving pastoralists' opportunities in non-pastoral areas and occupations.

1

The tendency in this study will be to concentrate detailed attention only on pastoralists' livestock activities.

The arid and semi-arid areas[1] of the earth, which together I call 'dry' areas or regions, cover some 50 million km^2 or 35 per cent of the earth's land surface area (Mundlak and Singer, 1975, p. 21), with a total human population of 500–600 million people. Of this total some 30–40 million are believed to have 'animal-based' economies, and the majority of these are pastoralists. Within the 30–40 million, 50–60 per cent are found in Africa, 25–30 per cent in Asia, 15 per cent in all of America, and less than 1 per cent in Australia. These figures, however, are subject to wide margins of error, since, even in countries with quite well-developed statistical services, different estimates vary very widely due to differences in definition of terms as well as to difficulties in counting. In terms of the number of pastoralists, the most important single countries are (in rough order of numbers) Sudan, USA, Somalia, Chad, Ethiopia, Kenya, Mali, Mauritania, India, and China, each with about 1 million or more pastoralists including men, women, and children (Sandford, 1976a; UNCOD, 1977a; UNCOD, 1977d).[2]

Many people believe that pastoral groups are gradually disappearing and that pastoralism is dying out as a way of life as people move into the cultivation of crops and other economic activities; and some people believe this trend to be not only inevitable but also desirable, a move from a lower, more primitive, to a higher, more civilized, way of life. In fact, the direction of this trend, as with many other trends, depends on where you measure it and from what point in time. In North America and Australia there are more pastoralists, and pastoralism is more important now in the economy than 200 years ago, but less than 50 years ago. In most other countries with pastoral populations pastoralism represents a lower *proportion* of total economic activity now than it did 50 years ago owing to the relatively more rapid growth of other sectors; but it is much more difficult to say what has happened to the *number* of pastoralists. For two contradictory tendencies have been at work, a natural growth rate in the population being countered by an emigration out of pastoralism into non-pastoral activities. What the balance, in terms of absolute numbers, has been between the two forces is in most cases obscure, because of both practical difficulties in counting and definitional problems in saying where the boundary between pastoralism and non-pastoralism lies. While in many countries pastoralists have become less nomadic and some land previously used by them is no longer accessible to them, there is little evidence that on a world scale the absolute number of people dependent on livestock has decreased. If one looks at the history of many dry areas, not over decades but over centuries, one sees not a trend in a single direction but an ebb and flow of pastoral and non-pastoral people and activities as political, economic, and natural conditions changed. This study is based on the belief that although great changes will and should take place in the ways in which pastoralists live, and although some areas now used for pastoralism will change to other forms of land-use, nevertheless most of the areas which are pastoral at present will continue to be so in the future and many millions of people will continue to be pastoralists. The study examines ways in which development can best take place for the benefit of these pastoralists and of other members of the nation state in which they are situated.

Pastoralists in dry areas use their livestock to harvest and convert solar energy captured and fixed in plants into products useful to man. For in these regions it is generally impossible, or at least uneconomic, to convert it directly to man's use through the medium of grain, legume, and oil crops as is done in more fertile areas; and conversion through livestock allows a higher level of production and of human population than do the alternative techniques of hunters and gatherers. Plant growth requires adequate sunlight, soil nutrients, and water; and while dry areas may have plenty of the first two, by definition they lack the last. Plant production expressed in terms of yields per hectare, therefore, is low. Pastoralists use their livestock to harvest and process these low yields into useful products more economically than can be done by hand or machine; and pastoral societies and systems of land-use are adaptations to local natural environments (and also to local political and economic conditions) whereby the yield of plant production can be exploited. Inheritance, marriage, and property laws regulate the combination of different species of livestock with water, land, labour, and other resources, and livestock and people move from place to place in such a way as to maintain the efficiency and security of the harvesters and processers and of the labour that tends them. This is not to claim that the actual social and land-use system in force in any pastoral situation is the only possible one or necessarily the best from all points of view; only that, unless it is a very recent arrival, or unless there has been some dramatic change in circumstances, it is at least not a chance freak of nature that any hasty and ill-thought change is as likely to improve on as to injure. 'Order out of chaos' is how one recent publication (Pratt and Gwynne, 1977, p. 76) describes the change from a traditional pastoral system of land-use to one prescribed by range-management experts. Nothing could be further from the truth.

Two factors dominate pastoralists' use of land in dry areas. The first is the extreme variability of rainfall, and therefore of grazing, that occurs between different years in the same place, and between different places with the same long-term average rainfall in the same year. An area that produces twice as much grazing as another in one year may produce only a quarter as much in the next. By the following year again the original relative positions may have been more than restored. To these variations caused by rainfall, other accidents such as disease or theft may be added. The second factor is regular intra-year seasonal differences in the relative productivity, and so attractiveness for livestock, of different areas. In some cases, as in the Horn of East Africa, this may be due to the different timing of the rainy seasons. In other cases, as in Iran and other parts of South-West Asia, the differences are due to temperature — to extreme cold on the mountains in winter and baking heat in the lowlands in summer. In yet other cases the differences are due to variations in type of soil, in liability to flooding, or the activities of cultivators which mean that grazing becomes available or persists at different times in adjacent areas. Pastoralists' usual response to these mainly uncontrollable factors has been one of opportunistic flexibility, of risk-spreading, and of mobility of livestock and people.

Pastoralists spread their risks in several ways. They may keep several different species of livestock (cattle, camels, sheep, goats) each with their own needs, strengths, and weaknesses. They may keep several different holdings of the same species in different places so that they will not all be struck simultaneously by the same disaster. Different members of a family or interdependent group may follow different occupations (livestock-keeping, crafts, agriculture, wage-labour) and share their earnings. Finally, pastoralists tend to maintain a network of social relations whereby the losses and gains suffered by particular individuals can be shared out, through a series of obligations and counter-obligations, over a wide circle of people. This network of social relations, therefore, plays the same role as an insurance policy in the industrial world.

DEVELOPMENT, MANAGEMENT, AND ORGANIZATION: SOME FURTHER DEFINITIONS

What should *development* mean in a pastoral context in the Third World? At this point it is enough to define it loosely so as to include the conscious pursuit of certain objectives with a view to increasing welfare. Chapter 2 will examine in greater detail whose welfare and what objectives should be pursued in different circumstances. Clearly, development involves some change; usually it involves technical as well as economic change, and the scope for new techniques is discussed from Chapter 4 onwards. But social and political change will also often be desirable, indeed without it technical and economic change may be impossible. At the same time, much that is of great value in the existing social structures of pastoral societies is not found, or has been destroyed, elsewhere. Pastoral societies are often, probably usually, well adapted to their physical environment, have effective social security systems for supporting the less fortunate, and provide a set of coherent beliefs and moral values, participatory social organizations and a social identity for the individual that contrasts sharply with the perplexity, alienation, and aimlessness found elsewhere. Social anthropologists have done much to demonstrate how practices and institutions among pastoralists that seem quaint, or based on ignorance or superstition, perform much the same functions as the state organization and bureaucracies in the supposedly more rational industrial world. Any sensible development policy will strive not only to provide better material standards of living for the pastoralists and to ensure that the pastoral areas supply some of the commodities needed by the nation as a whole, but also to conserve these traditional desirable social features or to replace them by an adequate substitute. Development, therefore, may mean change of all sorts, but should also include the deliberate conservation of what is valuable in the present.

Management is an elastic term which we shall look at again in more detail in Chapter 3. It may include some fundamental policy-making and planning which can be termed design. It also includes more specific short-term planning of the future provision of resources, such as annual budgeting in a government organization or attracting additional members to a pastoral encampment to share the burden of herding and watering. It covers organizing existing resources, for example sending field staff to the places where they are most needed or ensuring that someone will take the goat flock out tomorrow morning; and also reviewing operations from time to time to evaluate performance, for example listening to or preparing a monthly report, or checking the cattle as they return to camp in the evening. The relationship between management and *organization* needs elaboration. In one sense organization is the act of organizing, but a *social organization* is any durable grouping of more than one person with a common or definite purpose.

The design and management of new development cannot be viewed in isolation from those aspects of pastoral life which already exist. To take an obvious example, one cannot run a sensible range-management programme based on the construction of new water points if one ignores the old ones. Similarly, one cannot effectively put limits for the first time on the total number of livestock to be kept in an area without changing the rules of private property for the allocation of livestock between individuals in a clan or family. One cannot change the rules about the rotation of pastures without at the same time affecting the access of individual animals to the particular minerals contained in the grazing or water of those pastures. One cannot, in effect, just design and manage *new* technical features and expect everything else to carry on unchanged. This does not mean that government itself should try to intervene directly in all aspects of the management of pastoral life. Indeed, one of the main themes in this book is that governments cannot effectively do even those things which have hitherto been regarded as falling within their portfolios. What it does mean is that there is no clear-cut boundary at which the management of 'development' stops; and that if government wants the activities which it initiates to succeed it must provide a framework of laws, incentives, and organizations in which individuals and non-government organizations can effectively manage those aspects of pastoral life which government cannot or should not itself direct, in a way that is consistent with overall development policy. At the moment in many countries there are obvious contradictions in the policies pursued by different government departments, or even inside the same department, which frustrate the achievement of development objectives.

THE VALIDITY OF MODELS AND PRESCRIPTIONS

Certainly pastoral development should not mean slavishly trying to copy the American, Russian, Australian, or Chinese models. In much of the developing world where the influence of Western training and technical and financial assistance is strong, attempts to develop the pastoral sector have looked very much like attempts to copy the (North) American or Australian models of pastoral development. There has been a very strong emphasis on the production of beef, on commercial ranching,[3] on the specialized stratification of the production process in breeding, growing, and finishing enterprises, on auction markets, on processing facilities. Many of these elements may, in fact, be sensible enough, but the overall packages seem not to be tailor-made for particular circumstances but to be a reflection of an ideal of what pastoral development is about. The same also appears to happen in the Eastern bloc where, at any rate in its early days, pastoral reorganization in Mongolia largely followed the Soviet model (Lattimore, 1962, pp. 122–147). The American and Australian models are particularly unsuitable for most developing countries, originating as they did in peculiar historical settings where the interests of the previous inhabitants of pastoral areas were not taken into account, where the species of domestic livestock on which pastoral development focused did not previously exist on a significant scale if at all, where the general economy as a whole was characterized by labour shortage rather than by surplus, and where a large and wealthy non-pastoral sector could be called on from time to time to provide the resources with which to rebuild a pastoral sector suffering from collapse. Both the American and Australian pastoral sectors have been characterized during their brief existence by considerable environmental damage and economic instability. The Eastern bloc models also have still not solved the basic problems of making the herdsman give as much attention to communally- or state-owned livestock as he would if they were his own property.[4] Moreover, the initial social costs of reorganizing the pastoral sector along socialist lines have been enormous in terms of both human lives and livestock numbers (Caroe, 1953; Krader, 1955, p. 320).

Sensible pastoral development does not involve the wholesale adoption of stereotyped models; nor is it just a matter of devising a locally acceptable social framework within which to impose universal technical solutions. Neither the institutional framework nor the technical changes to be adopted are uniquely right. In pastoral development there are a number of choices to be made. One set of choices is between what the ultimate ends of development are, a choice between different *objectives*. In a particular pastoral situation, for example, should more emphasis be given to making the pastoral area a cheap and reliable source of meat for the nation's urban consumers or to creating within it sufficient opportunities for all its pastoral population to continue to make their living there? Another set of options relates to different *strategies* for the use of pastoral areas. Should, for example, emphasis be put on stability of livestock numbers or should they be allowed to fluctuate so as to be able to take advantage of periods of favourable climate? A third set of options relates to the particular changes or development *components* which should be introduced in a development programme. Should the land-tenure system, for example, be reformed? Is a new breed of sheep required? A final set of options relates to how the pastoral system should be *organized* and *managed*. Should, for example, government compel the pastoralists in a mandatory way to adopt new techniques or should it only try to persuade them, in a liberal way, by extension and demonstration? Should an animal health service be supplied only by government or should private veterinarians be permitted to practise? Or should groups of pastoralists train and employ one of their own members to provide them with an animal health service? This study sets out to show the criteria on which one should judge the appropriateness of choice and the particular circumstances under which one alternative is likely to be more appropriate than another.

I believe that from this study it will be possible to deduce how pastoral development should be carried out in a particular situation. We need to consider the question of why one should believe that these prescriptions are correct, and this resolves itself into the two further questions — 'What sort of conditions in general do we believe have to be fulfilled for a prescription to be valid?' and 'Have these criteria been fulfilled in this instance?' When it comes to technical and economic recommendations the situation is clear enough; for there are adequately developed and sufficiently well-known bodies of theory and techniques for appraising particular situations to guide us (e.g. theories concerning plant nutrient requirements and techniques for carrying out fertilizer trials). With recommendations about management and organization the situation is much more difficult both because theory is less well developed and because in the field of agricultural development we have only just started thinking about how to apply it to particular situations.[5]

Many of us are familiar enough with the situation in which one distinguished authority says, for example, 'The proper way to organise Range Management within the Ministry of Agriculture is for it to report direct to the top', or 'Pastoralists must be subject to strict government-imposed discipline which must be rigidly enforced', while another equally distinguished authority recommends a different government structure and that pastoralists should be allowed to make their own rules, which will (it is alleged) be both more appropriate and more authoritative for having been the object of pastoralists' participation. One authority may speak more persuasively than the other so that we are compelled to agree with him. But what objective reasons can we have for doing so? I believe we need to spell out in some detail the process by which we come to make organizational recommendations so that their validity can be tested in the same sort of way as we test recommendations in other spheres. We need not arbitrary rules of thumb but a statement of hypotheses and the conclusions drawn from them.

I believe that there are few, if any, universally valid prescriptions which can be applied to all pastoral situations, nor even prescriptions which can be applied to broad categories of such situations. I do not, for example, believe that one set of prescriptions applies to all 'arid overcrowded' situations and another to 'semi-arid and underpopulated' ones. Situations do not fall into such natural categories nor are they normally characterized by either having or not having some attribute such as aridity. Categorization, rather, is imposed by the mind of the observer, and there is no limit to the number of fresh criteria for categorization (e.g. population pressure, aridity, *and* accessibility) and hence categories that can be dreamt up; and the important characteristics are not discrete attributes ('with' or 'without') but variations along a scale. The appropriate set of prescriptions for development will be unique to each situation, and the purpose of this study is not, therefore, to provide a prescription of how to organize pastoral development in types of situations but, rather, to throw light on those factors which people planning and managing pastoral development need to bear in mind in taking decisions; it is up to them to decide to what extent and how the factors apply to their own situation. These factors I identify as follows: an overall vision of what the world can and should be like, the characteristics of the particular pastoral situation, and the availability of opportunities for technical, economic, or social change (hereinafter 'instruments') in that situation.

AN ANALYTIC STRUCTURE

This study attempts to establish an analytic structure in which it can be shown how different factors affect the way in which pastoral development programmes are likely to turn out and what choices should be made. The structure has three key elements. First, if one has a certain vision of what the world can and should be like — essentially a vision that believes that mankind can control its own destiny — then the different characteristics of pastoral situations will tend to make one want particular objectives. These characteristics, which will be further explained shortly, may give rise to contradictory tendencies. For example, the physical characteristics of an area may make it very vulnerable to environmental degradation and so make one want to pursue a policy that stresses caution and conservation of resources; but at the same time the acute poverty and isolation of its people may compel one to exploit the natural resources as intensively and as quickly as possible. Second, a government's instruments for pursuing its pastoral objectives lie in altering the general economic and social background of the nation, in incorporating particular components in pastoral development programmes, and in manipulating the way in which those programmes are managed and organized. Third, there are certain beliefs about the effects of these components, how these effects are modified by the characteristics of the pastoral situations, and how the components have certain organizational and management requirements. These requirements are, in turn, modified by the characteristics of the pastoral situation, and similarly the way in which the components are managed and organized affects their results.

These three elements of the analytic structure are composed of a multitude of propositions, some about the physical effects of physical events, e.g. the degree of immunization conferred by rinderpest vaccination, some about the factors affecting the behaviour of individual people, some about the way in which organizations as a whole behave. Some are almost of a metaphysical nature; for example, that if one is concerned for the poor one will wish to provide them with opportunities for making a living. The source and the strength of the evidence behind the various propositions which will be presented in this study vary enormously. Some of them are based on experiences of other kinds of rural development, or indeed of human behaviour generally. Some are based on my own direct experience working on behalf of governments in Botswana, Ethiopia, and Kenya. But the main basis has been a comparison of experiences with pastoral development in a large number of countries. This comparison was made from conversations, from written records, and from quite short visits to Iran, Afghanistan, India, Tanzania, and Nigeria.

In recent years attempts have been made to test hypotheses/propositions about organization and management in the agricultural sector of Third World countries by the use of quantitative indices of management variables and performance and of statistical techniques for examining relationships. Leonard (1977) has done this in respect of agricultural extension work in Kenya, and Gow *et al.* (1979) in respect of local organizations and rural development in a cross-country comparison. These attempts improve the precision of the statements it is possible to make about the validity of hypotheses, *given certain assumptions*, but at the cost, particularly I believe in the case of Gow *et al.*, of too great a trust that the quantitative indices really reflect what one hopes they do. At any rate in this study it was not possible, nor thought to be desirable, to use quantitative techniques. In the case of only very few of the propositions I put forward is it possible to say that the evidence in favour of a proposition is conclusive. In many cases it is very weak and the proposition is no more than a preliminary hypothesis put forward in the hope that it may provoke other people to review further evidence and to test it. But neither now nor in the future do I think that the material is of a kind which will submit to normal statistical techniques. The methodology involved is more akin to that of a historian, shuffling pieces of evidence around like parts in a jigsaw puzzle until a coherent and consistent pattern emerges. What the study aims to do is to challenge some of the ways in which people now think about pastoral development and to put forward some alternative suggestions that together form a coherent view of pastoral development.

Characteristics

Reference has already been made several times to the characteristics of pastoral situations; and to the way in which these characteristics affect the choice of objectives, the managerial and organizational requirements of development components, and the results which these components are likely to have. These characteristics are seen as being relatively unsusceptible to change by pastoral development programmes and can therefore be regarded as fixed rather than open to manipulation. Clearly, there are a near-infinite number of characteristics which may have some small effect in one way or another. But in trying to find broad patterns on which some comprehensible general theorizing can be based we must concentrate on a few key characteristics whose influence is very strong and which are important in several different ways. Some of these characteristics may mark off pastoral from non-pastoral situations, while in other cases they distinguish different pastoral situations from each other; and we can broadly define these characteristics into three groups — physical, social and economic, and political.

Among the most important *physical* characteristics are the timing, scarcity, and unreliability of rainfall and temperature; the susceptibility of the soil to erosion; the accessibility of the area to modern forms of transport; the physical potential for the development of irrigated or rain-fed agriculture. Among the main *social and economic* characteristics are the density of the human pastoral population; the degree of dependence of this population on its livestock both for income and for basic consumption goods; the ease and terms of trade with which livestock products can be exchanged for other goods; the degree of mobility of the human population and their livestock; and the nature of the existing social and economic system, e.g. the system of property rights in land, water, livestock, and labour, the system of social values, and the nature of the social organizations. (Of course some of these characteristics, e.g. systems of property rights, *can* be changed, but such change usually comes from political events and changes in the balance of power at the *national* level, and is not susceptible to change by particular or specifically pastoral development programmes. For our purposes they can, therefore, often be regarded as characteristics rather than instruments open to manipulation.) Among the important *political* characteristics are the relative sizes and rates of growth of the pastoral and non-pastoral populations in the nation as a whole; the present and past political relations of pastoralists with non-pastoralists and with the national government; and the degree to which a pastoral population straddles national boundaries and hence is regarded as a threat to the integrity of the state.

Clearly, the different characteristics are often not independent of each other. For example, pastoral groups may be highly nomadic for a combination of physical, socio-economic, and political reasons. What is important, however, is to see the way in which variations between the characteristics of two different areas will influence the choice of the sort of development programme which should be undertaken.

THE STATE OF THE RANGELANDS

A study that claims to have something to say about the appropriate way to carry out pastoral development is bound to be coloured by views about ecological trends in rangelands, about the causes of these trends and about the availability of technology to deal with them. There was a time when I believed, like many other concerned people, that the world's rangelands are suffering severe and rapid desertification. As this study has progressed, however, I have become increasingly sceptical about the general validity of this popular view — hereinafter called the Mainstream view. The Mainstream view is still held by a majority of those professionally concerned with the subject matter, i.e. academics and officials in national or international organizations, but not often by pastoralists. Over the last decade, however, a number of studies have begun to demonstrate how complex is the phenomenon of desertification and how uncertain the direction of any trend (see especially Horowitz, 1979; Breman *et al.*, 1979/80; Peyre de Fabregues, 1971; UNCOD, 1977c). The rest of this chapter will briefly review the main elements in the Mainstream view, what I believe to be the grounds for scepticism about it, and the consequences that often follow from holding it. There is no space here for a full review of the evidence; that will have to take place on another occasion elsewhere. It is not my purpose to show that desertification is *not* taking place, or that the cited causes cannot have the supposed effects; but only that the evidence and the arguments are so weak that no substantial reliance should be put on them, especially when such reliance is likely to injure the interests of weaker sections of society.

The main elements in the Mainstream view

As we have said, the Mainstream view holds that most of the world's rangelands are suffering from desertification and that, although in some cases unwise attempts to cultivate rangelands have been the culprit, in most cases the cause of desertification is overgrazing by domestic animals. Desertification has speeded up during the last century and overgrazing is due to an increase in the density of livestock, partly caused by a decline in the area of rangelands but mainly by an absolute increase in livestock numbers. This increase in livestock numbers is, in turn, attributed to one or more of a number of causes acting alone or in conjunction with each other. One cause is an increase in the number of pastoralists and this triggers both a demand for more livestock to support the extra pastoralists and also a greater supply of herding labour to look after the extra stock. Another cause is thought to be an improvement in veterinary medicine and services which has reduced or eradicated many of the previous causes of livestock mortality and thus removed the main limitation to the growth of livestock populations. A third cause is thought to be traditional economic and social systems which place a very high social value on the accumulation of livestock numbers rather than, for example, on the economic value of output from these livestock or on environmental conservation. Fourthly, it is believed by some people (e.g. Bonte, 1976) that the penetration of the international capitalist economy into pre-capitalist economic systems has led to the breakdown of previous self-regulatory mechanisms and an excessive pressure to increase both livestock and numbers and output.

Most proponents of the Mainstream view also hold that the technology is available with which to combat desertification, but that the principal reason why this technology is not applied is, once again, traditional economic and social systems, including systems of land tenure and the social institutions which accompany them. In particular, blame is put on communal grazing systems in which there is felt to be an inherent contradiction between private and public interests, because ownership and rights to use livestock are vested in individuals but the livestock consume forage on land which belongs to the community as a whole. In such circumstances, the individual livestock owner has a continuous incentive to increase the number of his own livestock even when this increase damages the communal grazing and land, because the damage is shared by the community at large, whereas the individual obtains a greater proportion of the total grazing through increasing his herd and the benefits from this increased proportion outweigh his share of the loss. This supposed inherent contradiction between private and public interest and the consequential overgrazing has been termed the 'Tragedy of the Commons' (Hardin, 1977a).

Some problems with the Mainstream view

There are a number of difficulties and uncertainties with the Mainstream view. One of these is that it is not at all certain that desertification, in spite of all the public alarm, is actually taking place on a great scale (Horowitz, 1979; Valenza, 1973; Peyre de Fabregues, 1971; Mortimore, 1978, pp. 35–39; Jacobs, 1977, pp. 2–3; Spencer, 1973). Part of the problem arises from differences between different definitions of desertification (Overseas Development Institute, 1977). One definition is that desertification is any change in the state, in terms of composition (by species) or quantity (biomass or ground cover), of the vegetation away from that which would be the case in the absence of any use of the land or vegetation by man or his livestock, away, that is, from what is sometimes called climax vegetation. If one adheres to this definition then desertification has undoubtedly occurred in the last 80–90 years, particularly in Africa, as livestock populations have recovered from the very low levels to which they were reduced by disease epidemics, especially rinderpest, and as previously unutilized areas have been opened up by water development. It is not, however, a very useful definition. Any use by man is likely to modify the climax vegetation, and unless man can use vegetation there may be little reason to conserve it. The climax vegetation in many areas is unproductive bush and it is only heavy use by man and livestock which has brought the land into a productive state (Pratt and Gwynne, 1977, p. 27).

Another way of defining desertification is in terms not of the state of vegetation at a point in time but of its productivity over a period of time. There are practical difficulties in measuring this, and important differences in conclusions can arise from whether one is measuring output in terms of energy content or protein, and whether one is measuring it over the year as a whole or in terms of its availability at critical times within the year (Breman *et al.*, 1979/80).

Part of the problem also arises from differences in the period of time over which desertification is measured. The state and productivity of rangeland vegetation at any time is largely determined by the rainfall in the current year. In arid and semi-arid areas rainfall is highly variable from year to year. The consequent variation in the state and productivity of vegetation far outweighs the effects of any long-term decline in productivity arising, for example, from soil erosion. Most people would not want to call changes brought about by year-to-year variations in rainfall 'desertification', but would want to preserve this expression for long-term declines. There is some respectable evidence for long-term changes in the state of the vegetation but none for long-term changes in productivity.

Most people agree that there is some level of overstocking at which range degradation and desertification take place. Hence it is often concluded that if desertification is taking place it must be due to overgrazing. There is, however, very little agreement in particular situations about what the right level of stocking is. Equally eminent experts can disagree, not by small percentages, but by factors of four or five, about the right stocking rate, and many estimates of overstocking are manifestly absurd because, if true, the livestock concerned would have been dead of starvation long ago rather than, as is simultaneously estimated, growing in number. Those with longest experience of particular range areas — the resident pastoralists — often deny that desertification has taken place or, if it has, that this is a result of overgrazing (Dahl, 1979, pp. 40–41; Botswana, 1977, p. A203).

One of the best-known 'facts' about pastoralism is that livestock populations over the last century have grown to unprecedented size, and with them the pressure on grazing. The real evidence for this is extremely poor. For most dry areas we do not know, within a margin of 30–40 per cent, for even one moment in time what the livestock population is. Mortimore (1978) has stated this of northern Nigeria, a comparatively closely and well-administered country. In any case, the figures are very unstable even over very large areas and quite short periods of time. In huge dry areas of 30,000 km^2 in Ethiopia (Watson *et al.*, 1973: Watson *et al.*, 1974) and Sudan (Hunting and Macdonald, 1976) the same observer, using the same estimation techniques, found, in different rounds of a repetitive survey, that the size of livestock populations varied, over the course of a few months or one or two years at most, by 100 per cent or more. Not only were there big changes, between different rounds of the same survey, in the numbers of each species (camels, cattle, goats, etc.) but both the proportion and even the direction of change varied from round to round between the species. Official estimates of long-term increases in livestock numbers tend to lie in the range between 50 and 250 per cent over 20–60 years. But these increases easily lie within the range of error and variation obtained simply by using different estimating techniques or different starting-points within a short period of a year or two. Livestock populations probably have grown; it would be unwise to rely on the statistics to prove this.

It is not so much changes in livestock numbers *per se* but rather changes in livestock density, i.e. numbers per unit area, that determine changes in the degree of overgrazing. In many countries either improvements in internal security or the development of new water supplies have opened up new areas to grazing. To some extent a growing livestock population has been faced not with constant or contracting but with expanding boundaries for its grazing. In Botswana both the area accessible to grazing and the number of cattle increased (allegedly) about two and a half times between 1965 and 1976 (Sandford, 1977a, pp. B16–B18). In Sudan the number of livestock quadrupled between 1937 and 1966, but the number of watering sites more than quadrupled (Sudan, 1976, p. 57), thereby alleviating the increase in grazing pressure. To some extent, especially in Africa, increases in the populations of domestic livestock have been matched by declines in the wildlife population. Domestic livestock and wildlife in part complement each other in their grazing habits (Western, 1973) and in part compete. To the extent that they compete, the increased grazing pressure from domestic livestock has been offset by declining pressure from wildlife.

The view that domestic livestock populations, especially in Africa, have reached unprecedented sizes derives partly from official statistics, partly from a feeling that now that many livestock diseases have been overcome by modern veterinary science there is nothing to control the continuous growth in population except starvation, and this occurs only after irreparable damage to the vegetation has been caused by overgrazing. In Africa rinderpest during the last 100 years has been by far the major killer disease; but it arrived there either for the first time, or at any rate in a new more virulent form, in the second half of the nineteenth century, moving south especially from 1885 onwards (Felton and Ellis, 1978, p. 3), often killing 80–90 per cent of domestic livestock populations. Its arrival frequently coincided with or slightly predated colonial rule so that the collection of livestock statistics started at a time of a peculiarly reduced population from which the growth thereafter has been, in part at least, simply a rebound. The only livestock disease which veterinary science, at any rate in the dry areas, has significantly defeated is rinderpest. Veterinary science has, therefore, found a new way of bypassing a control on livestock numbers, but the control itself is a new one. Before we conclude too definitely that overgrazing has been caused by the unprecedented growth in livestock numbers made possible by veterinary science we need to ask ourselves what controlled livestock numbers in Africa prior to the mid-nineteenth century.

Unfortunately, as regards the assessment of both desertification and growth in livestock numbers, the wide extent of the agreement about what is happening has now begun to affect the evidence itself, so that the two are mutually reinforcing. When the initial evidence in a particular situation does not support the conventional view it is regarded with suspicion and, in the best of faith, given the difficulties and uncertainties in the methodology of assessment, the evidence is then adjusted so as not to give a misleading impression, i.e. it is altered to come in line with the expected conclusions. The fact of this adjustment is then lost sight of, and the adjusted evidence is treated as fresh independent support for the Mainstream view. For example, in the early 1970s in Botswana the raw data on the size of the cattle population did not reveal the usual and expected rate of growth. There had been some experimentation with data collection methods and this was felt to have disturbed the reliability of reporting, so an increasing 'under-enumeration factor' was then built into the calculations but not reported when the final figures were published. (Source: Botswana Government officials.) In the same way, in the preparation of one of the country case studies for the 1977 UN Conference on Desertification the field data did not reveal much evidence of desertification and the draft report by the researchers did *not* say that it did. The draft report was then amended at a senior level in the ministry concerned to state that the evidence *did* reveal significant desertification.

The Mainstream view's distrust of traditional economic and social systems springs from two main sources. The writings, half a century ago, of the anthropologist Herskovits (1926) on the East African cattle complex have made many people believe that pastoralists' desire to accumulate large herds of livestock is not based on rational grounds related to their own material welfare, and that only a fundamental change in pastoralists' social values, and in their traditional institutions which reflect and support those values, can lead to a more rational emphasis on environmental conservation and material welfare. Allied to this suspicion of irrationality is the Mainstream view's overwhelming concern with control over and stabilization of livestock numbers. Most pastoral societies do not have institutions which directly regulate the size of their members' herds. In Chapter 2 we shall discuss whether stabilization of livestock numbers is always a sensible policy. Here we can note that the fact that proponents of the Mainstream view believe that stabilization is essential, and that pastoral societies usually do not, is the major cause of the former's poor opinion of the latter. Recent work by natural scientists (e.g. Brown, 1971; Western, 1973), social anthropologists (e.g. Dahl and Hjort, 1976), and economists (e.g. Fukuda, 1976; Livingstone,

1977) has done something to restore the image of the individual pastoralist as a rational person, but not much to show that the institutions and organizations of pastoral society at a level above the individual household are competent to ensure good management of the natural environment.

The Mainstream view is confident that the technology exists to prevent and repair desertification, and sees the reason why this technology is not applied as lying in economic and especially social 'constraints' (Ormerod, 1977). The techniques of range management and soil conservation will be discussed in more detail in later chapters (especially Chapter 5). Here we can note that considerable research to devise appropriate technology to stop desertification has taken place in the USA, the USSR, India, Israel, and possibly in China, but very much less elsewhere, especially in Africa south of the Sahara. In Africa, in particular, heavy reliance is put on technology and technical expertise developed in the USA. It is not very difficult to stop the spread of sand-dunes by very heavy expenditure and by preventing all access by livestock. But there is extremely little evidence to suggest that the stocking rates, rests, and rotations recommended for African rangelands on the basis of experience elsewhere enable any more productive or environmentally benign use of Africa's rangelands to be made than do traditional systems.

Some consequences of the Mainstream view

The prevalence of the Mainstream view has had a number of consequences. One has been the haste with which range-management programmes have been introduced. Since, it is thought, the rangelands are deteriorating fast, action must be taken urgently, there is no time for research, and, even if the programmes are not optimal, they are better than a continuation of the present situation. Another consequence is a desire radically to reform land tenure and institutions and organizations concerned with range management rather than to assist existing ones to adapt or to take on new functions. In the process much that is valuable in the existing system is lost and the new institutions and organizations do not cater for a whole range of problems and eventualities with which the old ones had learnt to cope. Organizational models are introduced (e.g. commercial ranches) which were themselves adaptations to the particular circumstances of somewhere else, and which then do not function at all in the new situation. One major problem has been an obsession with the doctrine of the 'Tragedy of the Commons' and a misplaced faith that the private ownership of land is the only answer to the dilemma that the doctrine poses. Seldom is it remembered that the alleged greater efficiency of private over communal land-ownership was initially based on evidence in fertile northern Europe not in arid tropical rangelands, and that in Europe also the social consequences were often dire.

In practice the alleged benefits stemming from the private ownership of grazing land have usually not occurred in dry rangelands. In Angola environmental degradation was worse on private commercial ranches than under the traditional communal system (Cruz de Carvalho, 1974). In Botswana new private ranches are unprofitable, overstocked, and environmentally damaging (Odell, 1980). In the USA the passing of the Taylor Grazing Act in 1934, which on parts of the public rangelands led to the issue of exclusive grazing permits akin to private property rights, was not attended by a stabilization of livestock numbers. Indeed, in a part of south-east Oregon, for example, livestock numbers on these rangelands actually increased by a further 20 per cent over the next 20 years, until a system of direct control by public regulation with penalties for infringement was enforced (Heady and Bartolome, 1977, pp. 25, 32, 64–67 and Tables 3, 11, 12). Neither in the USA nor in Australia have systems of property rights akin to private ownership of land led to a control and stabilization of livestock numbers at the level which range scientists believe to be right. But this lack of evidence for the proposition that private ownership of land leads to its better management has not diminished the clamour in favour of private ownership which is based on ideological rather than empirical grounds. We shall consider this matter more fully in Chapter 6.

A further consequence of the Mainstream view is an astonishing inhumanity towards the destitute of pastoral societies. Some documents explicitly refer to the folly of famine relief (e.g. Hardin, 1977b). Pastoralists are seen as destroying their environment, because either their own population growth or their social values require them to keep excessive numbers of livestock. When recurring natural disasters such as droughts and epidemics produce a class of stockless destitute, this is seen as an inevitable and desirable squeezing-out of the least efficient stockowners which it would be environmentally immoral to hinder. Yet the argument is built on dubious foundations. Pastoral populations may not be growing fast (Sandford, 1976b) and desertification may not be occurring. Where grazing pressure on rangelands is increasing this is often due to encroachment on the best grazing lands by cultivation by non-pastoralists, for which the pastoralists deserve sympathy rather than blame. I have seen no evidence to suggest that the destitute were more inefficient managers of livestock rather than more unlucky than the average, or more vulnerable because of circumstances unrelated to managerial ability.[6] When drought struck cultivating peasants in East Africa in the mid-1970s the most strenuous efforts were made by national and international organizations to rehabilitate them back into their peasantry. Similar attempts to rehabilitate pastoralists meet persistent obstruction from woolly-minded but otherwise well-meaning people who do not seem to be able to recognize that buying an animal from one pastoralist in order to give it to another does not alter the current grazing pressure, and that the long-term effects on grazing pressure are difficult to predict with much certainty. The short-term effects of rehabilitation back into pastoralism on the welfare of the destitute pastoralist are wholly desirable.

A final important consequence of the Mainstream view is the tendency for pastoral development programmes to assign a key role to firm intervention by government and to management of resources by government officials. There is much talk of need for *control* and for *discipline*. This follows from distrust of existing pastoral institutions and from the belief that modern science has already discovered the technical solutions to the problems of the pastoral areas. But this dominant role for government and its officials involves a number of major disadvantages. Few if any governments find that their pastoral areas are of major political or economic importance to them. Their commitment to the development of these areas is therefore likely to be small and spasmodic, and this is not a suitable background against which to propose energetic intervention and management. Finally, some very important decisions which fundamentally affect the lives of individual pastoralists have to be taken, in a government-managed programme, by quite junior officials. The nature of pastoral areas is such that close supervision of junior by senior staff is extremely difficult. There is, therefore, tremendous scope for abuse of power and corruption by low-level officials.

SUMMARY OF MAIN POINTS

This chapter has defined a number of important terms and concepts which will frequently recur in what follows, and it has given some indication of the present extent of pastoralism and of my expectations about its future. It has outlined an analytic structure, in which a number of beliefs — that mankind can control its own destiny, that possible ways of improving welfare exist, and that each situation, because of its own characteristics, requires its own prescriptions — lead on to the identification of ends, or objectives of development, and means, or instruments of development (strategies, components, and ways of organizing and managing these) whereby the ends can be achieved. It is a structure in which the different characteristics of situations, the different objectives, and the different instruments all interact, influencing and being modified by each other. The chapter has briefly outlined the methodology by which propositions will be drawn up and has indicated the evidence and the sources for this which will be used.

The chapter has also reviewed current beliefs (the Mainstream view) about the state of the world's rangelands and the causes of desertification. The chapter has not shown that desertification is *not* occurring, but it has drawn attention to problems in the definition of desertification and to the flimsiness of some of the evidence for it. The defects in the evidence relate both to whether desertification is occurring and also the causes thought to be responsible for it. The Mainstream view that serious desertification is occurring has tended to have certain consequences, among them a sense of urgency, a faith in private ownership of land, a carelessness for the welfare of destitute pastoralists, and a tendency to assign a key role to government intervention. These consequences are often undesirable.

NOTES TO CHAPTER 1

1. Arid and semi-arid areas can either be defined in terms of the relationship between rainfall and potential evapotranspiration or more crudely in terms simply of rainfall. One crude definition is that areas with an annual rainfall of less than 200 mm are arid and with a rainfall of 200–600 mm semi-arid (UNCOD, 1977a, p. 26). However, in West Africa the semi-arid zone is sometimes thought to reach the 800 mm isohyet, while in North Africa and the Middle East its maximum limit may be put at 400 mm.

2. It is possible that the pastoral population of China is seriously underestimated in these figures. Shen-Chang-Jiang (1982) estimates that 3 per cent of China's total rural population lives in pastoral areas, and while not all of these would be pastoralists by our definition, it seems possible that considerably more than 1 million of the implied 27 million rural inhabitants of pastoral areas are pastoralists.

3. By 'commercial' is meant that the output is for sale not for subsistence and that the basic goal of the enterprise is to make a financial profit. By a 'ranch' is meant a demarcated area of land reserved for the exclusive use of animals under the management of a single enterprise, an area from which these animals will not normally move except for sale or for a different stage in a stratified production process, e.g. for finishing elsewhere.

4. In Mongolia livestock owned by individuals have calving/lambing rates approximately double those of communal stock (*Far Eastern Economic Review*, 26 May 1978, p. 87).

5. For a recent attempt to provide some guidelines for the administration of agricultural development see Hunter (1978).

6. For a useful discussion of who gets rendered destitute see Haaland (1977, p. 183).

Chapter two

Objectives, strategies, and instruments

OBJECTIVES

We now turn to look at the objectives of pastoral development — the ends which individually and collectively we pursue. There can be objectives at different levels of generality. At a very general level we probably all of us individually pursue happiness, although that is not the only thing we seek. At only a slightly less general level we most of us seek material welfare, status, and perhaps power and even love. At such very general levels, however, these objectives do not give us much useful guidance for decision-making in our daily lives. At a very detailed level, in contrast, we may have short-term goals, such as my completing this study this year; or the x tribe recovering the cattle stolen from it by the y tribe. In this study objectives refer to aims of an intermediate level of generality that provide some guidance for action over a period of years. In the case of an individual this might be his ambitions for his own career and dynasty; and in that of a group it might be its survival as an independent entity during the lives of its members and their children. In the case of a government it might be the provision of its citizens with a defined minimum standard of living before the elapse of, say, 20 years. The first part of this chapter will examine what the objectives of pastoral development often are; and whether there are any principles which determine the circumstances under which one objective may be more appropriate than another.

This study is deliberately biased towards looking at pastoral development from the point of view of the government of the country concerned. Partly this reflects my own experience and partly the likely readership of the study. Of course the largest number of people affected by pastoral development are the pastoralists themselves. This study starts from a number of basic assumptions: that in pastoral development a government will and should give high but not exclusive priority to the welfare of pastoralists; that a government has a legitimate role to play in pastoral development, both in providing resources and in determining policy; that in carrying out its role a government would be well advised to listen to pastoralists' opinion, but that it does not simply have to respond to this nor is it under a moral obligation to defer to pastoralists' opinion beyond any general moral obligation to defer to the opinions of sections of the population; that, in pursuing its objectives, a government acts sensibly in modifying programmes, organizations, and institutions in a way likely to lead to the better achievement of its objectives.

All these assumptions are debatable, but they will not be debated here to any significant extent. For a discussion of some of them reference should be made to the early papers in Galaty *et al.* (1981). One consequence of these assumptions and the bias towards the government point of view is that the language and concepts of this study will tend to be the standard managerial ones of academic and bureaucratic thought about development.

Objectives of pastoralists[1]

To a pastoralist in the Third World 'development', in whatever language he is called on to discuss it, is probably something which has been promised to him (or her)[2] by politicians or government officials, something which they stress to him that he lacks and which they claim to be able to provide him with, often on condition that he makes some undertaking or contribution on his own part. In this way his concept is probably very strongly oriented towards government-supplied social services such as schools and clinics, perhaps also to more widely dispersed and cleaner water supplies. The spirit of the discussions with him about development may be disposed to contrast 'development' with traditional pastoral life as something incompatible with it. In many countries the phrase 'developing pastoralists' has, to many government planners, become synonymous with settling them in non-pastoral occupations such as crop-farming; and discussions about development with pastoralists then become discussions about settlement, a prospect that many pastoralists strongly resist for very good reasons.

A pastoralist's conception of the 'good life' or of 'desirable change', however, may be equally strongly set *within* the context of pastoral life as an improvement in his material standard of living in absolute terms, but also in his own personal position in relation to other pastoralists with whom he compares himself or in the welfare of the pastoral group with which he identifies himself. Depending on the degree of social or economic segmentation or stratification within pastoral society, he may compare and identify himself with that pastoral society as a whole or more particularly with one section or class of it. In considering the welfare of his group he may be concerned as much with its position relative to other pastoral or non-pastoral groups, particularly in respect of its control over natural resources and livestock, as with its welfare on any absolute scale. Some individuals, however, because of the economic or political position which they occupy, or through the influence of education, or through their experience of trade, employment, or travel, may view desirable change for themselves as a stepping out of pastoral life and society into some other social group.

Within a particular pastoral society individuals may have personal ambitions which are incompatible with the welfare of the society as a whole. Similarly, groups in that society, whether based on kinship, economic class, or something else, may have interests at variance with those of other groups; and one pastoral society may have different interests from those of another.

Not only may the interests of different societies be incompatible but their basic objectives and social values may also differ. It is a mistake to look for uniformity. Of course, there are ways in which the values of pastoral societies in general are likely to differ systematically from non-pastoral ones. It would be astonishing, for example, if pastoralists did not rate the status of livestock-keeping highly relative to crop-farming. But in many other ways the objectives and values of different pastoral societies will differ from each other, as a consequence of differences in their natural environment and their political and cultural history, in other words due to differences in their characteristics. There is nothing unusual about this; the same phenomena tend to appear in non-pastoral contexts as well. If the planner of pastoral development has a particular problem it may lie in the fact that he is unlikely himself to come from a pastoral background, and that the nature of pastoral systems of land-use, especially their unpredictability and their mobility, means that conflicts arise particularly often between different kinship groups. Modern states have a well-developed apparatus for dealing with conflicts between individuals and economic classes (family, marriage, and labour laws, economic and social theories) but tend to be ill-equipped legally and conceptually to deal with conflict between clans or tribes.

Should governments pay attention to pastoralists' objectives? There are two aspects to this. The first concerns the weight that a government should attach to pastoralists' objectives when these, in terms of political or moral ideology, clash with the government's own. We shall not discuss this aspect here. The second aspect concerns whether a government, in planning specific programmes for pastoral development, needs to discover what pastoralists' objectives (in the sense defined in the opening to this chapter) are, or whether it should merely consult them on specific operational details such as where new water points should be placed. I believe that governments should try to discover pastoralists' objectives, not only on moral grounds, but because failure to take such objectives into account in pastoral development programmes in the past has led to the failure of those programmes also in terms of the government's objectives. Not only do pastoralists not always share the government's main objective but they tend to have several others which it has not thought of; and if these others are not taken into account pastoralists have too little incentive to behave in the way government wants and expects. What needs to be done may seem very obvious to government officials, and there is then an inevitable tendency to regard an inquiry into what motivates other people as simply a waste of time. But trying to force pastoralists to behave in a particular way is tremendously costly in terms of both administrative and other resources; and if one is not going to force them then one needs to discover what might encourage them to conform voluntarily.

How do we find out what pastoralists' objectives are ? Even if we reject the view that all pastoral societies have the same objectives, can we nevertheless deduce what the objectives will be in a particular instance from a consideration of other characteristics of that society? Or do we need to mount a specific enquiry in each case? It seems likely that there are characteristics which influence the objectives which people pursue. It is probable, for example, that in particularly unstable natural environments, and where past experience has been that members of the society will not get help from outside when natural disaster strikes, the society will put a very high value on measures that ensure its survival and that of its members in bad times (e.g. risk avoidance, risk-spreading, and mutual help), and will disapprove of measures or behaviour (e.g. the sale of female livestock for private gain) which appear to threaten that ability to survive. It is probable that societies which have been exposed to the Islamic faith will tend to have some values which are systematically different from those societies which have not been thus exposed. And pastoral societies which have a long history of conflict with or political subjection to neighbouring cultivating societies are also likely to exhibit some common tendencies. Such cultural patterns, however, are beyond the scope of this study.

One way to find out pastoralists' objectives is simply to ask them. This presents difficulties. The interest at this point is not in responses such as that they want a school at point X or a well at point Y, but rather in some longer-term purpose for whose attainment alternative solutions can be compared. It is difficult enough to get governments familiar with the language of objectives and goals to be clear about what their objectives are (Moris, 1981, p. 20). A discussion with pastoralists along these lines is liable to bog down in conceptual and terminological confusions. Even if these could be overcome many, probably most, pastoral societies are not politically organized in a way that makes it possible to obtain one answer that in any way represents or commits the society as a whole. It may be no part of the function of any existing organization (e.g. a council of clan elders, a chief, a village meeting) to play a representative role in this field; and it may not be a role that any organization can quickly assume. If government or some other outsider then forces this role on an organization, old or new, neither the organization nor anyone else may take it seriously. Individuals called to a meeting to represent society at large will promote their private or group interests instead; and other members of the society will know that this is what they are doing and will not feel bound by their statements.

Other ways by which to elicit the objectives of individuals and societies are by attitudinal surveys or by observation of their behaviour and their culture and the institutions which bind their society together. New devices for testing attitudes in rural societies are constantly being worked out. While the declared basis of behaviour and of institutions may often be expressed in mystical or religious terms, an analysis of its effects may also reveal more secular purposes. For example, Almagur (1978) interpreted the practice of frequent sacrifices of cattle by the Dassenech of south-west Ethiopia as a means of regulating livestock numbers to the carrying capacity of the environment and hence as indicative of the high social value put on ecological equilibrium. One needs to bear in mind, however, that a society's objectives, as enshrined in its culture and institutions, may change quite rapidly over time. What we regard now as 'traditional' may in fact be quite a recent phenomenon which is already giving way to something else.

We can look at some of the main issues which are likely to feature among the objectives of pastoral societies. Listing them immediately leads one to want to pursue all of them simultaneously. In practice, this cannot be done. Some objectives are incompatible with others and in any case priorities have to be observed. The main differences between pastoral societies will lie in the importance which they attach to one objective in preference to another rather than whether or not an objective is totally rejected.

Members of pastoral societies will be interested in their material standards of living. In most cases this interest will include goods which are purchased, as well as goods which they produce for their own consumption. There seems to be little if any evidence that pastoralists have a more restricted range of desires than non-pastoralists, although the nature of pastoral life, especially its mobility, may restrict their ability to gratify them. Because of the inherent unpredictability and instability of production caused by unreliable rainfall in dry areas, pastoralists are likely to be particularly concerned with long-term viability — their ability to survive through bad periods. They are likely both to value the freedom of an individual to manage his own herds in the way which he thinks best, and to stress the importance of social relations and obligations because of the effect that these have in limiting the inconvenience which one man will cause to his fellows in the use of communal facilities such as watering points and in making possible the survival and rehabilitation into pastoral life of those who have fallen on hard times. Because of economies of scale in both consumption and management (Dahl, 1979, Chs. 2–4), pastoralists are likely to be very concerned about the way in which labour and livestock are distributed and allocated, particularly through inheritance and marriage customs. Their position in most countries, at any rate in the last 100 years or so, as a minority group under governments staffed by people with little understanding of pastoral life and whose major concern is with cultivators, is likely to make pastoralists particularly concerned about retaining management and control of key resources within the pastoral society. The tendency, in time of drought, for the prices of livestock to collapse while the prices of cereals soar, may make them put a high value on being able to meet all their subsistence needs from livestock products without having recourse to trade.

Objectives of governments and officials

While the language and concepts of government officials concerned in the planning of pastoral development may differ from those of the pastoralists, they share many of the same general concerns. We can distinguish four main themes — economic, environmental, social, and political — that lie behind current concepts of pastoral development held by those outside pastoral society who are concerned with its development. The *economic* theme tends, on the one hand, to see pastoral areas and their people as resources which can be used to contribute to the economic life of the nation by providing, for example, large and reliable supplies of animals for slaughter or for finishing elsewhere, of wool, hair, skins, butter, cheese, and milk, and of other range products such as honey or incense. These supplies can be used to meet directly the needs of the nation, or to earn foreign exchange which will purchase necessities from abroad. Pastoral areas also supply human labour which should be productively employed. This view is interested both in the volume of supplies to be obtained from pastoral areas, and in their reliability through time. On the other hand, the economic theme may also see pastoralists, or a section of them, e.g. 'the poorest' or 'stockless', as a *target* population, one whose material welfare needs to be increased or made more secure whether in pastoral or non-pastoral occupations, or within which income and wealth may need to be redistributed between members.

The *environmental* theme stresses the ecological vulnerability of pastoral areas and views pastoralists as both the victims and agents of desertification. This theme gives priority to development measures which protect and conserve the environment, and may regard attempts to increase output from pastoral areas as fundamentally incompatible with this priority. Officials of the organization in Australia with prime responsibility for rangelands research have written, 'Australians have tried time and again to develop arid Australia . . . with little if any success'. 'It has been our experience that development often leads to degradation and that it is often better to conserve what we have than to develop it' (Young, 1979); and, 'Some scientists believe, however, that there is no safe way to graze dry rangelands, that grazing can only lead to degradation of ecosystems. Certainly evidence is in their favour' (Newsome, 1971).

The *social* theme often manifests itself in a concern that pastoralists should have the predominant say in decisions that will affect their lives and in favour of the preservation of the integrity of pastoral society and its values against destructive and corrupting inroads by the outside world. Frequently it is the academic anthropologists who of all outsiders have lived most among pastoralists and best understand the dynamics of pastoral life, who campaign for the preservation of at least some parts of its social life and culture. It is not certain, however, that a partial preservation of existing cultures or social relations is either possible or desirable. It may not be possible because few societies are so isolated that links between them and the corrosive influences of the outside world can in practice be cut or frozen. In any case the members of these societies often have a strong desire for some elements of the non-pastoral world, especially Western human and veterinary medicine and, in some cases, education; and it may not be possible to be selective. At the same time, it may not be desirable to conserve traditional culture and social relations because they were formed as adaptations to other circumstances, and to freeze them in their present form may cause pastoral societies to become museum pieces, unable to compete on their own and existing only in permanent dependence on the unreliable benevolence of an outside patron. On the other hand, as pointed out in Chapter 1, pastoral societies often have very desirable social features and if these can be conserved they should be.

The *political* theme is often dominant. In many countries the pastoralists are a minority, often straddling national boundaries, often with a long history of conflict with their neighbours and with government. Inevitably, governments in their programmes for pastoral people are at least as much concerned with reducing the risks which pastoralists offer to national security as they are with promoting their welfare. In very few countries, Mongolia and Somalia are exceptions, do pastoralists account for even half of the total population — and only in these two countries and in Sudan and Botswana do they have significant political influence, although the problems that they pose are of political importance in several other countries such as Mauritania, Ethiopia, and Afghanistan. The political theme stresses the integration of pastoralists into the economic, social, cultural, and political life of the nation. In consequence it gives priority to breaking down rather than to conserving traditional pastoral culture and social relations, and to reducing rather than enhancing the self-sufficiency and self-reliance of pastoral society. Frequently it leads to the forcible resettlement of pastoralists in non-pastoral occupations.

What objectives are actually pursued? In few countries are the various activities of government in respect to pastoral areas fully integrated with each other so as to provide a coherent overall policy following a common objective or set of objectives. At the worst, different government agencies, in pursuit of diametrically opposed policies and objectives, compete with each other to provide the same service, e.g. new water points, in the same area. In pre-revolution Ethiopia, for example, two or more agencies were often preparing rival development programmes for the same pastoral area, not communicating with each other because neither wished to recognize the right of the other even to be consulted. In northern Kenya, although the range management department advocates destocking, the provincial administration allows livestock from overstocked areas to take over the grazing which has been preserved in areas which have been destocked. In several countries incompatible objectives are pursued simultaneously by several government agencies, or even by the same one, in the hope that the incompatibilities will somehow be painlessly resolved. This is particularly true in respect of pricing policies for livestock and meat. In most countries a clear definition of objectives does not exist, partly because those managing pastoral development do not recognize that there are any choices to be made between alternatives and that a clear definition of objectives is an important determinant of choice, partly, perhaps, because lack of clarity may help to preserve flexibility when things go wrong (Long, 1977, p. 182).

Where objectives do exist they may change over time. Where they are not formally stated they may sometimes be deduced. In Mongolia (Lattimore, 1962) and the USSR immediately after the revolutions political considerations were paramount, above all the need to break the power of the previous leaders. In Iran before the Second World War the same was true (Lambton, 1969, pp. 283–294); but in the last 10 years before the fall of the Shah, there had been, especially in the Forest and Range Organization, a shift in concern towards halting environmental degradation (Sandford, 1977b). Concern for the welfare of pastoralists was minimal. In India a desire to reduce the repeated burden of famine relief operations appears to have been the main initiating impulse behind the Drought-Prone Areas Programme, although in its implementation more emphasis seems to have been given to income-generating activities than to those reducing fluctuations in income and employment (Sandford, 1978a). In Botswana the motivating force behind the reform in tenure of rangelands, entitled the Tribal Grazing Lands Policy has, on the government side, been a mixture of concern about ecological degradation and the need for growth in the livestock industry and for more equality in incomes. To this has been coupled the interest of rich men in acquiring firm private title to previously communal land. In Australia (Williams, Suijdendorp, and Wilcox, 1977) and the USA (Heady and Bartolome, 1977), ecological considerations, allied in the Australian case to urban interests, currently hold sway. In Israel the need to fill its arid lands with people has been the most pressing need (Richmond, 1977).

The choice between objectives

Are there any principles which should govern which objectives should be pursued? What circumstances make one objective more appropriate than another? Is appropriateness determined wholly by the characteristics of the pastoral situation concerned or also, or alternatively, by the circumstances of the country or the ideology of the person designing development? This subsection addresses these questions.

Clearly the ideology of the person or organization designing development will play an important role. There are some issues of overall policy which are not susceptible to resolution by arguments conducted within the context of pastoral planning but are set, as it were, from outside. In almost all countries, for example, the decision whether to redistribute income and wealth from the rich to the poor, or vice versa, by high taxes on income, or by direct expropriation, is likely to be taken independently of circumstances in the pastoral sector; but it will have consequences inside that sector. The decision will largely depend on the ideology of the government. Quite separately from ideological issues, the circumstances of the country as a whole must also affect the appropriateness of objectives in the pastoral sector. If the country has a high level of demand for livestock products which is being met by imports which cause serious strain on the country's balance of payments, then it is rather appropriate that priority should be given to increasing the marketed supply from pastoral areas. If the government's budget is already severely strained, then any proposal to use the budget mechanism as a way of increasing the welfare of pastoralists, either through direct personal income supports, or through subsidized services or by supporting prices of livestock products, will not be very appropriate. If the rate of population growth is higher among non-pastoralists than among pastoralists, and if areas currently used exclusively by pastoralists in an extensive fashion have potential for more intensive use in crop-cultivation, and if alternative income-earning opportunities are not available for these increasing numbers of non-pastoralists, then it will not be very appropriate to provide security to pastoralists by a land-tenure system that precludes some transfer of land from pastoral into non-pastoral hands and use.

Important determinants of the appropriateness of objectives are the characteristics of the pastoral situation itself. If its human population is growing fast and exceeds the ability of the area to support it by traditional methods, then priority should be given to the objective of creating additional opportunities for earning a livelihood, through intensifying systems of production in order to employ and support more people. This could take the form of diversifying into other products by crop-cultivation, of introducing labour-intensive public works on roads or land reclamation, or of more labour-intensive methods of husbandry such as making hay. Incentives and opportunities will also need to be found for people to emigrate from pastoral life. If the area is particularly susceptible to irreversible, or at least difficult-to-reverse, ecological degradation, it will be appropriate to pay much attention to conserving the environment. If the area is isolated and difficult to reach and suffers from particularly unreliable rainfall, then it will be rather appropriate to lay emphasis on reducing fluctuations in output between good and bad years (e.g. by creating reserves of livestock feed) or to spread risks by mutual sharing and support arrangements between different individuals and areas. Where, however, although the climate is unreliable, easy opportunities exist for pastoralists to find alternative sources of income in bad times, or where famine-relief supplies can easily reach the area, then less attention need be paid to this aspect.

Where population pressure on resources is high and growing it will be rather appropriate to encourage a switch from reliance on home-produced animal products for meeting basic human dietary needs towards a system in which animal products are traded with non-pastoral areas in exchange for cereals. This is because normally, where the marketing system is reasonably well developed, a given quantity of animal products will acquire, through trading, a higher number of calories for human consumption through exchange for grain than it will provide by its direct consumption. For example, in northern Kenya in 1978 a litre of cow's milk, if exchanged for grain (by first transforming it into clarified butter which can be stored and transported for sale), would provide twice as many calories as if consumed directly; and a kilogram of meat would provide more than nine and a half times more calories by sale than by direct consumption (Dahl and Sandford, 1978, pp. 129–131). However, when the market system, because of inaccessibility, poor public security, unreliability of supply, or monopolistic traders, is not so well developed, or when the ratio of grain and livestock prices is very unstable, tending to shift sharply against the pastoralist in time of drought, then it will not be so appropriate to encourage the switch from self-sufficiency.

Where the political situation is such that a pastoral society presents a threat to the country's security, then, as already mentioned, it will be appropriate to aim to integrate the pastoralists as closely as possible into national life. But where the pastoralists are few in number and increasing only slowly, and where they are politically weak, possibly due to a past history of conflict with their fellow countrymen, then it would not be very appropriate to encourage forms of development which presuppose much continuing interest and support from the government since this is unlikely to materialize. It will be more appropriate to encourage self-reliance in both investment and management of resources; and it will also be important to obtain some security for pastoralists by protecting their land rights by law, since they are unlikely to be able to protect them through political influence.

If the present standard of living of the pastoralists is very low, clearly priority must be given to raising it. If the structure of a pastoral society, its system of property rights and its natural environment are such as to promote great inequality and exploitation of one pastoralist by another, then it will usually be thought rather appropriate to consider means of fundamentally reforming the social system. If, however, the existing system is equitable, one which has the resources to cope with the strains of a fluctuating environment and a changing world, and one with which the majority of pastoralists are content, it will be more appropriate to consider ways of preserving it.

Note how tentative and guarded are the prescriptions of the last few paragraphs. Particular objectives are described as being rather or not very appropriate; they are not firmly placed in one category or another. This reflects accurately the position in which those designing pastoral development are likely to find themselves, in pastoral situations not with one but many characteristics, surrounded by needs and pressures only some of which can be accommodated. They will need to balance one objective with another, trying, for example, to do something for pastoralists' incomes without putting unbearable pressure on the rangelands; to preserve a pastoralist's feeling of personal value and identity in his society without creating or reinforcing in that society separatist tendencies that pose a threat to the country's security; taking some risks without prejudicing the survival of the whole system. There will inevitably be some incompatibilities; incompatibility between two objectives both pursued simultaneously by the same person or group, incompatibility between the interest of the individual and that of the rest of his group, incompatibility between different sexes, groups, or societies in or outside the pastoral sector, between one generation and the next, or between pastoralists and government. There are no clear rules about which choices to make, or even useful techniques to help one to choose. It is one aim of this study to show the range of choice and that the appropriate choice will depend on the particular circumstances, including the characteristics of the pastoral situation.

SOME STRATEGIES

At the start of this chapter we defined objectives, for the purposes of this study, as medium-term aims that provide guidance for action over a period of years; and we have looked at a number of objectives in pastoral development. In subsequent chapters we shall look at some of the very specific components of pastoral development, such as range-management and animal health programmes, by which the objectives can be pursued. In this section of the study we look at some contrasting *strategies*. Strategies occupy an intermediate level between objectives and components. It is easiest to explain the meaning of the term 'strategy' by examples, and we shall give two. For purposes of definition, we can say that a strategy is a pattern of behaviour, on the part of individuals, groups, or organizations, in which a set of actions and decisions have a common purpose running through them and have a harmonious combined effect greater than the sum of their individual effects taken one by one. There are a large number of strategies that may be pursued in pastoral development. Johnson (1979b) gives several examples.

In this section of the study we look at two pairs of contrasting strategies. For the sake of brevity and clarity we treat the members of a pair as though they were mutually exclusive polar opposites. In practice, of course, a choice can be made so as to occupy a position at some point along a range between opposite extremes that best fits into the advantages and disadvantages of a particular situation. The two pairs of contrasting strategies are:
 (i) Mobile versus sedentary forms of pastoral land-use. The choice between them is often debated in terms of 'the settlement of nomads'.
(ii) Conservative stability versus opportunistic fluctuation in livestock numbers — the 'control of livestock numbers' issue.

SETTLEMENT OF NOMADS

A recurring issue in pastoral development is whether mobile forms of land-use should be abandoned in favour of settlement. Mobile forms of land-use are either pure nomadism, involving irregular movements of livestock by nomads living in tents or other transportable forms of housing, or transhumance, involving fairly regular and predictable movements by the livestock of people who may live for much of the year in fixed and permanent houses. For brevity we shall call both transhumance and pure nomadism by the same term, nomadism, and refer to the issue as one of settlement, that is the attachment of particular livestock to a particular piece of land, and putting pastoralists in permanent fixed habitations from which they do not normally move.

There is, of course, a difference between the mobility of livestock and that of pastoralists. In pastoral systems where milk and milk products are either directly consumed by pastoralists or sold by them, then people and their livestock will normally move and camp together, the reason being that, at least at certain times of day, there are, in these milk-based systems, very high labour requirements for milking, for separating young stock from dams, for processing milk. Even in milk-based systems some species of livestock, e.g. camels, may be herded separately from the pastoral family, or some classes of stock, e.g. males or dry cows (Dahl, 1979), or even the milking stock, may be separated from the pastoral families at some seasons to be reunited at periods of peak milk production (Nyerges, 1979, p. 14). Although neither country would regard itself as having a nomadic pastoral system, in parts of both the United States[3] and the USSR (ILO, 1967) livestock and their shepherds migrate hundreds of miles on foot between winter, spring, and summer pastures. Some of the arguments which follow apply particularly to the movement of livestock and some to that of the pastoralists themselves.

We can briefly summarize the reasons why some pastoralists practise nomadism while others oppose it. It is practised where seasonal variations in temperature, in rainfall, in the incidence of diseases and biting flies, in flooding, in the growing, ripening, and harvesting of crops, makes livestock-keeping in one area relatively more or less attractive than in another area according to a regular and predictable seasonal timetable. For example, in South-West Asia, e.g. in Iran, it is too cold during winter, and the snow is often too deep, for animals to graze on the high mountain pastures; and so at the end of summer they retreat to the lowlands. During the spring and summer they return to the highlands, both because of the availability of good pasture there and because the lowlands in turn have become inhospitable due to heat or shortage of water. In the Ogaden region of the Horn of Africa the second rains of the year fall in July and August in the north, but in October and November in the south. Livestock that move from one area to another according to the incidence of the rains can profit by feeding on the grazing when it is in its best condition as to palatability and protein content. Both in East and West Africa, areas which, due to tsetse and other biting flies which spread trypanasomiasis and other diseases, are unsafe during the wet season become usable during the dry season. In many countries of both Asia and Africa livestock may cause serious damage to crops in the cultivation zone around the pastoral areas during the growing and harvesting seasons; nevertheless they are welcome there after harvest because of their role in converting crop residues and other vegetation to manure and they can also obtain quite a high proportion of their annual feed intake there once the crops have been harvested. In some areas in both continents seasonal flooding from river banks may deny the use of certain areas to livestock during and just after the wet season but may provide a type and quantity of livestock feed which is extremely useful during the dry season. Nomadic movements of pastoral people may also occur to enable pastoralists to work at other agricultural activities such as crop- and tree-cultivation or at non-agricultural activities (Salzman, 1972).

In contrast to these regular seasonal movements between areas there are other less predictable ones. Certain water sources and certain kinds of vegetation supply minerals which livestock need, while others do not. These needs for minerals can not always be reliably predicted (Dahl, 1979, pp. 43–44). Yet the cost of replacing these natural and free sources of minerals with commercial manufactures can be substantial. In Ethiopia in 1975 the cost of meeting the annual mineral requirements of steers by using commercial products was estimated at over one-quarter of the annual increase in value of these steers under ranching conditions.[4] Livestock also move irregularly to escape from diseases, for example from outbreaks of rinderpest or from the gradual build-up of disease due to high livestock densities. The latter applies especially to camels. Nomadic movements are also made so as to produce high temporary densities of people and livestock where this is required for self-defence or because there are economies of scale, for example, in drawing water from deep wells. Perhaps most important of all, nomadic movements are made from one area to another because the one area has received, in this year or this season, relatively less rainfall than it normally does compared to the other.

The arguments against a nomadic form of land-use can also be briefly rehearsed. Movement is costly and inconvenient to pastoralists. They need to keep special and expensive livestock, for example baggage camels, in order to move their dwellings, possessions, and families. Even when such animals are available, movement is exhausting for both humans and livestock and may be dangerous if it incurs the hostility of people into or through whose territory it takes place. It limits the type and quantity of a family's possessions to what can be easily transported. Veterinarians and doctors dislike nomadic movement because of the way it can spread disease and reinfect areas once cleared, for example of foot-and-mouth disease or malaria. Political administrators dislike nomadism because it is often accompanied by violent clashes between competing pastoral groups and because they have difficulty in keeping control over their charges. They often also believe that it is pastoralists' nomadism that makes it so difficult to provide them with social services such as education and health. Where nomadic movements cross international boundaries further complications arise and may pose a threat to national security. Some people also believe that the practice of nomadism militates against pastoralists being adequately concerned with stabilizing and improving the productivity of rangelands, because, it is alleged, they feel that they can always move on to yet other areas if those currently used become degraded.

Some confusion has been caused by the alleged existence of a nomadic mentality that values movement for its own sake rather than for its practical consequences. This topic has been discussed elsewhere (Spooner, 1972). It seems probable that some nomads do indeed express strong feelings in favour of mobility as a cultural value that is good in itself; but this cultural value probably needs to be seen as an effect of the practical reasons in favour of mobility rather than as an independent cause of the mobility. Nomads have this strong cultural value precisely because restrictions on their movement threaten their survival. On the other hand, many nomads express a dislike of mobility and simultaneously stress how necessary it is to them. In contrast to the positive cultural value put on mobility by nomads is the strongly adverse feeling expressed by some settled people who regard the nomads' mobility as, in itself, evidence of their primitiveness and to whom pastoral development means settlement for its own sake.

The issue of settlement is not one that can profitably be discussed in terms of cultural values. Nomadic land-use is neither more (nor less) primitive[5] than sedentary; nor, incidentally, is it symptomatic, either in theory or practice, of a less socialist economy although this idea seems to lie behind a number of attempts to settle nomads forcibly. In the USSR a rigid policy pursued in the 1930s of stopping nomadic movements has been replaced by one in which livestock are fairly mobile over long distances but, except for the actual shepherds themselves, the people dependent on the livestock are relatively settled (ILO, 1967). In socialist Mongolia livestock may be more nomadic now than prior to the communist revolution, because people who, if operating on their own account, might have been too idle to move are now compelled to do so by the orders of their collective (Humphrey, 1978). There is no one universally valid answer to the question of whether or not nomads should be settled. All the reasons given by nomad pastoralists as to why they practise nomadism are valid in their own particular circumstances; and where settlement has been imposed on nomads compulsorily by government decree or in other ways, the results have been disastrous, witness the experience of the USSR and Iran before the Second World War, and of Algeria and Kenya during various periods of emergency in their pastoral areas in the 1950s and 1960s. Similarly, those who dislike nomadic mobility have good reasons for doing so. Whether settlement is desirable or not must depend on the particular situation. What we need to do is to consider the circumstances in respect both of objectives and of characteristics of pastoral situations which would make settlement more or less appropriate in a particular case.

Nomadism and rainfall: a simple model for maximum output

We shall now pursue in some detail, by means of a simple model, the point that movement from one area to another is needed to take advantage in cases where rainfall in a particular year or season has been relatively good in the one area in comparison with the other. For the sake of conceptual and calculating simplicity I make five assumptions which I shall not vary subsequently. These fixed assumptions are:

(a) The question at issue is whether or not nomadic movement is desirable between three areas, A, B, and C, which have long-term average annual rainfalls between 300 and 500 mm and each of which is 30 km² (3000 ha) in size.

(b) The critical factor which determines the amount of grazing available, and so the number of animals which can be kept in any year, is the total amount of rainfall which falls in the year as a whole.

(c) Livestock have fixed annual appetites. If they do not get enough to meet their appetite they die; and if they are offered more than this amount they refuse to eat it. The livestock involved are all of one type, age, sex, and weight. They have a single product, e.g. meat, which, provided they are fed to appetite, they produce in a fixed amount per animal per year.

(d) For every millimetre of rain that falls in one area in one year enough feed will grow to feed one animal the amount of its fixed appetite in that year. So if area A receives 500 mm of rain in year 1, enough feed will grow to provide for exactly 500 animals in that year.

(e) The rainfall recorded over a three-year period is wholly representative of the rainfall regime in the area over an indefinite period in respect of both average and deviations about this average.

These fixed assumptions are not particularly realistic, but they enable the calculations to be kept simple and clear conclusions to emerge. If I were to vary them, the calculations would become very complex, but the conclusions would remain broadly the same. I also initially make three other assumptions which can subsequently be varied, and the effects of this variation will be discussed later. These *variable* assumptions are:

 (i) The amount of rainfall received in a year affects only production in that year and not production in subsequent years; and any feed produced but not eaten in a year is wasted. It cannot be stored and used in subsequent years, nor will 'leaving it on the plant' affect the productivity of the plant in subsequent years.

 (ii) Although animals can be moved from area to area (i.e. between areas A, B, and C) they cannot be shifted out to, nor imported from, the rest of the country.

(iii) Animals do not die except of starvation nor do they reproduce themselves.

Under these assumptions the critical factors determining the desirability, or otherwise, of nomadic movements between the three areas are the extent of variation in rainfall in the same area between successive years, and the degree to which rainfall in the same year in different areas is correlated, i.e. whether, if rainfall in area A is below average in a particular year, there is a tendency for rainfall in areas B and C also to be below average. The purely hypothetical data of Table 2.1 illustrate three contrasting situations. The figures in the columns under the headings years 1, 2, and 3 represent both the rainfall measured in millimetres and, through assumption (c) above, the number of livestock that can be supported by an area. In Scenario One

Table 2.1 The capacity of three areas to support livestock under different rainfall scenarios

Area[a]	Rainfall (mm) and no. of animals for whom there is sufficient food			No. of animals which can be kept in the worst year
	Years			
	1	2	3	
Scenario One: Rainfall does not vary from year to year				
A	400	400	400	400
B	300	300	300	300
C	500	500	500	500
Total	1200	1200	1200	1200
Scenario Two: Rainfall varies from year to year and is highly correlated between areas				
A	400	600	200	200
B	300	450	150	150
C	500	750	250	250
Total	1200	1800	600	600
Scenario Three: Rainfall varies from year to year and is *not* correlated between areas				
A	400	600	200	200
B	150	300	450	150
C	750	250	500	250
Total	1300	1150	1150	600 or 1150[b]

[a] The mean annual rainfall of areas A, B, and C is 400, 300, and 500 mm respectively.
[b] If nomadic movement between areas is allowed 1150 animals can be kept in the worst year; otherwise only 600 can be kept.

rainfall does not vary from year to year and so each area's capacity to sustain livestock also remains constant. If each area is fully stocked to capacity initially, nothing is gained from nomadic movements that switch animals from area to area. The capacity of each area to maintain livestock is constant at 400, 300, and 500 animals in each of the areas A, B, and C respectively. In Scenario Two rainfall varies from year to year, but above-average and below-average years exactly coincide in the three areas. In the worst year area A can only support 200 animals, area B 150 animals, and area C 250 animals, and since the worst years coincide (see year 3 in Scenario Two) there is nothing to be gained by switching stock from area to area. The maximum capacity of the system (in the light of assumptions (ii) and (iii) which prevent restocking after bad years) is given by the total shown for year 3, i.e. 600 animals; this is also the sum of the figures in the last column of the table which indicate the number of animals which can be kept in the worst year in each area. In the case illustrated in Scenario Three rainfall varies from year to year, but annual rainfall in different areas is not correlated in time. If no nomadic movements are allowed then the maximum capacity of the system as a whole is 600, obtained from the sum of the figures in the last column of the table. This arises because, in the absence of nomadic movement, no area in any year will, by our assumptions, have more animals than it can keep in the worst year. If, however, movements of livestock between areas is allowed, then the maximum capacity of the system is 1150 animals, the total shown under years 2 and 3 in Scenario Three. For in year 2 excess animals from area C can be shifted into areas A and B, and in year 3 shifted from area A into areas B and C. We can generalize from this model and say that, in terms of the objective of maximizing output and total incomes, nomadism will be relatively more appropriate in regions where both inter-year variations in rainfall are greatest and rainfall is relatively uncorrelated between different areas within the region.

We can now turn to relaxing the variable assumptions set out previously. Sometimes, contrary to variable assumption (i), 'surplus' feed production, over and above the requirements of the animals present in an area in any one year, can be stored or carried forward, either as hay or because lighter grazing pressure in one year leads to better cover, composition, and vigour of the vegetation in subsequent years. In such cases the gains to be obtained from nomadism between areas will be less than they are when the surplus cannot be stored or carried forward. We can also relax variable assumptions (ii) and (iii). Where livestock can be sold to the rest of the country in bad years, and repurchased in good, or where the livestock themselves have very short breeding cycles and can rapidly reproduce themselves to take advantage of otherwise surplus feed, then again the benefits of nomadism will be correspondingly reduced; except in so far as the transaction and transportation costs of importing and exporting cattle to the rest of the country are much greater than the costs incurred where animals remaining in single ownership migrate between different pastoral areas. Advocates of settlement of nomads sometimes claim that only by settlement and the close identification of a particular person or group with a particular piece of land will it be possible to persuade pastoralists to invest in or to take an interest in improving the productivity of grazing land. Calculations such as those shown in Table 2.1 enable one to estimate how great this effect of settlement would have to be in order to overcome the disadvantages of the loss of flexibility.

Settlement and other objectives

We can also look briefly at the issue of settlement in respect of objectives other than those of maximizing output and incomes. The distinction must be emphasized between settlement as such, i.e. the mere immobilizing of pastoralism, and the diversion of pastoralists into other occupations such as crop-farming. It is the former with which we are concerned here. There is a good deal of evidence that immobilizing pastoralism does indeed sharply reduce the threat that pastoralists pose in the short term to the security of the state. Its main way of doing so is simply by impoverishing them, since almost universally such settlement has been accompanied by massive losses of pastoralists' livestock through starvation and disease. It is obviously much more difficult to calculate the long-term effects since so much else intervenes in the long term that it becomes impossible to trace through causes and their effects. As far as the social implications are concerned, clearly settlement of people previously nomadic will greatly change the nature of society's institutions and organization (for an example see Zghal, 1967), with some consequent loss of feelings of identity and continuity. Immobilization of pastoralists will not, of itself, make social services, such as primary education and health, easier to provide, for the main difficulty lies not in pastoralists' mobility but in their low density per unit of land; and nomadic movements permit (temporary) higher densities than can be sustained under sedentarized pastoralism (Sandford, 1978b).

Sedentarization may have an effect on social quality and stratification, although the direction of this is not certain. Some anthropologists (e.g. Barth, 1962; Irons, 1971) have seen in the need of pastoral societies in South-West Asia to have well-programmed and organized migrations between winter and summer grazing areas scope for the emergence of an authoritarian and hierarchical leadership. Settlement might abolish this particular avenue for individual aggrandizement, but the closer relationship with government that settlement normally entails, and any rearrangements of rights in grazing land that might follow on settlement, seem likely to provide fresh opportunities for the emergence of a powerful broker class for managing relations with government or for controlling the procedures by which rights to land are required or sustained (for an example see Bates, 1973). It seems particularly difficult to generalize on this issue, nor is it possible to identify characteristics of pastoral situations which will tend to influence the effect of pastoralists' settlement on social stratification in one direction or another.

Settlement is likely to have a considerable effect on the pastoral economy's demand for labour and the consequent opportunities that it offers for useful employment. Where shortage of labour occurs in a pastoral society nomadism often gives way to settlement, implying that nomadism in those situations has the higher demands for labour and, conversely, that where settlement takes place less employment is likely to be afforded. But the chain of causation is not likely to be the same everywhere. Where, under conditions of nomadic pastoralism, different species, ages, and conditions of livestock (e.g. camels, dry cows, milking cows, lambs, etc.) can be sent off separately in search of the vegetation and grazing conditions which best suit them, the demand for herdsmen will be high (Dahl, 1979, Ch. 4; Torry, 1977). Where, however, livestock are territorially closely constrained, one herdsman will suffice for several different classes of stock. On the other hand, settlement may make both necessary and possible an intensification in land-use, by the planting of grass and browse, through works for conserving soil and water, by hay-making, which increases the demand for labour. Areas of relatively high potential, due to better soil and rainfall, offer more opportunities for intensification of land-use.

CONTROL OF LIVESTOCK NUMBERS

Dry pastoral regions are characterized by great, and generally unpredictable, variations in rainfall between successive years, and consequent large variations in the growth of natural vegetation available as forage for livestock. Variations in the availability of forage cause fluctuations in the maximum number of livestock which can be kept and in the output of useful products from these livestock. This section of the study will examine one of the ways in which pastoralists can respond to these fluctuations, that is, the way in which they adjust and control the number of their livestock. For simplicity, I contrast two extremes, a *conservative* strategy in which a constant number of livestock graze an area through good and bad years alike, and an *opportunistic* strategy in which the number of livestock grazing is continuously adjusted according to the current availability of forage. In practice, pastoralists are unlikely to pursue either of these two extremes exactly, but usually veer more in the direction of one than the other. A conservative strategy implies that the number of animals is not allowed to increase in the good years to utilize all the forage available, as they would then be too many for the subsequent bad years. Thus, under a conservative strategy some surplus forage may be wasted in good years. An opportunistic policy, in contrast, enables the extra forage available in good years to be converted directly into useful products, or into productive capital in the form of a bigger breeding herd. It encounters practical difficulties over exactly how the variation in livestock numbers is to be effected, and the risk that too many animals may be kept for too long after a period of good weather has ended, with consequent damage to the environment. In order to distinguish it from the usual way of applying an opportunistic strategy, i.e. to adjust too little and too late, I define an *efficient* opportunistic strategy as one which adjusts livestock numbers to exactly the right extent at the right time.

Zoologists and ecologists have noted that many invertebrate and vertebrate wild populations (i.e. not herded and tended by humans) successfully pursue an opportunistic strategy — sometimes referred to as an 'r' strategy (May, 1976, p. 35) — and some of these scientists have warned against pursuing culling policies that would dampen fluctuations in these populations (Phillipson, 1975, p. 199). On the other hand, among range scientists there seems to be little disagreement that a conservative strategy is preferable for a population of domestic livestock. This contrast in prescriptions may spring from a variety of causes. It may arise because the criterion for success in a wild population is different from that in the management of a domestic herd by symbiotic or parasitic man. Or it may arise because some self-regulating mechanism controls wild populations in such a way that the population never reaches a level that causes environmental damage, or because it rebounds from such a level before damage occurs;[6] and because no such self-regulating mechanism works in the case of domestic livestock populations.[7]

The risks of conservatism and opportunism

Range scientists, in advocating a conservative strategy, frequently recommend that estimates of carrying capacity — the number of animals, or animal biomass, that an area of rangelands can support without a downward trend in the productivity of vegetation and soil resources — should be set at a level which will not subsequently prove to have been too optimistic. For example, Box and Peterson (1978) write: '. . . carrying capacity is limited by that harshest period during the climatic cycle. For instance the carrying capacity of the Sahelian desert areas would be limited to the number of animals able to sustain themselves during the driest year of the drought', and 'all development schemes must be examined against historical or simulated time periods long enough to insure that carrying capacity at any site will not be exceeded'. However, in general too little attention is paid to the probabilistic aspects of a conservative approach. Droughts, here defined simply as deficiencies in rainfall, are not of uniform severity, nor do climatic cycles exactly repeat themselves. We need to think not of a level of carrying capacity, i.e. an estimate of the number of animals which can be safely kept, that will *never* be excessive, but rather of the probability or risk that any selected level may prove to be too high. In this context we can think of a *mildly conservative* level of carrying capacity that will prove to be too high (i.e. the amount of forage available is inadequate for that number of animals) in only 20 years out of every 100, a *moderately conservative* one that will prove too high in 5 years in 100, and an *ultra-conservative* one that turns out too high only once (on average) in a century. For every selected level of carrying capacity for a particular pastoral area there will be a corresponding risk that it will prove too high.

The choice of the degree of risk to be accepted is important. For every degree of risk that the carrying capacity will be too high there will be a corresponding risk that it will be too low. For if in 20 years out of 100 it is too high, and there is insufficient forage to support that number of livestock, then, unless the statistical distribution of rainfall in that area is very peculiar, in about 79 to 80 years in every 100 it will be too low, in the sense that there will be more forage available than the minimum necessary to support that number of animals. Whether the forage that is surplus to this minimum is actually left ungrazed depends on whether the minimum is defined in terms of the amount that the livestock will eat if allowed to (hereinafter 'fed *ad lib*') or the amount required for bare survival. The first of these two alternatives is the relevant definition if we are concerned with the damage that livestock will cause to the environment if too many of them are kept; and in that case all the surplus above the minimum will be left ungrazed.[8]

The cost of conservatism

Some of the important relative disadvantages of the two strategies, in terms of potential environmental damage and waste of ungrazed forage, have already been mentioned. A sensible choice of strategy will depend on the balance between these two and between other factors, and on the extent to which either strategy is feasible in practice. These points are pursued in more detail in the next section. Elsewhere (Sandford, 1982) I have demonstrated that, under a reasonable range of assumptions,[9] a conservative strategy can have very high costs in terms of the value of useful output from livestock foregone, through waste of unused forage, in relation to the value of output attainable under an efficient opportunistic strategy. The results of this demonstration for different variants of a conservative strategy and different degrees of rainfall variability are shown, in summary form, in Table 2.2. This shows, for example, that in an area with only moderately variable annual rainfall (coefficient of variation = 20 per cent) a conservative strategy that aims to keep a constant size of herd that is too large on average once in five years will, on the assumptions made, provide an average annual income only 17 per cent less than the average income obtainable by pursuing an efficient opportunistic strategy. If one wants to be more conservative and to have a herd that is too large only once in 100 years, then average income will be 47 per cent less than that under an efficient opportunistic strategy. However, in another area of much less reliable rainfall (coefficient of variation = 50 per cent) the income of a 1 in 5 risk strategy will be 42 per cent less than that of efficient opportunism, and a 1 in 100 risk strategy will mean, in effect, that practically no livestock are kept at all, and so no income derived from them.

Table 2.2 The costs of conservatism (costs are expressed in terms of output foregone, because of understocking, relative (%) to output attainable (=100%) under an efficient opportunistic policy)

Variant of conservative strategy (expressed in terms of the risk — 1 in n years — of the level of carrying capacity selected proving too high)	Cost of variant where coefficient of variation[a] of annual rainfall is:		
	20%	35%	50%
1 in 5 years	17	29	42
1 in 20 years	33	58	82
1 in 100 years	47	82	100

[a] Coefficient of variation = standard deviation ÷ arithmetic mean × 100.

Two points are of critical importance in determining the balance of advantages. The first is whether livestock numbers can and will be varied at the right moment, by natural increase, by purchase, by slaughter, and by sale. The second is whether there is any 'carry-over' effect from year to year, whereby overgrazing or undergrazing in relation to forage availability and a proper degree of use in one year affects availability in subsequent years. A positive 'carry-over' occurs where forage surplus to requirements in one year can be cut and stored as hay; or where undergrazing has a positive effect[10] on the amount of forage produced in subsequent years through an influence on species composition, ground cover, and vigour of the vegetation. A negative carry-over occurs where, under either strategy, too many livestock are kept in a pastoral area with consequent overgrazing leading to a decrease in range productivity in subsequent years. The heart of the range scientists' argument is that under an opportunistic strategy livestock numbers are not in practice adjusted appropriately and that both positive and negative carry-over effects occur in forage availability from year to year. The quantitative estimates in Table 2.2 show some of the advantages of opportunism over conservatism, and present a challenge for a similar quantification of the countervailing advantage of conservatism.

Factors favouring conservative or opportunistic strategies

In practice few if any pastoral groups can pursue either wholly conservative or wholly opportunistic strategies. Probably the general tendency is more towards the latter than the former. Nevertheless, some societies are relatively conservative; the Dassanech of East Africa, for example, are alleged to keep their livestock population stable by slaughter (Almagur, 1978). Capitalist pastoral enterprises, however, are not necessarily more conservative than traditional pastoral societies, and both in Australia and the USA many ranchers see opportunism as their only way to survive (Heathcote, 1969). It is not proposed to list here which groups pursue relatively more opportunistic or more conservative strategies but instead, on the assumption that there is a diversity of behaviour between more conservatism or more opportunism, to identify the factors which are likely to influence behaviour towards one or the other.

Clearly physical factors will be important. The greater the degree of variability in rainfall over time, the greater will be the opportunity cost of conservatism. The figures in Table 2.2 show just how much greater, and the point can be illustrated by a simple model. Let us imagine two sites with the same *average* annual rainfall and the same *average* annual production of forage, but with one site having a far greater degree of variation (indicated by a far higher coefficient of variation) in rainfall and forage above and below average. For example, the less variable site may have a 1 in 10 chance of not producing enough forage to feed four animals, and a 1 in 20 chance of not feeding two. The other, more variable site, however, may have a 2 in 10 chance of not producing enough forage to feed four animals and a 2 in 20 (1 in 10) chance of not feeding two. To balance its greater likelihood of not having enough forage to feed even small numbers, the more variable site, in order to have the same *average* annual production as the less variable, will have a greater likelihood of producing more than enough forage to feed large numbers. But these aberrations on the higher side will be of no use to it if our strategy is based on taking, for example, only a 1 in 10 risk of the selected level of carrying capacity proving too high. For in this case the less variable site can be stocked with four animals, but the more variable with only two. Because of this extra 'opportunity cost' in terms of forage not grazed, a greater degree of variation in rainfall is likely to influence pastoral strategy in the direction of opportunism. However, if variations in rainfall over time at different sites within a pastoral region are relatively uncorrelated, then the temporal variations can be mitigated by moving livestock from one site to another, and the cost of conservatism reduced in this way, making it relatively more attractive.

The nature of the soil, the topography, and the type of vegetation will also determine the extent to which under- or over-grazing will affect productivity in subsequent periods. Some soils are inherently more susceptible to wind and water erosion, and soils on slopes will be more vulnerable to water erosion than soils on level ground. The reverse is probably true of wind erosion. Different species of vegetation have different effects in protecting the soil from wind and rain and in binding it together with their roots, and will respond in different ways to fluctuating grazing pressure.[11]

Both the nature of the physical environment and economic and social factors will determine the species of livestock which pastoralists keep, and this in turn will influence the possibility and desirability of a more conservative or opportunistic strategy. If, for example, the pastoralists are mainly relying on camels, opportunism will be largely impractical, for camels have a maximum potential natural growth rate, in terms of numbers, of between 1 and 7 per cent per year, and this prevents a rapid response in stock numbers to periods of favourable rainfall. Maximum potential annual growth in numbers of goats, however, may be as high as 45 per cent, of sheep 25 per cent, and of cattle just over 10 per cent (Dahl and Hjort, 1976). Each species, therefore, presents a different capacity for adjusting stock numbers upwards and therefore a slightly different balance of advantage between the two strategies. However, although sheep and goats may be better able, because of their high reproduction rate, to pursue opportunistic strategies, they may also, through their greater efficiency as grazers, create the very instability which makes opportunism necessary in the first place (Noy-Meir, 1975, p. 470).

The influence of the rate of natural population growth will be modified where pastoralists can sell, exchange, and repurchase different species at different points in the cycle of droughts and good years from areas not affected by the same rainfall regime. For in that case loss of camels, for example, during drought can be compensated by a switch into small stock which, when their numbers have grown rapidly after drought, can be re-exchanged for camels (Dahl and Hjort, 1979). The existence of a reliable potential for switching will favour opportunism. This is also the case where, in the event of a disaster to his livestock enterprise, a pastoralist can rely on relief from within his own community or from government, or on paid employment, or on self-employment in some non-pastoral enterprise, to meet his subsistence needs and to enable him to restart his pastoral enterprise after the drought is ended. For in these cases the existence of alternative means of survival will remove much of the advantage of conservatism.

Pastoralists' objectives will also influence their choice of strategy. If their main concern is assurance of survival, whether physically as individuals or socially as coherent groups with an identity of their own, or if government or business is concerned with the need to secure reliable supplies of meat from dry areas, then the choice will be for conservatism. If, however, an ideology of performance and competition in respect of income, wealth, and status prevails, opportunism is likely to predominate. In contrast, a government or society may be concerned to minimize inequality between individuals. Fluctuations in livestock numbers that are a consequence of an opportunistic strategy are often identified as the occasions on which the rich get relatively richer and the poor poorer (Devitt, 1979). This is not always so, but, where it is, the tendency will be towards conservatism.

INSTRUMENTS OF DEVELOPMENT

We now turn to look at the instruments that can be used in pastoral development. Given that we wish to achieve certain objectives and to pursue one set of strategies rather than another, what practical steps can we take to turn our intentions into reality? One set of instruments that can be used are broad political, economic, and social policies which affect the nation as a whole as well as the pastoral section of it. Among such policies are those concerning the political constitution and institutions of the nation, ethnic discrimination, the pricing of industrial and agricultural goods, the location of industries, personal and indirect taxation, the public health and education system, and so on. Often these broad national policies are not susceptible to change by particular or specifically pastoral programmes. In such cases they are 'characteristics' rather than 'instruments'. They are briefly referred to again in Chapter 11.

Another set of instruments consists of legislation and rules, together with the means for their enforcement such as enforcement officers and courts, that are specific to the use and management of pastoral areas. Such rules are likely to include the allocation of rights to grazing, water, livestock, and labour, and the control of these resources. Another set consists of investments and programmes specially designed for pastoral development. Among the investments will be new roads, new water supplies, perhaps some fencing, firebreaks, and planting of forage species, and some buildings. Among the programmes will be some to provide livestock to the poorest who have none of their own, to improve animal health, breeding, and husbandry, to manage and control the growth and use of forage, to move, market, and process livestock and products, to provide social services to the human population. All these sets of instruments, except for the broad national policies, we can describe as *components* of pastoral development. Such components may be introduced and implemented by government organizations, by a group of pastoralists, or by individuals. We shall be looking at some of the potential components in detail in Chapters 4–9.

The various components of pastoral development, when implemented, have effects that may be intended or unintended. Some effects will be the consequence of the components' technical elements; for example, livestock mortality is likely to fall as a consequence of vaccination against diseases. Some effects will be the consequence of new incentives offered by these programmes to pastoralists and to others. New marketing programmes, for example, are likely to affect the class and number of livestock sold; and new tenure arrangements may induce pastoralists to alter the number, quality, and species of their livestock. But one of the factors which will influence the effects of components will be the way in which they are organized and managed. Essentially the same components may be organized and managed in a number of different ways. In Chapter 3 and subsequent chapters we shall examine in greater detail what constitutes 'different ways' or forms of organizing and managing something. One difference lies in whether a function is carried out by government, trader, or community; another difference is the degree of centralization of decision-making. It is legitimate, therefore, to regard *management and organization* as a different kind of instrument, and different forms of organization and management as a separate category of factors to be taken into account in designing pastoral development. In Chapter 3 we shall look at some general points in organizing and managing pastoral development and at the criteria for choice between different forms. This will be followed by a more detailed look at management and organization of different components in later chapters.

AN ANALOGY

In our framework for analysing the appropriateness of different forms of pastoral development we have identified characteristics of pastoral situations, objectives, strategies, instruments, i.e. components and alternative forms of organization and management, as the key categories of factors which affect and interrelate with each other. Such categorization can be merely muddling or it can be a help in clarifying and ordering our ideas. An analogy may be helpful in promoting clarification. Let us take the analogy of a family of tourists visiting a country and preparing their programme. The geography of the country, its mountains, valleys, and extent, and the age, sex, education, and interests of the tourists are akin to our *characteristics* of a pastoral situation. The particular places which the different members of the family wish to visit are akin to our *objectives* of development. Different members of a family, like different individuals, classes, occupational or ethnic groups within a nation state, may have conflicting objectives and wishes and may quarrel about these. The route which the family follows between these places is akin to our *strategies*, and the vehicles in which it travels are the counterpart to our *components*. Finally the choice of drivers is the equivalent of our choice of different forms of *organization and management*. In the same way as the geography of a country affects both where the family wants to go, its route, and the vehicle in which it travels, and in the same way as different drivers are more suited to particular vehicles and routes, so in pastoral development, there is an interaction between characteristics, objectives, strategies, components, and forms, with each in turn influencing and being influenced by the others. These interactions are particularly emphasized and illustrated at the end of Chapter 4 which deals with water development. Analogies can be misleading as well as helpful. Nevertheless, this one may go some way to illustrate the nature of the choices to be made in pastoral development.

NOTES TO CHAPTER 2

1. Throughout this section I am strongly indebted to the ideas of several members of the ODI Pastoral Network. Some of these ideas were set out in ODI Pastoral Network Paper, 2b and in Oxby (1975).

2. Both females and males are pastoralists. The English language does not have a neutral pronoun to describe the case where neither sex is particularly indicated, and it is tedious and pedantic always to say 'him or her'. Following common practice I hereafter use the masculine form to include the neutral case.

3. The source of this information is discussion with officials of the US Bureau of Land Management in Utah in 1982.

4. The source is an unpublished memorandum of the Ethiopian Government's Livestock and Meat Board.

5. Of course this depends on one's definition of primitiveness, currently an unfashionable word. One crude way of testing whether one thinks that mobility is in itself primitive is to rank pastoral societies in some sort of subjective order of primitiveness and then to see whether this ranking is correlated with their relative mobility. When I do this, it is not so related.

6. In conversation, Dr Hugh Lamprey has suggested to me that domestic livestock may be less sensitive than wild ungulates to changes in protein content in the forage, and will continue to graze forage with a lower protein content than will wildlife.

7. Some Somali pastoralists have talked to me along lines which suggest that some density-dependent mechanism controls the appetite and disease-proneness of camel herds.

8. If we define the minimum in terms of the amount required for bare survival the fate of the 'surplus' will be somewhat different. Let us assume that the accepted degree of risk of (the estimate of) the carrying capacity turning out to be too high is 5 years in 100. For convenience let us also assume that annual rainfall is normally distributed, with a coefficient of variation of 40 per cent (quite usual for very arid areas), and with a linear relationship, passing through the origin, between annual rainfall and annual forage production; and that livestock, if offered the opportunity, will eat twice the amount they need for bare survival. These assumptions, although rough, are reasonable approximations to reality. In these conditions the 'bare survival' requirements of the number of livestock present at the accepted estimate of carrying capacity will amount to 34 per cent of average annual forage production and these requirements will be surpassed by production in 95 years in every 100. However, the same number of livestock will be prepared to eat each year, if allowed, 68 per cent of the average annual forage production, an amount which will be surpassed, leaving an ungrazed surplus, by actual production in only 79 years out of 100 — a major decrease in the frequency of wasted surplus.

9. Among the assumptions are: normality of annual rainfall; a linear relationship between annual rainfall and forage production; livestock are fed ad lib; there are no

significant costs of livestock production that vary with the number of livestock kept; value of livestock output varies proportionately with the number kept.

10. A 'positive' effect occurs where undergrazing in one year leads to more and/or better forage being available in subsequent years than would have been the case if the pressure of grazing in the first year had been proper. 'Undergrazing' *may* even have negative effects where the consequence is invasion by less desirable species.

11. Noy-Meir (1975) discusses other plant characteristics which make some grazing systems inherently unstable even where exogenous shocks such as poor rainfall do not disturb them. Such systems may benefit from fluctuating grazing pressures.

Chapter three

Management and organization in pastoral development

THE SCOPE OF MANAGEMENT

This chapter, after a brief review of what management involves in a pastoral context, will examine the ways in which some pastoral situations pose particular difficulties or peculiarities for effective management that systematically distinguish them from other pastoral situations or from other forms of agricultural development. It will also discuss some of the kinds of choices that can be made between different forms of management and organization, the criteria on the basis of which appropriate choices can be made, and the general factors that are likely to influence choice in one direction or another.

The management of pastoral development includes both its design and its current management. The design of pastoral development involves making decisions about the emphasis to be put on different objectives, defining —in the case of a government — the target area or group, and selecting certain strategies, components, and forms of organization and management. The process of designing may require that some very detailed investigation, e.g. hydrogeological surveys, be carried out, and will certainly include negotiations — within and between pastoral groups, between pastoral groups and government or other non-pastoral groups, between different government and quasi-government organizations, and possibly between government and an external financing agency. This process of designing may, on occasion, appear to be finite, as when a government and an external agency sign an agreement to undertake a project on the basis of a feasibility study. In reality, design and redesign is a continuous activity.

Current management involves short-term planning and allocation of resources. The actual process may include the drawing up of rules, regulations, and orders, providing a framework of both material and non-material incentives to motivate people to act in a desired way, as well as the direct implementation of the work by the person or organization doing the managing. It will involve a great deal of detailed programming and co-ordination of labour, livestock, money, and other resources to make sure that things are done in the right place at the right time. Programming the expenditure of money requires also that provision be made to raise it, through user-charges or taxes levied, probably, on pastoralists, or through loans and grants raised, probably, from outside pastoral society. Reviewing and evaluating performance are also part of management and may be as simple as checking

47

the number and condition of a herd at the end of a day's work or as complex as a formal, statistically based, monitoring of a project's impacts.

The 'manager', i.e. the one who carries out management functions, may be a private individual or an organization. If the latter, it may be a household, an encampment, a clan, or any other group of pastoralists (or their officers), a commercial firm, a part of government or some other non-government organization. Although many activities in pastoral life and development may be carried out by individuals working on their own, e.g. a herdsman tending a group of animals, a range officer patrolling a boundary line, an engineer drawing the design of a dam, nevertheless some organization will be involved, be it the household and its head allocating daily duties, or the range-management organization of government hiring, training, and disposing its staff. This study is not primarily concerned with the way in which the herdsman allocates his own time in looking after the animals, and only marginally with how pastoral households organize their resources on a daily basis. It is mainly concerned with how a pastoral group or society or a government organization carries out its functions. However, I do not believe that there should be a hard and fast division between the functions of the individual, the community, and the government. It may be appropriate that the same function should be performed by an individual in one set of circumstances and by government in another. Moreover, in any case the 'grass-roots' levels cannot be wholly divorced from those above them, since one of the functions of the upper levels will be to change behaviour at the grass-roots, and the behaviour of the grass-roots levels can totally frustrate other functions at the upper levels. For example, if certain pastures or water points are closed, as part of a rest-and-rotation grazing system, this will affect the herdsman's concern to ensure that his camels obtain the minerals they need from particular wells or types of vegetation. If he disregards the closure the proposed grazing system will be ineffective.

Some pastoral development programmes are very simple, include only one component, and have consequences which are useful but which do not fundamentally change relations between individuals or the structure of pastoral life. Other, more ambitious, programmes have many components, e.g. new water points, control of livestock numbers, rotation of pastures, etc. and involve enormous changes not only in the way in which pastoral production is carried out but also in the way in which its benefits are distributed and in the social relations between different individuals, sexes, ethnic and occupational groups, or economic classes. For such ambitious programmes to be successful (in terms of their objectives), a very wide range of management functions must be undertaken. Among such functions are the allocation of property rights, operating or managing resources and services, collecting and disseminating information, procuring supplies from outside pastoral society, recruiting and training staff, managing political and other relations between pastoralists and the rest of the economy, etc. Some of these functions are specific to particular components of pastoral development and some are common to many of them. Some are not an integral part of any particular component, but their performance must form part of the background against which development projects can be successfully pursued.

SPECIAL FEATURES IN THE MANAGEMENT OF PASTORAL DEVELOPMENT

Management in an industrial concern, in the army, in a ministry's headquarters in a capital city, on a farm or agricultural estate, in the extension service in a crop area, and in pastoral development all have some features in common; but they also each have special features and problems of their own. The management of agricultural and rural development is now attracting a growing volume of interest and study.[1] The management of pastoral development shares some features with the management of other forms of agricultural and rural development which it does not share with industrial, military, or bureaucratic management. It also has some peculiar features of its own which pose particular problems for good management. The next few paragraphs identify some important features. For the most part, these features are peculiarly apparent in pastoral situations in contrast to non-pastoral ones; but they are variables, present in greater or lesser degree, rather than attributes which can only be present or absent. Development in some pastoral situations may not exhibit these features at all or only to a lesser degree than in some non-pastoral situations, while in other pastoral situations it exhibits them to a strong degree.

The density of the human population in most pastoral areas is low, and with it the density of pastoral production units from whom information and marketable commodities have to be collected and to whom information, commodities, and services have to be distributed. Not only is the population sparse, it is often mobile also, and its movements cannot be predicted with certainty. In many pastoral areas with traditional social and economic structures the only social unit that coheres, that is, that moves and camps together as neighbours, for any long period of time, is the household or the encampment of several households, often with a total human population of less than 200 people.[2] The low natural productivity of the environment can justify only a low level of investment in transport and communications. Large interannual variations in climate and, associated with this, variations in productivity and livestock numbers, cause large fluctuations in the supply of and demand for services and commodities. These factors all raise substantial problems of management. Fluctuations over time mean there will either be under- or over-capacity in terms of staff and permanent structures. The low density and poor communications network mean that the cost of transport is high in terms of both money and staff time; and the unpredictability of movement and location means that many journeys are undertaken fruitlessly. The mobility of the population and its low cohesion mean that organizing the provision of services on the basis of either geographical areas or social units can lead to the ratios between, for example, veterinary staff and livestock becoming rapidly very unequal in different areas or in different pastoral groups.

The mobility of the population, its frequent lack of cohesion above household or encampment level, and the difficulty of communications raise two further problems for management. The first is that if a participatory management structure is established to manage public facilities, e.g. a council or committee to supervise the use of a well or pasture, the membership of the organization may have to change very frequently or else it will be found that it has dispersed elsewhere and can no longer function and no longer represents current users of the facility. The second problem is that close supervision of junior employees by their seniors in public service is very difficult and expensive. The seniors may not know where their juniors are and it is very expensive for one to travel to meet the other.

In many countries pastoral populations, if not currently oppressed minorities, nevertheless have a long history of hostility to the government of the state and to their fellow citizens. Moreover, overall national policies, for example in respect of property rights, education, or health, are often thought up primarily with the circumstances of the urban or crop-cultivating population in mind. There are often substantial cultural and linguistic barriers between pastoral people and the government officials with whom they deal or who decide on pastoral affairs. These barriers arise because very seldom do these officials originate in pastoral society. This may be due to deliberate discrimination against the employment of pastoralists, or because the late development of education in pastoral areas has meant that too few pastoralists had the necessary educational qualifications for government employment, or because of a national policy against government officials serving in the area of their own origin. The consequences are that it is very difficult to obtain a good understanding by either pastoralists or government of the needs or expertise of the other side or of what constraints it labours under; and the national policies are quite inappropriate when applied to pastoral areas. These problems are also found in other non-pastoral situations but seldom to such a degree as in pastoral ones.

As we have seen in Chapter 2, there are circumstances in which the best strategy may be one of nomadic movements by pastoral livestock over very large areas of land. This normally implies that different pastoral groups with their own distinct herds of livestock and their own distinct economic interests may be wanting to use the same piece of land (i.e. the forage on it) at the same time. The fact that there are economies of scale in providing certain services, for example that a well or dam sufficient to supply 1000 head of cattle will cost much less than twice as much to construct as one supplying 500 head, also means that different pastoral groups may simultaneously want to use other facilities besides land. Pastoral human populations normally have a positive natural rate of growth although it may not necessarily be a very high one (Sandford, 1976b). At the same time, the size of their pastoral grazing lands may be decreasing due to incursions by outside interests. The technical possibilities for expanding the per-hectare output of pastoral land seem to be more limited than in high potential cropland areas. All these factors have the result that neighbouring pastoral groups, even when closely related in terms of kinship, tend to be in continuous and increasing competition with each other,[3] far more so than is the case in rain-fed cropland areas where the allocation of rights to use of land, even when this is very unequally distributed and very scarce, tends to take place at definite points in an individual's life cycle or at worst at particular dates in the crop year.

In nomadic pastoralism not only is the competition much more continuous and unpredictable, but at the same time the use of common facilities requires a high degree of co-operation and management between different groups. In some respects it is quite like irrigated agriculture where many farmers are drawing water from the same source, but in the case of pastoralism there are more limited possibilities than in the case of irrigation for everybody to become better off simultaneously through technical advances. These factors raise very serious problems for participatory forms of self-management, but at the same time it is even more difficult in pastoral than in crop areas for government successfully to pursue an authoritarian style of management imposing strict externally generated discipline on the population. This difficulty arises both from the nature of the physical environment and also because governments know so little about the pastoral societies they seek to control. The critical question for participatory management is at what level of society, for what functions, and in what circumstances, is a sufficient degree of co-operation likely to exist to make participatory management possible.

ALTERNATIVE FORMS OF MANAGEMENT AND ORGANIZATION

The preceding section has stressed some of the peculiar problems of the management of pastoral development. If there was only one *form* which management and organization could take, then there would be little point in a recital of the difficulties, for all that could be done would be to struggle on regardless of them. It is because there are different ways (forms) of organizing and managing pastoral development that it is useful to draw attention to some of the special features of pastoral situations and to see how these may affect our choice of management and organization. The next few paragraphs draw attention to some important different forms of managing and organizing pastoral development.

There are, of course, a near infinite number of respects in which the way something is managed or organized in one situation is different from the way in which it is managed or organized in another. In selecting a handful of these respects for categorizing into different 'forms' I am implicitly — and now explicitly — making two claims; first that the different forms correspond to real choices that have repeatedly to be made, for example that a choice between more or less centralization is one that comes up again and again and can be recognized as such; secondly that the choice of one option rather than another has important and consistent consequences — consistent in the sense that, other things remaining unchanged, the same option chosen twice or more in succession will have the same consequences on each occasion. The consequences that matter are mainly calculated in terms of their impact on objectives (see also the next section in this chapter).

One obvious option concerns who should do what — the nature of the organization to carry out particular functions. In particular, should the organization concerned be a government one (e.g. the veterinary department), a community one (e.g. a co-operative or the council of elders of the X clan), a commercial firm or trader, or an individual pastoral household or herdsman? For example, veterinary treatment of livestock can be provided by the central government's veterinary department, by veterinarians in private practice, by community-employed livestock assistants, or by individual stockowners to their own animals.

Another option relates to the basis on which organizations should be constituted. One possibility is to constitute pastoral groups (or field services of government) on a *territorial* basis, to include, for example, as members of an organization or as its clientele, all those who live in a particular district or in the area around a particular water point — but this raises problems where nomadic movements cross territorial boundaries. Another possibility is on a *social group* basis, e.g. a kinship basis, to include, for example, all the members of clan X; or a *social class* basis (e.g. the poorest or stockless). And another is on a contract basis, to include those who have agreed to join a co-operative or company. Community organizations can be inclusive or exclusive; inclusive ones are open to anyone; exclusive ones can regulate their own membership.

Another option relates to whether organizations should be multi-purpose or specialist. A ranching co-operative is multi-purpose, as is a district pastoral development agency. Alternative organizations may be specialist, specializing either by function (e.g. in animal health *or* range management) or by *product* (a meat organization *or* a dairy organization). Specialization applies not only to branches of government but also to organizations of pastoralists. Parallel to this option are those relating to scale and complexity of both organization and technique, and to whether new organizations should be set up to undertake new functions and to cope with new conditions or whether use should be made of existing or traditional organizations.

Several options relate to matters of management. One such option is whether decision-making and executive action should be centralized at a level in an organizational hierarchy where economies of scale and high levels of technical expertise exist, or should be decentralized to lower levels at which speed of decision-making and local expertise can be mobilized. Centralization and decentralization are options which can apply both to purely 'hierarchical space', i.e. between the top and bottom of a large organization wholly housed in a single building, and to 'physical space', for example where staff of a given level of seniority can either be dispersed to work on their own throughout the rangelands or concentrated in a single team at district headquarters. A related option is whether staff and services should be fixed in one location or themselves be mobile.

Parallel to this option about the degree of centralization, but not identical with it, are questions about the style of management that is to govern relations between manager and managed. The style may be *mandatory*, as where a government range department issues regulations whose infringement by pastoralists will lead to their punishment; or it may be *liberal*, that is permissive but manipulative, with one or a whole bundle of incentives designed to influence the managed to behave as the manager wants, but with the former free to ignore the incentives if he wishes. Such incentives may be financial, with grants to induce investment, or with high prices to encourage sales, or they may offer increased honour or status. The style may be *contractual*, as, for example, where a private veterinarian provides the services a pastoralist wants against payment, or where a group of pastoralists jointly use land on the basis that individuals will accept decisions made by the group as a whole.

Another option in management style is between authoritarian and participatory management — especially in respect of decision-making. Under a participatory style of management lower levels in a hierarchy, or the customers and clients of a monopoly or government service, are consulted and may initiate discussion; but not under an authoritarian style. There is no necessary correspondence between centralization and mandatory or authoritarian styles of management, although in practice they often go together. Nevertheless it is possible for lower levels to be fully consulted (participatory), for decisions then to be taken at very high levels in a hierarchy (centralization), and for the results to be embodied in contractual agreements or in a series of liberal measures which pastoralists are free to take part in or to ignore.

A further management option is between more or less management intensity, measured (easily) in terms of staff ratios (staff in relation to land area or production or livestock or pastoralists), or (with difficulty) in terms of the proportion of time spent by staff on managerial rather than technical functions. Managerial functions include planning, budgeting, and report-writing, personnel matters, supervision and training of more junior staff, liaison with pastoralists. In the case of pastoralists, managerial intensity can be measured by the proportion of their time spent on community affairs rather than on those simply pertaining to their own livestock. Management intensity is also indicated by the existence of written plans and of codified operating procedures and formal systems for monitoring and evaluating progress.

THE CRITERIA FOR CHOICE OF FORM

How should we decide what form of management and organization is appropriate in a particular situation? The natural answer of the 'practical' man is to choose the form that 'works' in carrying out the management functions set, that 'produces results' and that does not cost too much. But these are not unambiguous concepts. Commercial ranches, in some countries, may produce higher sales of beef per hectare than traditional pastoralism; but the effects of these ranches on rural poverty or on the integrity of traditional cultures are usually negative (see, for example, Cruz de Carvalho, 1974). Similarly decentralization to individual owners of livestock or herders of decisions about where livestock should graze at particular times may enable the most thorough exploitation of the vegetation, and consequently, the maximum average level of output, but such decentralization may be disadvantageous in respect of considerations of equity, environmental conservation, and the stability of output. Nor is the concept of minimizing the cost of management, which is tantamount to minimizing management intensity, appropriate. The minimum cost will occur when no management or any other activity takes place at all.

Impact on objectives

Fairly obviously, the most appropriate form of organization is one that facilitates the greatest degree of achievement of all the development objectives that are being pursued on a particular occasion[4] with the greatest margin over the costs involved in that particular 'form'. We can call this criterion the one that maximizes the impact on objectives. The methodological problems involved in calculating the relative impact on objectives of different 'forms' are the familiar ones involved in any kind of social benefit–cost analysis. Almost all such formal decision-making devices tend to be much more useful as aids for shaping our general attitudes to decision-making than as practical tools on particular occasions. In our search for the most appropriate form of organization and management the problem is not only a question of the criterion for choice. Often what seems to work or to have one set of consequences in one country or situation does not work or has other consequences in another. We also need evidence that shows us how different conditions affect the results of different forms of organization and management.

As a conceptual model one can conceive of a scoreboard in which different forms of organization and management are listed on lines down the side of the board, and different objectives are written across the top at the head of columns. Each form of organization (line) can then be given a score in terms of its impact in achieving each objective. Table 3.1 illustrates such a conceptual scoreboard, where Form A1 stands for a form of organization in which pastoralists are organized on a kinship basis, and government services on a territorial and universal basis; where A2 stands for a form in which pastoralists are also organized along kinship lines but where government services are organized on a kinship but also on a contractual basis, etc. Form B1 may stand for co-operative ranches run by pastoralists and B2 for commercial ranches run by outsiders. The first column of the table then shows how good (i.e. how many points it scores) each organizational form listed down the left-hand side of the table is at increasing the quantity of output; the second column does the same thing in respect of stability of output; and so on.

Table 3.1 A model for assessing forms of organization and management

| Form of management and organization | Objectives | | | | |
	Quantity of output (1)	Stability of output (2)	Integrity of pastoralists' culture (3)	Environmental conservation (4)	etc. (5)
A1	5	5	8	−2	3
A2	1	−2	8	−1	−1
B1	10	6	−9	0	−3
B2	10	6	−9	+1	−2
etc.					
etc.			etc.		

By this model the choice of form will depend on each form's aggregate score across the board. As an *operational* model, of course, this is far too crude. We need to introduce further columns for different kinds of costs. Moreover, the scoreboard is only two-dimensional, and we need at least two other dimensions, one to represent different characteristics of pastoral situations, and the other to represent different components, or combinations of components, of development programmes. Even as a conceptual model it suffers from the drawback of treating forms of organization (and characteristics of pastoral situations if we add a third dimension) as discrete attributes rather than continuous variables. In any case, we do not have enough experience, nor the right kind of studies of that experience, to enable us to separate the effects of different management and organizational forms from other differences between pastoral development programmes so as to generate the 'scores' to fit into each of the boxes on the board.[5] We need not, therefore, worry about what the figures might be scores of, i.e. what units they are expressed in and whether they are really the same units in each box, thus allowing us legitimately to sum across the board to obtain an aggregate score. The model has, however, some utility in giving an idea of how one might tackle, in a formal and rationalizing way, an all-embracing approach to the choice of organizational form.

In practice we shall have to be much more modest. The main criterion for our choice of form must be the impact on objectives, and the costs (drawbacks) involved. In Chapters 4–9 we shall look at the actual experience of pastoral development in respect of particular components and try to start the mapping-out of the results of different forms in terms of objectives and costs under different conditions. It will be a very tentative sketch of a few patches in a multi-dimensional scoreboard of the kind just indicated. No attempt will be made to look at financial costs. Firm scores cannot be put in any boxes, but a few pluses or minuses begin to emerge. Probably this is as much as we shall ever get. It would be nice to pretend that more research would lead to a complete and accurate picture with the possibility of precise conclusions about what to do. More, and above all in-depth, field research is required and this will enlarge the area of the patches in which we can at least discern the sign (positive or negative) of the score, and maybe the order of magnitude. But precision is likely to remain for ever beyond us.

Minor criteria

There are, however, a number of minor criteria by reference to which we can make provisional judgments about the merits of different forms of organization and management where direct evidence is lacking about the impact on objectives. Some of these minor criteria represent qualities which one would look for in the way in which a programme is managed and organized, and the absence of which would lead one, *prima facie*, to suspect that a particular way is not likely to be effective. These qualities are flexibility, viability, acceptability to pastoralists, congruence in incentives, and incorporation of available knowledge.

Flexibility is required in space, time, and target. Blanket systems of approach based on mathematically convenient assumptions about squares, circles, straight lines, and averages are not going to be able to cope with the realities of pastoral diversity. Beautiful square, hexagonal, or circular grazing blocks (models which minimize fencing and firebreak costs), homogeneous vegetation (which responds uniformly to particular techniques of pasture management), water points spaced at distances of exactly 30 km, these are all features of plans and management systems which are not going to work in practice. They are useful devices for ordering one's thoughts, but worse than useless in making plans for implementation. The system of organization and management must be geared to be able to cope with spatial heterogeneity.

Flexibility over time is required to cope with the great climatic variability of pastoral areas and with other factors which change over time; and the system adopted must contain provision for the speedy reversal, whether temporary or permanent, of previous decisions and policies. For otherwise pressures will build up, for example, to open up emergency water supplies or fodder reserves in time of drought, and if the development programme's own decision-making system cannot adapt to these it will be swept aside and will probably lose influence beyond the period of the immediate crisis. Flexibility over time is also required to cope with demographic pressure and with rapid changes in social structure due to the impact, for example, of education.

Flexibility in target is needed to deal with the requirements of different kinds of livestock and different classes of people. Camels, for example, have quite different needs from cattle for fodder, water, and minerals, and respond quite differently to restrictions on movement and to increased proximity to other animals (Dahl, 1979, pp. 41–52; Torry, 1974). People with few livestock or with children at day-school will not be able to follow the same management regime as owners of large herds or those with plenty of herdsmen. A system designed solely for the 'average' man or beast will be wrong for the great majority of the population.

We can look at viability, acceptability to pastoralists, and congruence in incentives together. By viability is meant the ability of a programme, in the long run, to generate its own sources of technical expertise, political support, and finance so that it can continue without constant recourse to these resources from outside pastoral areas and society. Since pastoralists are quite a small minority in most countries it is not realistic to expect much political stamina in central government to continue on a large scale any initial interest in and support of pastoral development. The acceptability of pastoral development to pastoralists is also relevant here. Of course governments can force highly unpopular measures on pastoralists. Sometimes it may be necessary and desirable to impose measures (e.g. land reform or expropriation of livestock) on the current political and social leadership of a pastoral group, measures to which that leadership is violently opposed. In the long run, however, unless those who will exercise dominant political influence in pastoral society accept and agree with what is being done, it is improbable that any government will continue with a development programme supposed to be in the pastoralists' interests if this requires a continued politically unrewarding effort from government. The situation may, of course, be quite different where the programme is merely a means of exploiting pastoralists in the interests of a government's political supporters.

The inclusion of the quality of congruence in incentives follows from the same general line of reasoning. If sole reliance is placed on government orders and legislation or on financial incentives, leading to a conflict of pulls between the chosen instrument and other influences, not only will progress be slow but any faltering in the chosen instrument may lead to a total reversal of direction. The fate of controlled grazing schemes in Africa at the end of the colonial era and the campaign to sedentarize nomads in Iran in the 1920s and 1930s illustrate this. In the manipulation of behaviour of both pastoralists and the staff of development programmes several different kinds of incentive all need to point the same way. Rural development in communist-ruled China is often held up as a model of success, and great stress in explaining this success has sometimes been laid on the role of ideology, self-discipline, and the level of consciousness among the Chinese rural people. It is now becoming more apparent that such success as there has been was due to the fact that these factors and more material incentives all pointed behaviour in the same direction, and that where they were at variance success was lacking (Unger, 1978).

Spatial and temporal variations in rainfall, topography, vegetation, and other factors make blanket solutions, as already pointed out, singularly inappropriate in pastoral development. Yet some decisions do have to be taken which affect large blocks of land and large numbers of people. In most of the world's pastoral areas very little scientific research has yet taken place on the management of pastures, and on appropriate animal husbandry and breeding, and only a modest amount on problems of animal health. Answers based on proper (according to Western ideas) scientific research into technical problems are not yet available in any quantity, but pastoral societies have generally successfully used these areas for centuries. They have often evolved techniques for evading the problems if not for overcoming them, whereas technically well-trained newcomers from outside often do not even suspect the existence of the problems. For these reasons of spatial and temporal heterogeneity and of the absence of 'technical' solutions, it is particularly important that forms of management and organization be adopted which facilitate flows of information from bottom to top, i.e. from pastoralists to range and veterinary officers upwards to ministries, and laterally between pastoralists and inside the organs of government. These flows should receive at least as much attention as the extension of government's expertise downwards. It is not only a question of technical information but also of information about the functions that individuals or groups are expected to undertake within a development programme, about their problems, and even about their physical whereabouts.

If some of the minor criteria for choice of form represent positive qualities such as acceptability and viability, others represent negative ones — drawbacks and costs. Financial costs are only one element in this, although an important one. Many pastoral development programmes currently being implemented have an organizational structure excessively dependent on vehicles, on radio-telephones, and on mechanical bulldozers and graders. The prices offered for livestock products in the developing world, and the relative prices of labour and machinery, make inappropriate these transfers of technology from the USA and Australia. Other costs are really negative objectives, feelings by pastoralists that they are being shut out from the management of their own resources, an increasing loss by them of control over their own future. Some forms of organization and management currently being implemented in pastoral development are putting excessive opportunities to take bribes, and to build up personal power and wealth at the expense of others, in the hands of people (mainly but not only outsiders to pastoral society) not subject to adequate bureaucratic or social control. Some forms envisage a quite inappropriate kind of personal relationship between officials and pastoralists or between pastoralists themselves, or even between officials. For example, newly graduated schoolboys 'instruct' experienced elders; or range-guards recruited from one clan or tribe arrest pastoralists from another for trespassing on their own rangelands (Spencer, 1973, p. 194). These relations are quite alien and offensive to local tradition and in the long run will defeat their own purpose.

SUMMARY

This chapter has been concerned to discuss in a general way some questions about the organization and management of pastoral development which will arise in dealing with particular components of development in subsequent chapters. The scope of management has been defined to include not only the day-to-day supervision of operations but also the design of pastoral development and its review and evaluation. The more complex the programme of pastoral development that is to be implemented, the wider the range of management functions which need to be carried out. Although this study is not substantially concerned with the management of individual animals, nevertheless no sharp dividing line can be drawn to distinguish the management of development from the management of the herd.

Many of the issues of organization and management which arise in pastoral development also arise in agricultural development as a whole and in other sectors of the economy. Nevertheless, there are some special features in the natural, social, and political environment of pastoral development which are not so common or present to such a degree in other environments and which therefore pose particular problems or require special solutions. Low population density, fluctuating levels of production, the mobility of the human population, and the degree of competition between different groups, and misunderstandings between pastoralists and governments are the most important features.

An interest in improving management and organization in pastoral development presupposes that it is possible to distinguish and choose between different ways of organizing and managing. This chapter has identified a number of different forms of organization and management between which choices can be made and has examined the appropriate criteria for choice. Usually this will be in terms of the effect that making one choice or another has on the objectives of development. Although analytically sophisticated techniques for choosing can be proposed, and help us to grasp the nature of the issues which arise in making a choice, in practice only very rough-and-ready answers to some of the questions about choice are likely to become available in the foreseeable future. In some cases even rough-and-ready answers about likely direct effects on objectives will not be available, in which case reliance will have to be put on other minor criteria.

NOTES TO CHAPTER 3

1. For some important examples see Chambers (1974), Leonard (1977), Hunter (1978), Gow *et al.* (1979), Honadle *et al.* (1980), Moris (1981).

2. For a fairly full discussion of the functions, size, and durability of groups of nomadic pastoralists at different levels see Tapper (1979a).

3. There is a fuller discussion of competition between pastoral groups in Salzman (1978). This looks at the relationship between territorial and genealogical closeness and their effects on competition and co-operation.

4. Possible objectives were considered in Chapter 2. We can summarily recollect them here. The main ones were concerned with: the quantity and stability of output; the conservation of the environment; the integrity of pastoralists' culture; the political integration of pastoralists; equity; the self-reliance of pastoralists; the security, status, and achievement of wealth or basic needs of pastoral societies as a whole or of individuals and social groups within them.

5. Leonard (1977, especially pp. 72 and 84) has shown that this approach is feasible both in theory and practice at a local scale where the number of variables can be reduced and where it is possible to select a reasonably convincing proxy (number of visits paid to each farmer) to represent one's objective. In contrast the attempt by Gow *et al.* (1979) to do this on a global scale is less convincing.

Chapter four

The development of pastoral water supplies

INTRODUCTION

This chapter starts with an outline of some important aspects of water development: the kinds of changes in water supply that it can bring about, the technical and administrative devices that give rise to these changes, the impulses from which water development springs, and the low success rate and durability of some technical devices. It goes on to list the main managerial functions which are involved in water development and illustrates with examples some of the issues which arise in carrying out these functions. Following the general analytic model of Chapter 1, it then examines interactions between characteristics of situations, objectives of development, forms of management and organization, and the different technical and administrative devices which constitute the water development component. It first discusses the way in which technology requires certain forms of organization and management; the example of labour-intensive water development is looked at in some detail. It then examines the impact, under different conditions (i.e. characteristics of situations), of water development on different objectives. It proceeds from there to analyse the advantages and disadvantages involved in one particular organizational option, the choice between a government or non-government form of control over new water supplies. Finally, it draws together in summary form the various propositions about interactions which have been developed in the chapter.

The development of water supplies involves not only physical changes in the number, location, output, and type of supplies but also changes, whether intended or not, in the way in which existing supplies are used and in the relative advantage which different people derive from the use, control, and ownership of both new and old supplies. The development of pastoral water supplies is very closely connected with range management because access to water is a key factor in controlling access to pasture. Range management is being treated separately in the next three chapters, because pastoral water development does raise some specific issues of its own which are additional to those connected with range management, and which deserve attention in their own right. However, placing the subjects in separate chapters should not obscure the inextricable relation between them and the folly both of developing water supplies in range areas without tying this development in to the development of range management and of ignoring the impact of new water supplies on existing range management systems.

SOME ASPECTS OF WATER DEVELOPMENT

The development of pastoral water supplies has several different aspects. Supplies can be installed in new locations and at a greater density than hitherto. The quantity (flow) of water at each location can be increased (decreased) over the year as a whole and water can be provided at different seasons within the year from hitherto. The provision of water can be made more reliable in respect of technical breakdowns, public security, and the degree of its immediate dependence on current weather conditions. The mineral content of water can be changed, making it more potable and beneficial to people and livestock, and its cleanliness can be altered with a consequent effect on health. Changes in the way in which water is delivered to animals, for example changes in the number and size of troughs, can affect the number of animals watered at one time, or during a day, the hours at which they are watered, and for how long they have to wait at the watering place. This, in turn, will affect their ability to graze at the best times of day and in the best places. Changes in the delivery system, e.g. the installation of wind-power, diesel or electric pumps, can affect the amount of labour required to water livestock. Changes can be made in the relative access to water of different pastoral groups (e.g. different clans or social classes) and individuals, and of different species of livestock (e.g. cattle or camels). Limits can be put on the number of livestock watered in total and by each individual or group.

These various aspects of water development can be brought about by a variety of technical and administrative devices. Deep boreholes, reaching down beyond the limits of open wells, can tap aquifers which yield fossil water stored for thousands of years or more recent water collected in different areas or in previous years and which is not, therefore, dependent on current or recent rainfall. Dams, *hafirs*, and cisterns (for definitions see note 1) can be built, with or without devices to prevent pollution, leakage, and evaporation, which supply water for a few weeks or even year-round and which depend on current rainfall or, at most distant, on that of the previous year. Supplies can be piped in from tens or hundreds of kilometres away, or can be brought in by ordinary lorry or tanker as happens, for example, in Syria (Chatty, 1980), Saudi Arabia (Ibrahim and Cole, 1978, pp. 30–31) and, in bad years, the Ogaden region of Ethiopia (Cossins, 1971, p. 44), and Somalia (Lewis, 1961, p. 35). Small desalination plants can make over-mineralized waters potable. Open wells can be dug by hand down to depths of 90m (Bernus, 1981, p. 46) and lined with timber, stone, bricks, or concrete to make them more permanent and secure; and troughs and manually or mechanically operated pumps or other lifting devices can be fitted to a number of different water sources. The physical characteristics of the environment, its rainfall, topography, soil, and geology largely determine which of these devices will be technically feasible in particular places. Administrative and legal as well as physical devices can be used to allocate water to different individuals and groups of users.

The impetus for the development of pastoral water supplies can come from different sources. Sometimes what will trigger development is newly acquired access to technology not previously available in the area. The manufacture of borehole drilling equipment and mechanical pumps and expertise in hydrogeology or desalination techniques are beyond the technical competence of most pastoral societies. It is the intervention of government, or in some cases, as in Botswana, of commercial firms which not only bypass but actually evade government, which opens up the possibility of this kind of development. Sometimes the development of new water supplies is sparked off by the intervention of outside sources of finance or by new ways for pastoralists to accumulate the resources required for investment. In Saudi Arabia, pastoral Bedouin can borrow from a bank, for a period of 10 years, to finance the purchase of a water tanker (Ibrahim and Cole, 1978, p. 31). In southeast Ethiopia and northern Somalia pastoralists went off and accumulated funds by working in towns and abroad and returned to invest these in cement-lined cisterns (*birkedus*) (Mirreh, 1978). In some cases it is not technical but social change, whether imposed by external forces or by internally generated evolution, which brings about new patterns of ownership and control of water.

Spending money on new water supplies is the easiest form of pastoral development. In many pastoral development programmes it is the only planned activity which actually gets carried out (examples are north-east Kenya, Tanzania, and a pilot range project in Ethiopia). In many countries different government organizations backed by different aid agencies actively compete with each other for opportunities to scatter new water points around the pastoral areas without any clear conception of what is there already or why they are adding to it. While this is a great waste of money, it has less serious environmental and social effects than one might fear, since after a few years few new water points still function.

In remote north-east Kenya, for example, only 25 per cent of 54 boreholes drilled since 1969 were still operating in 1976 (source: internal reports of Ministry of Water Development); of the 100 *hafirs* or *hafir* dams constructed, many were silted up, some completely, by 1979 (Axin, Birkhead, and Sudholt, 1979, pp. 29 and 55). In Kenya Maasailand, not far from the national capital, only 62 per cent of new water points constructed on group ranches in the 1970s still functioned at the end of the decade (White and Meadows, 1981, p. 5). In Botswana 40 per cent of boreholes never function, and a survey in central Botswana found only 65 per cent of water points (85 per cent of these are boreholes) functioning, with 19 per cent completely abandoned and 16 per cent not functioning because of some temporary breakdown (Hitchcock, 1978, pp. 143–175). In 1977 Jacobs, who had known Tanzanian Maasailand over 20 years, commented: 'Most of the former permanent water supplies of Maasailand, such as boreholes, dams and improved spring catchments and water points are either broken down, clogged up, working at reduced capacity or in need of hardware and repair to permit them to work effectively' (Jacobs, 1977, p. 8). In the same area a large range-development project constructed or rebuilt 25 major dams in the 1970s. In 1977 all of these were breached or destroyed (Jacobs, 1980) as a consequence of unusually heavy rainfall. In the Ogaden region of Ethiopia in 1974 only 9 out of at least 17 boreholes known to have been drilled were still functioning (Livestock and Meat Board, 1974, Annex II). In Niger out of 23 boreholes installed between 1961 and 1969 only 15 (65 per cent) were still functioning by the latter year (Bernus, 1977, pp. 56–57). In Sudan out of 145 boreholes in one area of southern Darfur 44 had never operated and 28 had broken or malfunctioning pumps in the mid-1970s (Hunting and Macdonald, 1977, pp. 13 and 61). The poor performance in Kenya and Botswana is all the more notable because these countries have both governmental and private sectors of the economy of higher than average efficiency in Africa. The examples given have not been deliberately selected to paint a gloomy picture; they are simply those for which data are available, and other examples which have not been selected might prove to be even worse.

FUNCTIONS IN THE MANAGEMENT OF WATER DEVELOPMENT

We now turn to look at some of the management functions which need to be carried out. The first step, in logic if not necessarily in timing, is the application of a water law in pastoral areas which lays down the ground rules about the overall level of exploitation and about who, under what conditions, may exploit water resources in a pastoral area by continuing to operate existing water points or by developing new ones. The application of a water law may involve the enactment of a new law, or the recognition *de facto* or *de jure* of an existing law or custom. Omission by government to legislate will mean either the continuation of existing practice or the licensing of a free-for-all for anyone to develop water without any conditions. If a free-for-all is allowed, and particularly if there is access to sources of funds and technical expertise from outside pastoral society with which to construct new permanent water points, the result is liable to be an expansion of the area that can be used by livestock throughout the year, and environmental degradation. If a form of water law is applied in which only a restricted *number* of licences to develop water supplies are issued, as happened in the past in Botswana where no one was allowed to drill a new borehole less than 5 miles from an existing one, and if no further conditions limiting capacity or period of use are attached, then the result will be that those who obtain the licences will be given *de facto* rights of exploitation over the land around their water supply, and will be able to earn profits from their herds or to charge fees for watering from their supply which reflect not only the value of the water they supply but also of the extra communal forage resources which they have been able to expropriate.

Early in the consideration of water development for a pastoral area the purpose of any proposed new water development needs to be clearly defined and this purpose understood and accepted by those who will carry out construction work in the field. This is especially the case where expensive equipment and technically skilled teams of workers from outside the area are to be involved. Those activities which need to be carried out before construction work begins, e.g. the exact siting of new points, agreement on the size and on other technical specifications, decisions and agreement on the responsibility for financing and control of construction, operation and maintenance, need to be substantially complete before a construction team is assembled. Once assembled, construction teams acquire a momentum of their own. They have their professional reputations to consider and so they cannot afford to be associated with protracted delays. Often they are paid on a piece-work basis, or at least for time spent at a construction site, and so they need to get into the field. In one country such a team, frustrated by inactivity, hijacked earth-moving equipment from another project several hundred kilometres away and started work with it on their own project without the knowledge of their own ministry or of the local people and before any water development programme for the project had been approved. Once equipment has arrived all sorts of arguments can be raised about the high overhead cost of keeping it idle; and this leads to inappropriately designed facilities being put in the wrong place and their benefits being captured by the wrong people.

We shall look at some of the effects of water development programmes in a later section of this chapter which will make clearer what their purposes can sensibly be. In the case of several of these purposes, for example where new water supplies are to be used as an instrument for controlling use of ranges, the design phase needs to include a survey of existing water supplies — their location, their potential seasons of use, their relative importance, who owns them, and who uses them on what terms. Such a survey needs to be done as well as the more usual technical studies that are intended to ensure that construction can be carried out with the greatest prospect of success and at the least cost. The existence of alternative supplies often means that the expected demand for, and hence revenue derived from, new supplies fails to materialize (Hunting and Macdonald, 1976, p. 59). Attention also needs to be given to the question of who will be adversely affected by new water supplies, whether these people ought to be compensated or helped to adjust, and whether their reactions are likely to affect the success of the programme. In Algeria wealthy flockowners, who had previously had sole use of certain grazing lands because they alone could afford to transport water there by lorry for use by their flocks, sabotaged windmills put in by the government which were intended to open up these grazing areas to use by other people (Coudere, 1975). Several public boreholes in the Ogaden region of Ethiopia located near existing private supplies were sabotaged, presumably because of the competition offered to these supplies. Attention also needs to be given to the likely effect of possible future development of further water supplies on the performance of the supply currently under consideration.

While great attention is usually paid in the process of technical design of government-owned water supplies to how to extract water from the ground, or how to store it in a dam, often almost no attention is paid to how to distribute it physically to livestock. As a consequence water gets polluted and structures get damaged by improper use caused by inadequate facilities. This neglect of the physical facilities for distribution is matched by neglect of the question of how to organize people and their livestock at watering — who is to use which point, how often, in what order and with what obligations. In contrast, privately owned supplies, or those constructed or owned by a traditional community of pastoralists, often have quite elaborate structures for distributing water to livestock, and meticulously enforced rules to ensure proper maintenance and use (Helland, 1980, pp. 47–75; Holy, 1974, pp. 106–109; Hatfield and Kuney, 1976). We shall return to this point later. Here the need is being stressed for proper consideration of these matters at the design stage.

At the design stage most government-sponsored water development programmes in pastoral areas appear to have been characterized at best by a one-way flow of information from government to people and often by no flow of information at all.[2] It seems probable, however, that local pastoralists can provide a large amount of information of great importance for technical design, for example about flood levels in stream beds, about draw-down in shallow wells during dry seasons, about which classes of livestock are likely to be present in the highest numbers in particular seasons and areas, about what physical facilities are necessary to water livestock, about how watering is organized at existing facilities, and whether this form of organization can also be used at new ones.

Yet, useful as such information would be, it is seldom collected and incorporated in technical plans. The reasons for this are complex and not only, if at all, due to arrogance on the part of water engineers. Engineers' job descriptions and time budgets seldom include provision for this sort of activity, nor are engineers likely to be singled out for promotion for showing zeal or competence in it. Moreover, they are ill-equipped to carry it out. They may not know the local language, and they seldom are able to stay long enough in one pastoral area to learn about its politics and personalities and to know which biases and special interests influence the views which they hear. Relations between government and pastoralists in most countries are not structured in a way in which the interests of all the groups in a pastoral society are adequately represented. Furthermore, engineers feel ill-at-ease in an activity which they feel is 'sociology' not 'engineering'. Yet sociologists cannot effectively carry out the activity either. They are not employed in sufficient numbers nor do they have sufficient engineering expertise or status in engineering departments for them to be able to carry on a dialogue with any authority or for the information they provide to triumph over conventional design criteria of least-cost. What is required is not a sociological 'washer' holding engineer and pastoralist apart, but a method of bringing the two into closer contact. Since the mid-1970s attempts have been made in southern Ethiopia to get a continuing dialogue going between pastoralists and technicians, but it is too early to judge their success, and in any case these attempts have been interrupted by political events.

We have so far dealt with management functions in the design phase of water development, but this has already begun to identify some of the functions in succeeding stages. Estimates have to be made of the financial and material resources required for the construction, operation, and maintenance of water points, and these resources have to be raised in cash and kind. This involves collection, storage, transmission, and audit. Some materials, equipment, and staff will often have to be provided from outside pastoral areas and these will have to be procured and delivered. Construction work has to be carried out according to the design. Staff have to be trained in their technical and administrative tasks. Except where an individual operates a water point solely for use by his own livestock, rules have to be drawn up governing the use of the facility and the conditions in respect of fees and day-to-day maintenance. These rules will have to be applied and administered, and bent in the face of emergencies, perhaps by a well-attendant, headman, or elder, perhaps by a committee or by a distant official. Claims by individuals to use the facility have to be adjudicated and rosters for use drawn up. Someone must ensure that the rules and rosters are communicated to and understood by the users. Infringements of the rules have to be checked and if necessary punished. Drinking troughs and their surrounds have to be kept clean, fences, pipes, and taps repaired, and pump-engines refuelled and maintained. Wages of staff have to be paid. Whatever the size and complexity of the facility and whether it is owned by individual, pastoral group, or government, essentially all these functions will in one way or another have to be carried out if the facility is to be effectively and peacefully used.

THE ORGANIZATIONAL IMPLICATIONS OF PARTICULAR TECHNIQUES

To a large extent the choice of techniques for obtaining water, that is, whether it should be a borehole, a dam, or a piped supply, will be determined by the physical characteristics of the area where water is required. The geology of some areas makes it possible to obtain water from boreholes, in others it prevents it. Similarly, the potential for dams and *hafirs* depends on the amount of rainfall, on slope, type of soil, and vegetation cover which will determine run-off, and on the soil and rock structure at the dam site which will determine whether water can be stored. In many cases, therefore, there is little option between one technique or another. In other cases there may be. Among the reasons for deciding to choose one technique rather than another, or, where no choice is possible, whether to develop a new supply at all, will be the organizational implications. For particular techniques tend to impose particular patterns of organization and management.

The installation and operation of boreholes, for example, imposes a quite different set of requirements for organization and management from that of shallow wells. The choice of site may require the expertise of a qualified hydrogeologist. Further technical expertise will be required in deciding on the type of drilling equipment to be used, where such equipment can be found, what diameter the hole should be, and what operating equipment (pump, engine) will be most suitable. Either bureaucratic or commercial skills will be required to get all this work done on satisfactory terms. More-over, the installation of even one borehole will be quite a substantial financial investment and in many areas there is a high degree of risk that a borehole will fail to find water. Even for the installation phase, then, we find that boreholes require that funds be available on a large scale and that some dependence be put on technical and commercial expertise. Small traditional pastoral groups will usually not be able to mobilize such resources them-selves, although in eastern Botswana nearly 60 per cent of all boreholes are owned by individuals or groups (syndicates) of individuals (Fortmann and Roe, 1981, p. 26). However much participatory self-management and self-sufficiency is one's ideal, the technology of boreholes implies some alienation of decision-making into outside hands and a high degree of dependence on, or interdependence with, the modern sectors of the economy.

In the operation of boreholes once established the same tendency persists. Even routine operation and maintenance means dependence on fuel, spare parts, and some mechanical expertise and equipment (e.g. gear for lifting pumps for maintenance) from outside traditional pastoral groups, although pastoral collectives in the USSR, with a technically fairly well-educated membership of 1500–2000 families (ILO, 1967), may be able to provide the expertise and equipment from their own resources. Dependence on boreholes reduces uncertainty from climatic, but increases it from mechanical and social, causes. Whereas a shallow well, stockpond, or dam normally gives reasonable notice that it is about to dry up, and is not vulnerable to other sudden accidents during the dry season, a borehole can be in full operation one minute and totally useless the next. Boreholes are susceptible to ordinary mechanical breakdown. They can also easily be sabotaged (Bernus, 1977, p. 56). Moreover, they give to one man, the borehole operator, very consider-able power over the fortunes of the pastoralists who use the borehole. He may refuse to work 'overtime', he may fail to order enough 'official' fuel but be able to supply 'some of his own' at an inflated price, he may claim that the equipment 'is not working properly today'. It is true that if he presses his advantage too far the pastoralists may (and do) react violently. Oxby (1975, p. 6) records visiting a borehole and being told that the last 'well official' in charge of turning off the taps had been murdered by herders. But since pastoralists generally know little about the system they may find it safer to bribe the operator and avoid a showdown. The capital cost of boreholes requires, if they are to be economic, that they be very intensively used and this may necessitate a larger number of pastoralists and livestock using each water point than is convenient or feasible to organize in a participatory fashion.

This ability by the operator to control the use of a borehole, simply by 'switching it off' against the wishes of pastoralists, has sometimes been cited as an advantage in that it provides an instrument for regulating the use of pastures for which a borehole is the sole source of water. For, by denying water to livestock in some pastures and providing it in others, rests and rotations of pastures can be enforced by managers even when herders and pastoralists are hostile to such a management system. In practice, however, this advantage fails to materialize. For if the amount and quantity of forage appears to be much higher in the 'closed' than in the 'open' pastures, bore-hole operators may in some cases be terrorized into reopening wells which they have been ordered by their superiors to close (Eddy, 1979, p. 168); while in many other cases the range-management agencies of government have been overruled by the political administration who are unconvinced by the range managers' arguments and are unwilling to face a confrontation with pastoralists on this issue.

Open wells exhibit very different qualities from boreholes. Local expertise probably exists that can indicate where water is likely to be found. Such wells can generally be dug by the pastoralists or at least by locally recruited labour if any such is looking for work. Since the main input in construction is human labour, this can be easily recruited and supervised by the pastoralists' own organizations. The overall costs of constructing an open well are usually quiet modest and can be met from within the pastoral community. However, for the rather elaborate wells in southern Ethiopia, Helland (1980, p. 63) records a cost, simply for re-excavating an old well, of 280 herd of cattle which makes it of the same order of magnitude as the cost of a borehole. While some expertise is required to water livestock from open wells, it is the kind which every competent pastoralist is likely to possess rather than the technological magic involved in operating a borehole. The normally low capital cost of open wells, and their usually low yield of water, means that each one can probably serve the needs of only a few encampments, making participatory forms of management much more feasible. Control by the range managers of the use of open wells against the wishes of pastoralists is unlikely to be effective. Locks on well-heads can be easily broken and pumping machinery which has been disabled by the authorities can be substituted by a bucket and rope.

Dams and *hafirs* share some features of boreholes in the construction phase, but if human population density is high and a considerable degree of unemployment exists, then labour-intensive rather than mechanical tech-niques of construction can be employed. In their operating phase such surface supplies may be maintained by labour-intensive techniques and require a high degree of discipline by the users to prevent pollution of the water and damage to the structures. In this respect they are well suited to participatory forms of management except in so far as there are economies of scale in their construction so that it may be necessary for large numbers of pastoralists from several different groups to use the same facility. Inter-group competition may then prevent satisfactory management. In northern Kenya fairly satisfactory participatory systems of management were in operation at new government-constructed *hafirs* while these were used only by the Borana tribe. When government no longer prevented members of the Somali tribe from using the same stockponds the management system collapsed.[3] While range managers are likely to find it impossible to close surface supplies against the pastoralists' wishes, it is possible to design such supplies in a way that makes them partially self-regulating. For if their volume and depth are deliberately kept low then the water will dry up, through seepage, evaporation, and use by animals, before the surrounding pastures are overgrazed. Such a system of self-regulation was applied in southern Ethiopia and in north-east Kenya in government-sponsored programmes in the second half of the 1970s. However, such self-regulation is inevitably somewhat crude, since rainfall in the hydrological catchment of the water point may not be exactly correlated with that over all the pastures it serves and it can only provide against over-use and not for complete rest of a pasture.

Pipelines share many of the qualities of surface supplies, although they require a rather lower degree of user discipline. Experience in northern Tanzania, however, illustrates the difficulties that arise where competing groups share facilities. There, although the different Maasai groups have their own offtakes, they share a main pipeline which, according to Tanzanian officials, has suffered recurrent sabotage as different groups tried to block the offtakes of others.

Labour-intensive development and maintenance of water supplies

Hafirs, cisterns, dams, and open wells can be built and maintained by labour-intensive methods. In the Ogaden region of Ethiopia group- or privately owned hand-dug *hafirs* may be up to 1600 m³ in capacity and concrete-lined cisterns average 2500–3000 m³ (Cossins, 1971, pp. 39 and 42). The capacity of these structures will be roughly equivalent to the amount of earth that has to be shifted in their construction. In Tanzanian Maasailand about 40 dams were built by machinery under a government programme during the 1970s which ranged in capacity between 13,000 and 1,140,000 m³, with the amount of earthwork involved ranging between 700 and 46,000 m³ each. On average each cubic metre of earthwork gave a storage capacity of about 21 m³ (US-AID, 1976). In Sudan the average size of *hafirs* has increased from about 25,000 to 40,000 m³ over the last 20 years (Shepherd and El Neima, 1981, p. 23). Figures of 2000 m³ of earthwork have been quoted for the construction of a traditional shallow well in southern Ethiopia (Helland, 1980, p. 63). In addition to the earthworks involved in construction of these structures, a considerable amount will be required in their maintenance, in removing the soil transported into them by water erosion and by the feet of livestock. Probably the annual requirement for maintenance will be between 3 and 10 per cent of that required in the original construction. The amount of earthwork that can be carried out per man-day of labour obviously varies enormously, depending on the amount of equipment available to help the labour, the nature of the earth to be moved, the distance it has to be moved, and how fit and well organized is the labour force. During the construction of the British railway system in the nineteenth century a figure of between 5 and 12 m³ (depending on the nature of the work) per man-day for fit and well-organized teams using wheelbarrows and hand-trucks was achieved (Coleman, 1965, pp. 39 and 50). In the early days of a famine relief programme among unfit and ill-equipped Afar pastoralists in Ethiopia in the mid-1970s, the figure was 0.25 m³ per man-day. (Source: Ethiopian Government officials.) A standard figure for African conditions is 1 m³, but in pastoral conditions where the labour is neither trained nor fed for high and sustained outputs of physical energy, 0.5 m³ per man-day would be a more probable level of achievement.

Extremely large amounts of labour are required for water development programmes involving labour-intensive methods of construction and maintenance. As an illustration we can use a hypothetical example based on technical data from Sudan where a *hafir* with 30,000 m³ capacity is estimated to provide dry-season water for 3500 livestock units (lu) (Hunting and Macdonald, 1976, p. 62). Among nomads in this area the average number of lu per head of the human population is 6.3 and we can estimate that active adult males (aged 15–50) constitute 25–30 per cent of the human population.[4] If the water-holding capacity of the stockpond is equivalent to the earthworks required in its construction, and the labour output is 0.5 m³ of earthwork per man-day, then we find that each adult male in a population using such a stockpond will have to contribute about 400 man-days of labour to its construction and 10–40 man-days annually to its maintenance. The reader can himself modify the results in the light of alternative assumptions.

There appears to be rather little recorded experience of such labour-intensive programmes of water development; and therefore much of what follows is inevitably more in the nature of hypothesis than evidence. In some pastoral societies there is no reservoir of underemployed labour available to undertake this kind of work. The livestock system of the Gabra of East Africa, for example, generates a demand for labour equivalent, on average, to about 2500 man-hours per household per month (Torry, 1977, p. 13). This is considerably in excess of the supply and consequently the Gabra neither export labour to other parts of the economy nor have underemployed labour resources within the pastoral society. In contrast, other pastoral societies do not fully employ their total potentially available labour in pastoral activities;

for example, the Borana of Isiolo District in Kenya export about a third of their young adult male labour force to other parts of the Kenya economy (Dahl, 1979, p. 212); and in Mauritania, in the 1960s, an overall 20 per cent of the pastoral population of Adrar region was elsewhere in search of work, with much higher proportions in some social groups and ages and sex categories (Bonte, 1975). In Saudi Arabia 67 per cent of the available pastoral Bedouin labour force is unoccupied in pastoral activities (Cole, 1979). Yet the mere availability of labour, in aggregate, will not of itself make labour-intensive works viable. The reward offered to labourers for working and the way in which society is organized will also determine whether underemployed labour will actually take part in labour-intensive construction programmes.

We can examine some of the organizational implications of labour-intensive development and maintenance of water supplies. Where the facility to be constructed, and hence the labour requirement, is quite small in absolute terms, for example with the stockponds in the Ethiopian Ogaden already mentioned, group ownership and construction by the unpaid labour of members of the group is feasible, although even in the Ethiopian case the system is breaking down because of the difficulty of relating the amount of work done (in maintenance) by any individual with the benefit which he derives from it (Cossins, 1971). As the size of the facility increases such self-help becomes more difficult. The amount of labour required, and the period of time over which it will be required, means that its provision cannot be fitted in as a part-time addition to an individual's routine pastoral activities. It can only be done at all where a proportion of the labour force is 'free' of the task of herding its own property. That freedom may occur where the nature of the economic system (capitalist, feudal, slave-owning), or some recent disaster such as drought, has produced a class of more or less permanently stockless proletariat; or it may occur where the social system is one in which young adult males go through one or more stages in their life cycle (an age-grade system) when they have neither effective rights over nor responsibilities for livestock. In the case of a property-less proletariat, the labour involved will have to be paid only the equivalent, in cash or in subsistence consumables, of what it could get in an alternative occupation. Such wages could be contributed either directly by stockowners or by government funds which may or may not be recouped from stockowners. In the case of an age-grade system the labour is only likely to be forthcoming if its provision could be linked to earlier or more substantial acquisition by young men of their own breeding herd than would otherwise occur. In effect, the 'wage' would have to be paid in female animals by the older generations.

The larger the facility, the larger the segment of pastoral society from which labour will have to be drawn to construct and maintain it. When the labour is contributed by a stockless proletariat paid subsistence wages, this presents no further problems other than the raising of the necessary resources. But where labour is contributed on some other basis, this may require a high degree of co-operation between groups normally in competition with each other. Such competition may not be intense in areas of seasonal movements with well-defined and respected rights in pastures being allocated to quite small groups. Where the system of exploiting the environment is highly opportunistic and unpredictable within and between seasons, competition is likely to be intense and co-operation in constructing and maintaining a common facility difficult to attain. This is particularly so when neither individuals nor groups know how much future use they will want to make of a facility. In such cases they will not want to invest much labour in either its construction or routine maintenance (other than day-to-day cleaning), and in these circumstances either the pastoral society itself needs to be organized or reorganized on authoritarian, mandatory, and hierarchical lines, or a substantial degree of intervention by government or by a specialist, function-oriented, and possibly commercial concern seems necessary not only in providing funds but also in organizing the work. If pastoralists are required to reimburse expenditure this will have to be done on the basis of charging them on a short-term basis (e.g. a daily watering fee per head of stock) in accordance with the use they actually make of a facility.

THE IMPACT OF WATER DEVELOPMENT

The impact on production

This section will review a few of the effects of water development. We shall start by looking at the impact of pastoral water supplies on the objective of increased pastoral production. Easier access to water can improve the productivity of individual livestock in several ways.[5] When water is provided closer to where livestock are grazing they are enabled either to water more frequently or to spend less time and energy in walking to water than hitherto. Time saved walking to water can be spent grazing instead. More frequent watering tends to increase productivity, for example in terms of milk yield or liveweight gain per head, by increasing an animal's appetite and hence, when feed is available, the amount of feed it eats. Experiments in Australia indicate that, depending on ambient temperature, breed, and type of feed, sheep eat between 25 and 75 per cent more (in terms of dry matter) if watered daily than if watered every three or four days (Wilson, 1970). Similarly, cattle with a water intake restricted to 40 per cent of what they would otherwise have drunk cut their feed intake by 40 per cent (Thornton and Yates, 1968). However, an experiment with Indian sheep, which are possibly better adapted to water shortage than those used in the Australian experiments, showed only a 10–15 per cent reduction in feed intake when the watering interval was increased from one to three days (Singh, More, and Sahni, 1977).

Where no extra feed is available for livestock to eat when their appetite is stimulated by the provision of extra water, then this water may have negative rather than positive effects on production. This seems to be because reducing an animal's water intake causes, in Zebu cattle at any rate, a corresponding reduction in the animal's minimum requirement of energy intake for long-term survival (fasting metabolic rate). Conversely, raising water intake raises this minimum energy requirement, leaving less available, under a restricted diet, for conversion into useful product. There may be a similar effect in relation to nitrogen requirements (J. M. King, pers. com.). It has also been found, under experimental conditions, that easier access to water tends to be associated with a slightly lower efficiency of food use, measured in terms of the proportion of dry matter eaten that is digested. This lower efficiency tends to be of the order of 5–10 per cent (i.e. a decline in digestibility from, say, 65 per cent with infrequent watering to 60–62 per cent with more frequent), but it is not clear whether this decline is due directly to more water (in relation to feed) or to the associated increase in the amount of food consumed, since an increase in feed intake itself decreases digestibility (Thornton and Yates, 1968).

Owing to difficulties in measurement there are no reliable data available on the effect of watering frequency on the quantity of food consumed or the efficiency of food use by domestic livestock under field conditions in dry areas in developing countries. However, indigenous sheep owned by commercial ranchers in East Africa are alleged to have shown only very disappointing improvement in performance when more water supplies were installed (Brian Hartley, pers. com.). In Rajasthan in India cows with easy access to water had a milk yield in the driest seasons 55–60 per cent higher than those with less easy access (Jodha and Vyas, 1969, p. 8). It is not, however, possible to determine from these field examples the relative contributions to the results of changes in appetite and in efficiency of feed conversion.

Better distributed water supplies can reduce the distance that livestock travel, and therefore the amount of energy they expend in obtaining water. One trial has suggested, under experimental conditions, an energy expenditure on walking of about 4 kJ (kilojoules) of metabolizable energy per kilometre walked per kilogram liveweight of animal (Ledger, 1977), although other work (Ribeiro, Brockway, and Webster, 1977) suggests a lower rate of about 2 kJ. The higher rate implies that a 300 kg (liveweight) animal that has to walk, on average, 5 km per day has a total energy expenditure, for purposes other than the production of milk, meat, or fibre, about 15 per cent lower than one walking 10 km, or 25–30 per cent lower than one walking 15 km.[6] We have very few detailed or reliable studies as yet of how far herded livestock move in a day or how much of this is in looking for forage and how much for water.[7] In Nigeria nomadic cattle herds are recorded as walking an average of 16 km daily over the year as a whole with a minimum of 9 and a maximum of 30 km. Cattle belonging to settled pastoralists walked only about one-half of this distance (Van Raay, 1975, pp. 111–116). In northern Kenya the position is reversed with camels attached to more sedentary villages walking an average of 27 km daily while those at more nomadic camps walked only 15 (Tanaka and Sato, 1976). For Mali we have information specifically on distance walked to and from water (Swift, 1979, especially p. 155). In the hot season camels walk a daily average of 14 km for water, cattle 17, sheep 13 and goats 15 km. All these daily figures are averages covering both watering and non-watering days.

Precise evidence is usually not available, and clearly there are very large differences between different seasons of the year. It seems that, overall, in those dry regions where drinking water is sparse in the dry season but not in the wet, about 30 per cent, say 5–10 km, of the average daily distance walked may be spent specifically in obtaining water, and the balance in foraging. At any rate in Africa there is less difference between areas and species in this respect than one might expect, because well-adapted livestock appear to offset greater distances to water by watering less frequently. Under 'ideal' conditions doubling the number of water points in an area will reduce the distance walked to water by only about 30 per cent, and a typical 300 kg animal's total (metabolizable) non-productive energy expenditure by perhaps 5–10 per cent. While this reduction at first sight appears small, it may represent a potential for doubling the balance of energy available for useful production (meat, milk, and fibre), since typically only 5–10 per cent of a herd's total gross energy intake is available for expenditure on useful production, the remainder being absorbed in various non-productive 'overhead' expenditures. Stoddart, Smith, and Box (1975, pp. 224–225 and 248–250) and Sandford (1978a, pp. 8–16) give detailed calculations of the partition of energy intake between different forms of energy expenditure. In practice an animal, for short periods in the dry season, may expend a higher proportion on productive purposes than the 5–10 per cent quoted here, but where it has to 'fund' this expenditure by drawing on its reserves of fat it will not be able to keep up a high rate of productive expenditure for very long.

The most significant effect of the development of water supplies is to open up to pastoral use areas not previously used at all, or only used by certain species (e.g. camels) or at certain times of year before surface pools or temporary springs dry up after rain. By developing water in these areas it may be possible to use fodder that would otherwise not have been used by domestic livestock at all. For example, between 1965 and 1976 the area of land in Botswana accessible to domestic livestock approximately doubled as a consequence of borehole drilling programmes financed from both public and private sources (Sandford, 1977a). In Saudi Arabia, drilling of boreholes has proceeded to such an extent that it is now reported that 'there are no ranges that are considered inaccessible to pastoralists (except in the Empty Quarter) because almost every range site can be reached by lorry from one or more water points' (Al-Saleh, 1976). In Sudan the number of watering sites for livestock was allegedly quadrupled between 1957 and 1968 by constructing nearly 1000 water points equipped with boreholes, reservoirs, and dams (Sudan, 1976). Probably in most cases, however, water development does not bring land previously totally ungrazed into use, but rather it increases the grazing pressure on it by allowing more and different species of livestock to graze the land, and it changes the season of use and the length of the period in the year during which it is used. In north-east Kenya, for example, a range water development programme has allegedly doubled the area of land now accessible to grazing in the dry season (US-AID officials, pers. com.). Previously it had been restricted to wet season use.

The impact on the environment

Clearly, increasing or changing the nature of the grazing pressure will change the vegetation — its composition, standing biomass, and ground cover, and its productivity — and the size and composition of the wildlife population that use it. Such changes can be desirable or undesirable. The areas which, in terms of the quantity and nutritional quality of the feed which their vegetation provides at particular periods,[8] are best suited for grazing during the dry season may not be those whose existing endowment of water points permits their use at that time, whereas other areas less suitable from the point of view of vegetation may contain the permanent water points. The work of the UNDP range-planning teams in northern Kenya a decade ago was mainly concerned with trying to match, by planning the location of new water points, the seasonal availability of water in different areas with their seasonal comparative advantage in feed.

In the more distant past excessive claims have been made for the benefits that water development could bring by opening up new land to grazing, whereas in fact this land was often already used to a limited, but not necessarily optimal, extent. The pendulum now appears to have swung too far the other way and any water development that leads to a change in the existing pattern of vegetation (as it inevitably will) is condemned as 'desertifying'. What is needed is an assessment of the effect of the water development on the total productivity of the whole pastoral system within which a new water point and its surrounding area is situated. In general, the development of additional water supplies is likely to be a prerequisite of a range-management system that depends on a programme of rest and rotation and that seeks to achieve a relatively even pressure of grazing throughout a pastoral region.

Domestic livestock populations have an inherent tendency to expand in numbers. When forage is in very plentiful supply annual growth rates in cattle numbers, as high as 26 per cent per year, leading to a doubling in numbers in three years, are possible for a few years after the end of a drought (Meadows and White, 1979). Over longer periods and in more normal times the maximum rate of growth in numbers possible from the natural reproduction of the herd is about 11 per cent per year (Dahl and Hjort, 1976). Much higher rates than these are possible in the case of sheep and goats. When forage supplies are on average only barely adequate for survival, then much lower rates of growth in herd numbers are usual as calving rates fall and mortality rises. Nevertheless, growth rates are normally positive. Ultimate control, in terms of actually reducing livestock numbers to a lower level, is then generally triggered off by some natural event.

In the past and in some areas epidemic livestock disease may have been the mechanism which controlled livestock numbers. In Central Asia it tends to be the availability of forage in a severe winter. In much of Africa ultimate control is exercised by the availability of water at the height of the dry season in years of drought. In some cases it is the total volume of *water* at that time which is critical, and when this proves inadequate surplus livestock die of thirst. In most cases, however, it is not the volume of water but the quantity of *forage* within reach of a dry-season (i.e. permanent) water point that is the critical factor, and what controls the population is starvation (or forced and rapid sales) when this forage runs out. In the process of starvation the circle round the water point in the centre of the area accessible to permanent (dry-season) water is devastated, and such circles of devastation are aptly called 'sacrifice areas' (Stoddart, Smith, and Box, 1975, p. 212). The size of the area accessible to a permanent water point is itself elastic and its extent depends on the time within the dry season, the harshness of the season, and the class of stock involved. In bad years instances of cattle grazing as far as 40 km from their water point have been recorded (Dahl and Sandford, 1978, p. 40). For camels a figure of more than 90 km is possible (Asad, 1970, p. 29). However, towards the end of the harshest dry seasons animals probably lack the strength to walk so far and the accessible area contracts. In normal times the radius of the real sacrifice area is probably only about 1 km, but in times of acute drought this may expand up to 8 km.

The development of new water supplies increases the proportion of the total pastoral zone that sacrifice areas and their associated areas accessible to permanent water occupy. The optimum proportion will depend on such factors as the fragility or resilience of the environment (soil and vegetation) in the sacrifice areas, the length of the dry season in relation to the rest of the year, the variability of rainfall in terms of severity and frequency of drought, and the intrinsic growth rate of the livestock population. The more resilient the environment, the longer the dry season, the more variable the rainfall, the slower the intrinsic growth rate in numbers, then the lower the risk and the greater the advantage involved in accessible and sacrifice areas forming high proportions of the total zone. When, in contrast to this, the indications are that the proportion should be low, then the appropriate form of water development is the construction of shallow dams, stockponds, and seasonal wells, where these are technically feasible. These will extend the area and period of grazing in good years, improving the condition of a limited number of livestock in those years, but will not permit any long-term and substantial rise in the total population carried, because they do not affect the ultimate control, which is the amount of accessible forage in the dry season in bad years. Although livestock tend to die in the dry season, the most serious damage to the vegetation occurs when there is overgrazing during the wet or growing season during seed formation, and not in the dry season, when seeds are already in the ground. This indicates that accessible and sacrifice areas of dry-season grazing need to form a lower proportion of the total than a mere calculation of the relative seasonal availability of forage would indicate as the appropriate balance; and that an even distribution of temporary supplies in wet-season areas is as important as that of permanent supplies in sacrifice areas.

The impact on equity

We now turn to look at the way in which water development affects the fortunes of particular groups of people. One effect of the installation of reliable permanent water supplies is that it makes possible the growth of permanent settlements of people around the water point. Often these are people who do not have the baggage animals or other means of transport to enable them to move from one pasture or water supply to another. This ability to settle may help impoverished pastoralists who are trying to rebuild their herds after drought and who, starting with subsistence animals necessary to assure their food supply, have not yet time or resources to accumulate baggage animals. Often, however, the settlers are not poor pastoralists but officials, shopkeepers, and immigrant cultivators who gradually increase in numbers until they shut out the pastoralists, by creating pasture 'reserves' for their own animals or by harassing pastoralists whose livestock pose a threat to their crops. Around the towns of north Kenya townsmen are trying to demarcate 'town-dairy' reserves. In Niger the government administration supports cultivators against pastoralists even in areas where cultivation is forbidden by government decree (Bernus, 1977, pp. 54 and 86). In north Somalia the growth of urban settlements is excluding some of the pastoral clans from their traditional water points, e.g. at Hargeisa. A report on Tanzanian Maasailand sums it up (Hatfield and Kuney, 1976, p. 18):

And once a potentially stable clean water supply is introduced into an area it almost automatically introduces a new population centre composed of representatives of the institutions of modern society. At time [sic!] agriculturalists as well as outside pastoralists are attracted to the water. Thus what may have been originally designed for a relatively small pastoral population in the end has to supply an entirely new community.

It does not seem to make much difference whether new permanent water supplies are owned by individuals or by governments. An individual owner, even if he installed the supply for the purpose of watering his own or other pastoralists' livestock, is likely to succumb to selling water to the highest bidder unless traditional community pressures against this are reinforced rather than restrained by government action; and government administrators everywhere are more susceptible to the constant political and social pressure that settled people can exert on them than to the intermittent pressure of shifting pastoralists. Even where officials do not themselves occupy offices in settlements around water points, it is at the water point that they will stay, drink coffee, and listen to complaints during their visits.

In some pastoral societies labour is in superabundant supply. Among Bedouin pastoralists in Saudi Arabia, for example, a substantial degree of underemployment has been reported with only 30–40 per cent of the available labour force being actually required (Cole, 1979). But in other pastoral societies shortage of labour is a major constraint on the growth of herds; and this shortage of labour also represents an important mechanism for bringing about a more equal distribution of livestock between households than would occur simply as a consequences of marriage and inheritance laws or of other processes for redistributing from richer to poorer households. People who do not have large enough herds of their own to set themselves up as viable self-sufficient pastoral households enter into contracts with those with too many livestock to provide labour in return for some share in the increase of the herd (see, for example, Irons, 1975, Ch. 7; Dahl, 1979, Ch. 4; Swift, 1979, Ch. 5). The precise nature of the contract differs between different pastoral situations, but the underlying rationale is the same.

Similarly, the particular task which is the most labour-intensive, and constitutes the bottleneck which forces owners of larger herds to enter into these contracts, differs. In some cases it may be the milking of animals, in others protection against predators. But in some cases it is the amount of labour required in the watering of livestock which is the critical task. One study in East Africa indicated that 10 per cent of all time spent on looking after animals is spent simply on watering them at deep wells, but the addition to the number of herders required is probably greater than the proportion of time (Torry, 1977, pp. 10–13). Swift (1979, pp. 206 and 222) has shown that among the Twareg of Mali over the year as a whole the amount of labour required specifically for watering livestock only amounts to between 5 and 15 per cent of total labour required, and that *overall* labour requirements are substantially less than labour supply. Nevertheless, peak labour demands on watering days place limits on the number of animals of any one species that a household can manage with its own labour force. For example, although one man can look after 50 camels throughout the rest of the year he must be assisted by a second man for watering tasks every five or six days between January and June. As a consequence, rich households have to enter into co-operative arrangements and ones in which they swap food in exchange for labour from poor households or in which they (quasi) adopt poor kinsfolk. In planning the development of new water supplies, therefore, attention needs to be paid to whether the particular techniques involved (e.g. the installation of mechanical pumps) are likely to affect the demand for labour and so this redistribution mechanism between rich and poor.

Increasing the density of water supplies, especially dry-season ones, will alter the balance of advantage between owners of different species of livestock. Easier access to water means that areas which could previously only be used by camels are now open to use by, for example, cattle, which need to water more frequently and can therefore range less widely than camels. The precise extent to which camels and cattle compete with each other for scarce resources of forage is not clear and no doubt differs from place to place. Camels mainly eat browse and cattle mainly eat grass, but there is some overlap in feed sources,[9] and further competition also occurs at surface-water supplies where water fouled by camels is unacceptable to other species of livestock. If all livestock owners owned all classes of livestock in identical proportions, all would be equally affected. In practice, within social groups such as clans and tribes some people tend to specialize more in one species than another; and certain social groups, for example the Rendille of Kenya, specialize in camel-keeping. If the balance of advantage between different species substantially shifts as a consequence of water development, then the balance of specialization will also shift, but the more specialized a group as a whole was previously, the more difficult and slow will be the shift.

GOVERNMENT CONTROL AND NEW WATER SUPPLIES

One of the options between different forms of organization and management discussed in a general way in Chapter 3 concerns whether a particular function should be carried out by government or by some other kind of organization, for example by a community, by a trader, or by individual pastoralists. This section discusses some of the advantages and disadvantages which arise, under different circumstances, when a government intervenes to develop pastoral water supplies.

Interventions by governments tend to concentrate on those supplies which are relatively complex and expensive, and which have not, for these reasons, already been installed by private or group enterprise. Apart from their technical complexity and expense, such large water supplies are, in any case, very difficult for non-government organizations, especially community organizations, to manage. These difficulties are the more acute the more mobile the human population and the more opportunistic and less predictable it is in its movement. For in these circumstances competition between individuals and groups tends in any case to be extremely high. The very size of large water points attracts large concentrations of livestock from many different groups, and the importance of the new resource further increases competition among those seeking to control it. There is no real sense of being a community; moreover, it is very difficult for a community's management committee to provide coherent leadership since both the users of the supply and the members of the committee are constantly changing. In these circumstances, therefore, governments have preferred to manage these supplies directly through a government organization.

However, government organizations have also found such supplies difficult to manage partly because of the incompatibility of different aims. Large supplies tend to be boreholes, *hafirs*, or dams where there are considerable economies of scale in construction, and so a constant temptation to put in one big supply rather than two smaller ones at different sites. Provided the aquifer yields enough water, it costs much less than twice as much to drill and equip a borehole capable of watering 2000 head of livestock as one watering only 1000 head per day. In general the capacity of dams to store water rises more than proportionately to the amount of earthwork involved in the construction (Carruthers and Clark, 1981, p. 141), although local peculiarities of topography prevent this relationship being a very close one. Such supplies therefore often yield water sufficient not only for more live-stock than the area previously supported but for more than its forage supplies can safely support. Water supplies are put in not only to ensure more appropriate use of the range but also often as a way of buying political support for government from pastoral groups — sometimes general political support, sometimes specific agreement to a range-management programme. Sensible range-management policies and long-term political considerations require that the use of a water supply be restricted to a limited number of livestock and to one social group. But a desire to economize on resources, to water the maximum number of livestock that a supply can provide for, and to obtain the political support of as many groups as possible for the least expenditure, means that government often fails to impose these limitations.

For example, in Niger, although the government started off a water de-velopment programme with the policy of restricting the use of each supply to a maximum number of livestock and to members of only those social groups with traditional rights in the area concerned, this policy has either been abandoned or never put into practice. As one report put it: 'To give good quality water to some and refuse it to others has always been an insurmountable obstacle, in principle and in practice' (Bernus, 1977, p. 63). The same thing happened with a pilot range-management project in southern Ethiopia, where pastoralists who had traditionally used the area concerned complained that new government supplies had attracted pastoralists from as far as 300 km away, indeed from another country, and that the traditional control systems had collapsed as no organization within pastoral society could deny a pastoralist access to government water, and government itself would not do so. In north-east Kenya since Independence, a very large programme of water development has been matched by a progressive reduction of re-strictions on the movements of different clans in areas round the new water points previously closed to them. In spite of the government's hopes of gaining political popularity by developing water supplies, very often such supplies are deliberately sabotaged by pastoralists. Such at any rate has been the common experience of Algeria, Niger, Ethiopia, Kenya, and Tanzania, although the precise reasons no doubt differ in each case.

In addition to difficulties arising from incompatible aims, a government also encounters a number of practical difficulties in managing water supplies. Even where it decides to restrict the number of livestock and the social groups using water, it has difficulties in doing so. One such difficulty lies in the criterion for discrimination between who should and who should not use a supply located in public or communally used lands. In areas of opportunistic and mobile systems of land-use, place of residence is not a useful way of distinguishing social groups. Individuals in those circumstances often define their social identity mainly in terms of kinship. But often, also, governments in these areas are trying simultaneously, for other political reasons, to play down distinctions in terms of kinship, and while most governments at least recognize officially that such distinctions exist and have a role to play in the allocation of property rights, they find it unacceptable to use kinship as the criterion for access to a facility provided by government itself. Even once the question of the right criterion of group membership has been settled, there are pitfalls in the adjudication procedure for determining which individuals or livestock belong to the privileged group. For adjudication questions in nomadic areas cannot be settled on a once-and-for-all basis by a visiting, senior, and (one hopes) incorruptible, official but may arise at any time as livestock move between herds, families between encampments, and encampments between areas. Inevitably the adjudication function gravitates down to a lowly paid water-guard or borehole operator, who is neither properly supervised by his supervisor nor fully accountable for his actions to the social group he is supposed to serve. Such a low-level official will find it difficult to resist both bribes and threats (Bourgeot, 1981, p. 174).

Difficulties experienced in keeping boreholes and surface-water supplies in operation have already been mentioned. Fuel runs out, pumps break down, and installations are damaged. Government procedures for procurement and financial control are ill-adapted to the task of speedy repair or quick response to changes in demand. Often no watering fees are charged either for political reasons or for lack of an efficient administrative machinery for collecting them. Even when fees are collected by government the money is often not available for running the facility but gets paid in to some central fund; and when increased demands for water lead to higher requirements for funds for repairs and running costs, these will be met only in subsequent financial years when the demand may have fallen again. While some of the problems of running water supplies in pastoral areas, for example those due to remoteness and climatic fluctuations, are faced by government and non-government organization alike, government faces some peculiar difficulties of its own. The financing of pastoral water development from funds provided by foreign 'donor' agencies often means that inappropriate equipment is used for which regular commercial channels for the supply of spare parts do not exist. Where a private entrepreneur operates a water supply himself he has a direct incentive to keep it functioning, and he can provide such incentives even where he hires an operator. In contrast, government finds it very difficult to provide a system of rewards and incentives whereby all in the long chain of those who must contribute to ensuring the proper running of a supply (the pastoralists, the borehole operator, the vehicle driver, the stores clerk, the procurement officer, the financial controller) find that they have a strong interest in making it function efficiently rather than being uninterested or even preventing its efficient operation.

SOME PROPOSITIONS ABOUT RELATIONSHIPS

In Chapter 1 the outline of an analytic structure was sketched in which prescriptions for pastoral development could be evaluated on the basis of a multitude of propositions about behaviour and causes and effects. In Chapter 2 the analogy was used of a family of tourists visiting a country and choosing the places to visit, the route, the vehicle, and the driver, in order to illustrate the relationship between characteristics of pastoral situations, objectives, strategies, components, and forms of organization. In Chapter 3 this idea was further developed in considering an ideal conceptual model (visualized as a multi-dimensional scoreboard) within which relationships concerning forms of organization and management could be systematically examined. In the final section of the present chapter some of the propositions about the development of pastoral water supplies set out earlier in the chapter are drawn together. The purpose of this is to show explicitly that the ideas put forward in a rather abstract way in earlier chapters really can be applied to a particular component. For reasons of space it will not be possible at the end of subsequent chapters to draw the propositions together in this explicit framework. Nevertheless the same framework exists implicitly in each of the chapters dealing with particular components.

This final section will not repeat all the earlier propositions but will pay attention to those with the most important implications for choice of organizational form. We should recollect, however, the warning given in Chapter 1. Establishing the validity of a general proposition does not necessarily lead to an unequivocal conclusion about what should be done in a particular situation. For the implication of one general proposition which is applicable in the circumstances of a particular case may be more than counterbalanced by the implications of another applicable proposition.

The influence of the characteristics of pastoral situations

(a) On choice of techniques

(i) The main determinants of the choice between different types of water supply (borehole, dam, etc.) are the physical characteristics of the proposed site, e.g. its geology, topography, type of soil.

(ii) Highly fluctuating and unpredictable environments tend to cause intense competition between different pastoral groups; and this intense competition often leads to sabotage, misuse, and neglect of technically complex and shared water facilities.

(b) On form of organization

    (i) Where, because of the physical characteristics of a situation (as well as for other reasons), different pastoral groups within it are strongly competitive with each other (see above), participatory group-management is not a viable style of management; nor are labour-intensive methods of construction and maintenance, unless done on a strictly commercial (i.e. paid-labour) basis.

    (ii) Highly fluctuating environments have highly fluctuating demands for water at different sites. Government organizations find it particularly hard to manage such fluctuations in demand.

The influence of technology

(a) On form of organization

    (i) The technical complexity and expense involved in the construction and running of boreholes make them unsuitable for participatory forms of group management. In contrast, open wells are suitable for this; while dams and *hafirs* occupy an intermediate position, being technically complex and expensive to construct but simple to operate.

    (ii) The size and expense of boreholes and some dams, with their economies of scale, often mean that several competing pastoral groups have to use a particular supply. Where this is the case, participatory group-management is difficult. In contrast, open wells are usually used by only one group.

    (iii) Dams and *hafirs* require a high degree of discipline among users to prevent pollution and damage.

    (iv) Boreholes, and other technically complex supplies, give a great deal of power and opportunity to borehole-operators and other officials to exploit those who use the supply.

    (v) If designed for this effect, dams and *hafirs* can be automatically self-regulating as to intensity and duration of use.

    (vi) In general, large supplies, i.e. those which are expensive and have large outputs of water and which attract large concentrations of livestock from competing groups, are not suitable for participatory group-management.

    (vii) The use of open wells cannot be effectively controlled by government organizations.

    (viii) Open wells, and to a slightly less degree, small dams and *hafirs* can fairly easily be constructed and maintained by labour-intensive techniques, but in the case of large ones it depends very much on the general economic and social system of the pastoral society concerned.

(b) On objectives

  (i) Increasing the density and output of pastoral water supplies improves the productivity of individual livestock by increasing their appetite, and by reducing losses of energy incurred by long treks to water. It opens up for use by livestock areas of land which were previously unused or only used partially or not at the most appropriate time of year.

 (ii) However, the availability of grazing within reach of permanent water is often the key factor that limits the growth of livestock numbers. Increasing the number of water supplies removes this limitation and the consequent growth in numbers may cause environmental degradation in areas previously grazed adequately but not excessively.

(iii) Increasing the density of water supplies may further the interests of the owners of some types of livestock (e.g. cattle) at the expense of owners of other types (e.g. camels).

 (vi) The installation of permanent water supplies makes possible the settlement of people round about them in areas which previously only nomads could utilize. The new settlers may be ex-nomads; but more often they are immigrant cultivators, officials, and traders who, in time, exclude pastoralists from around the new supplies. Governments are more susceptible to political pressure from these settlers than from nomads; and so the supplies may ultimately harm the interests of nomads.

 (v) In pastoral areas where labour is in relatively short supply, installing mechanical pumping devices at water points, by reducing the demand for labour, may destroy traditional mechanisms for redistributing livestock from richer to poorer pastoralists.

 (vi) Boreholes are less dependent on current weather than other forms of water supply, and are therefore more reliable from that point of view. But this is counterbalanced by their greater vulnerability to breakdown and sabotage.

(vii) In comparison with private entrepreneurs and with community organizations, governments find it very hard to provide the right incentives to all levels of staff involved in the maintenance and operation of government water supplies.

The influence of organization

(a) On technology

  (i) Where government undertakes a programme for the development of pastoral water supplies using funds supplied by foreign donors, this often involves the use of equipment which is otherwise inappropriate for the purpose.

 (ii) The nature of the social system partially determines the feasibility of using labour-intensive techniques of construction and maintenance. Large dams and *hafirs* cannot be constructed or maintained by labour-intensive techniques unless fairly large parts of the labour force are free, either permanently or at some point in their life cycle, from responsibility for, and rights over, livestock.

(b) On objectives

(i) If the law on developing water supplies allows a free-for-all — and particularly if there is access to technology and funds from outside pastoral society — the result is likely to be environmental degradation. On the other hand, if the water law only imposes a restriction on the *number* of water points developed but on nothing else, the result will be *de facto* allocation of pasture to those who have obtained a *de jure* allocation of water.

(ii) In the design of government-owned water supplies little attention is usually given to the physical and administrative distribution of the water to livestock. In contrast, privately or communally owned and organized supplies pay a great deal of attention to distribution.

(iii) In the design of government-owned supplies there tends to be an inadequate upward flow of information from potential users to designers, due to inappropriate incentives in most government organizations. Prematurely appointed construction teams drawn from outside pastoral society tend to construct badly designed structures in the wrong place and for the benefit of the wrong people.

(iv) For a variety of reasons water supplies constructed and owned by government tend to be big, and this leads to an incompatibility of aims in their management such that in practice government finds it very difficult to manage these supplies effectively. In particular, government finds it difficult to discriminate, when it ought to, between pastoralists from different groups, or to close down supplies completely when range conditions dictate this but pastoralists oppose it.

NOTES TO CHAPTER 4

1. In this chapter the following terms for different types of water source and supply have the meanings indicated.

Borehole A machine-drilled hole of less than 300 mm diameter, often lined with casing pipe.

Open well A shaft deeper than it is wide, usually dug by hand.

Dam In a dam the dam wall holds back the water and *more* than half of the water, at full storage, lies above the ground level that existed before the dam was built.

Hafir In a *hafir* the wall, if any, is just a convenient place to put soil taken out of the hole. The wall does not hold back any standing water. All of the water, at full storage, lies below ground level in a hole or pit.

Hafir-dam In a *hafir*-dam the wall holds back the water, but *less* than half the water, at full storage, lies above the original ground level.

Cistern   A *hafir* or *hafir*-dam with a rock, masonry, or cement lining.
Stockpond   A dam, *hafir*-dam, *hafir*, or cistern.
These definitions are largely based on Fortmann and Roe (1981).

2. Two recent papers (Shepherd, 1981; Shepherd and El Neima, 1981) have described in some detail the process of popular participation in the planning of water supplies in pastoral and agricultural areas in Sudan. Unfortunately, they became available too late to have a substantial influence on this study.

3. This information comes from Borana pastoralists involved. It is subject, therefore, to ethnic bias.

4. These are figures for Hausa and Twareg populations in Niger (Bernus, 1977, p. 41).

5. In revising the original version of this chapter I have been greatly helped by having access to the draft of a monograph by J. M. King entitled *Ungulate Water Turnover in Africa*. Remaining errors are mine alone.

6. This is based on the assumption that such an animal's daily fasting metabolism amounts to about 22 MJ (megajoules) of net energy and that it uses a further 3.5 MJ in eating, ruminating, and digesting.

7. There is more information about *un*herded livestock in Australia. See, for example, the lists of references in Squires (1976) and Hodder and Low (1978).

8. See Stoddart, Smith, and Box (1975, pp. 232–240) and Breman *et al.* (1979/80) for analyses of seasonal changes in the relative nutritional value of different feeds; and see Dahl and Sandford (1978, pp. 43–44) and Van Raay (1975, Ch. 5) for pastoralists' appreciation of these changes.

9. For example Field (1979, p. 12) found that 11 per cent and 10 per cent respectively of the diet of camels in north Kenya were composed of grass and herbs, compared to 83 per cent and 13 per cent of the diet of cattle in the same area (Lewis, 1977, p. 32). Field's study took longer and was, therefore, much more complete than Lewis's.

Chapter five
The scope of range management

INTRODUCTION

This and the following two chapters discuss range management. The term 'range management' has a very wide scope and is used to describe a variety of different technical as well as institutional aspects of human interventions in the rangelands. Many of these aspects fall well outside the definition of management set out in Chapters 1 and 3 of this study. In the present chapter the variety of different aspects of range management (in its wide sense) are set out and a brief description is given of the factors, including some of the technical factors, involved in the three main aspects. Some account is also given of the extent to which these aspects are being implemented in different parts of the world. The next chapter (Ch. 6) looks at organization and management (in its narrow sense) of two of these aspects — the allocation of land between different uses and the allocation of land between different users. The subsequent chapter (Ch. 7) looks at organization and management of the third main aspect — the improvement of range productivity.

ASPECTS OF RANGE MANAGEMENT

In this study 'range management' will be defined to include almost all aspects of land and livestock tenure and some aspects of herd management, as well as the detailed manipulation of the vegetation to increase its productivity. The different aspects that fall within the broad definition are very closely intertwined, and many difficulties have arisen in pastoral development programmes from failure to appreciate that tinkering with one aspect will have indirect consequences on other aspects which may be much more important than the direct results in terms of the first. Thus, plans to rotate pastures or to impose limits on the total number of animals that may graze an area, may have consequences in terms of the ability of livestock to avoid disease, or to obtain access to the right kind of nutrient at the time at which they need it, which will far outweigh the direct effects on the productivity of the vegetation. Government range-management organizations are frequently set up which are incompetent in terms of both qualifications and physical resources to deal with aspects in the wider definition, and whose planned activities in manipulating the vegetation are not matched by corresponding activities on the part of other organizations to cope with these other aspects.

In its broad definition range management comprehends: allocation of the use of land and vegetation between different uses and between different users; increasing the area of land available for grazing, by clearance, for example, of tsetse fly or by the development of water supplies in areas otherwise inaccessible; maintaining and improving the productivity of rangeland in terms of forage as well as of products such as fuel and gum, by manipulation of soil, water, and vegetation resources; stabilizing soil, vegetation, and water to prevent flooding or sand-storms and shifting sand-dunes; managing herds, that is, moving and herding domestic livestock, and sometimes wildlife as well, in a way that ensures that each animal obtains the nutrients, water, and health conditions which it needs at the time that it needs them. In pastoral areas where rangelands and cultivation are spatially mixed, or where livestock use feeding-stuffs on cultivated land for at least part of the year, range management also involves, to a certain extent, management of the use of cultivated land and of the relations of livestock owners with cultivators and other sectors of the economy. This study will concentrate on three main aspects: the other aspects mentioned will be discussed only tangentially or not at all.

ALLOCATION OF LAND BETWEEN DIFFERENT USES

Some pieces of land can be used in a number of alternative ways, for cultivation, for pastoralism, for forestry, or for exclusive wildlife use. The choice of uses raises a number of issues. One is a conflict between short- and long-term productivity. In much of the Middle East and North Africa, for example, previously pastoral land was brought under cultivation which yielded high returns for a few years until productivity declined due to soil erosion and exhaustion. The land then returned to pastoral use, but at a much lower level of productivity than previously. A second issue arises because it is in fact very difficult to predict which use will have the highest long-term productivity, due to uncertainty both about the future physical yields under different uses and about the future economic value or prices of these yields. Thirdly, the benefits from different uses tend to accrue to quite different groups. The benefits from wildlife use, for example, accrue to tourists, to hoteliers, and to those able to tap the increased government revenue accruing from the tourist trade. These are seldom the same people as the pastoralists or hunter/gatherers who are expelled from game reserves. Even where arrangements arise for tourist fees and taxes to be spent on local development, the beneficiaries from this are probably not those displaced (Dahl and Sandford, 1978, p. 109). Cultivation in previously pastoral areas is often started by non-pastoral immigrants or by only one section of a pastoral group, and this cultivation displaces pastoralists. Often when pastoralists do start to cultivate it is not because they want to do so, but because only the rights of cultivators to land are recognized by government and protected by law. This is, or was, the case, for example, in pre-revolution Afghanistan, in imperial Iran (Tapper, 1979b, p. 109) and in Ethiopia. In such cases cultivation may be taken up by pastoralists not because it is a more productive form of land-use (the reverse may be the case) but because this is the only way they can maintain their rights in land.

A fourth issue arises because the choice between pastoral and non-pastoral use may often not be best made according to the relative long-term productivity in different uses of small patches of land. There are economies of scale in land-use and administration, and complementarities in use between different qualities of land, which require that productivity be measured not on small patches but over large or balanced areas. For example, where too close and mixed a patchwork of cultivated and pastoral use of land develops this may lead to conflict over damage to crops and over access by livestock to water supplies, a conflict that debilitates both systems (Frantz, 1975). Moreover, investment costs per hectare or per animal rise sharply the smaller the piece of land concerned. As we have already noted, it probably costs little more to drill and equip a borehole at which to water 2000 than to water 1000 animals. The cost per hectare of a perimeter fence to keep livestock out of cropland will be one-tenth as high for a 100 km^2 piece of land as for 1 km^2. The costs of administration, whether in terms of herding animals or of supervising rotation and stocking of pastures, rise sharply as grazing land is broken up into smaller patches. For example, in the open rangelands of South-West Asia one shepherd can look after between 250 and 500 animals, whereas in the densely cultivated area of the Central Highlands of Ethiopia the figure can be as low as 1:5–10 (Cossins and Ymrou, 1974, p. 19 — zone 2), although other factors are involved here too.

All this means that where cultivation in range areas is allowed to start up in penny packets dotted around all over the place, range management can become unviable, whereas if the same total area of cultivation had been restricted to one corner of the pastoral area it would not have raised such a problem. In the central mountainous area of Afghanistan aerial photographs (on display, in 1977, in a government forest and range institute) revealed that while cultivation occupied quite a modest proportion of the total area it was so dispersed throughout the pastures that planning for range management under any form of centralized control over large blocks of land would no longer be credible. Where new cultivation is dispersed in this fashion its location is not haphazard or irrational; it will almost certainly be picking out the most fertile pieces of land. But it will be doing so in a way that is detrimental to the best use of the other pieces. The same problems that arise in respect of haphazard allocation of land to different uses may also apply where it is allocated to different users. In the USA 'the Bureau of Land Management and Forest Services likewise are handicapped by the existence of small tracts of patented land throughout areas that they administer. These areas are owned by individuals or corporations which in many instances have too little land to justify close supervision. Obviously such conditions make any efforts at control of land use difficult' (Stoddart, Smith, and Box, 1975, p. 98).

Often the viability of a pastoral system requires that livestock which use very large areas of land of one type (often of very low productivity) during most of the year should have access to natural vegetation on small areas of another type, often of very high productivity, for quite short periods of time, for example at the height of the dry season. If this access is interrupted by cultivation, which if the small area of high potential is viewed in isolation from the rest may seem the more productive form of land-use, the whole pastoral system may collapse and the productivity of the area as a whole be lowered. This excision of key areas from pastoral use has had very serious effects on pastoralism in both East and West Africa, and was a major factor in the disaster that hit some pastoralists during the 1973 drought.

Allocation of land to different uses can be done by centralized administrative fiat or by ensuring that under a decentralized system those who make the decisions, whether they are direct users of the land or merely control its use, will reap both the costs and the benefits of the decisions which they make. A decentralized system is likely to have more of the necessary flexibility to adapt to changing circumstances, but clearly raises obstacles where equity requires that both the use and the user be changed.

ALLOCATION OF LAND BETWEEN DIFFERENT USERS

Improving the productivity of rangelands cannot be treated in isolation from decisions about who is to use the land and to what degree. One cannot control the number of livestock, how they use an area or what investment shall be made on it, without knowing whose livestock they will be or who will use and benefit from the investment. Land management and land allocation cannot sensibly be separated. Yet a surprising number of range development programmes are started in which attention has been paid only to the technical aspects of range productivity, and the question of whom the programme should or will benefit (or injure!) has been either unconsciously or deliberately ignored.

Sometimes the reason for this is sheer lack of understanding that the issue of allocation arises, and in such cases there is a tendency to treat the pastoralists as an undifferentiated mass with a common interest and a common mind. In other cases it is appreciated that what is involved is indeed land reform, but it is hoped that this can be dealt with subsequently and feared that, if it is raised at the outset, administrative and political inertia will prevent anything being done. Often the reason for ignoring the land allocation issue is that so few pastoralists are expected to be willing to participate in the new programme proposed that it seems obvious that priority should be given to the first volunteers. But often it is precisely because it is unclear who will benefit (and who will lose) and to what extent (or, if clear, not accepted), that there is so much opposition from the pastoralists in the first place. For example, in Nigeria a range reserve was set aside for use by a limited number of animals, and licences to use it were allocated on a 'first come first served' basis with no limit put on the number of animals which the first comers might choose to register. In north-east Kenya a water and range development programme on communal land was started at the same time as government ceased to enforce the previous clan and tribal territorial boundaries. Subsequent attempts to register the users of particular blocks were then quite unsuccessful, since the previous occupants of the area saw this merely as an attempt to make them pay grazing fees to use their own land, while the new immigrants saw it as the revival of an attempt to identify them so that they might again be excluded. In neither the Kenyan nor the Nigerian case was there the slightest success in controlling livestock numbers. (Source: field level officials in both countries.)

A new programme for the management of rangelands will have to provide answers to such questions as: which groups (settlers or nomads, tribes, clans, encampments) or individuals will be entitled to use the land; will the land be split into individual allotments for households or family groups, or will the livestock from many households use the land in common; to what extent will existing property rights in land and livestock be respected, perhaps with minor modifications to the degree and manner in which they are exercised (e.g. by limiting the number of animals or insisting on a rotational use of pastures), or to what extent will they be radically altered? Many, probably almost all, pastoral societies have extremely rigorous rules about property rights in livestock, governing who (e.g. father, wife, daughter) may do what (e.g. milk, slaughter, sell) to which livestock (e.g. camels, cattle, cows, steers) in what circumstances (e.g. marriages, divorces, deaths). Such rules, however, seldom envisage circumstances in which an absolute limit (quota) is put on the number of animals an individual or household may keep, although in conditions of extreme scarcity of water or grazing those with the biggest herds may have pressure put on them temporarily to send some animals elsewhere.

Where new regulations impose 'quotas' this is liable severely to disrupt the existing pattern of property rights, and to raise such questions as: does every individual man, woman, or child have an equal right to be registered as a user and to receive an individual quota, or do certain individuals (e.g. heads of units such as households or camps) 'represent' their units; does every individual or unit have the right to keep the same number of animals (i.e. the same quota) or does it depend on existing wealth when the new regulations start, or on age, status, or some other qualification; if the aggregate number of livestock kept on communal land is to be increased or reduced how is this alteration to be shared between the quotas of individuals; can quotas be sold, transferred, or split; what happens when existing quota-holders retire, emigrate, or die, and when new claimants are born, grow up or return from elsewhere; what happens to quotas on marriage or divorce and when illegitimate children are born and survive; are quotas, once allocated, intended to be permanent or is it expected that they will be redistributed by administrative intervention at regular or irregular intervals; what system of law is to guide these matters, national law, tribal law, or newly introduced regulations specific to range development; who will decide disputes and enforce judgements; and which is to prevail when national and tribal legal systems contradict each other or when a rule about quotas conflicts with another law of property in livestock?

These are not minor technical points which range scientists on their own can deal with as afterthoughts to programmes mainly concerned with the technical elements of improving range productivity; and it is not reasonable to expect either that an individual pastoralist, in order to obtain generally rather modest increases in the overall productivity of rangelands, will be prepared to provide a blank cheque of approval to a vague programme that may result in someone else gaining at his expense, or that a group of pastoralists will be unanimous in their response to specific proposals about how quotas or other benefits should be distributed. Obviously, one group may give unanimous approval to a proposal from which it will gain at the expense of another group. In Kenya, for example, the Maasai responded enthusiastically to a policy of allocating land to group ranches because this seemed to secure the claims of Maasai pastoralists to land in danger of encroachment by neighbouring cultivating tribes (Galaty, 1980). In northern Kenya Borana pastoralists support the concept of grazing blocks to the extent (and only to this extent) that they provide a device for keeping Somali pastoralists out of certain areas, and the Somali pastoralists dislike the proposals for the same reason (Dahl and Sandford, 1978, pp. 160–161). Obviously, the larger and more certain the potential gains in overall productivity offered by a technical programme, the greater the proportion of pastoralists who can be tempted by a gain in absolute terms even if they lose a little in relative terms. But a profound concern with one's position relative to other people is a universal phenomenon, and any new proposals are likely to alter the balance of advantage between, for example, settled and nomadic, men and women, one generation and another, first-born and later children, rich and poor.

We can look at the example of rich and poor. In many pastoral societies relative wealth and poverty are ephemeral conditions and individuals move back and forth from one to the other as part of a normal life cycle of events or as the result of chance. If, as part of a new programme, quotas are allocated to individuals on the basis of their initial herd sizes at the inception of the programme this may, for the first time, 'freeze' the poor in an unchangeable condition of relative poverty, whereas to provide equal quotas for all condemns the rich to instant and premature poverty. For the poor individual the prospective improvements in overall productivity offered by the technical aspects of a range-management programme that requires the imposition of quotas might conceivably just double his standard of living. This is a small shift compared to the normal prospects of fluctuations in relative herd size over a number of years which he will now have to abandon. Obviously, the precise degree of force of this argument depends on the extent to which pastoralists are able to invest and earn livelihoods only in the pastoral economy or are able to diversify into other activities. On the one hand, the effects of allocating permanent quotas (in terms of freezing the existing distribution of wealth) will be greater in more purely pastoral societies. On the other hand, such societies may already have more highly developed mechanisms for stock sharing and redistribution (Burnham, 1979, p. 356).

These are not arguments against change or against quotas, but arguments in favour of facing squarely up to the implications of range-management proposals for social harmony and the distribution of wealth and power. The proposals for group ranches in Kenya did so more than most, in explicitly providing that the poorest be allocated quotas of at least minimum subsistence level (Pratt, 1968, p. 199); however, even the academic literature on this scheme has been strangely silent on potential conflicts over quotas and their transfer which may arise between members of a household or family.[1] In India, under the Drought-Prone Areas Programme, up to half the common grazing land of villages has been reserved for use by members of new sheep co-operatives. Membership of these is limited in total number and is allocated to those who, on a first-come-first-served basis, are able to subscribe two sheep as a membership fee. The programme is clearly at the expense of those whose livestock would otherwise use the area, and in particular of owners of cattle and buffalo, and also of those who cannot and dare not risk this high initial subscription to a new and untried enterprise. There is no reason to believe that this shift in balance of advantage is desirable or, indeed, intended. It is simply the consequence of failing to think about distributional issues and in particular about the criteria by which beneficiaries ought to be selected. Depending on circumstances, potentially defensible criteria would be: justice, defined perhaps in terms of legal rights or past usage; need, defined, for example, in terms of lack of opportunity to follow any other form of livelihood; or efficiency, defined perhaps in terms of producing high and sustained levels of output at least economic or environmental cost. The last of these criteria is sometimes explicitly embraced, although far too often attention is focused on marketed offtake of beef animals to the exclusion of other forms of output, and it is all too readily assumed that existing wealth is sufficient evidence of efficiency, a claim strongly asserted by the wealthy and rejected by the poor. It is a claim for which empirical evidence is lacking.

Establishing criteria also implies establishing the conditions under which selection by these criteria can be implemented. A strongly egalitarian objective will not be compatible with leaving decision-making or executive functions in the hands of an existing or emerging élite in a highly stratified society; and any sharp rearrangement of the existing distribution of property rights is likely to be accompanied by grave internal social stress.

IMPROVING THE PRODUCTIVITY OF RANGELANDS

The distinguishing characteristic of rangelands is their low and unreliable supply of moisture for plant growth; and so improving the productivity of rangelands is largely a question of improving the management of this limiting factor. We can categorize improving rangeland productivity into three main processes, reducing waste of moisture, getting maximum plant production per unit of moisture, and getting maximum economic use from each unit of plant production. The three processes can be set in motion by a number of range-management activities, such as mechanical or physical work on soil and vegetation, burning, regulating grazing pressure, etc. which affect both the species composition of the vegetation and its physical environment. These various activities can be carried out by a number of different techniques. This section of the study will briefly review the processes and activities and their potential, and describe some experiences with techniques in particular countries.[2]

PROCESSES IN RANGE IMPROVEMENT

The first process is to ensure that the maximum amount of such moisture as is available is productively used by plants, mainly in transpiration, and is not lost. Such loss may arise as a result of surface run-off of rainfall which then escapes from the rangelands in river courses; or it may arise from the evaporation of rainfall from the soil or from ponds and lakes; or it may arise from the percolation of rainfall into the soil but down beyond the reach of plant roots, although this form of loss in most cases then reappears as a benefit in the form of livestock drinking or irrigation water in permanent streams and wells. The overall extent of such loss obviously varies according to topography, type of soil, the climatic factors which determine the rate of evaporation, and the nature of the vegetation cover which determines the balance between evaporation from the soil and transpiration from plants. The proportion of rainfall lost as run-off tends to decrease the larger the area being considered. In larger river basins (greater than 1000 km^2) in arid or semi-arid regions it may amount to as little as 1 per cent or even less, whereas on very small-scale plots it may be as high as 40 per cent or more (UNESCO/UNEP/FAO, 1979, pp. 81–85). Evaporation from soil and water surfaces may account for as much as 50 per cent of rainfall. Range-management activities seek to reduce these losses. This may be done by improving the infiltration of rainfall into the soil, or by increasing run-off in one place (thereby reducing the scope for evaporation there) in order to trap the water and use it more productively elsewhere. Evaporation may be reduced by application of chemicals such as ethyl glycol and bitumen to water and soil surfaces, or by planting shelter belts that modify the advective drying action of the wind. For example, in China a 20–50 per cent drop in evapotranspiration has been claimed to result from an effective network of shelter belts

(UNCOD, 1977e, p. 16). Vegetation can be managed in such a way as to optimize the balance between evapotranspiration by plants and evaporation from soil surfaces, by encouraging varieties that grow at seasons of lower evaporation, that cover the ground quickly, or that have the right balance between the surface area of soil that they shade and the volume of soil which their roots can tap.

The second process is to ensure that the moisture which is made available to plants is used with the highest possible efficiency in terms of the greatest production of plant material per unit of water supplied.[3] To a limited extent this can be achieved by the selection and propagation of plant species which, mainly by reason of their greater ability to take productive advantage of high levels of solar radiation, have a higher intrinsic efficiency of water use. Plants that possess the C-4 photosynthesis pathway of carbon fixation exhibit water-use efficiencies up to 100 per cent higher than C-3 plants in identical conditions.[4] But not many range plants in desert conditions are C-4 plants (although *Atriplex* species are an exception to this as are most Sahelian grasses — see Breman *et al.*, 1979/80, pp. 234–235) and the reason may lie in their greater vulnerability to *fluctuations* in moisture supply.

Greater water-use efficiency can also be achieved by manipulation of the plant's physical environment. Water-use efficiency is higher when plants are under some moisture stress than when they are freely supplied with moisture; and the ability of plants to make effective use of solar radiation and moisture can be limited by deficiencies of some nutrients, especially nitrogen. Hence the supply of nitrogen, by artificial fertilizers or by the introduction of suitable legumes, can increase the efficiency of water use. Where potential evaporation rates vary significantly between seasons in the year it may be possible to ensure that plants grow at times when evaporation rates are relatively low yet solar radiation is adequate, rather than at times when evaporation rates are very high and solar radiation more than adequate; and water-use efficiency will thereby be increased. Under experimental and simulation model conditions potential increases in efficiency of water use of perhaps 300–400 per cent can be demonstrated from a combination of selection of plant species and manipulation of the physical environment.

The third process in improving rangeland productivity lies in getting the maximum economic use from each unit of plant production. Partly this is a matter of ensuring that mainly edible and nutritious plant species and varieties grow. In the bush-dominated Tsavo National Park in Kenya even in a drought year only 18 per cent of net, above-ground, primary production of vegetation is consumed by mammals of all kinds (Phillipson, 1975, p. 193). In contrast to this low utilization figure, the sustainable yield (proper-use factor) of a grass-dominated pasture is of the order of 50–70 per cent of net primary production (Pratt and Gwynne, 1977, p. 95). The production of inedible bush is normally a waste of scarce moisture. Unless hay can be made there must be a balance between the growth and harvesting of nutritious and palatable annual grasses and of perennial grasses which provide a more reliable source of forage outside the main growing season (Breman *et al.*, 1979/80, p. 249). Partly it is a question of managing the desirable species in a way that ensures that they grow and are harvested at a time and in a form that optimizes their useful quantity and quality. The right succession of grazing by different species of herbivore can increase the total quantity that is harvested rather than trampled or ignored (Western, 1973). It is necessary for herbivores to obtain forage that is adequately spaced in quantity and quality throughout the year. This may involve conserving hay, or moving animals from one type of vegetation to another, or burning off standing hay of low protein content in order to obtain a regrowth of grass with a higher protein content on the residual moisture.

ACTIVITIES IN RANGE IMPROVEMENT

We can distinguish six broad sets of activities by which these processes of improving range productivity can be set in motion. These are: mechanical or physical work on soil, vegetation, or structures; planting, seeding, or reseeding with selected species and varieties; burning the vegetation; application of chemicals; altering the timing, length, and succession of use by livestock of particular pieces of land; and regulating grazing pressure in terms of numbers, species, and movement of animals. Each set of activities may affect several processes and can usually be carried out by a variety of different techniques. Mechanical work, for example, can be used to level or contour the land, so as to reduce run-off, to clear bush to allow more nutritious grasses to spread more abundantly, and to conserve those grasses as hay. Burning may be used to increase run-off of rainfall from some less useful areas so as to trap and use it elsewhere, to reduce bush infestation, and to replace standing hay of low nutritional value with green grass of high protein content. Mechanical work can either be carried out by the most modern machinery, in the form of bulldozers and scrapers, or by camels and oxen with ploughs or earth scoops, or by hand labour. The same process of improving productivity may be set in motion by one or a combination of these activities, and the same activity by one or a combination of different techniques. The reason for identifying and distinguishing the different sets of activities is that each set has certain managerial and technical features which are common to the alternative techniques for carrying out that activity. We shall come back to this point in Chapter 7.

One of the factors which will determine whether any of these processes will be deliberately set in motion, and, if so, by which activities and techniques, will be the relation between the costs involved and the benefits to be obtained. We can call this, using rather a narrow definition of economics, 'the economics of the case'. Very generalized claims are often made about particular range-management techniques, that they are 'economic' or 'uneconomic'. The economics of a particular case will be determined partly by the physical relationships (technical coefficients) between inputs or practices, such as bush clearance, and outputs, such as increased forage yield; and partly by the ratio between market prices or social values of the inputs and outputs. While, no doubt, there *are* very general economic patterns,[5] particular cases can show substantial departures from these, which make any transference of experience about the economics of increasing range productivity from one country to another extremely unreliable. We can give some illustrations of this from some price ratios set out in Table 5.1.

Table 5.1 The ratios between market prices of selected inputs and outputs in four countries

The ratio between the prices[a] of:	Western USA (1978)	Iran (1977)	North Kenya (1978)	Arid India (1977)
Daily wage of labourer/ 1 litre of diesel fuel	220 : 1	66 : 1	3.25 : 1	5.7 : 1
Daily wage of labourer/ 1 litre of milk	116 : 1	11.8 : 1	10.7 : 1	6.67 : 1
1 litre of diesel fuel/1 litre of milk	0.53 : 1	0.18 : 1	3.28 : 1	1.17 : 1
1 kg of live sheep/1 litre of milk	6.74 : 1	3.67 : 1	6 : 1	3.33 : 1
1 kg of live sheep/1 kg of live cattle	1.31 : 1	1.25 : 1	1 : 1	4.0 : 1

[a] As far as possible prices used in this table are those paid to or by pastoralists at or near their enterprise.

The table indicates that the ratio between the prices of different pastoral commodities, such as milk and live animals, varies much less than does the ratio between prices of inputs, such as labour and diesel, and those of commodities. Nevertheless, even in the case of commodities it shows that it may be two or three times more profitable to concentrate on one commodity rather than another in one country compared to another; and hence that experience of the kind summarized in statements such as 'that sort of management practice is all right for beef-raising but not for sheep' cannot be reliably transferred. But the greatest instability is displayed in the ratios between the prices of different inputs, and between inputs and outputs. In particular, labour-intensive practices which would be inconceivable in the USA can be justified in low-wage countries such as India, whereas fuel-intensive practices (e.g. patrolling range boundaries in big pickups) which may seem sensible in the USA may be extremely uneconomic in poorer countries.

Mechanical and physical work

Mechanical and physical work to increase the proportion of rainfall used by range plants has been carried out on a field scale at least in the USA, China,

Iran, and India. On government land in the USA contour furrowing and range pitting, to impede surface run-off of rainfall and to increase infiltration, and water spreading, to direct water which has already run off in streams back on to floodplains and terraces, have taken place since 1935 over perhaps 100,000 km^2 or 12 per cent of the dry rangelands of the western USA (Hadley, 1977). In China one measure adopted to halt and reverse desertification is to enclose areas of pasture land (*kuluns*) with stone walls or fences inside which the land may be levelled. As an example of work reported to have been carried out on a very large scale we can cite the case of one commune in Inner Mongolia, with a total population of 4000 people and 1600 km^2 of land, which is reported as having treated more than 300 km^2 of its land in this way (UNCOD, 1977f; UNCOD 1977g). In Iran some contour furrowing and range pitting has taken place on government-owned rangeland, but the extent of this is reported as being less than 1 per cent of the area on which range improvements of all kinds are being attempted (Shaedaee and Niknam, 1975). In India action appears to be on a relatively much smaller scale but, under the Drought-Prone Areas Programme, both on areas of community land reserved for sheep co-operatives and on state-owned forest land used for the production of grass, some range pitting and contour furrowing is being done. But the areas affected represent probably less than one-tenth of 1 per cent of the total area of the districts involved, and rather less than 1 per cent of the total forest and pasture areas concerned (in 1977).

The most important other kinds of mechanical and physical work are bush-clearing and haymaking. It is not possible to make satisfactory quantitative estimates of the extent of these. In the western United States 'several million hectares' are said to have been converted during the last 25 years from sagebrush to grasslands by a combination of mechanical and chemical means of bush clearance (Hadley, 1977, p. 547). In southern and eastern Africa mechanical bush clearance, both by hand labour and by machinery, has taken place on commercial ranches, but the extent of such clearance for the purposes of pastoralism (rather than cultivation) has been tiny in relation to the total area of rangelands or even of bush-infested rangelands. In Asia bush clearance does not seem to be important but, in contrast to Africa, much effort is expended in cutting and conserving forage. This is true not only on the collectives, communes, and state farms of areas in Central Asia, in the USSR, in Mongolia, and in China which suffer bitter winters and therefore need supplies of conserved forage above snow level, but also in India where grass is cut on government forage and forest reserves and conserved for use not only in the dry season in each year but also as a drought reserve to be carried over from year to year. On a much more limited scale, firebreaks to prevent the spread of fires are also a form of mechanical or physical work.

Planting and seeding

Planting and seeding of forage, which includes not only the reseeding of indigenous species but also the introduction to an area for the first time of new species of forage trees, shrubs, legumes, and grasses, has also been practised on a significant scale in a number of countries. In China shelter belts and networks of trees, shrubs, and grasses have been planted in desert areas on a vast scale. One report tells of one such network 800 km long and 500 km wide (UNCOD, 1977f, p. 6). The main purpose of these shelter belts is to reduce the force of the wind, and therefore the amount of wind-borne sand; however, at the same time the shelter belts achieve not only a great reduction in rates of evapotranspiration, and the more effective use, therefore, of scarce rainfall, but also production of forage in the belts. In the USA bush clearance over millions of hectares has been accompanied by grass seeding. To a limited extent in some countries planting and seeding has reduced the run-off of rainfall and has promoted the growing of range species of high water efficiency at the expense of others. In Iran, for instance, and in North Africa *Atriplex* species have been among those planted. But the main purpose of planting and seeding has been to substitute more for less nutritious species and to reduce soil erosion. In Tunisia more than 500 km^2 of forage plantations of cactus, *Atriplex*, and *Acacia* have been planted during the 1970s (Ionesco, 1975). In Iran an official record suggests that 28,000 km^2 of forage have been planted under a government programme, but this figure is somewhat suspect when compared to a figure from the same source of only 8000 km^2 for the total of all range-improvement projects (Shaedaee and Niknam, 1975). Alternative figures by another Iranian official are 220 km^2 of rangelands reseeded with forbs and grasses and 450 km^2 planted with shrubs, mainly *Atriplex* (Nemati, 1978). The cause of this substantial discrepancy is not known.

In sub-Saharan Africa much less planting and seeding has taken place. There has been a limited amount of planting of cactus on private farms in South Africa as a drought reserve; and in Eritrea the Italian colonial authorities started some cactus plantations for feeding livestock. In India a number of programmes are under way. In some of these, government forest reserves of low value for timber are being planted with grass, mainly *Cenchrus ciliaris*, but in some cases with fodder trees such as *Acacia arabica* (Babul). In a few cases where timber is being planted in such reserves the trees are being undersown with grass species, the hay from which will be sold off and carried away for consumption elsewhere for some years until the timber trees are fully established. At that point, if the grass is still able to compete with the trees, livestock may be allowed in to graze. Some land on previously undeveloped and largely uncontrolled village grazing areas is being allocated for exclusive use by newly formed sheep co-operatives, and grass and browse species are planted on them. This is being financed and carried out by government departments. Some individual farmers are planting grass and fodder tree species on their private land, often on the sides of irrigation ditches and in some cases on land susceptible to deterioration into active sand-dunes. In Australia legumes are being sown on a substantial scale in pastures, not only to raise directly the protein content of the livestock's diet but mainly to improve, through their effect on nitrogen availability in the soil, the composition (in terms of species), growth, and yield of the accompanying grasses.

Burning

Burning, as a tool for range management, can be used to alter the species composition of range vegetation, for example by controlling bush encroachment, and to remove unutilized herbaceous material left over from the previous growing season in order that new growth, of higher nutritional value and greater vigour, may develop and be accessible to livestock. In West Africa, for example, burning towards the end of the dry season stimulates growth of material with a crude protein content of 5–9 per cent compared to 2–4 per cent in the material burnt off (De Leeuw, 1979). Similar effects on the availability of digestible energy can be obtained. The effects of fire on the vegetation differ markedly according to the season or climatic conditions (humidity, wind, temperature) under which it is carried out, and the quantity of the material to be burnt, as well as on the type of vegetation and the stage in its development at which it is being burnt. Burning of vegetation may greatly increase the subsequent run-off of rainfall and the rate of soil erosion. Burning, both as a tool for manipulating forage supplies and as a way of lessening the incidence of parasites and predators, is extensively used in Africa, but apparently to a much less extent in Asia. Although previously range scientists tended to regard burning as a wholly undesirable practice, its useful role is now recognized by some of them both in Africa and elsewhere. It is now believed, for example, that the highly productive open plains of East Africa are a consequence of natural or man-made fire: and where administrative pressure has been used to discourage burning, bush encroachment has commenced (Jacobs, 1977, p. 3).

Application of chemicals

Chemical herbicides are extensively used in the USA for brush control (Hadley, 1977, p. 347) and research on their use has taken place in East Africa. They are not yet, however, being used on a significant scale in Asia and Africa. The application of chemical fertilizer is also now a widely accepted practice in North America (Goetz, Nyren, and Williams, 1978), and is beginning to be carried out by commercial farmers in South Africa (Theron and Venter, 1978). The use of chemical herbicides and fertilizers does not yet, however, appear to be widespread in dry rangelands elsewhere in Asia and Africa, although even in dry regions soil nitrogen, rather than

102

soil moisture, can be a limiting factor for plant production over many years. For example in the Sahel region in Africa application of nitrogen (and phosphorus) led, under experimental conditions, to annual dry-matter production, in a year when only 200 mm of rain fell, 1.5–4 times higher than on untreated fields; but under the same treatment in an area where only 100 mm or less of rain fell no response to fertilizer was found (Breman *et al.*, 1979/80, p. 235). In the USA the price ratio, at farm level, between 1 kg of live sheep and 1 kg of nitrogen in nitrogenous fertilizer is 3.2 : 1 (US $ 1.28 : 0.40), whereas in India it is 1 : 1 (Rs. 4.0 : 4.02) and in Niger (Sahel) 2.56 : 1 (CFA 200 : 78). These variations in price ratios (valid for 1977/78) go some way to explain the variation in fertilizer use.

Rotation of grazing

Altering the timing, length, and succession of use by livestock of a particular piece of land, which for short I shall refer to as *rotation* (defined here to include deferment and resting), is considered to be an important part of range management by range scientists and pastoralists alike. But the particular emphasis put by each group is somewhat different. Range scientists emphasize the effect of rotation on the productivity of the *vegetation*; and stress the effect of defoliation and trampling on different plant species at different stages in their life cycles, and the consequence of this on the composition of the plant community and on its overall vigour.[6] They devise grazing regimes that defer grazing of a particular piece of land until, for example, after the time in the year when its seed has set, that alternate grazing between different pieces so as to ensure uniform use, and that rest parts of the range from time to time for an entire year or more. Different regimes have different consequences on different plant species and on different plant communities, or on the same community in years that are climatically different. What may be suitable for a particular plant community in one state of use or over-use may be less suitable in another. In conditions where the intake of the individual animal can not be directly controlled, compromises have to be made between having land-management units so small as to be quite uneconomic and so large that the vegetation thereon is too heterogeneous to benefit from a particular regime. In all these matters a great deal of research has taken place in North America, and a moderate amount in Australia and southern Africa. Very little has taken place in the rest of Africa or Asia.

The literature on traditional pastoral societies is fairly well sprinkled with references to the way these societies deliberately manage their use of the rangeland under some rotation imposed by social control, i.e. control exercised by a higher level in society than the individual household. But whereas range scientists emphasize the effects of such rotation on the *vegetation*, pastoralists in traditional societies put much more stress on the effects of rotation on *livestock*. Of course, much of such social control of rotation in traditional societies is a reaction to climatic and political factors. Where movement of individual herds up and down mountains in South-West Asia (Barth, 1960), or in and out of cultivated areas in West Africa (Gallais, 1975), is socially controlled (as to its timing and duration), rather than being left to the initiative of the individual herdsman, this is generally because of the need of the pastoral groups concerned to manage their political relations with other groups rather than because of the effect of untimely moves on the productivity of the vegetation. But even where political relations are not involved it would appear that social control of rotation is more concerned with the distribution of an exogenously (independently) determined stock of forage between selected livestock and selected livestock owners, rather than with the effects of the rotation on increments to the stock. A number of societies, for example, regulate the use of areas of dry-season grazing around permanent water supplies, not allowing either members or outsiders to use up this dry-season reserve while there remain sources of available and accessible forage outside these reserves (see, e.g.: Marx, 1978; Bourgeot, 1978 and 1981).

There may be one or two examples unknown to me in which rotation is practised by traditional pastoralists because of its effect on plant productivity, but the contrast between range scientists' obsession with this effect and traditional pastoralists' lack of interest remains very strong. In the absence of social control these pastoralists constantly move their individual herds round the pastures, in search of vegetation which is both palatable and rich in energy and protein. Obtaining for their livestock an adequate and timely supply of minerals, either through the vegetation or directly at 'salty wells' or 'salt licks' is also a constant concern; and different species and classes (in terms of age and sex) of animals have different needs for these minerals (see, e.g., Bernus, 1979; Dahl, 1979, p. 43). Traditional pastoralists also move their livestock to different pastures in order to avoid risks of disease, for example trypanosomiasis, which there may be greater danger of contracting in one pasture than another at particular seasons.

The apparent failure of traditional pastoralists to practise rotation, along with other techniques, in order to improve the productivity of the vegetation, tends to be attributed to three main causes: to their ignorance of range science and the benefits to be derived from rotation; to lack of forethought or concern with range productivity — sometimes ascribed to the fact that such pastoralists allegedly believe that they can always move on elsewhere; to a system of land tenure under which the fact that the land belongs to the community at large prevents its efficient and disciplined management. Two further possibilities need to be borne in mind. First, that there may in fact be no significant gains in the productivity of vegetation to be derived from systematic rotation. The evidence on this is mixed, but two recent reviews state that 'research trials by and large fail to justify the tremendous enthusiasm for rotational growing, but rangeland administrators and conservationists continue their enthusiastic commentary in support of them' (Hyder and

Bement, 1977); and 'with the possible exception of the deferment scheme in the north-west of Western Australia, grazing rotations do not improve vegetation cover or animal production over that recorded under continuous grazing' (Wilson, 1977). Yet in one country in Africa both national and expatriate range officials justified to me their proposals for a rotation system by saying that, although no local research had been done to evaluate the system proposed, it could be provisionally recommended, pending local testing, on the strength of a US-based knowledge of plant physiology. But in the large number of years since this programme started no testing had taken place or monitoring of range trend, and interaction with local pastoralists was seen as a process whereby the range scientists 'teach' the pastoralists about range science.

The second possibility is that even if some increase in overall primary range productivity could be achieved by rotation this would be more than offset by the losses in secondary productivity of livestock caused by curtailing the ability of pastoralists to search out and bring their livestock to the pockets of vegetation and minerals that they most need at that particular moment. In North America and Australia livestock are not generally closely herded. In Asia and Africa, in contrast, due to lower labour costs, the movement of livestock can be very closely guided by a herdsman so that they concentrate on quite small patches of high quality or relatively unutilized grazing, thereby ensuring relatively even use and making the best of what is available; and this gives a great advantage to a flexible decentralized management system. Where pastoralists have milk as the main item in their diet they will be immediately aware, through variations in milk yield, of fluctuations in the nutritional status of their livestock. Such very close monitoring is much more difficult in pastoral systems oriented to meat or wool production. In northern Kenya pastoralists, especially those specializing in camels, feel strongly that any rotation system in which binding decisions were made governing the movements of all herds and animals would be extremely harmful to the productivity of their animals whose nutritional needs must be considered on an individual basis, or at least according to type (age/sex) or species basis (Dahl and Sandford, 1978, p. 164).

Adjusting grazing pressure

Adjusting the overall grazing pressure, in terms of the numbers and species of livestock, and the way they move and congregate (i.e. the physical impact of their hooves on soil and vegetation), is also a key activity in range improvement. While there is room for considerable differences of opinion as to the precise level of grazing pressure that is associated, in any particular situation, with the maximum yield from the vegetation, there is virtually universal agreement that there is some level with reference to which overstocking damages rangeland productivity; and some agreement that insufficient grazing pressure may also, in some situations, have undesirable effects on the productivity of the vegetation, particularly in respect of its composition in terms of different species (see, e.g., Conant, 1982). Agreement on general principles, or even on the precise effect of grazing pressure on range productivity in a particular situation, does not, however, necessarily lead to a coincidence of views about what level of grazing pressure is the *optimum*. Partly this is because of different views about the appropriate exploitation strategies (opportunistic or conservative) in the face of an unpredictably fluctuating environment, which we have already looked at in Chapter 2. Partly it is because a level of grazing pressure which gives the maximum (primary) yield of forage *per hectare*, and therefore potentially also the maximum (secondary) *total* yield of livestock products, may not be the one that gives the maximum yield *per head* of livestock, or, which is more relevant, represents an economically optimum combination of inputs and resources such as land, livestock, labour, and purchased inputs (Stoddart, Smith, and Box, 1975, pp. 271–276).

We can look briefly at the techniques available for implementing decisions on rotations and adjustment of grazing pressure. Where those whose function it is to make decisions about rotation systems and grazing pressure themselves directly herd and own (or *de facto* control) the livestock and pastures, and where reasonable prices for livestock can be obtained in easily accessible markets, there is little difficulty in making decisions effective. However, when the decision-makers do not themselves herd and own the livestock and pastures, or where, due to poor market conditions, herd numbers can only be reduced by slaughter or by selling at a loss, divergences of opinion can arise between the decision-makers (e.g. the Range Management Department of government) and the owners and herders, and a system of controls, sanctions, and incentives will have to be introduced to bring practice into line with the decisions. Such a system may include conditional grazing licences, quotas, legal sanctions, livestock taxes, grazing fees, price incentives, and bonus payments to owners and herders. Instead of trying to align the conflicting interests of decision-makers and implementers in this indirect fashion it may be more effective to do it directly, for example, by nationalizing livestock and pastures, or by transferring ownership or *de facto* management control to some organization (e.g. to collective farms in the USSR or to ranching companies in market economies) whose actions can be more easily influenced by, or whose views more closely coincide with, those of the decision-makers. In some cases control can be exercised in a more physical way, by the construction of fences, and by the siting, regulating of capacity, opening, and closing of water points, or by the location of supplies of salt, minerals, and other feed supplements. We have already looked at the use of water supplies as an instrument in range management in Chapter 4. Finally, livestock numbers may be controlled by the provision, or absence of provision, of animal health services, to which we shall turn in Chapter 8.

SUMMARY OF MAIN POINTS

This chapter has concentrated on three aspects within the very broad scope of range management. When parts of dry regions are allocated to one form of land-use rather than another, one group of people may benefit at the expense of another. When the users of a piece of land adopt a form of land-use on it, the choice may be determined by the relative security of tenure that the use confers rather than by its relative ecological or economic merits. Several components of range-management schemes, e.g. fencing, involve economies of scale which require that the land be allocated in quite large blocks to one use or another rather than being broken up into little pieces with the use of each piece being determined on its own independent merits. Where, contrary to this requirement, the land is broken up into separate small pieces with different uses, any kind of centralized system of management becomes unfeasible.

Range-development programmes too often concentrate on technical issues in land management and ignore the fact that these benefit some people and injure others; in effect, the changes, especially when they involve limitations on livestock numbers through the use of livestock quotas, constitute land reform. The benefits to be expected from the technical improvements may be small in relation to the losses some people may suffer from changes in their rights to use land; and uncertainty about who will suffer and who will gain may be an important cause of the lack of enthusiasm on the part of pastoralists for range improvements. There is not only a potential conflict between owners of large and small herds but also between people of different ages, sexes, and other categories. At any early stage in range-improvement programmes the criteria need to be established which determine how rights to use the improved rangelands are to be allocated; and a mechanism for adjudicating the rights of individuals needs to be used which is consistent with these criteria.

Improving the productivity of rangelands and dry regions is principally a question of improving the utilization of the scarcest resource — moisture. Three processes in doing this are distinguished: reducing waste of moisture, getting maximum plant production per unit of moisture, and getting maximum economic use from this plant production. The available evidence is that these processes have the technical potential, in combination, for raising the productivity of rangelands several-fold. This is in contrast to the often expressed view that there is only small scope for improvement in rangeland productivity. Six sets of activities are distinguished for implementing these processes and some account is given in this chapter of the extent to which these activities have been carried out in selected countries. The relative prices of the different inputs to these activities and of the different pastoral products largely determine the extent of these activities.

NOTES TO CHAPTER 5

1. The academic literature which is silent on this subject includes Davis (1971), Halderman (1972), Hedlund (1971), and Galaty (1980). Helland (1980), however, does mention the problem although without any substantial discussion.

2. This section draws heavily on: Mundlak and Singer (1975); especially papers therein by Noy-Meir, Orsham, Fuchs, and Koller; Pratt and Gwynne (1977); Stoddart, Smith, and Box (1975); and my own observations in several countries.

3. Production of plant material can be assessed in terms of dry-matter weight or energy content. Fuchs (in Mundlak and Singer, 1975, p. 140) defines water-use efficiency as the ratio of dry-matter production rate over evapotranspiration of the plant.

4. For further discussion of C-4 plants in this respect see Whyte (1974).

5. Such very general economic patterns arise because of international or inter-regional trade and movements in products and inputs. The more isolated a pastoral region is the more likely it will be to show a divergence from the general economic pattern.

6. For a review of the North American and Australian literature on rotation see Australian Rangelands Society (1977), especially papers by Trlica, Arnold, Hyder and Bement, and Wilson.

Chapter six
The management of land allocation

INTRODUCTION

This chapter is one of three (Ch. 5–7) concerned with range management, and it will deal with two out of the three main aspects identified in Chapter 5. In looking at the allocation of land between different uses it will do so in the context of an option between the allocation being done by government or by some sort of community organization of pastoralists. It will then look at the allocation of land between different users — again in the context of a number of options between different forms of organizations and management which have already been identified in Chapter 3.

MANAGEMENT OF THE ALLOCATION OF LAND BETWEEN DIFFERENT USES

The important issues in the management of the allocation of land between different uses, e.g. to grazing or to cultivation or to wildlife use, are the criteria on which the decision between different uses are made, the way in which decisions taken about the appropriate form of use determine who are the gainers and the losers, the flexibility with which decisions about the appropriate form of use can adjust to changing circumstances, and the way in which decisions once reached can be enforced.

The decision about the appropriate form of land-use should not be taken on physical criteria alone, e.g. according to the rainfall amount and regime or to soil type. The technical criteria for assigning land to one use rather than another are somewhat arbitrary. In any case whether, for example, land deteriorates depends at least as much on *how* it is cultivated as on whether it is cultivated or grazed; and how it is cultivated will depend on the availability of labour and capital for investment in the control of soil erosion and in moisture conservation, on the crop rotations chosen, etc. and also, of course, on political security. Land classified now as complete desert or as suitable only for light grazing, and which degrades even under that use, may under different political and economic conditions be capable of fairly intensive cultivation without degradation. For example, Evenari (1975) has described a productive and labour-intensive agricultural system, based on the run-off of rainfall, which existed between 2500 and 3000 years ago under an annual rainfall of only 100 mm in what is now the Negev Desert. Since social, political, and economic conditions change quite quickly the appropriateness of different forms of land-use will also change.

It is often claimed that only government, and in particular a land-use planning unit within it, possesses both the expertise necessary to evaluate the physical and socio-economic factors and the breadth of vision to look at the interests of the nation as a whole rather than of a narrow section within it. In practice governments have difficulty in living up to this claim. Placing land-use decisions in the hands of government imposes considerable inflexibility on the system in terms of both time and space. The expense of sophisticated land-use planning will mean that the exercise will take a very long time to mount, and cannot be repeated at frequent intervals; it will require that allocation be done on a very broad basis, probably using small-scale maps; this broad basis may ignore important micro-variations in suitability (although, as we have also seen, too patchwork a pattern of different uses can introduce diseconomies of its own); and there may be great difficulty and confusion in relating boundaries on a map to actual demarcation on the ground. But the experience is also that governments are very unreliable in applying land-use decisions, that different branches of government make conflicting decisions and that short-term crises and political pressures override long-term considerations. In this respect governments do indeed show considerable flexibility, but not flexibility based on well-thought-out environmental or social criteria.

As an example of the delay involved where governments undertake detailed land planning in pastoral areas one can cite the experience of the Tribal Grazing Land Policy in Botswana. The most distinctive feature of this policy was that tribal grazing land should be zoned into three broad land-use categories, and that land in one of these zones should be allocated for commercial ranching. The policy was adopted in 1975. It was not until 1979, four years later, that in any district the planning of land-use had progressed far enough to allocate any specific pieces for ranches. By that time much of the initial political impetus and goodwill for the policy had evaporated. By the end of 1981 on only 19 ranches had proceedings reached a stage where a formal land lease had been signed; this figure (19) represented an insignificant addition to the number of commercial ranches that already existed in Botswana prior to the formulation of the new policy. The government's desire to carry out the zoning of land-use in a way that seemed efficient from the technical, administrative, and legal angles led to requirements for staff and equipment that could not be met at a satisfactory rate. Now that the initial zoning is complete in most districts, some of them are already beginning to want to revise the original zone boundaries.

For the tendency of governments to contradict themselves we can look at the examples of Niger, Tanzania, and India. In Niger official policy to exclude cultivation from pastoral areas was simply ignored by administrators on the spot (Bernus, 1977). In Tanzania a general background policy by government to exclude cultivation from Maasai rangelands on environmental grounds is subject to hiccoughs as local officials pursue short-term political priorities to form *Ujamaa* cultivation villages and to plant food crops for national self-sufficiency (Hatfield, 1977; Hatfield and Kuney, 1976). In India land reserved for grazing by village livestock is constantly being allocated away by officials desperate to provide cropland for the poor while land reform laws remain unimplemented. (Source: discussion with Indian officials.)

Government officials are generally reluctant to give powers over land-use planning to local communities; even when a high-level political decision to do so is made they often frustrate its implementation. For example, in Tanzania in spite of political ideology and the stress on public participation since 1961, there appears to have been less control by pastoralists over land-use planning in the 1970s than in the 1950s. (Contrast the situations described in Jacobs, 1961, p. 24, and Hatfield, 1977.) One observer reports 'opportunities for participation were literally grabbed away' (Hatfield, 1977, p. 31).

In contrast, not surprisingly, pastoralists are keen that land-use planning decisions be placed in their own hands. In some cases, this is because they recognize that zoning land as 'grazing land' is often the only defence they have against its being alienated into the hands of people from intruding non-pastoral groups. In other cases, where pastoral society is socially highly stratified and especially where it is under economic or political stress that appears to threaten its long-term viability, or where the power of pastoral leaders is supported by the nation state, these leaders often head the rush to alienate key pieces of land from pastoral use. This was the experience of pre-revolution Kazakhstan (Tursunbayev and Potapov, 1959, p. 514), the Aussa Sultanate in Ethiopia (source: consultants' report to the Ethiopian Government), and Twareg Ahaggar of the Sahara (Bourgeot, 1975). These leaders' actions were not motivated by considerations of socially optimal land-use but by private interest. It appears that in the change from one use to another there is an opportunity for private gain that social institutions restrain in a more stable situation. There is little evidence, as yet, as to how well the socially rather egalitarian post-revolution communities of the USSR, Mongolia, and China have taken land-use decisions. Mongolia's *negdels* (pastoral collectives) have received generally sympathetic treatment from Western writers. In the USSR and China it seems that excessive attention has been paid to grain production in areas ecologically better suited for grazing. It is likely, however, that this poor land-use has arisen from interference by government rather than from misjudgement by local collectives or communes.

Cases can occur, however, where the desire to change from a pastoral way of life to cultivation may arise among those poor pastoralists who, due to either long-term factors or some sudden disaster, have lost all or most of their herds; and the move may then be resisted by the better-off herd-owners who want a cheap supply of labour to look after their herds and who see in a move to a cultivating way of life a threat to this supply. They will then try to prevent any part of pastoral areas being converted to cultivating use.

Few governments in Third World countries have the means, by direct government intervention, to control the form of land-use practised. The areas concerned are too vast and government officials are frequently quite unaware of the extent of cultivation being practised in a rangelands area. For example, at one time in southern Ethiopia a survey revealed that a third of pastoral families were also cultivating (AGROTEC–CRG–SEDES, 1974, p. 46), at a time when government officials concerned believed the number to be negligible. Even where officials know what is going on they may be unable to control or prevent it. The more inaccessible and sparsely populated the area, the more difficult direct government control becomes.

The conclusions to be drawn from a review of these issues are straightforward. Governments may have some staff who are technically well qualified to consider questions about the appropriate form of land-use in dry regions. However, these staff are usually too few for their views to form the basis of sufficiently fast or sufficiently flexible decisions. In practice, whatever the expertise available to them, governments have a poor record for consistency, over a period of time and between different government departments, in decision-making about pastoral land-use. Pastoral communities may show greater consistency and be able to respond more quickly and flexibly, but if their social structure is highly inequitable the community's decisions on land-use are likely to benefit the powerful members at the expense of the weak.

MANAGEMENT OF THE ALLOCATION OF LAND BETWEEN DIFFERENT USERS

The allocation of land between different users will be discussed in the light of a number of options between different forms of organization and management. The first of these concerns the size of the areas of land and of the organizations (measured in terms of people) which should be the basic allocation units. The issues involved are largely ones of centralization or decentralization of decision-making or other functions. The other options concern the type of organization to which allocations should be made. Three distinctions of type are discussed; one distinction is whether ownership and interest over livestock are unified in the same decision-making body as those over the land which these livestock graze — a distinction which is often discussed under the title of 'The Tragedy of the Commons'. A second distinction is whether the organization is inclusive, i.e. admits practically everyone, or exclusive, i.e. can determine its own membership. The third distinction is whether the organization is single- or multi-purpose.

THE SIZE OF ALLOCATION UNIT

The size of the basic allocation unit can be measured in the case of land either by its area (e.g. in km^2) or in terms of the number of livestock it can support, although this figure is usually less easily available. In the case of size of organization it can be measured in terms of the number of people drawing a substantial part of their livelihood from the organization whether as owners (owner-operators or absentee shareholders), employees, or as members of a pastoral community. At one end of a range of combination of size and complexity is a family homestead of one household occupying, say, 65 ha of land which is reserved for the continuous, self-sufficient, and exclusive use of that household's livestock. At the opposite end of the range will lie the complex pastoral systems of parts of Asia and Africa where members of different ethnic groups, either simultaneously and intermingled, or in temporal succession, sometimes in peaceful co-operation, sometimes in violent competition, all range over the same huge area of tens of thousands of square kilometres comprising land at different altitudes, in different rainfall regimes, and where some of the land is under cultivation and some under permanent natural vegetation.

Certain broad patterns emerge. The size of the basic land-unit which can be treated as a reasonably self-sufficient management block, and which tends, therefore, to be the unit allocated to some group or person to use, is only partly determined by the immutable physical characteristics of the situation, by its rainfall regime and its endowment of water, soil, and mineral resources. We have already discussed these in the section on settlement in Chapter 2. However, the size of unit allocated is also largely influenced by the social and economic factors. The effects of these are both difficult to estimate in advance and tend to change over time. For example in Australia, the USA (Heathcote, 1969), Mongolia, and the USSR there has been a tendency for an increase over time in the size of the land-unit seen by the government concerned as most appropriate for a self-contained operation run by a particular kind of social organization. In Kazakstan (USSR) the number of pastoral collectives was reduced, largely through amalgamations (and the average size of land-unit consequently increased in proportion) by two-thirds in the 10 years after 1958 (FAO, 1970). In Mongolia the number of *negdels* was more than halved between 1958 and 1975 (Lattimore, 1962, p. 180; Humphrey, 1978, p. 141).[1] In contrast, in Tanzania Maasailand the ranching associations encouraged by government in the 1960s were superseded by smaller 'villages' in the 1970s, although the reason for this change was not so much fresh ideas about what constituted viable self-sufficient units as a desire to impose the same uniform pattern on agricultural and pastoral areas alike. Whatever the direction or reasons for change, however, the point remains the same — the optimum size changes over time.

The size of basic land-unit chosen for allocation as a management block may be selected by a number of different criteria. It may be the smallest area that will maintain enough livestock to provide an adequate standard of living for one household; or it may be the smallest unit area, or a multiple thereof, that enables certain economies of scale to be reaped, for example in fencing, in water supplies, in machinery, or management. It may represent the smallest area within whose boundaries particular livestock can satisfy all their food, mineral, and water requirements on a year-round and permanent basis except in exceptional circumstances where emergency movement elsewhere is required. Single-function capitalist ranches, on the Western model, tend to operate a system in which all significant managerial functions are centralized at one level in the person of the ranch manager. He will decide, for example, on which pasture the livestock will graze each day, on the grazing pressure, and on other techniques to maintain and improve range and animal productivity. Even where some decisions of detail are delegated to herdsmen, the ranch manager will probably supervise them on a frequent, often daily, basis. He will usually also select the timing and number of animals to sell. Where Western-trained technicians draw up government-directed programmes for pastoral development in circumstances where the complete model of a capitalist ranch with unified ownership of livestock, land, and other assets is not possible, they still tend to advocate the same centralized management structure.

In contrast, in pastoral systems in Asia and Africa which have evolved over time by interaction between pastoralists and their neighbours (hereinafter 'traditional pastoral systems') rather than being imposed by paternal governments, management functions, and consequent rights in respect of both use of land and livestock, tend to be divided up and exercised at different levels in the system.[2] All or part of the land that a major political or ethnic group (a 'tribe') uses may be said to belong to the whole tribe, and a central political authority of the whole tribe (the 'chief') may negotiate on behalf of the tribe as a whole the timing and extent of its access to other resources of feed, water, and right of way which are at least partially controlled by people outside the tribe. In some cases the chief may also have some arbitrary powers to control the allocation of pieces of the tribe's own resources to individuals or sections within the tribe, although more often this sub-allocation, where it occurs, will be governed by customary rights or by the relative armed strength of different sections.

In some cases a tribe's land may really be equally accessible to all members of the tribe. Often, however, subdivision of the tribal land between major sections occurs, and within these subdivisions there may be further sub-subdivision; but at each level of subdivision the nature of the rights and restrictions allocated tend to differ. It may be very difficult for someone not a member of the tribe to obtain permission to graze his animals within tribal territory, but relatively easy for a member of one section to acquire rights to graze his animals on the land of another section with its permission. At successively lower levels of subdivision the allocation of rights, and the contrasting restrictions on those without rights, may become more specific, for example, as to the class of livestock, the season of use, or the duration of the right allocated. At the lowest level the 'camp' (group of households living or moving together) may only have the right to the first growth of pasture in a season on a particular piece of land, or the reservation of a piece of land for use by its own young stock may apply only for the period of days or weeks while the camp is located at a particular site and will not apply to the same place in subsequent years. Corresponding in most cases to the level (e.g. clan, subclan, camp, household) in the social structure at which rights are allocated will be decision-making powers to decide whether to enforce the rights and restrictions at a particular time or whether to enlarge, temporarily or permanently, the circle of right-holders.

Information on land allocation and decision-making within pastoral collectives in the USSR is not available. But on *negdels* in Mongolia a system of flexible decentralized allocation of land and resources to units within the *negdel* appears to exist similar to that found in traditional pastoral systems. The allocation of land to a *negdel* is fairly permanent and exclusive of the livestock of other *negdels*. Within a *negdel* land is sub-allocated to brigades, and within brigades subordinate levels of *kheseg* and below this *suur* (camp of three to four households) exist. Each lower level of social organization within the *negdel* is more impermanent, and the allocation of land to it more partial and of shorter duration than that to the level above (Humphrey, 1978; Rosenberg, 1974).

Table 6.1 summarizes some data about the allocation of pastoral land under government programmes in various parts of the world. The data are not always strictly comparable; for example, in some cases the land allocated is only used for grazing purposes, while in other cases, e.g. on the collectives in the USSR, quite substantial areas of cultivation exist on the land allocated. In most cases the households participating are expected to devote all their time to, and obtain all their livelihood from, use of the land allocated, but in the Indian case this is not so. In a number of cases, e.g. Mongolia or Kenya (Kajiado), government either consciously as an act of deliberate policy, or for lack of an immediately obvious alternative, adopted the same land-units and unit boundaries as had existed under a traditional system. The figures in Table 6.1 are of interest simply as pieces of information. No very clear pattern emerges from them. Even within the same general region of the USSR, for example, the number of households in a collective ranges from 90 to 1900 and additional information, not available in Table 6.1, but probably related to topography, would be needed to explain the causes of the differences in size.

Where the availability of forage and water does not fluctuate much in either time or space, then it may be appropriate to allocate single and quite small pieces of land for the exclusive use of a particular small social organization. The same is true where fluctuations occur but affect the whole of a vast region simultaneously to the same extent. Where fluctuations occur, but these are on a predictable seasonal basis and affect different ecological zones

Table 6.1 Allocation of pastoral land under government programmes

Country, region, and period	Social organization to which land allocation made	Area of land (km²) allocated to this organization	No. of households participating in organization	No. of livestock units[a] grazed on allocated land
Australia (NSW)				
1880	Pastoral homestead	24[b]		
1890s	Pastoral homestead	41[b]	1	NA
20th century	Pastoral homestead	82–247[b]	1	NA
China				
Inner Mongolia 1975	Commune	1600[c]	c.800[c, d]	90,000[c, e]
Inner Mongolia *c.* 1975	Commune	5000[c]	c.3000[c, d]	NA
Inner Mongolia 1979	Commune	1800[c]	1000[c]	36,000[c]
India				
Drought-prone areas 1977	Sheep co-operative	1[f]	80[f]	80[f]
Kenya				
Kajiado 1976–77	Group ranch	230[f] (40–690[g])	160[f] (30–420[g])	8000[f] (550–89,000[g])
Mongolia 1970s	*Negdel* (collective)	5000[f]	700[f]	c. 26,000[f]
Rwanda				
Mutara 1970s	Group ranch	4[f]	15[f]	NA
Senegal				
East Senegal 1980s	Pastoral unit	264[f]	c. 83[f]	NA
Tanzania				
Maasailand 1960s	Ranching association	1675[f] (500–2700[g])	484[f] (250–1000[g])	23,000[f] (19,000–30,000[g])
USA				
Federal Land pre-1916	Pastoral homestead	<1[b]	1	NA
Federal land post-1916	Pastoral homestead	3[b]	1	NA
Texas pre-1906	Pastoral homestead	11[b]	1	NA
Texas post-1906	Pastoral homestead	21[b]	1	NA
USSR				
Kazakstan 1969	Collective farm	740[c]	1900[c]	27,000[c]
Kirghizia 1966	Collective farm	280[c]	1000[c]	7000[c]
Pamir 1967	Collective farm	NA	90–210[g]	NA
Turkmenia *c.* 1975	Collective farm	880[c] (270–6700[f])	NA	c. 2600[d]

[a] Livestock units (lu) are estimated on the basis 1 lu = 1 bovine or equine (of any age) = 5 sheep or goats of any age = 0.77 camel (of any age).
[b] Maximum amount allowed by law.
[c] Figure for one example quoted.
[d] 'c.' before a figure indicates that the figure concerned has been derived by secondary calculation rather than by direct quotation from the original source.
[e] This figure is very high for this environment; and it is possible that in translation from an original document sheep and goats have been confused with bovines.
[f] Average figure.
[g] Range of several figures quoted.
Sources: Australia — Heathcote (1969); China — Ho Chi (1977), UNCOD (1977f), Huang Zhaohua (1982); India — Sandford (1978a); Kenya — ILCA (1979a); Mongolia — Humphrey (1978); Rwanda — Oxby (1981); Senegal — Oxby (1981); Tanzania — Parkipuny (1972); USA — Heathcote (1969); USSR — Monogarova (1978), FAO (1970), ILO (1967), UNCOD (1977h).

within a region at different times, then it may be appropriate to allocate separate pieces of land in different ecological zones for the exclusive use, at the appropriate time, of single and quite small organizations. For example, in north-west Iran (Tapper, 1979b) a particular block or collection of pieces of winter pasture (termed an 'estate' or '*yer*'), and of an average size of 4–5 km^2, is allocated in the plains on a permanent basis to a particular winter camp (*oba*) of 10–15 households. In summer time the winter camps regroup into smaller units of 4–5 households, with each unit having a permanent allocation of about 1 km^2 (sometimes in two–three separate pieces) of summer pastures in the mountains, some 150–200 km away from their winter pastures. In the USSR a collective farm may have its own separate summer pastureland as much as 400 km away from its residential base and winter pastures, or several collectives with their own winter/summer bases may share a distant summer/winter one (ILO, 1967, p. 73).

Where, however, forage and water supplies are not predictable, and especially where adjacent pastures within the same general ecological zone may simultaneously experience quite different weather, then the allocation of small pieces of land for the exclusive use of particular social groups is inappropriate. Either the unit of land allocated to a single social organization needs to be so big that it encompasses within its boundaries enough land for pieces that do badly at one time to be counterbalanced by those that do relatively well within the same unit, or if the units allocated to single organizations are quite small then there needs to be a flexible and speedy system whereby social organizations whose land is doing relatively badly in one year can borrow grazing from an organization whose land is doing relatively well. This borrowing can be recompensed either in money terms, as in the agistment system between ranches and regions in Australia, or on a reciprocal basis when need arises.

Traditional pastoral systems may incorporate elements of both these alternatives. For example, a tribe may occupy a huge area which is subdivided among segments of it. Each segment will normally exclude the livestock of another segment; but where that other segment is suffering a disaster, such as drought or disease, not of its own immediate making, then the better-off segment will admit the worse-off, not only because it chooses to accumulate reciprocal rights for the future but also because it acknowledges that the worse-off segment, through disaster, has actively acquired a 'right' to intrude on its land. Neighbouring pastoralists, who do not belong to the tribe, however, are not considered to have any *right* to intrude, although they may be permitted to come in under a specific agreement whereby the host tribe will obtain reciprocal treatment in due course. For such a system to function effectively there has to be reasonable parity of power between neighbouring tribes, or a government administration which can ensure that the rights of the weaker are protected, and considerable flexibility. For example, in northern Kenya the British colonial administration enforced inter-clan grazing boundaries on pastoralists of the Somali tribe. The principle of this was popular with the weaker and unpopular with the stronger expanding clans. However, at the same time the administration took away from clans and reserved to itself the power to decide whether to admit the livestock of other clans to graze on the home-clan's land for particular periods. This transfer of decision-making to a higher level imposed an inflexibility on the system which was unpopular with weak and strong clans alike.

TYPES OF SOCIAL ORGANIZATION ALLOCATED LAND — THREE DISTINCTIONS

We can now turn to the choice of type of social organization to which allocation of pastoral land should be made. This issue is often discussed in terms of the brand names of particular examples, e.g. pastoral homesteads or family stations (for individual households) in Australia and the USA, collectives or communes or *negdels* in communist Asia, or company ranches, group ranches, traditional tribes, or clans in the rest of Asia and Africa. But these brand names often disguise the true nature of the differences between them; and we discuss here three major distinctions that tend to be inherent in the initial constitution of different types. The first of these is whether ownership or interest in livestock is vested or unified in the same decision-making body as that in land. In terms of this distinction, pastoral homesteads, company ranches, and communist bloc collectives are rather like each other and are in contrast to most traditional pastoral societies or to some forms of statutory co-operatives in which ownership and decisions over livestock remain in the hands of individual members of a co-operative, but those over land in the co-operative as a whole.

The second distinction is whether the organization is 'inclusive', that is, it is open to, and offers approximately the same terms to, all those who want to participate, or whether it is 'exclusive', that is, it is restricted by some selection process which confers special rights and responsibilities on some people from which it excludes others. In this respect many traditional pastoral societies are relatively inclusive organizations, but family homesteads and commercial companies with long-term leases or permanent rights over land are exclusive, while the position of collectives has tended to vary over time.

The third distinction lies in whether the organization has one single purpose or is multi-purpose. Company ranches basically aim to maximize profits by the extensive raising of livestock; and the system of rewards and sanctions for those individuals who are employed on such ranches is aimed to forward this purpose. In contrast, the institutions of traditional pastoral societies serve many purposes. Members of such societies not only herd livestock, they also often cultivate, trade, and sell their labour. Collectively, they often provide mechanisms for defending their persons and property from internal or external attack and for a social security system to maintain the weak. Their concern is not only with physical well-being and security but also with cultural integrity. There is a fourth important distinction, but of a rather different kind, between social organizations, namely, whether they are intended to constitute a sharp break with the past — a radical reorganization of pastoral systems and society — or to provide a continuity which makes use of and builds upon what was useful in a previous system while dispensing with those elements which are no longer appropriate. This fourth distinction is not dealt with in this chapter, but the issue will be discussed in Chapter 10.

UNIFICATION OF INTEREST IN LAND AND LIVESTOCK — 'THE TRAGEDY OF THE COMMONS'

Many other studies of pastoralism and range management have identified a conflict of interest that arises where land and grazing are owned and used by the community as a whole but the livestock are owned by individuals, as a major cause of problems in management of the rangelands. Among the problems believed to arise in this way are desertification and economic disruption brought about by uncontrolled increases and subsequent collapses in livestock numbers, and lack of investment in improving the rangelands. This conflict of interest and its associated problems have been called 'The tragedy of the commons' (Hardin, 1977a).

'The tragedy of the commons' argument emphasizes that where several individuals graze their livestock on communally owned land, then each individual can make a short-term gain by increasing the numbers of his own livestock on the land, even if too many animals are already grazing it, since he will receive the full benefit from the production of that extra animal, while the cost, in terms of the amount by which the feed intake (and so also the production) of the animals already there is reduced by competition from the extra animal, will be shared by all the users of the land. Hence, even when the aggregate costs exceed the benefits, the individual who pays only a small part of the total cost but receives all the benefit will continue to increase his herd. Moreover, no individual will be very interested in improving the productivity of the communal land, or in arresting its deterioration, since he can have no guarantee that his neighbours will not, by increasing the size of their herds, capture the main benefit from any improvement.

Hardin, the most eloquent spokesman of this school of thought, has written (1977a, p. 20):

The tragedy of the commons develops in this way. Picture a pasture open to all. . . . As a rational human being each herdsman seeks to maximize his gain. Explicitly or implicitly, more or less consciously he asks 'What is the utility *to me* of adding one more animal to my herd?' This utility has one negative and one positive component.
1. The positive component is a function of the increment of one animal. Since the herdsman receives all the proceeds from the sale of the additional animal the positive utility is nearly +1.
2. The negative component is a function of the additional overgrazing created by one more animal. Since, however, the effects of overgrazing are shared by all the

herdsmen the negative utility for any particular decision-making herdsman is only a fraction of −1.

Adding together the component partial utilities the rational herdsman concludes that the only sensible course for him to pursue is to add another animal to the herd. And another. . . . But this is the conclusion reached by each and every rational herdsman sharing a commons.

Therein is the tragedy. Each man is locked into a system that compels him to increase his herd without limit — in a world that is limited. Ruin is the destination to which all men rush, each pursuing his own best interest in a society that believes in the freedom of the commons. Freedom in a commons brings ruin to all.

Two things should be noted. Firstly, that this is a highly formalized model of human behaviour that comes down deductively from *a priori* assumptions about how people behave; it is not a model built up from anthropological field studies of particular herdsmen in particular situations. Such deductive models can be extremely useful, but they need to be checked regularly for their consistency with the real world. Is it true, for example, that each herdsman 'seeks to maximize his gain' in the way posited? Does he conclude 'that the only course for him to pursue is to add another animal to his herd'? Is each man 'locked into a system that compels him to increase his herd without limit'? Are there really no alternatives to doing so? If it is, in fact, true that herdsmen see the world in this way and do try to behave in the way posited, i.e. if the model correctly describes a part of human behaviour, does it, nevertheless, provide an adequate description, does it explain enough about changes in livestock numbers, environmental deterioration, and under-investment for us to want to be substantially guided in our actions by the conclusions which seem to spring from it? Are there several other factors which also need to be taken into account which might lead us to other conclusions?

The second point to note is that two major alternative options spring equally from the model's analysis of the contradiction that arises from the communal ownership of land and the private ownership of livestock. One solution is to put both land and livestock into private ownership, i.e. into the hands of individuals; the other is to put livestock into the ownership of the community as a whole. Hardin's own thought processes are quite clear, but his language misleading when he writes, 'the tragedy of the commons as a food basket is averted by private property or something formally like it' (Hardin, 1977a, p. 22).

'The tragedy of the commons' argument, where the implicit and explicit assumptions on which it is based are fulfilled, may be formally correct. Nevertheless, not only are the argument's assumptions often not fulfilled in practice in particular cases but its importance has been exaggerated to the point where it sometimes appears as the only factor to be considered in deciding on land-tenure policy in pastoral areas; and a number of unjustifiable conclusions have been drawn from it. For example, overstocking and environmental deterioration appear to be just as common and serious in areas of rangeland where, as in parts of the USA and Australia, both land and livestock are individually owned. Too often a jump is made from the proposition that where ownership of land and livestock are divorced a conflict of interest may arise, to the conclusion that ownership of land should be by individuals, even in circumstances where fragmentation of grazing units into large numbers of small units is ecologically as well as economically inappropriate, and the alternative of a few large ranches is socially unjust. Too little recognition has been given to the fact that, at least since the enclosure of the English commons starting a couple of centuries ago (and probably earlier), 'the tragedy of the commons' argument has been used by a rapacious élite to justify the expropriation of the resources of the poor for the benefit of the élite. Writing about the enclosure of the commons in England, Moore (1974, p. 23) has commented 'the rural capitalist justified the misery he caused by appealing to the benefits he created for society at the same time that he made immense personal gains'. In the USA since access to public grazing lands came under government control with the passing of the Taylor Grazing Act in 1934, the system of licensing and management of these lands has been deliberately slanted so that those who already own the largest amounts of private land are allocated permits to graze the largest number of stock on adjacent public land.

The argument goes beyond the evidence when it claims as a general case that in acting in a way that is against the interest of the community as a whole the individual is behaving 'rationally' — with the implication that because such behaviour is rational it is also inevitable. Such behaviour is only 'rational' where it is impossible to get legislation or common agreement within the community of a kind that allocates the benefits in the same way as the costs, and that prevents actions which lead to a decrease in the total wealth of the community and the productivity of its resources. Otherwise such behaviour is no more rational than are theft, murder, or other anti-social activities. Rational men do not pursue collective doom; they organize to avoid it, witness traffic management and the control of industrial pollution in industrialized countries.

The proponents of the argument often appear to assume that pastoral societies, for reasons peculiar either to their natural environment or to their internal social structure, cannot devise or impose appropriate rules of behaviour on their individual members. This may have been true of the new and inexperienced pastoral communities that grew up during the anarchic phase of capitalist penetration of the rangelands of the USA and Australia during the last century. It is not true of most traditional pastoral societies of Asia and Africa, as their very strict rules concerning marriage, inheritance, and consumption patterns, for example, show. If such traditional societies have not devised rules for controlling livestock numbers and holdings, we need in the first instance to look for the reasons elsewhere than in social incompetence. It may be that such control would not, in fact, be to their benefit, either because of the implications for average income which we have already looked at in the discussion on opportunistic and conservative strategies in Chapter 2 (implications which apply equally under communal or private tenure), or because the environment is not in fact deteriorating as a consequence of overstocking. It may be that it is not the internal structure of pastoral society which prevents the drawing up and imposition of rules on members about livestock numbers and investment, but external forces (e.g. an uncomprehending government or pressure from a powerful neighbouring tribe) which make the imposition of such rules impossible or inadvisable.

Not all pastoral societies, even those where the vast majority of forage is obtained from communally exploited grazing lands, approve or permit expansion by individuals of the size of their herds. The mainly pastoral Dassenech of south-west Ethiopia, for example, 'keep their livestock population stable and do this by regular slaughtering' (Almagur, 1978, p. 54). Nor in those societies where increases in the size of individual herds are socially approved will all individuals succeed, or even strive, to increase theirs. Clearly, there are likely to be systematic differences between individuals within a society, and between societies, differences which are related to specific characteristics of the individual and the society that influence the tendency to accumulate.

We can speculate about the effect of some of these characteristics. Households or enterprises where the livestock:person ratio is low are likely, both because of subsistence consumption needs and because of the availability of herding labour, to have a relatively greater incentive to increase herd size, although they may find it particularly difficult to do so. Families, or societies, specializing in relatively fast-breeding animals (e.g. goats) will be following general strategies based on a system of rapid reproduction and growth (probably followed by rapid collapse). Those who rely on camels will be following another strategy. The more variable the environment, and the less this variability can be offset by spatial mobility, the more will people need to invest in livestock numbers as an insurance against catastrophic losses. The more access pastoralists have to other forms of saving and investment, the less the need and convenience of investing only in more livestock. The more socially and politically isolated the pastoral society is from the rest of the nation state, and therefore the less likely that it will receive relief or be given access to alternative livelihoods in times of disaster, and the more inherently fragile the natural environment, the less risk will it want to take of damaging its habitat by overstocking. That factor probably explains stability of livestock numbers among the Dassenech. On the other hand, closer economic integration on fair terms with the rest of the nation's economy may encourage a greater exchange of livestock for purchased foods and other goods. It is possible that, the more widely separated the ownership and control over livestock from those over the land that the livestock use, the greater the divergence between private and social costs and benefits and the greater the tendency for individuals to overstock. This is 'the tragedy of the commons' argument. This last factor, however, is only one among many.

In the dry regions of the world the alleged social benefits of the privatization of land are, too often, illusory. The institution of private property 'or something like it', in the form of long leases or permits for the exclusive use of government land, has not by itself led to an adjustment in livestock numbers to the level which range scientists believe to be desirable. For instance, prior to the 1934 Taylor Grazing Act the publicly owned rangelands of the USA were, in effect, open to uncontrolled communal use by graziers. The Act, although not giving long-term security of interest to individuals, at least allocated the short-term costs and benefits of particular pieces of government land to individuals whose stock were given exclusive access to them by permits. Yet, for example, in one grazing district in Oregon State, the number of livestock using the public land under the new exclusive access system actually *increased* in the first 20 years after the passage of the Act by about 20 per cent above what it had been at the time of the Act, until it reached a level some 75 per cent above the estimated grazing capacity of the land. In those 20 years the graziers themselves had largely determined the number of livestock using the land. It was only when the government strongly asserted its powers to control directly the number of livestock that this was finally reduced to the level of the estimated grazing capacity (Heady and Bartolome, 1977, pp. 25, 32, 64–67; Tables 3, 11, 12).

The picture is no different for those rangelands in full private ownership in the USA,[3] or under long-term leases from government and individuals in Australia. The vesting in the same individual of both the short-term benefits and costs of keeping livestock and the long-term costs in term of land degradation is insufficient to induce him to keep numbers down to the estimated carrying capacity of the land. It is difficult to the point of being impossible to calculate the precise degree of influence of different factors in determining decisions as to the level at which to stock grazing land. But it is clear that factors other than maximizing long-term profit of the enterprise play the dominant roles. On ranches owned by commercial companies it has been the need to pay regular dividends giving a return in line with other investments, and on family enterprises the necessity of earning enough to meet the needs of the family in the short term. Hence, fluctuations in relative market prices and in rainfall, the extent of subsidization of prices of inputs and products, the size of holdings, and changes in the returns to capital and labour which could be earned in other sections of the economy have outweighed considerations of the long-term productivity of the land. (For accounts of the roles played by these factors see Heathcote, 1969; Young, 1979; Williams, Suijdendorp, and Wilcox, 1977.)

The discussion so far has been mainly in terms of the effect of private ownership of land on livestock numbers and the environment. The argument has been further confused by statistics which tend to show that those enterprises with unified systems of control and ownership that are commercial (capitalist) ranching organizations, whether owned or run by companies or single individuals, market a higher proportion of their livestock herd each year than those enterprises that do not have unified systems in respect of land and livestock which are in allegedly traditional or non-commercial societies. The statistics have been misleading in a number of ways. Where more traditional (communal grazing) and more commercial (private land tenure) systems really coexist alongside each other, as in Botswana and Kenya, what the traditional sector sells to the commercial for the latter to resell in due course has sometimes been counted as the offtake of the commercial and not of the traditional sector. The offtake of commercial ranches has also sometimes been calculated on the basis of a theoretical potential, or what has happened in other countries, rather than on actual local experience. But the most common cause of confusion has been to take the number of animals marketed as being identical with the potential or actual economic productivity of the two contrasting systems.

The numbers of animals marketed, expressed as offtake rates in relation to the number in the herds, are not a proper assessment of the relative productivity of different pastoral systems. Commercial ranches tend to employ a much smaller labour force in relation to the size of their herds and so also have fewer non-productive dependants. As a consequence these enterprizes do not need to retain large amounts of produce to feed their human populations. Because they lack labour they usually specialize in the production of animals for meat rather than in more labour-intensive dairy products, and so a higher proportion of total enterprise output takes the form of animals sold for meat and is counted as offtake, whereas the amount of dairy produce sold is often totally ignored in the statistics. Finally, the relative shortage of labour on commercial enterprises induces them to invest in labour-saving devices such as pumps, fences, and vehicles which have to be paid for by selling output for cash; whereas traditional systems feed their relatively larger labour force directly through the produce of the pastoral enterprise. Where capitalist and traditional systems are compared by other indices of efficiency, for example, in terms of the dietary calories which they produce for human consumption or the economic value of all their produce (meat and milk, sales and home consumption), the results tend to favour the traditional rather than the capitalist systems. When output is expressed in monetary terms, however, an additional complication arises from the fact that capitalist enterprises have sometimes, through the political process or through manipulation of the marketing system, managed to obtain higher prices for their output than traditional enterprises are able to obtain for the same output.

We can give only a very few examples of comparisons between the productivity of traditional and commercial systems which illustrate these results. Western (1974) has suggested that in East Africa the Maasai pastoral system has a higher food chain efficiency (at 7.8 per cent) than well-managed commercial ranches (at 6.5 per cent). However, the definition of food chain efficiency used in this case favours the high stocking rates normally practised by pastoralists. A comparison by Ellis, Jennings, and Swift (1979) of different production systems in different countries gave a communal grazing traditional pastoral system in Uganda low marks by a variety of efficiency criteria (expressed in terms of energetics) in comparison with both an intensive peasant farming system in India and a grazing system in North America which was not too dissimilar from a commercial ranching system. However, that kind of across-country comparison raises formidable methodological problems.

Very recently White and Meadows (1981), have carried out the most detailed and thorough economic comparison that has been attempted so far of different systems operating under similar conditions. They compared three kinds of system in Kenya Maasailand. One system, which we can call 'un-developed group ranches', is probably not significantly different in its land-use, animal husbandry standards, and productivity from what the traditional system would have been if the land-tenure system had not been altered by the introduction of a 'group ranch' form of land tenure. The second system, which we can call 'developed group ranches', continues with a communal grazing system (i.e. communally owned land, privately owned cattle), but has some modern inputs, e.g. improved water supplies, cattle dips, etc. The third system is one of individually owned ranches. The productivity of the systems is compared in 11 ways in Table 6.2.

The offtake rate (expressed as a percentage) shows the number of livestock disposed of by sale, consumption, or both, as a proportion of the number of animals in the herd. The gross output/herd-capital ratio (expressed as a percentage) shows the gross value of output (before deducting the cost of purchased inputs) as a proportion of the value of the herd. The net output/herd-capital ratio shows the net value of output, i.e. where the cost of purchased inputs (excluding labour) is deducted from the gross value of output. Different rates are shown as far as possible for different kinds of livestock (i.e. cattle, small stock) and output (i.e. meat/live animals and/or milk) and for sales and subsistence. The expression 'basic' indicates that the results refer only to the 'domestic' herd and excludes animals purchased to graze for a limited period before resale. 'Aggregate' indicates that the results include those of both the basic and purchased herds. The figures quoted are the unweighted averages of different enterprises. Unfortunately, it has not been possible to express the results on a per-hectare basis. Probably the livestock of individual ranches have access to more land and grazing than do those on the group ranches. Nor is it possible to comment on the relative degree or speed of environmental degradation in the different systems.

The results shown in Table 6.2 illustrate a number of the points made in preceding paragraphs, particularly about the importance of the distinction between offtake rates which do (basic) or do not (aggregate) make appropriate allowance for animals purchased for resale and of the inclusion of milk produced for domestic consumption (described as 'subsistence' in the table).

Of course if one's (government's) prime concern is to provide meat for the urban population regardless of the cost of doing so in terms of the welfare

Table 6.2 Comparison, by different criteria, of the productivity of livestock systems
in Kenya Maasailand

Criterion of productivity	Undeveloped group ranches	Developed group ranches	Individual ranches
Offtake rate (%)			
Cattle			
(a) Aggregate			
(i) Sales only	10.1	8.1	15.2
(ii) Sales and subsistence	11.9	8.4	15.8
(b) Basic			
(i) Sales only	10.1	8.1	8.9
(ii) Sales and subsistence	11.9	8.4	9.5
Small stock			
(i) Sales only	8.5	6.9	10.8
(ii) Sales and subsistence	19.9[a]	12.4[a]	23.3
Gross output/herd-capital ratio (%)			
Cattle (basic) excluding milk			
(i) Sales only	14.9	11.8	13.5
(ii) Sales and subsistence	16.8	12.2	14.0
Cattle (basic) including milk			
(i) Sales only	14.9	13.2	17.6
(ii) Sales and subsistence	25.1	25.0	23.2
Net output/herd-capital ratio (%) (all livestock including milk, sales and subsistence, basic cattle)	23.1	21.4	21.8

Source: White and Meadows, 1981.
For definitions see text.
[a] Suspected underestimate.

of the pastoral population, it may precisely be the quantity of animals *marketed* for their meat which is of the greatest interest. However, again some caution is required in interpreting the figures. To the extent that enterprises with split interests and control in respect of land and livestock (i.e. under a traditional communal grazing system) do stock the ranges at higher rates than those with unified interests and control, then a higher *rate* of offtake from the latter may still be compatible with a higher *absolute* offtake from the former.

This section of the study has cast some doubt on the validity of any general assumption that a system of private property, which unifies in a single decision-maker or owner control over both livestock and land, is usually more efficient, in terms either of controlling livestock numbers or of other energetic or economic criteria, than communal (community land, private livestock) or socialist (community land and livestock) systems. On the other hand, it has not established any reverse general propositions — i.e. that communal or socialist systems are more efficient than private property. We must avoid generalizations of this kind which try to apply the same solution to a wide variety of pastoral situations faced with different circumstances. Where rainfall is unreliable in both time and space, livestock need to be able to wander over huge areas of land to wherever the grazing is better at a particular time. To give such huge areas of land to individuals would be inequitable; community ownership of land is therefore indicated unless a sufficiently perfect information system and market can be established between owners of individual small pieces of land that grazing elsewhere can easily be purchased in time of need for livestock whose own home-base is suffering a bad season. Where the vegetation is not uniform but very patchy, or where livestock of different kinds (species or classes) have somewhat different nutritional requirements, then a highly decentralized system of livestock management is required in which the herdsman can move each group of animals to the patch of grazing which suits it best. Communal grazing systems, as defined above, fit these requirements for huge blocks of land coupled with both equity and decentralization. We explore some of the issues of decentralization further in Chapter 7.

Where control of livestock numbers is vital, then a communal grazing system requires the application of quotas to the size of individual livestock holdings. In societies which are socially stratified in other ways, livestock quotas are also likely to be unfairly distributed or ignored. (This issue also is further discussed in Chapter 7.) In such circumstances, a more socialist system, in which both land and livestock are owned by the community as a whole, may be the only way to achieve a number of different objectives. In some socialist countries (e.g. Mongolia) a mixed system exists in which the majority of the livestock are owned by the community as a whole and a minority by individuals. In practice (although not by intention of the governments concerned) in such situations when natural conditions (e.g. drought or severe winters) require a downward adjustment in livestock numbers, it is the community herd which has to adjust most because individuals manage to secure much of the scarce forage for their private livestock.

Where there are economies of scale in the provision of certain facilities, e.g. boreholes and fencing, community ownership of land and of these facilities may enable their provision at lower cost than would be possible under a system of small private ownership. Where such economies of scale do not exist, but what is required is careful management and maintenance of numerous scattered small facilities, e.g. open wells, then private ownership may be preferable. By itself private ownership is not enough to control livestock numbers at the low levels usually desired by range scientists. But strict enforcement of government laws about livestock numbers is more feasible on private land where the livestock can be identified with the owner of the land. However, where the size of land-unit owned by numerous individuals is very small, strict enforcement is likely to be too costly to be feasible. It is doubtful if any general propositions can be made concerning the effect of different forms of property (private, communal, socialist) on the willingness to invest in improvements to the grazing or on the supply of funds for this investment. Where (as in the USA) private owners have installed land and grazing improvements on a substantial scale on their own ranches, it has often been by using public funds in the form of grants or loans on very favourable conditions. Often the level of investment in facilities on communal or government land is far higher than could be justified by criteria of profit which would guide a private entrepreneur. Sometimes the supply of loan capital from the private banking sector to private ranches has itself, because of the need to service the loan, caused a level of overstocking. In Kenya investments financed by loans on private ranches are having to be refinanced by government grants in order to avert the ranches' financial collapse.

EXCLUSIVE ORGANIZATIONS — CRITERIA FOR MEMBERSHIP

If the social organization to which rights to use land are allocated is an exclusive one, in the sense in which we have defined exclusive, then questions arise as to the criteria by which people are to be selected for admission; and to how and by whom the adjudication procedure for vetting individuals or groups in terms of these criteria is to be carried out. At the 'inclusive' end of a spectrum of possibilities we have the situation which apparently existed during the initial phase of collectivization in the USSR (ILO, 1967, pp. 28–30) and Mongolia (Lattimore, 1962, p. 180), where anyone who wanted to, regardless of his (or her) ethnic group or sex, or whether his neighbours wanted him or not, or whether at the time he possessed any livestock, was entitled, and in many cases was compelled, to join a pastoral collective. Current place of residence seems to have been the only, and even then not a very important, criterion for admission. Once a member, each person's claim on the annual proceeds from the collective's wealth and operations tends to be proportional to the amount of labour he contributes in that year.

At the other, exclusive, end of the spectrum, we have the situation in Botswana at the end of the 1970s, where ranches of 60 km^2 of land already in pastoral use are being allocated by government on very long-term leases to individuals who, in theory at any rate, have to undergo a rigorous set of tests to determine their eligibility.[4] The tests include whether they come from an already overcrowded area, whether they have already invested in fixed assets on the land in question, whether they have a large enough existing herd with which to stock the ranch, whether they are likely to be able to manage the ranch properly, etc. As a consequence of this selection procedure only about 3 per cent, it has been estimated for one important part of Botswana (Hitchcock, 1980, p. 26), of those who currently derive their livelihood from the land in question will be given rights to it. These rights will enable them to exclude the rest, although they will need to continue to employ some of them, as they do at present, as labourers on their ranches. The selected ranchers can bequeath the ranches to their heirs, but have only a circumscribed right to sell their leases to the highest bidders. They are not supposed to permit the livestock of other people to graze on their ranches under sub-leases, and it is hoped that they too will restrain their livestock within the boundaries of their own ranches.

In between these extremes of inclusiveness and exclusiveness lie most of those traditional pastoral societies in Asia and Africa where membership of a group to which pastoral land belongs is determined in principle by kinship, often in terms of one's ability to trace one's descent from some common ancestor of the group.[5] This principle is often confused, and made more flexible in practice, by the admission to membership of other individuals or subgroups for strategic or similar purposes, who are then allocated a position in the group's genealogical chart which is based on myth rather than on fact (Burnham, 1979). The general effect of this criterion of kinship is to define membership in a way which gives relatively equal opportunity to use the fixed resource, land, to all existing members of the society and to all their offspring; and to allow the admission of new members where the existing membership agrees that this is desirable. This has also been the position with pastoral collectives in the USSR after the initial phase already referred to (ILO, 1967, p. 70). Just how equal the opportunity is varies from society to society, depending not only on customary law on access to land, but on the rules for inheritance and access to the variable resources of livestock and water. But in very few cases in traditional societies are restrictions put on the amount of these variable resources that an individual can acquire by his own efforts.

Most people believe that, unless there is some degree of exclusiveness, in the form of an association between a defined group of people and a particular piece of land, sensible management of the land for long-term productivity will not be possible because an open-ended community will not be able to devise or enforce rules of good husbandry on individuals; nor will a remote government be able to do so except at prohibitive administrative cost. Nevertheless, occasionally governments believe that the existing forms of linkage, in the form of tribal territories under the authority of traditional tribal leaders, are so undesirable on other grounds, mainly connected with the security of the state, that an absence of a link between defined groups and particular pieces of land is preferable to continuing with the existing forms. For such political reasons traditional forms of tenure have been deliberately destroyed in, for example, the USSR, Iran, and Saudi Arabia. In the latter case, at any rate, the resulting free-for-all exploitation by undifferentiated graziers of undivided pastures led to a sharp increase in the rate of environmental degradation (Al-Saleh, 1976, pp. 227–238).

Place of residence

Where some degree of exclusiveness is desirable in order to promote environmentally sound management, possible criteria for inclusion of some people and exclusion of others from the organization to which land is to be allocated are: evidence of past lawful use, current place of residence, kinship, need, potential efficiency in use of the land, ownership of livestock currently using the land, and so on. In regions where the existing system of land-use is a highly mobile and opportunistically nomadic one, and where different social groups, defined in traditional terms, may all use the same piece of land either in succession throughout the year, or simultaneously, then it will not normally be appropriate to base the criterion on 'place of residence'. Firstly, one will have to choose a particular reference date to determine place of residence, and the choice of date is likely to be arbitrary; for choice of a day in one month will favour one set of people and in another month a different set. Secondly, where dwellings themselves are mobile, as in the case of tents or portable huts, it may be impossible in practice to determine who was residing where on a particular date. Thirdly, if one suddenly groups, according to place of residence, people who were previously grouped by some other criterion, e.g. kinship, one will cause tremendous social dislocation, by separating people with close ties of property and other interests and by forcing together people of different cultural background and interests.

Nevertheless, such arbitrary regrouping of population *can* be carried out although it may be costly, and other interest groups may encourage it for reasons quite different from those of the planners. One pastoral collective in the USSR in 1969 is reported as having 29 different nationalities (tribes) among its 1900 constituent households (FAO, 1970). There is some evidence that during the regrouping of the population that accompanied the formation of group ranches in Kenya Maasailand in the 1960s and 1970s some close relatives deliberately arranged to be incorporated into different ranches precisely because they wished, as a kinship group, to spread both their risks and their influence as widely as possible, and because they calculated that by having different members of the family in different ranches it would be easier to move livestock from ranch to ranch in contradiction of the planners' intention to make the system less fluid and mobile (Hedlund, 1971).

Efficiency

Quite frequently it is proposed that only 'efficient' pastoralists should be permitted to use grazing land and that the inefficient should be excluded. Such a policy might make sense if it were possible to distinguish between pastoralists in this way, in conditions where alternative opportunities to earn a satisfactory livelihood were available elsewhere in the economy. Under these conditions exclusion of inefficient pastoralists might be in their own long-term interests as well as those of society in general and of efficient pastoralists in particular. Such conditions have prevailed at times in the USA, Australia, Iran, and in parts of North Africa and the Middle East where there has been a strong demand for labour in other parts of the economy. In much of pastoral sub-Saharan Africa, however, either no alternative livelihood to pastoralism exists for these people at all, or only of the most degrading kind. In any case the concept of efficiency is not unequivocal. An *environmentally* efficient user may be defined as one whose use of the range causes no decline in its long-term productivity. An *economically* efficient user, however, may be defined as one who manages his productive activities in a way which conforms to society's preferences (Scitovsky, 1952, p. 70). There is no necessary correspondence between the two (or between them and other kinds of efficiency) for a number of reasons, both theoretical (in particular relating to the way society 'discounts' future production) and practical, relating to the difficulty of measuring the environmental consequences of different productive activities

Often efficiency is confused with wealth and with size of herd. Clearly, one of the factors that may determine the present size of a man's herd is his ability and diligence as a stockman. However, there are other important determining factors such as the number of livestock he initially inherited from his family, how many wives he has whose acquisition cost him livestock (or in some cases increased the size of his herd), how much family labour he has to look after his herd, how long he has had to build up the size of his herd, and, in an uncertain environment, sheer chance which causes disease to break out, or rain to fall, or raiders to pounce in one place rather than in another. I know of no studies which have attempted to estimate the relative importance of these different factors in determining herd size or the heritability of the trait 'good stockmanship'. There are, however, a number of cases where the current size of a man's herd was taken to indicate his efficiency as a stockman (see, e.g. Ward, 1979, p. 240).

There may be circumstances where, in theory, efficiency of the individual pastoralist might be an appropriate criterion for inclusion in or exclusion from the group of people to be given access to pastoral land. But the process of firstly defining this efficiency and then of adjudicating the relative efficiency of individuals seems so fraught with opportunities for corruption and special pleading, at the expense of the weakest but not necessarily the least efficient sections of society, and so unlikely to succeed in selecting individuals who will really use the resources in the optimum way for society that it is difficult to think of a situation in which it could be recommended in practice. However, once some selection has been made of privileged individuals who are to receive access to land, then, provided these individuals are relatively equally endowed with resources, allowing them to compete with each other in bidding to purchase land or grazing rights is probably administratively the most feasible way of assessing their relative economic efficiency.

Kinship and past use

Kinship and the evidence of past legal use, as criteria for inclusion, can be considered together, since they are to some extent both complementary and alternative to each other. The governments of many modern states are reluctant to accept kinship, as manifested in the institutions of pastoral clans or tribes, as being a suitable basis for the organization of pastoral development programmes. Partly this arises from the difficulty that government officials drawn from non-pastoral cultures have in understanding the structure and rationale of traditional pastoral institutions. They find them complicated, and, not seeing the purpose behind the complications, they believe it better to sweep them away and to start with a clean slate. Partly the reluctance arises because government officials tend to see clan-based systems as being the *cause* of the intra-pastoralist violence endemic in many pastoral areas rather than the symptom and the consequence of the competitive tension inherent in trying to make a livelihood from a fluctuating natural environment. Partly it arises from the fact that the clan system has also been the way in which pastoralists have organized themselves in hostilities against the non-pastoral groups from which the government officials themselves often come. In some cases the government officials do come from pastoral societies; they may then see the clan system as the way in which the society which they themselves have left is continuing to make claims on them, claims on their salaries, their time, and their patronage. The pastoral society sees these assets as being community property arising from the community's financing of these officials' education, whereas the officials see them as their private property arising from their own efforts. This general reluctance to accept kinship- or clan-based organizations of pastoral development tends to be characterized by criticisms of such organizations as 'primitive' and 'not suited' for the management of development in the modern world.

It makes little sense to try to freeze pastoral institutions, which have continuously adapted themselves to changes in the past, into the particular shape in which they happen to find themselves at the onset of a development programme, on the grounds that this shape is 'traditional'. On the other hand, traditional, and particularly kinship-based, institutions have certain characteristics which it is foolish to ignore. One of these is their persistence. Even when governments attempt to establish institutions based on new arrangements, the old — both the power of the old élites and the old territorial divisions and customs — tend to persist. There are rumours that this has happened even in the USSR pastoral collectives where violent efforts were made to smash the power of the old élites. It has certainly happened in Mongolia (Rosenberg, 1974, p. 65; Humphrey, 1978, pp. 152–157), in Kenya (Galaty, 1980) and, although possibly to a lesser extent, in Tanzania (Hatfield, 1977, pp. 20–27). Another characteristic of traditional pastoral institutions is that they tend to be all-embracing, to provide not only for all aspects of life but also for the livelihood of all members of the society, whereas new institutions and organizations imposed by government often produce a class of dispossessed people who no longer have either rights or role in the pastoral system. The tendency for traditional institutions to provide for all members of society is not an absolute one but one of degree. In some societies institutions exist whereby all people born into the society will be given some access to livestock and land on terms not markedly dissimilar from other people of the same age. In other societies some people may be expelled altogether and others given subordinate roles.

In an attempt to displace traditional clan-based institutions by those based on 'more modern' lines, governments sometimes try to substitute new procedures for determining access to communal resources. One such procedure is that of inviting volunteers, whereby membership in a new organization allocated pastoral land is given to those who first indicate their desire to join until all the available space is filled up.[6] This has happened, for example, in the sheep co-operatives formed under the Drought-Prone Areas Programme in India (Sandford, 1978a), where an upper limit was put on how big a part any one person could play, and on the Runka Range Reserve in Nigeria (source: a former official) and the ranching associations in Tanzania Maasailand (Maasai Range Project, 1975, p. 2), where little or no limit was put on the extent of an individual's participation. It has also been proposed for some group ranches in Botswana. Government officials often advocate the 'volunteer' principle, although they realize that it may be inequitable for late-comers, because they regard conservatism and reluctance on the part of pastoralists to undertake innovations as the key constraints on the success of their development proposals; and because they see this conservatism as a defect in character rather than imposed on the individual by his current material circumstances. In practice, it generally happens that only the better-off can afford to take the risk involved in innovation, and the educated, who are generally the children of the well-off, and the well-connected, hear of volunteering procedures earlier and are better placed to get their names on the lists.

Another procedure favoured by governments is that of registering and adjudicating, through official machinery, the customary past rights of individuals to use a piece of pastoral land, and then to base future access to the land on the result of this adjudication in so far as it identifies right-holding individuals, and on new regulations governing the conditions on which these rights can be maintained and transferred in the future. Such a procedure ought, in theory, not only to get rid of traditional social organization and hierarchies but also to ensure that none of those individuals who already have rights have them inadvertently cancelled. However, even if the rules for the future adequately protect the rights of all sections, including the absent, the illegitimate, the unborn, and not least, the women, the process of transition from the old system to the new provides opportunities for the extinction of existing rights. In the first place, it is often assumed that a register of existing right-holders is identical with a register of existing livestock-holders. But this is generally not true even in principle (e.g. in the case of the temporarily stockless), and in any case the drawing up of lists of stockholders is a notoriously difficult enterprise not only because of practical difficulties in finding livestock and their owners in inaccessible areas, but because of classification problems where several different people may have layers of rights in the same animals.

Secondly, the formal codification of customary law, whether in writing or merely verbally, tends to work to the disadvantage of marginal cases who would, under customary procedures, have been admitted on grounds of equity. Thirdly, those called on to advise government on the state of customary law are often precisely those traditional élites who will benefit by a reduction in the number and status of existing right-holders. However, in their new role as advisers on customary law they are both able to dominate adjudication procedures and are also not subject to the same restrictions as would have bound them in their traditional roles. It seems that, at any rate in Iran, Kenya, and Botswana, the government's adjudication procedures have been improperly influenced in this way. However, the Kenya Group Ranch Programme in Maasailand appears to have been fairly successful in initially identifying all those with rights (Galaty, 1980), although perhaps less successful in subsequently protecting those rights (Campbell and Mighot Adhola, 1979).

Adjudicating rights is not just a question of drawing up a list of right-holders, but also of specifying the extent of the rights of each; and this aspect manifests itself most clearly in the matter of allocating stock quotas to individuals. Questions of efficiency, equity, and administrative feasibility are all involved. On the grounds of equity some people might want to allocate an equal quota to each individual, while efficiency might require that the highest quotas be allocated to those who make best use of their quota, in terms of the volume or value of livestock production, or who keep the kind of livestock that best fit into an environmentally sound management plan. Others might argue that the least possible disruption should be made to the existing pattern of distribution of livestock holdings which reflects the pastoral society's social values. In practice, all these objectives fade before the issue of how stock quotas on individuals are to be enforced. In the USSR it took a most bloody struggle in the pastoral areas to bring about a redistribution of livestock from the old élite. In Mongolia it took some 30 years after the revolution, of less bloody struggle than in the USSR, before effective redistribution and the application of individual stock quotas took place (Rosenberg, 1981); and even now there is a tendency for private holdings to rise illegally above quota levels (*Far Eastern Economic Review*, 26 May 1978, p. 87). Attempts in Africa, both in colonial and post-colonial times, to enforce quotas have foundered on the fact that governments have relied, both for information and for means of enforcement, on precisely those pastoral élites who would be most severely injured by the application of any quota system which was not grossly inequitable.

What general conclusions can be drawn on the question of the exclusiveness or inclusiveness of social organizations to whom pastoral land is to be allocated? Clearly, some form of exclusiveness is likely to be necessary if any form of ecologically sound management is to be applied, for in the absence of exclusiveness anyone can come in to graze his animals for short-term benefit on a piece of land and then, after ruining it, return whence he came. Beyond that, conclusions will mainly depend on the priority given to the objectives of social equity and the provision of an assured meat supply for urban areas. Exclusivity, in circumstances where alternative good livelihoods are not available, is likely to lead to the formation and increase of a property-less class of people dependent only on the wages they can earn from their labour for others. Inclusiveness is likely to lead to a greater human population dependent on the rangelands who will probably consume a greater quantity, per caput, of livestock products there than they would as wage-earners in towns; so that their continued dependence on the rangelands decreases the supply that would otherwise be available to other consumers.

SINGLE- OR MULTI-PURPOSE ORGANIZATIONS

The final main issue in the choice of the type of organization relates to whether it should be single- or multi-purpose. This is partly a question of how many different kinds of products and forms of production it should take part in — just livestock for meat and dairy products; or livestock products and rain-fed or irrigated cereals for subsistence consumption; or cash crops for sale. Partly it is a question of how many stages in the production of a single product the organization carries out: for example, whether it has just a breeding herd; or fattens animals as well; or also slaughters, processes, and packages them. Partly, also, it is a question of whether the organization should specialize only in production, or also provide social services, such as health and education, or social security in the form of old-age pensions.

To a limited extent the answer will be dictated by the physical characteristics of the environment if these are such that only one form or stage of production is technically feasible. Such cases are probably exceptional, and in most environments alternative products can be produced. Single-product or single-stage organizations are likely to be more reliable sources of supply of individual commodities than multi-product ones in the same physical environment, because even when economic factors such as prices move adversely it takes time and substantial new investment to change the production pattern. They are likely, however, to be very much less efficient in absorbing demographic change, in providing occupations for more people under conditions of high population growth, or in releasing people to alternative occupations when need arises. This is because their ability to absorb or release labour is dependent on technical factors at only one level in a single production chain. In contrast, multi-purpose organizations can switch labour and other resources from one line of production to another when economic factors change and can take advantage of alternative techniques in several different chains of production.

Pastoral development programmes in which government plays a leading role are likely to be less multi-purpose, or, if multi-purpose, to be less flexible and worse managed than those where the dominant role is played by the pastoralists themselves. For government departments are normally structured on lines of professional specialization, and narrowly specialized professionals have little incentive to expand their programmes and encompass work lying in the domain of other departments. Where they do so they have great difficulty in recruiting staff with the necessary experience and in co-ordinating at local level activities in which the key decisions are usually taken at higher (and often differing) levels remote from the local scene. Traditional pastoral societies and their organizations are often, although not always, multi-purpose, as are the collectives and *negdels* of the USSR and Mongolia.[7]

SUMMARY OF MAIN POINTS

This chapter has been concerned with two main aspects of range management, the management of the allocation of land between different uses and between different users. In the first of these aspects the main focus was on the relative advantages, under different circumstances, of government or community organizations carrying out the allocation. A fairly sceptical view was taken of governments' ability to assess optimum land-use at the speed and with the flexibility needed. Nevertheless, it was noted that in socially stratified communities decisions about changes in the form of land-use are often occasions on which the powerful, by using their positions in social organizations, can advance their private interests at the expense of the weak. Governments frequently fail to follow a land-use policy consistently even when it is founded on sound technical judgements.

In looking at the allocation of land between different users, four main options in organization and management were considered. In examining these options the experience not only of government programmes in different parts of the world but also of the way in which traditional pastoral societies tackle the issues outside the context of government programmes was reviewed. In looking at the question of size of unit and organization it was noted that in traditional pastoral systems a variety of different functions and powers over land allocation tend to be exercised at different levels in an organizational hierarchy, a pattern also followed in socialist Mongolia's *negdels*. In contrast, Western-style ranches tend to concentrate functions at a single level. It was also noted that judgements about the optimum size of allocation unit in a particular environment tend to change over time.

One major section looked at the choice between private ownership, communal grazing, and socialist ownership of livestock and land — the issues which are often discussed under the title of 'The tragedy of the commons'. Private ownership, contrary to what is often claimed, does not have a superior record in terms of controlling livestock numbers. Although most communal grazing systems do not control livestock numbers, some do, and the fact that others do not may not so much reveal an inherent institutional incapacity as a lack of good reason to do so or external pressures. Doubt was also thrown on whether private ownership necessarily is accompanied by greater resource productivity or more self-financed investment. This general scepticism suggests that the choice between tenure systems cannot be generalized on a global scale but should be determined by a number of important factors which vary between different situations.

One section looked at three criteria which may be used for determining who should be members of a particular organization to which an area of pastoral land is allocated. The criteria are place of residence, efficiency as a pastoralist, and kinship or past use. The advantages and disadvantages of the criteria and the reasons why they are adopted in particular circumstances were reviewed. The chapter ended by looking at the choice between single- or multi-purpose organizations as the basic units to which pastoral land should be allocated. The choice is partly determined by the natural environment, partly by the question as to whether a reliable source of supply of particular commodities is the main objective or the ability to absorb or release surplus human population or labour.

NOTES TO CHAPTER 6

1. Another source of information (Foreign Broadcast Information Service: Mongolia Report No. 258) shows a slightly smaller proportionate decline in numbers of *negdels* from 354 in 1960 to 259 in 1975 (255 in 1979).

2. A useful summary account of this stratification of functions in a number of societies within one broad region has been given by Tapper (1979a).

3. In the USA 60 per cent of non-federal rangeland (mainly privately owned) is said to be in 'poor' or only 'fair' condition. The corresponding figure for pastoral (public) land is 75 per cent. The difference between the two figures is insignificant when one recollects that the non-federal land would have been selected for private ownership at the outset because it was the best land. 'Condition' in these cases is calculated in relation to resemblance to 'climax' vegetation which may be an inappropriate criterion. Between 10 and 15 per cent of non-federal land is estimated to be 'exploitatively grazed' and 70 per cent 'properly grazed' (Perry, 1978; Pendleton, 1978).

4. In practice, emphasis tends to be put on only one criterion — whether they have an existing fixed investment in the land.

5. This is just one example of a wide variety of groupings where the unifying element is kinship.

6. In the USSR and Mongolian cases cited earlier all those who volunteered in an initial phase *had* to be given membership; and only later was the entry of additional members made contingent on the existing membership agreeing that there was room for more.

7. It appears that collectives in the USSR also provide social services to their members, whereas *negdels* in Mongolia do not, although these services are provided by government authorities to the population on the basis of administrative subdivisions at the lowest level which are identical with *negdel* territories (Humphrey, 1978).

Chapter seven

Managing the improvement of range productivity

INTRODUCTION

This is the third of three chapters concerned with range management. In Chapter 5 a variety of different aspects of range management were outlined and a brief description given of the factors involved in the three main aspects. In Chapter 6 the management of two of these aspects, the allocation of land between different uses and between different users, were discussed in some detail. The present chapter will discuss the management of the third main aspect — the improvement of range productivity.

In Chapter 5 we classified improving the productivity of rangelands into six activities: physical and mechanical work on soil, vegetation, and structures; planting, seeding, and reseeding; burning the vegetation; the application of chemical herbicides and fertilizers; altering the timing, length, and succession of use by livestock of a particular piece of land, i.e. rotation of pasture; and regulation of grazing pressure by adjusting stock numbers and types. In this chapter some important issues in the management of these activities will be discussed. Some of these activities involve strong linkages with the non-pastoral economy, in terms of physical inputs, advanced technology, and the need for large investments which it may be beyond the capacity of pastoral society to raise from its own resources. The first section of this chapter focuses on the consequences of these linkages on the choice of certain forms of organization and management, i.e. management by pastoralists in a participatory style. The remainder of the chapter focuses on the other activities which do not involve such strong linkages with the rest of the economy. Two main issues are discussed. The first is the need for information by both pastoralists and government and the ways in which it can best be passed in both directions between them; this raises the whole question of extension work. The second main issue is the day-to-day management of activities; who this should be done by, the extent to which decentralization of decision-making is required, the appropriate style of management, and the way in which a mandatory style can be enforced.

ACTIVITIES WITH STRONG LINKAGES OUTSIDE THE PASTORAL SOCIETY

Physical and mechanical work, planting and reseeding, and applications of chemicals often involve strong linkages between pastoral society and the rest of the economy. These linkages may arise partly because of the need, in some although not in all cases, to call on outside technical expertise, for example to survey and lay out soil conservation works, to advise on and supervise the application of chemical herbicides, and to operate earth-moving machinery or to erect fencing. Partly they arise from the need to procure physical inputs such as fencing wire, machinery, herbicides, or seeds and other planting material and partly from either a reluctance or an inability to raise investment resources from the current production of the pastoral society concerned. Sometimes the physical work, for example of bush-clearing, contour-furrowing, fence-post cutting and erection, can be done by manpower drawn from within pastoral society, and sometimes such manpower can be fed or remunerated from current pastoral production. More often the use of pastoral labour for physical work will lead to a decline in current pastoral production as a result of less labour-intensive and effective herding practices; and this decline will have to be made up by the import of other forms of food. Alternatively, the labour will become available because recent drought or other disaster has left much of the labour force without livestock to herd or to depend on for subsistence. In either case the imported food will have to be paid for either by selling off part of the herd capital or by utilizing external resources in the form of bank loans or government grants.

Reliance on outside sources of expertise, physical inputs, and investment resources tends to bring about a management system in which effective participation by ordinary members of pastoral society in decision-making is reduced. This tendency is stronger where the levels of formal education among the pastoralists are lower. The concepts and the organizational needs of the technicians, the suppliers, and the financiers start to crowd out understanding by ordinary people. Even where formal decision-making is left in pastoralists' hands this often takes the form of their being presented with a decision-making process so structured as to what are accepted as relevant kinds of argument and evidence that the views of technicians and financiers are bound to prevail (Conlin, 1981). Outsiders find negotiations with participatory management structures very time-consuming, unpredictable, and, thus, costly. The tendency, therefore, is either for a government to step in and to appropriate part of the rangelands on which to carry out the work on its own behalf, or for it to try to establish management structures inside pastoral society in which decision-making can be highly concentrated. This may be done either by restructuring land tenure so as to concentrate ownership in the hands of relatively few private ranchers, or by trying to establish centralized and authoritarian management structures in tribal society.

For example in imperial Iran the Forest and Range Organization expropriated large areas of land from tribal use to carry out physical works and planting operations (Sandford, 1977b). In India the government has preferred to do these works on land in forest reserves already under its control, but it is also beginning to do so on more communally owned village grazing areas after alienating these to co-operatives tightly controlled by government (Sandford, 1978a). In Botswana, where fencing has been seen as the key to increasing range productivity, sizeable chunks of previously communal land are being alienated to private ranchers to whom banks can make loans and suppliers of fencing material can sell with relative ease. In order to hurry the work along, and because it believed it could do the work to a higher technical standard if left in sole charge, the Botswana Government itself undertook the physical works on the first of the ranches before handing them over to their new owners (Odell, 1980, p. 53). In Kenya the government authorities, not apparently with much success, have tried to establish on group ranches management committees with much greater power over the livestock of individual ranch members — and over relations between the group and the rest of the economy (e.g. in incurring loans) — than had traditional social organizations.

The management of these activities (physical and mechanical work, application of chemicals, reseeding, etc.) involves not only the initial phase of investment and physical development but also the subsequent operation of facilities, use of the land, and repayment of loans where these have been incurred. The Iranian Forest and Range Organization, having carried out the development works, had not, after up to 10 or more years and by the time of the Shah's fall in 1979, thought of a way in which to ensure that the facilities would be properly used by traditional pastoralists, and therefore continued to exclude them. Instead it was trying to encourage the establishment of large, centrally managed corporations to take leases on the land. The Botswana Government's turn-key ranches have subsequently faced acute problems, not only because the structures erected by government were not always completed to a high standard, but also because their subsequent owners proved incompetent to manage and maintain them.

Many of the issues concerning the development and management of water supplies which we have already discussed in Chapter 4 arise also in connection with these range activities. Where the environment is fairly productive and homogeneous, allowing a relatively densely populated and sedentary form of pastoralism, and where the physical work does not involve substantial economies of scale in construction or operation, then quite small and simple management units, small in terms of both area and the number of people, with a high degree of participation in decision-making will generally be possible. In such circumstances, also, it should be possible for the social organization concerned either to raise the investment resources itself by the sale of capital assets or to service a loan if the activity is potentially economic. The Maasai of northern Tanzania, in raising resources to construct water supplies and dip tanks, and in managing these, demonstrate this point.

However, where the environment is relatively heterogeneous, in soils, vegetation, and climate, requiring large-scale nomadic movements, and especially where it is spatially and temporally unreliable so that the nomadic movements are opportunistic rather than predictable, the management units will have to be large, allowing several different social groups and their herds to use the same facilities simultaneously if circumstances dictate. Under these conditions participatory self-management is difficult. For the managing body, whether committee or general meeting, will have a changing membership lacking continuity, and pastoralists are unlikely to want to invest their own resources in an activity whose benefits they may not subsequently use. The competition for resources between social groups will mean that co-operation between these groups in managing the resource will be unlikely. In such circumstances either direct intervention by government in providing and managing the facility, and in charging a fee on the basis of actual use made, or a somewhat authoritarian social organization, overarching all the competing social groups concerned, would appear to be the appropriate organizational forms. Where there are economies of scale in the construction or maintenance of physical works it may be necessary for a number of different groups to share a single service or facility. Pastoralists may be particularly reluctant to provide resources for investment in facilities which they will have to share with members of other groups.

OTHER ACTIVITIES

Resource-raising, technical expertise, and procurement are the main issues in relation to the three activities dealt with so far. In the case of the other activities — burning, rotation and regulation of grazing pressure — the important issues relate to the functions of collecting and communicating information, and the detailed execution of decisions including the enforcement of regulations. The rest of this chapter will deal with these issues.

INFORMATION

The communication of information is often seen, in pastoral development, as an activity to be carried out by government range extension workers, in which they instruct pastoralists in the basic principles of range management and the evils of overgrazing. I have come increasingly to see this, in the case of traditional pastoralists at any rate, as a wholly ludicrous activity in which people from urban backgrounds, who have often taken up positions and training in government range-management services only because they were unable to find employment in urban-oriented services, expound with desperate zeal the lessons that they have learnt in a classroom to an unwilling audience of experienced pastoralists who understand far better than their teachers the composition, productivity, and dynamics of the local vegetation. An example will illustrate this. On one occasion I and a colleague were looking at a hillside in Africa in company with a range extension officer and an interpreter who had also been a herd-boy in the area. The extension officer was able to identify, by their scientific names, just two of the species of forage on the hillside but could add no further information beyond this, while the interpreter/herd-boy was able to identify, by their local name, 10 species and the particular advantages and drawbacks of each plant to different types of stock. In any case, the principles of range management that the extension officers learn and expound as though they were universally valid are too often found to be based on a North American experience whose interpretation is itself being challenged at its own place of origin.

There is indeed a great need for the collection and dissemination of information, but the scope of this should be far wider than that of conventional range extension work. In the subsections which follow we shall first discuss research, then pastoralists' need for information and the circumstances which usually attend its provision, and finally the needs of government officials. We shall then briefly review some experiences of methods ('arms length') other than conventional face-to-face extension work in the field of delivering information to pastoralists. The section after that deals in some detail with extension in the field, paying particular attention in the case of nomadic groups to identifying the right kind of group to serve as the focus both for disseminating information from government and for collecting it to pass to government. The relative advantages of different kinds of groups under different circumstances are examined.

Research

In most of Africa and Asia there is a great dearth of knowledge about the effects of livestock on vegetation, and vice versa, and about the consequences of new range-management practices and investments. Not much research has been carried out, and what has is often made irrelevant by following procedures adapted for research on annual crops in stable environments, so that the gap between the conditions under which research is carried out and those in which its results are to be applied is even wider than usual. Such research usually lacks the dynamic element required of a situation in which rainfall, vegetation, and livestock interact with each other. Most of the research is woefully divorced from an appreciation of the history of land-use and climate in the area, nor does it make use of oral history that would partially substitute for the absence of scientific records.[1] The expense of conventional research, in terms of fencing, water supplies, and herds of livestock, means that it can only be done at a very few places; and this physical separation from the areas where its results may be applied, the difference between research and field conditions, and, in most countries, the organizational location of range research in a separate national research institute without strong linkages to the executive or extension officers at district and provincial level of government's range-management department, mean that these officials and the pastoralists are neither aware of the results of the research nor, if they are, believe them to be relevant to their own concerns. This general case appears to be true, for example, of imperial Iran, Kenya, Tanzania, and Nigeria.

An exception arises in India. There the work of some of the national research institutes appears to be as remote as elsewhere; but in the case of the Drought-Prone Areas Programme administrative arrangements have been made to devolve responsibility both for initiating and carrying out some experiments and pilot trials to district-level organizations and officials who are able to obtain occasional advice from national bodies and local universities and research institutes. Although in technical terms the experiments are rather crude, they seem to be very successful in arousing interest among district-level officials in improving the techniques of range management, in questioning their existing methods, and in stimulating inventiveness, circumstances which I have not seen elsewhere. Certain kinds of more basic research will have to continue to be done in a few national centres.[2] But some district-level research work is required not only to test the local applicability of results obtained elsewhere but also to stimulate the interest of local people and officials in the potential of new technology.

Pastoralists' needs for information

The results of research need to be communicated not only to officials but also to pastoralists, as does much other information. Pastoralists need to be informed about what general government policy is in respect to the management and development of the rangelands; about land-tenure reform in pastoral areas, and about the details of registration and adjudication of rights in their own particular areas. As well as learning about the relative effectiveness of different methods of improving range productivity, as demonstrated by research, they also need to be taught particular skills whereby they can play their part in introducing the new methods. Such skills may include fencing, techniques for reseeding and planting, how to lay out flood spreading and soil and moisture conservation works, and so on. They must be informed about regulations concerning rotational grazing and adjusting grazing pressure, for example about the dates at which particular water points and grazing blocks are to be opened and closed, and about limitations as to numbers and types of livestock to be admitted to a particular piece of land in the coming season. Pastoralists will continue to need to know, as they have in the past, about grazing conditions in particular places, where the concentrations of livestock are, where rainfall has recently fallen, and where better grazing can, therefore, subsequently be expected.

The special circumstances of providing information to pastoralists

Most of these types of information which pastoralists need to have are not markedly different from those required by settled crop-cultivators and which agricultural extension workers seek to provide. But the circumstances under which they have to be provided in pastoral areas are different. The lower density of human population means that, for face-to-face contact between client and extension worker, a much greater distance must be travelled. The mobility of herds and herdsmen means that, even if the extension worker is himself nomadic, regular contact between him and his clientele will be difficult unless he can be attached to some fairly permanent pastoral group which moves and camps together. We return to this point later. There is more often a language barrier between extension workers and their clients in pastoral than in cultivating areas, because the poor access to education which pastoralists have had in the past and the high minimum educational qualifications required for entry into government extension services have caused most extension workers to be recruited from non-pastoral groups speaking a different language from that of the pastoralists. The same poor access to education means that pastoral groups often have a high rate of illiteracy and therefore cannot be reached by the written word.

The fact that many innovations to improve range productivity need to be introduced on land subject to communal use has the consequence that extension work that reaches individuals one by one may be ineffective because of the necessity of agreement and co-operation in implementation by the group as a whole. Possibly to a slightly higher degree in pastoral than in cultivated areas, information is a commodity which enables individuals to profit at the absolute as well as the relative expense of their neighbours. This is the case in respect of information about current and prospective grazing conditions in different areas, and perhaps particularly so in respect of information about procedures for registering and adjudicating claims to grazing and watering rights. For in this case well-informed individuals can sometimes acquire exclusive private rights to communal land while the less well informed are unaware of what is going on. Possibly also more frequently in pastoral than in cultivating areas, responsibility for managing enterprises (i.e. livestock herds and farms) is split between different people. In such cases of split responsibility, one person (the 'owner') may make decisions about which animals shall be sold, about which general areas the herd shall graze during a period of time, and about the expenses which the enterprise will undertake; while another person (the 'herdsman') may make day-to-day decisions about which particular animals shall graze where on that day, or about when mineral and other supplements shall be fed. Management is frequently divided between many more than two people. Information must be channelled specifically to the person who needs it.

Government officials' need for information

It is also necessary that there be an easy flow of communications from pastoralists to government as well as the other way round. Partly this arises from a general diagnostic need by governments to know what pastoralists see as their problems, how they would like them solved, and what the opinion and extent of agreement is of different groups and sections within pastoral society as regards government proposals. Partly it arises from the specific requirements for management information in the particular system for managing development that government seeks to impose. Many government programmes to develop and manage pastoral areas imply more centralized decision-making than under the systems which they are intended to replace, and this centralized system can only be efficient if it is based on adequate information. Some of this information may be collected on a once-and-for-all basis during the project-planning phase of development, although in practice it is extremely difficult to know in advance precisely which information is going to be most useful. While such pre-project surveys habitually concentrate on mapping the vegetation, it is really much more important to find out what the rationale of the present system of land-use is, and how use of the resources is divided up between different people.

In any case much of the information needs to come to decision-makers regularly and frequently during the course of implementing the programme. If, for example, a district range officer wants to rotate the grazing between different pastures in a block of public or communal land, to adjust grazing pressure, or to burn the vegetation, and to do these things in a sensible way with regard not only to the condition of the vegetation but to the productivity of the livestock which use it, then he is going to need to know the present condition of the water supplies in different pastures, and of the vegetation there, its quantity, its nutritional (i.e. protein) content, its dryness (if he wants to burn it); he must know where rainfall has recently fallen, how many animals belonging to whom are in what pastures and for what reason, and what the present condition of these animals is and their probable future nutritional needs, e.g. for pastures or water with particular mineral contents. Unless his district or grazing block is remarkably homogeneous he needs to have this information in a good deal of detail in respect of quite small patches of land. While some of this information may be collected from his own staff, or in some indirect mechanical way (e.g. satellite imagery), some of it can only come from the pastoralists concerned. Almost all of it could come in this way if proper communication channels were established.

Arms-length systems of communication

A number of different schemes have been tried for communications between government and pastoralists. Mostly these stress communications from government. In Iran a good deal of information work in special areas, e.g. river catchments, where new range programmes are being introduced, has been done among children in schools, where the audience is fairly captive and facilities exist to make use of audio-visual aids. Also in Iran a limited use has been made of radio broadcasts, using the general agricultural programme which is (1977) broadcast for an hour daily, to provide occasional programmes on pastoral matters, mainly relating to animal health. In Botswana, when the new Tribal Grazing Lands Policy (on land tenure) was introduced in 1975, a special effort was made to use radio broadcasts to explain the policy to the nation. Some 10 broadcasts on this topic were made over a period of two months, and the target audience was first organized into about 3000 radio listening groups, with a total membership thought to account for more than half of rural households.³ Prior to the inception of this service of broadcasts a selected leader from each group was given a residential training course of two days' duration; and each group was provided with a radio and written background material to assist its members to understand the whole programme. Groups were encouraged to make comments and to raise questions by post for further discussion in subsequent broadcasts, and about 90 per cent of groups responded in this way, 50 per cent of them responding to nearly every broadcast. These comments and questions not only enabled obscurities in the presentation of the policy to be cleared up, but provided some feedback to the government authorities of people's reactions to the policy (Botswana, 1977).

A considerable amount of time had to be invested in these broadcasts by officials concerned in drawing up and implementing the policy, as well as by a special team organizing the radio listening groups. The scheme probably reached a high proportion of the population with a more accurate presentation of government policy than could have been achieved by any alternative programme in Botswana. Nevertheless, complaints continue to be raised of a general misunderstanding by the population of the policy, and there is some evidence that the most isolated sections of the nation, and often those most adversely affected by the new policy, i.e. the hunter–gatherers who are also often employed in casual herding jobs, were not reached by these radio broadcasts, partly because they had no access to radios and partly because they were too physically isolated to be incorporated in the organization of the radio listening groups (Hitchcock, 1978). The radio does, however, present a way of getting simple messages across to a part of the pastoral population quickly without the risk of deliberate distortion by intermediate links in a communication chain. For it to reach a large proportion of the pastoral population requires that ownership of radios be fairly widely distributed, and that the population be led to expect to hear a broadcast at a particular time. Such expectation can be brought about through the establishment of regular programmes of interest to them broadcast in their own language at a particular time in the week or month.

In Kenya, for example, some use has been made of mobile motorized extension units using films and similar audio-visual aids to communicate general policy and ideas or specific techniques. They are one way to gather an initial audience which is attracted by the novelty of the techniques. But the units themselves are very difficult and expensive to keep operating in rugged terrain because of mechanical breakdowns; and it is also difficult to keep a flow of up-to-date and relevant material reaching pastoralists on a programmed basis. The material available for showing may be irrelevant to current concerns in the area, and the pastoralists may, at the time the unit is available, be out of reach of motor transport. It is much easier and more convenient for the crews concerned to organize an itinerary in which such mobile units serve non-pastoral populations of towns or trading centres in pastoral areas rather than the pastoralists themselves. Nevertheless, such units have a use in putting forward entirely new ideas, for example for soil and water conservation works or flood spreading, which are difficult adequately to convey in words and of which local examples do not yet exist. They have to be backed up, however, with a more permanent and closer arrangement.

Mobile units may also be appropriate in an initial development phase, where the existing political structure in the pastoral areas is such that government is finding it difficult to make contact with the weaker sections of pastoral society because an intervening pastoral élite is preventing such contact from being made. In these circumstances isolated junior extension officers stationed inside the pastoral community are liable either to be totally ignored or to be taken over and monopolized by the élite on whom they become dependent for their day-to-day comfort and conveniences. A mobile unit, whose staff are more senior and more independent of the local élite because normally resident elsewhere, may be better able to reach and communicate with the weaker sections. An example of this can be seen in the case of the Red Caravans in the pastoral areas of the USSR in the 1920s when the Soviet Government was trying to break the power of the traditional nomadic leaders (ILO, 1967, p. 34).

Residential training courses for pastoralists are run in some countries; and visits by pastoralists to see development schemes outside their own areas are also frequently arranged. The trouble is that they foster an air of unreality. Residential training courses are often held on demonstration ranches where the stocking rate is, perhaps, one-quarter of that in the traditional pastoral area, exotic or improved stock are kept under a level of veterinary supervision not available elsewhere, and the ranch is equipped with an uneconomic level of equipment. The instructors on such ranches are not forced to grapple with the problems with which the pastoralists are faced; and the pastoralists often come away from such demonstrations with an entirely different impression from that which the visit was meant to foster. 'I saw a lot of people and animals in prison' was the comment of one pastoralist after being taken to see some ranches in another area. Too often such training is seen as 'changing pastoralists' attitudes' and not as transmitting information of the kind set out a few paragraphs previously, that is, actually useful to pastoralists and seen by them to be so. Pastoralists resent interactions with government officials in which they are credited with knowing nothing and are lectured by people who actually know less. Consequently, it has proved difficult, for example in northern Kenya, to fill the vacancies in the local training centre, and the majority of those attending from one area, at any rate, were alleged to be townsfolk persuaded by considerable pressure from their chief. (Source: a local range official.)

EXTENSION IN THE FIELD

A communication system between government and pastoralists will be required not only in respect of range management but also for other development components such as veterinary, water, and marketing programmes. In the context of crop cultivation in densely populated areas it is common for separate field services with extension functions each to try to be in direct contact with individual farmers; and the more technically complex the information to be transmitted, and the more that extension work in a particular component is combined with the enforcement of rules and regulations (policing), the more desirable it will seem for each service to have its own direct link. In pastoral areas, however, the ratio between the time spent travelling to look for a pastoralist and the time spent actually in contact with him will inevitably be higher than in crop areas, because of the lower density of population and therefore the greater distance to be travelled. This element due to distance will be aggravated further the more nomadic and opportunist the pastoral system and the greater the uncertainty about where particular individual pastoralists or groups are to be found. The high ratio between travelling time and contact time implies that each extension worker will be able to serve a relatively low number of pastoralists. Provided that the messages to be transmitted can be kept simple, and that policing functions can be kept separate, there is a strong economic argument for using multi-purpose extension workers in pastoral areas, making each 'occasion of contact' an opportunity to exchange information of more than one kind. Each extension worker will still only be able to serve a small number of herders, but overall fewer extension workers will be required.

In a number of different countries there are field officers of the range-management organization with functions which are largely those of extension rather than of regulation or research. It is a fairly common experience that such extension officers suffer acute difficulties in maintaining effective contact with pastoral groups, partly because they have little to communicate that is useful to pastoralists, partly because of barriers of language and culture, partly for lack of transport with which to make and maintain contact. The situation described by one such extension officer aptly summarizes the unenviable position they occupy. He had been in his present post for six months and was responsible for extension work in an area of 13,000 km², to cover which he had no means of transport except his own feet. He did not know the language of the local pastoralists nor, except for a very few, did they know any language known to him. The furthest he had so far travelled into his present posting was to the airstrip a kilometre from the town where he lived and the only people to whom he had made a serious effort to provide advice on range management, emphasizing especially the need to limit stock numbers, were a group of cultivators on an irrigation scheme on the edge of the town who had previously been pastoralists but who had lost all their livestock in a series of disasters. When asked why he did not go out on foot into the rangelands to meet pastoralists in their camps he admitted that he was afraid to do so. 'They hate me and will kill me', he said. 'They say that I only know about cultivation; but I know everything.' It is little wonder that in these circumstances absenteeism, alcoholism, and mental breakdowns seem to be common problems among range extension officers.

These extension officers may try to make contact with pastoralists one by one, although the low density and unpredictable movement of individuals may make this very difficult; or they may seek to spread their messages to individuals *en masse* at public meetings or through intermediaries such as representative committees of pastoralists, or traditional or government-appointed pastoral authorities such as clan elders or chiefs. Too seldom is adequate attention paid to the way public meetings are called or to the composition of attendance, in terms of which sections of pastoral society are represented. Pastoral society is not homogeneous, nor is it divided simply along clan or kinship lines although such divisions may be very important. There will also be divergences of interest between people of different sex, age, place of residence, and occupation (e.g. agro-pastoralists in contrast to pure pastoralists), and according to the species of livestock in which they specialize. Often such so-called public meetings are summoned at short notice, and tend to be attended by the better-off and elderly (whose sons or hired labourers are looking after the herds), frequently by those who also have non-pastoral business interests in urban centres which is where it is easier to pick up news of a meeting.

Similarly, committees to represent pastoralists, whether they are simply appointed by government officials or are elected, are unlikely to represent the full range of interests in pastoral society. Members may have been selected primarily because they are well located to attend frequent or suddenly called meetings and because they are able to understand better than others the language which officials speak. They may well also be owners of large numbers of livestock, but they are unlikely to represent the full range of interest groups in pastoral society. Information passed from government to pastoralists through meetings of such people is unlikely to reach all corners of pastoral society, partly because it may be against the interests of those who attended to tell those who did not, partly because to spread information involves time and energy on their part for which they will not be compensated. The accuracy with which information is relayed is a further problem. Nor are such meetings and bodies likely to relay accurately to government the views of those not represented on them.

An efficient communication system will not arise by chance, but needs to be designed and then carefully maintained and monitored. Such a system is likely to require several different channels and different techniques. The appropriate one to use will depend on the nature, novelty, and complexity of the information to be imparted, which people need to communicate with each other (is it veterinary officer and herdsman or marketing officer and owner?), on the regularity, predictability of timing, frequency and speed of communication required, and the extent to which communication needs to be carried on with several people simultaneously or to which links in a communication chain may have a vested interest in passing on or holding up information. While special channels will therefore need to be set up for particular purposes — e.g. special briefings of the kind illustrated by Botswana's radio programmes on land tenure — there is also a need for a permanent and basic channel, to pass certain routine information, e.g. about pasture rotations or the whereabouts of particular groups of people and animals, and to provide the starter mechanism for establishing other channels, e.g. by calling for special meetings or by generating nominations for special training courses.

EXTENSION AND SEDENTARY PASTORALISTS

In pastoral areas where the population, although sparse, is sedentary, each extension worker can, as in crop areas, be resident in a local settlement and be responsible both for a particular area of land round his home and for a particular group of people — those resident on the land. In this case people are defined and categorized by where they live. The number of extension workers required in such a system will depend on their means of transport, the extent to which they need to visit their clients at their homes, the productivity of the environment, and the way in which their clients' homes are dispersed over the countryside, as well as on the nature of the common messages to be transmitted and the diligence of the extension agents.

We can give some simplified examples of how these factors influence the calculations of the desirable number of extension workers. If the extension worker has to travel on foot or bicycle, and to visit his clients in their homes (which we can for simplicity assume is where they pen their cattle overnight) and to return daily to his own place of residence, he is unlikely, even if unusually dedicated, to be able effectively to travel more than 8 km from his place of residence. Let us assume that the average pastoral household has a herd size of 50 head of cattle, equivalent of 36 livestock units (lu) of 250 kg each.[4] If the homes of these households are uniformly dispersed over the countryside, then, if the environment is very productive with a carrying capacity of, say, 4 ha/lu, each extension agent will be able to serve about 140 households who use an area of about 200 km^2. If the carrying capacity of the environment is a more normal 16 ha/lu he will be able to serve only 35–40 households, a very low figure. If the pastoral homesteads are not evenly distributed but lie (conveniently, this model is for purposes of illustration, not realism) on the perimeter of a circle of radius 8 km, with the extension worker's home at the centre of the circle, and with the cattle able to graze up to a further 15 km from their overnight pens outside this perimeter, then the extension worker will be able to serve up to 1100–1200 households (who use an area of about 1700 km^2) in a very productive environment (4 ha/lu) or about 300 households in a more normal one (16 ha/lu).

How many households will actually be served is, of course, dependent on other factors than mere physical accessibility. We can cite an agricultural example for two such factors. In western Kenya, with a population density of 15–100 households per km^2 (in contrast to the 0.2–0.7 per km^2 that we are talking about for pastoral areas), junior extension agents spent 60 per cent of their working time on visiting individual farms but only visited about 20 farmers per month, in contrast to the figure of 50 farmers per month which they themselves believed would represent a fair effort. Moreover, a minority of 'progressive' farmers, accounting for 10 per cent of the total, were receiving, at three visits per year, six times the average number of visits per farmer (one every two years), and were, in effect, at a ratio of 45 progressive farmers per junior extension worker, the only ones to receive an effective service in terms of individual visits. (Leonard, 1977, Chs. 2 and 9).

It is difficult to predict precisely what effect a lower density of population will have on the number of farmers or pastoralists that an extension agent will visit in a given period of time. The west Kenya figure quoted, in a densely populated area, is less than one farmer per working day. It seems certain that lowering the density of farmers must have some negative effect, but possibly, at such a very low frequency of visits, it may not be very great provided that farms are within a radius of 8 km from the extension agent's house. In that case extension agents in pastoral areas may, in practice, serve as many sedentary farmers as in high potential areas. But if the negative effect is strong it seems unlikely that an extension service involving personal visits to sedentary pastoralists' homes could have any significant effect on pastoral productivity.

EXTENSION AND NOMADIC PASTORALISTS

In areas of nomadic (including transhumant) pastoralism a system of dispersing extension workers to reside permanently in local settlements and to be responsible both for a particular area of land and for a particular group of people is unlikely to be very effective. For in these circumstances an extension worker's clientele will change through the year, with the group for whom he is responsible moving out of his reach and possibly some other group for whom some other worker is responsible coming into his area. Much of the time he may find himself without any clientele at all, while at other times he will be surrounded by people unfamiliar with him and lacking confidence in him. In these nomadic circumstances it is likely to make more sense either for extension workers to be centrally based, e.g. at district or provincial level, and to be sent out for several days or weeks at a time to where the pastoralists with whom they are familiar are camped for the time being; or else for the extension workers themselves to be nomadic, moving always with groups to whom they are assigned. In either case the lowest (i.e. most grass-roots) rung in the extension system will be based on social groups instead of on territory, although at some higher level in the administrative system group-based extension workers will have to be connected into the territorially based services and hierarchies of the state.

What kind of social grouping presents opportunities for being the point of contact for receiving, for example, through the attachment of an extension worker, information from above or outside, and for collating information, including expressions of opinion, of needs or of agreement from pastoralists? Several criteria are relevant. Such groupings need to be fairly permanent, in the sense that roughly the same people continue to be members. The members need to be able to meet fairly frequently and to communicate with each other at only moderate cost in terms of time, effort, and money; and they need to be fairly united in the sense either that their interests coincide or that at any rate they can all expect to benefit or lose in the same way from the matters to be communicated. Where members are not united, in this sense, they will either be unable to express agreed or consistent community opinions, or if they do it will only be because the minority opinion is constantly overruled. Probably none of these criteria is either a necessary or sufficient condition for a group to act as a successful link in a communication chain. But where none of the criteria are fulfilled the chances of success are low.

It is possible, and may be necessary, to create entirely new groupings for particular purposes pertaining to new development programmes, including groupings whose main purpose is to act as channels of communication. But such specially created groupings appear to have quite a high chance of proving to be either élitist organizations (I shall return to this point later) or sickly creatures who never achieve a self-sustaining life but perish as soon as government's original interest in them wanes. The executive committees of ranching associations (average land area of association was 1700 km^2 and average membership about 500 families) in Tanzanian Maasailand seem to have functioned less well as general communication links with their members, although this was one of their supposed main functions, than did the management committees of dipping tanks. The area and membership they covered was too large, their meetings (quarterly) too infrequent, and the membership of the executive committee too busy on their private affairs. In contrast, management committees of dipping tanks met often with each other and with the members they represented because of everyone's weekly need to attend at the tank. (Source: local range officials.) Similarly in northern Kenya, grazing committees, appointed to represent pastoralists on grazing blocks and to advise government on the acceptability of government proposals to the pastoralists and to inform the pastoralists of government decisions, were ineffective because they covered too large an area (up to 6000 km^2), with too diverse a collection of competitive interest groups, and no one had the responsibility or incentive to maintain communications between the grazing committees and the pastoralists they were supposed to represent. (Source: local officials and Helland, 1980, pp. 135–171.)

There are three sorts of existing social groupings which can also be used as the basis for a communications link: the group of people who migrate together and who camp in the same general vicinity (which we shall here term a *camping* community), the group who use a water point or a cluster of wells (which I shall call a *watering* community), and traditional political and social structures based on criteria other than co-residence, co-migration, and joint use of facilities. I shall use as an example of such traditional structure a lineage — a kinship group — members of which trace their descent from a real or mythical common ancestor; and here I shall call such lineages 'clans'. In many pastoral societies the important social and political structures are not based on kinship groups or clans. For example, in East Africa age- and generation-sets are sometimes important. I use clans here simply as one example. Occasionally these three forms of groupings — camping communities, watering communities, and clans — coincide where a water point is used by one and only one camping community whose household heads are all of the same clan, although it would be very exceptional if all those able to trace descent from a common ancestor however distant, i.e. the whole clan, were to camp together. More often, more than one camping group forms a watering community (the opposite is also possible); and though in some societies camping communities are normally constituted by households headed by people from the same clan, in others they are not.

Camping communities

Camping communities have the greatest facility for members to communicate with each other and are where an extension worker, if he were attached to one, would find it easiest to carry out his work of distributing technical and other information passed down from above to pastoralists, and for collecting opinions and information from pastoralists to pass up. This arises from the physical closeness to each other of members of a camping community, and from the fact that such communities normally already have some communal decision-making structure which decides, for example, when and where major migrations should take place. Camping communities tend to be rather small, however, normally less than 50 tents and sometimes less than 10. Moreover, although camping communities may be permanent in the sense that, at the same season each year, the same households tend to congregate together, at other times of the year they may disintegrate into much smaller units of only two or three tents.[5] Clearly, if such camping communities are to be used as a formal link in a chain of communications between pastoral people and government (or a higher level in an association of pastoralists provided with resources and rights to manage their own affairs), it is not one at which it will be possible to post a full-time, paid, and highly trained technician. The costs would be too high.

Camping communities may, however, be a link at a level at which an identified member of the community is vested with specific functions and responsibility for providing extension and other services to his neighbours and for passing information up to government. The member so identified might be the camp 'leader' or some other individual to whom some special training in his duties has been given; and he might be remunerated either by his neighbours for his services to them or by government or by a combination of the two. It would be unrealistic to suppose, however, that such individuals would give information to government (e.g. about non-adherence to stocking quotas or invasion of pastures officially closed) which might cause inconvenience to their neighbours. Any remuneration that government paid might be subject to satisfactory performance, at least in respect of the downward flow of information, and some system to monitor this would be required. Moreover, the opinions communicated by such individuals would inevitably reflect those of the politically influential members of their communities, and where such communities are sharply differentiated in power and wealth minority opinions would not be voiced.

Watering communities

Watering communities, that is, the collections of households who use a common water point or cluster of wells, present another possible link in a communication chain between government and pastoralists. Watering communities may consist of as few as two or three households, in which case they have no advantage over camping communities in this regard. But they may consist of many more. If we assume that livestock (other than camels) can graze up to 20 km from water, if necessary, then a single centrally located water point or a cluster of these can water up to 11,000 cattle in a normal environment (carrying capacity of 16 ha/lu) and up to 44,000 cattle in a more productive one, permitting the existence in the area served by the water point of a human population of 220–870 households respectively. In Niger the equivalent of more than 20,000 head of cattle were found to be drinking at a single borehole (Bernus, 1974). However, watering communities in nomadic areas are likely to be less long-lived — both in respect of their period of use within the year and in the persistence of their membership from year to year — than are camping communities; and the degree of co-operation and confidence between members is also likely to be less. If members are watering their stock only every two or three days they will meet each other quite seldom and when they do they will often, especially at the bigger water points with watering communities of any size, be in competition with each other.

We have already seen, in Chapter 4, that participatory management of large water supplies by nomadic pastoralists may not be possible. Hence, although the potential larger size of watering communities may make it more economic to attach full-time, better-qualified, extension workers to them than to camping communities, nevertheless such extension workers will probably only have access to their clientele for a part of the year, and may find that their clientele comprises groups of both competing and divergent interests from whom a clear and agreed expression of communal opinion cannot be obtained.[6] Moreover, the time at which animals are being watered is not the best time for the transmission of any kind of technical instruction to the individuals looking after the animals, although other kinds of information, e.g. about rotations, can then be satisfactorily passed. Water points do, however, provide a possible intermediate link, for the period of the year during which they are in use, at which part-time extension workers attached to camping communities can exchange information with higher levels in a more territorially based extension hierarchy.

Kinship groups

Where pastoralists are sedentary they can be defined or categorized in terms of their place of residence — they are the inhabitants of such and such a place. We have also seen that, if nomadic, they can be defined as members of particular camping or watering communities — which can also be named. But if we look for social organizations of a greater size than these we often find it difficult to discover anything, other than kinship groups — what I have called here, for short, 'clans'. Governments tend to dislike the categorization of nomads by clans because they often see the clan structure as being an actual or potential focus of opposition to government authority, and they wish, therefore, to do nothing to reinforce or sanction this structure. It is probable, although this is to stray somewhat outside the scope of the present study, that such hostility as the clan structure focuses against government is a result of a real clash of interest between pastoralists and government rather than an independent consequence of the existence of a clan structure. Be that as it may, how else, than by clan, can one define and identify nomadic people in organizations bigger than camping or watering communities?

Some governments try to reorganize nomadic society along the lines of voluntary self-selecting associations. We can call these 'co-operatives'. Of course such co-operatives may simply be clans under another name and will then simply repeat clan-based divisions and decision-making structures. Little is gained or lost by such change of title except clarity of understanding by those who are not aware of what has happened. Governments often see such co-operatives as being opportunities for 'progressive' individuals to leave their conservative fellows behind them and to reap the benefits of their greater willingness to innovate. This has already been discussed in relation to land allocation in Chapter 6. While one cannot rule out differences in 'character' between individuals as a cause of greater or less willingness to innovate, it seems probable that differences in innovativeness also tend to reflect rather closely differences in power and wealth, and so the ability to take the risks of innovating without hazarding one's very survival. Hence, to base extension services to pastoralists on such voluntary co-operatives is systematically to favour the rich over the poor.

Without judging whether or not a clan-based organizing of pastoral society is desirable in other ways, we can consider whether it presents a feasible foundation on which to base a satisfactory system of transmitting information relevant to pastoral development. In practice, it is often used in this way, for the only entry point that government officials may have to pastoral society is through chiefs or elders who hold political authority among pastoralists through a clan (or similar traditional) structure, an authority which government administrators, albeit often reluctantly, have had to recognize. These traditional leaders are sometimes asked directly what pastoralist opinion is, or to pass information to their clansmen; and are sometimes requested to summon meetings of their people at which government officials can speak, or otherwise to help in establishing communications links. This sort of use of the clan structure as a channel of communication is not usually approached in anything but a haphazard way. It is not planned or programmed. It simply occurs because it appears to be the only thing that is feasible.

Clan structures in pastoral society tend to be concerned with one or more of the following functions: to determine the access of individuals, or subgroups, to the resources of land, livestock, and water, and to uphold those with right of access against those without; to regulate the giving and taking of partners in marriage and the upbringing of children; to represent, through negotiations or the deployment of force, the interests of members of a clan against outside interests; to resolve conflicts between members of a clan. They may also have ritual functions related to the upholding of social values and group identity. It seems reasonable to suppose that clan structures are well suited to carry out these functions, in terms of the channels of information (e.g. meetings) available to assist in coming to and announcing decisions, and in the powers given to clan authorities to enforce them. Sometimes the existing channels of communication and powers may, as a coincidence, be suitable also for carrying out other functions such as resource management; but general institutions and particular organizations adequate and efficient for some functions are not necessarily so for others for which they were not designed. One sometimes hears suggestions that 'traditional institutions' be used in the implementation of development programmes. That may often be sensible. But, to adopt a Western analogy, the fact that a certain village or city has a highly successful football team which has won all its matches is not a good reason for giving the team responsibility for managing the new sewage works. Clan institutions are likely to be less specialized — more multi-purpose — than football teams; but before extra functions are loaded on them their present ones, and the ways in which they carry them out, need to be analysed to see how well suited they are to a particular new one.

Where the new function is the collection and transmission of information to and from lower and higher levels in a resource-management system (e.g. between pastoralists and officials of a range-management department) one needs to enquire with what frequency and regularity, with what complexity of content, and by what channels (e.g. word of mouth, letters, casual or regular messengers) the traditional institutions pass information. Is it just a question of holding *ad hoc* meetings of the elders of particular subgroups when disputes arise between their members? Or are there regular meetings of representatives of all subgroups or specialized messengers (such as Cossins, 1972, records for Afar pastoralists in Ethiopia) taking instruction from higher up to lower down in a clan hierarchy? There is no point in attaching an extension officer to a particular clan, or in formally designating existing authorities in the clan structure as information links, if there is no way for these people to use clan channels to pass the information with the precision and frequency required.

Traditional institutions are unlikely to adapt themselves to meet new needs unless those on whom additional duties will fall are given some additional incentive (not, of course, necessarily a financial one) to undertake them. Nor is there much point in asking traditional leaders what the opinion of their group is, or that the group express its agreement to a new proposal through them, if they neither have the means to discover the opinion nor are vested with authority to express an opinion or agreement on the part of the group that will bind it for the future. Agreements or opinions expressed by leaders without authority may satisfy the letter of bureaucratic requirements that pastoralists be consulted about and agree to development proposals before they are implemented, but they will not lead to any greater respect by members of the pastoral society for the observance of the management system than if no such agreement had been obtained.

THE DAY-TO-DAY MANAGEMENT OF RANGE IMPROVEMENT

We now turn to look at the day-to-day management of range improvement. Three main options in organization and management will be examined in successive subsections: firstly, the question of the circumstances under which centralized or decentralized (dispersed) management systems are preferable; secondly, the question of who should manage, in terms both of whether it should be the government or an organization of pastoralists and also of who within pastoral society should do the managing; thirdly, the question of the appropriate style of management — seen in terms of a range of possibilities from a more mandatory to a more liberal one. A final subsection discusses systems for ensuring that management decisions are carried out by pastoralists and that those who ignore the decisions are brought into line. These options arise in the case of all the different activities that improve range productivity, but it is the cases of rotating pastures and regulating grazing pressure to which we shall give attention. We shall assume that certain policy decisions have already been taken: about the appropriate type of rotation system (continuous grazing, deferred, alternate grazing, deferred- or rest-rotation, etc.[7]) for particular local vegetation communities; about the general strategy (e.g. opportunistic or conservative) for regulating grazing pressures and the appropriate levels of grazing pressure for particular local vegetation communities; about the general principles according to which livestock quotas are to be allocated between individuals. Day-to-day management then includes such things as: defining and demarcating the boundaries of individual paddocks;[8] deciding on the precise dates on which paddocks shall be opened and closed to particular animals, and the exact degree of grazing pressure to which they shall be subject while open; and determining the rights of individuals to pasture specific numbers of particular types and classes of livestock in particular pastures at particular times.

Centralized and dispersed management systems

We can contrast centralized and dispersed (decentralized) systems of day-to-day management. The terms are relative to each other rather than describing absolute values. A centralized system of management is one where decisions are taken, and activities organized, on a scale that affects very large areas of land and very many people and their livestock. Centralized management systems are, therefore, inevitably rather remote from most of the individual livestock and people concerned, and they depend on information provided by some other person or instrument to the decision-maker rather than on the decision-maker's own personal observation. A dispersed management system may be dispersed at the level of the individual herder or camping community, or to the individual homestead ranch. In any day-to-day management system some tasks and responsibilities may be more centralized and others more dispersed. Although there are interesting exceptions — the annual movement of livestock into the Niger delta of Mali is one such exception (Gallais, 1975), and the twice-yearly migration of the Baxtyari of Iran another (Digard, 1979) — in most traditional pastoral situations very dispersed systems of day-to-day management prevail.

In a spatially variable and temporally uncertain environment, where different vegetation communities are interspersed with each other in response to local variation in slope and soil, where rain falls unpredictably in time and space, where grass fires may totally remove all forage from an area overnight, where water points break down and sudden outbreaks of disease occur, a highly centralized system of day-to-day management is unlikely to show adequate flexibility unless coupled with a very rapid, extensive, and sensitive system of monitoring and communications which can enable rather precise information about conditions and sudden changes in them to come quickly to decision-makers. Such a monitoring and communications system is likely to be expensive in relation to the production potential of dry regions. Hence, rather often one finds, under centrally managed systems, that boundaries of paddocks are demarcated in straight lines, instead of following, as they should, the ragged edges of vegetation communities which make sensible management units because of their homogeneity and the uniformity of their palatability to livestock and response to different treatments. The straight lines have advantages from a bureaucratic point of view. They can be easily drawn on maps, or spotted from aircraft, or put in on the ground by drivers of graders and bulldozers who are ignorant of vegetation types. They are cheaper to put in and for officials in their vehicles to inspect than are ragged boundaries; but from the point of view of manipulating pasture productivity they are less suitable.

In centrally managed systems in such environments it is extremely difficult for the managers to know enough either about the condition of the vegetation or the needs of the livestock. Different species and classes of livestock, or even individual animals, may vary widely in their requirements, at a particular time, for different minerals or other nutrients. Where a pasture rotation system is imposed, in ignorance of their requirements, that prevents their access to the forage or water that suits their needs best, their performance will deteriorate unless their needs are otherwise met by the purchase of expensive supplements. Similarly, inadequate knowledge about the condition of the vegetation hinders its proper management. For example, for safe and useful burning of the vegetation, to prevent bush encroachment and to improve productivity, extremely up-to-date and detailed local knowledge is required, about the quantity (per unit area) and dryness of the material to be burnt, and about relative humidity and wind speed and direction (Wright, 1978). The availability of forage for grazing will often be very patchy and not ascertainable by rapid and sparse reconnaissance by air or land vehicle. Sensible rotation of pastures does not involve automatic adherence to inflexible rules but a constant review of conditions and vegetation management decisions in the light of up-to-date information. Reviewing conditions and decisions may imply changing opening and closing dates for particular paddocks and switching grazing pressure from more heavily to more lightly used areas.

The greater efficiency of a more dispersed day-to-day management system applies also to dealing with people and their stock quotas. One often finds that on centrally managed range schemes the managers do not know where the people and livestock are or why they are there; and the herdsmen do not know where the managers want them to be now or where and when they should move next. All the complications raised by questions about who should be allocated the stock quotas in respect of, for example, temporary absentees from the pastoral area, illegitimate or stepchildren, widows or divorced women, require more and more formal, rigid, and hence potentially inequitable rules to solve them the more remote the decision-maker is who will decide how big a stock quota an individual pastoralist should receive. Remote officials have the greatest difficulty even in identifying the owners of particular animals, partly because pastoralists' concepts of ownership and property rights are often different from those of range officials, partly because members of a pastoral group may be reluctant to give outsiders information that may be used to the disadvantage of a member of the group.

The same general difficulty applies where an individual pastoralist wishes to leave one pastoral group or area and to attach himself to another. These things can be decided at rather low cost by people who already know, from direct personal acquaintance, why someone wants to move, what justice there is in his claim to join another group, and how great will be the advantages and disadvantages to the communities he is leaving and joining. A remote decision-maker can only decide such issues either arbitrarily in the absence of proper information or at great cost in ascertaining all the facts.

One set of experts on range projects in East Africa have suggested that, while flexibility in day-to-day management is a desirable feature for private ranches with experienced managers, government-operated schemes, such as communal grazing block schemes or government-assisted co-operative ranches, should adopt much more rigid plans (Pratt and Gwynne, 1977, p. 120). It is clear that these experts fear that any flexibility in day-to-day management of government-operated range-management schemes will be abused so as to subvert their whole purpose. One sees here a fear by the expert of losing control to pastoralists who do not share the expert's belief in how to manage the rangelands. The same point was made by a range-planner in Kenya, who, recognizing the need for flexibility in an uncertain environment, nevertheless said, 'I am not against nomadic movements in principle provided that *we* have planned them'. But there is some evidence that the consequence of their precautions is the exact opposite of what the experts desire. Government's scepticism and ignorance about pastoralists' own systems for managing grazing lead to its sabotaging existing systems operated by local grazing communities; while a major reason for pastoralists' resistance to government's programmes is their fear of the inappropriate inflexibility that government appears to be intent on introducing (Dahl and Sandford, 1978, pp. 164 and 208; Draz, 1978).

Who should manage?

So far we have contrasted centralized and dispersed management systems and have seen that in most day-to-day management activities the advantages tend to lie with a decentralized system. We can now turn to look at *who* should carry out the various tasks. Even in a decentralized system it may not be appropriate for all of these to be given to pastoralists. For example, where different pastoral groups are in strong competition with each other, then it is unlikely that either a representative management committee or an individual manager whose authority derives solely from his joint appointment by competing groups will be able to make and impose sensible management decisions. For each of these decisions will be scrutinized for the way it appears to favour one or other of the groups, and the manager's authority will be challenged by, and be unenforceable on, whichever group feels itself disadvantaged. In such cases of competitive use even quite low-level decision-making and execution of tasks may have to be done by a manager appointed by and responsible to an authority (e.g. government) superior to the competing groups; and this manager will have to have the possibility of using the power of the government to back up his decisions.

In some pastoral situations different groups do not compete, but some groups or classes, defined in ethnic or occupational terms or by degrees of wealth, dominate others. In such circumstances if a government wishes to promote social equity it will not, even where a decentralized management system is appropriate on other grounds, want to allow much power and responsibility in management to be exercised by pastoralists since it will certainly be exercised by the dominant group to bolster its own position. This is not a phenomenon unique to pastoralism but is common to all sorts of development programmes. In pastoralism the issue arises particularly in respect of the allocation of grazing quotas. If the initial distribution of these between people is inequitable and if government wishes to regulate grazing pressure by allocating maximum livestock quotas to individuals, then however democratic the process by which such allocation is to be made appears to be, if it is left to pastoral society itself to administer it is likely to end up by maintaining or bolstering the position of the wealthy and powerful against that of the weak.

So inevitable is this that many governments do not see the *principle* on which quotas are to be allocated as an issue at all. In imperial Iran the Forest and Range Organization in certain selected areas established an aggregate grazing quota for a village as a whole and left it 'to the village' to determine its sub-allocation between individuals. Officials did not see it as their responsibility to lay down or even to enquire about the principles of sub-allocation. They assumed that sub-allocations would be in proportion to the size of existing holdings. (Source: local range officials in catchment areas.) Even in socialist Tanzania, government range-management plans simply assumed that any necessary destocking required to relieve grazing pressure would be done in a way that left existing relative inequalities in size of holdings unchanged (Maasai Range Project, 1975). The Tribal Grazing Lands Policy adopted by Botswana in 1975 did in theory provide for equal livestock quotas for all in communal areas; but since no mechanism was established to enforce these quotas the policy in this respect has remained unimplemented. On the group ranches of Kenya Maasailand a policy of a two-tier quota system was established, whereby all members of the ranch, whatever the size of their present holding, would have the right to a basic quota sufficient to support them, with supplementary quotas being given to richer members if the aggregate of basic quotas was less than the carrying capacity of the ranch. However, enforcement of quotas was left to each ranch's management committee, which was dominated by the rich who have taken no steps to enforce destocking by themselves or to bring the poor's actual holdings up to the basic minimum (Helland, 1980, p. 192). In contrast, in Mongolia and the USSR social revolutions provided situations in which the central government supported the pastoral poor in enforcing, through collectivization, redistribution of the livestock holdings of the rich, although the incidental consequence was often huge livestock losses.

Many of the tasks in the day-to-day management of range improvement involve making decisions in which communal participation is not only possible but actually desirable, both because such participation is felt to be good in itself and because it is efficient in respect of other objectives, through the increase in sources of information that such participation provides. Such communal decisions can be made by the whole pastoral community (or all the adult males) if the management system is dispersed enough to allow them to meet together regularly, or by a group of representatives from different parts of the community. Some decisions may be taken by universal and others by representative participation. But in the execution of these decisions not only does common sense tell us that a responsibility narrowly focused on individuals is likely to be more conscientiously discharged than if diffused too broadly, but there are some actual historical examples from areas where livestock were important where a change from a narrowly focused to a more broadly dispersed responsibility led to a decline in effectiveness.

One such example comes from Rajasthan in India where, prior to Indian Independence, the administration of a village's grazing area was the responsibility of a village official — the *jagirdar*, a combination of landlord and headman. After Land Reform in the mid-1950s this post was abolished and an attempt to transfer its responsibilities for managing the grazing to a representative system of local government (panchayat raj) in which responsibility was diffused among several elected councillors was unsuccessful (Jodha, 1979). In northern Scotland prior to the end of the nineteenth century an elected 'constable' of each township kept careful note of each person's stock on the communal grazings and ensured compliance with quotas. A change in legislation replaced this official with a grazing committee and a clerk with no executive or disciplinary power and thereafter the rules tended to be neglected (Fraser-Darling, 1955, p. 207). It appears likely that focusing responsibility for action unequivocally on one individual leads to effective action because the individual will be blamed for doing nothing as much or more than for doing something which, although against the interests of some individuals, is for the common good (e.g. enforcing grazing quotas). In contrast, where responsibility is diffused among members of a committee, far from being able to shelter behind anonymity when they take stern action, the identity of the member of a committee who initiates stern action will quickly be betrayed to the victim, whereas responsibility for ineffectively doing nothing can be shared.

Management style

Decisions can be taken at a high level in a remote bureaucracy in the national capital, or by officials at district level, or by camp-level organizations, or at various levels in between. But whatever the level at which decisions are taken or at which other management functions are exercised, the question of management style also arises. Management style can be classified in several ways, but in the section on alternative forms of organization and management in Chapter 3 two major ways of categorizing the style of management that is to govern relations between manager and managed were distinguished. One way focuses on the extent to which, and the way in which, the opinions of the manager or the managed are to prevail once the manager has formed his opinion. Under a *mandatory* style the manager's opinion is enforced by regulation and penalties if necessary; in a *liberal* style the manager may offer incentives but the decision remains that of the managed; in a *contractual* style negotiations between manager and managed result in an enforceable agreement on the rights and duties of each party. The other way of categorizing management style is in respect of the way in which the manager's opinion is formed — the extent to which subordinates or clients are consulted or can take the initiative in raising issues. Under an *authoritarian* style the manager's own role is predominant; under a *participatory* style subordinate levels have a great influence. In this subsection we shall mainly be concerned with management style in the first of the two ways of categorizing it set out in this paragraph.

We can spell out the differences between mandatory, liberal, and contractual a little further. In the veterinary field, compulsory vaccination of livestock against certain diseases is an example of a mandatory management style. At this end of the range those who ignore the decisions which have been taken at higher levels in a decision-making hierarchy, are punished and are given little or no opportunity to escape from them. At the other end of the range we have a liberal management style in which the higher level essentially only offers incentives to lower levels to behave in the way which the higher level wants. The provision of optional vaccination for livestock free of charge is an example of a liberal management style. It is one in which lower levels not only can make their own decisions about how much of the higher level's view to accept but are free to reverse their decisions at any time. In the middle between the extremes of mandatory and liberal styles is a 'contractual' style in which higher levels offer to a lower level a package of incentives in return for an agreement by the lower level, which the lower level cannot then unilaterally abrogate, to behave in a particular way. Some of the arrangements to provide security of tenure to group ranches or other organizations of pastoralists (e.g. pastoral units in east Senegal), or to lend money to these or to private commercial ranches on the condition that certain rules of good management are observed, are examples of attempts at a contractual style. However, usually the unequal status of the two parties and the difficulty of enforcing agreements (a point to which we shall return) make them not very successful examples. Obviously, at the margin different styles tend to merge into each other rather than to have clear-cut boundaries between them. Moreover, even in respect of the same function or range-improvement activity it is possible for a manager to exercise several different management styles simultaneously, although in practice it is extremely difficult for the same person or service to combine both stick and carrot approaches without one fouling up the other.

On rangelands in the United States and Australia all three styles of management have been tried. In the USA, for example, the federal government has provided financial assistance to ranchers on private land to install, to the extent they choose, such improvements as range-seeding, contour-furrowing, control of undesirable plants, and facilities for protection from fire (Blaisdell and Sharp, 1979). In a more contractual style loan funds have been provided to ranchers to acquire grazing land on condition that they follow a management plan devised by the Soil Conservation Service (Payne, 1979). Both on public (federal- and state-owned) and on private land in districts where the land-users have collectively agreed to this, more mandatory measures involving the laying down and enforcement of land-use regulations have been applied. In Australia some liberal measures have been used, as for example with state subsidies to transport costs and livestock prices, to encourage ranchers to destock temporarily by agistment to other areas, or permanently through slaughter or sale of stock at the right time. In the conditions that have been attached to leased land, administrators have blended more contractual and mandatory styles to induce ranchers to invest in the development of their ranches and to follow appropriate management practices (Young, 1979).

In Africa and Asia a variety of management styles has also been tried, although it is rare for any country to try such a wide range of styles all aimed simultaneously at the same type of pastoralist as has been done in the USA and Australia; and overall there has been less emphasis, as far as the management of range improvement is concerned, on a liberal approach. This low priority given to liberalism reflects: the greater prevalence of communal types of land tenure, coupled with governments' low confidence in the responsiveness of such tenure systems to economic incentives; the weak financial positions of the governments concerned which make them constantly want to reduce the financial burden of development on government; and the fact that it is not always clear to governments how pastoralists will respond to liberal incentives. The particular case of the response of livestock sales to changes in price levels is discussed in Chapter 9. Nevertheless, there are examples of liberal approaches which involve incentives that are more positive than simply offering advice.

In Rajasthan in India, for example, both planting and fencing material for the production of forage and for the prevention of wind-erosion are offered virtually free of charge to farmers on private land under the Central Arid Zone Research Institute's operational research programme; and some farmers have availed themselves of these. In Botswana both loans and long-term leases over 6000 ha ranches are being provided to encourage farmers to paddock the land and to adopt approved rotation practices and control of grazing pressure. It was originally the aim of the technicians that their facilities should be provided on a contractual basis with conditions being written into both loan and lease agreements to ensure that the farmers carried out the approved practices; but political intervention has greatly liberalized the contractual obligations. Similarly, with group ranches in Kenya Maasailand it was originally intended that both the administrative arrangements under which the land was allocated to groups by the Registrar of Groups, and the agreement under which loans would be extended by the Agricultural Finance Corporation to groups for the development of their ranches, would contain provisions under which the land and loan allocations were conditional on the management of the land according to methods approved by the range-management authorities. In practice, neither the Registrar nor the Corporation have been prepared to invoke the sanctions which in theory they had available against breaches of the conditions. (Source: discussions with Kenya Government officials.)

A contractual style of management involves considerable difficulties.[9] One of these is that a contract has to be between two identified parties each of whom is able to make a commitment as to its own future activities; and in pastoral development one normally has government on one side and pastoralists on the other. But whereas governments are experienced in committing themselves long term to *international* agreements, or short term to paying contractors for specific pieces of work, they are usually quite unable to commit themselves to the continuing provision of a package of internal services to their citizens; and governments' record in fulfilling promises made to pastoralists is a poor one. In the first place, as far as *internal* affairs are concerned, staff and budgets are allocated to individual ministries and departments, none of which can speak for other departments; so that a promise by the Range Management Department of government that, for example, government will provide water at a certain place does not, in practice, commit the Ministry of Water Affairs which is the only organization which can honour the undertaking. Moreover, it is a tradition of many governments, especially those with a British colonial administrative history, that no forward financial commitments can be made for more than one financial year at a time; and in any case changes in political leaders of governments or of ministries tend to negate commitments entered into previously. There are few countries in which citizens are able to enforce government's own promises by legal process.

On the other side also there are difficulties. Except when agreements are made with individual pastoralists occupying their own private property, it is often not clear with whom among pastoralists government is trying to obtain agreement. Governments often say that they have reached agreement with the 'elders' of a pastoral clan or tribe. But insufficient attention has been paid to whom these elders represent or with what authority they commit them; and the government's own reluctance and inability to commit itself militates against the recording of an agreement in writing which specifies the obligations of each party and the remedy available to one side if the other defaults. Oral agreements made in an *ad hoc* way tend to break down in a welter of counter-accusations. Furthermore, the timing of commitments by each side may not balance; so that, for example, a government, on its part, may undertake to provide water points such as stockponds which, once constructed, are difficult to remove if the pastoralists fail to honour an undertaking on their part to restrict livestock numbers. Sometimes a government's only sanction, in case of non-compliance by pastoralists, is not a credible one, e.g. to deprive pastoralists of their land. A government may do this when the incentive is strong enough, for example, to reward its non-pastoral supporters with grants of pastoral land. It is unlikely to summon up the political courage to do so simply because pastoralists have defaulted on, for example, an agreement to destock.

While governments do sometimes adopt quasi-contractual styles for the management of public or communal grazing resources, the most commonly favoured style, at least in the past, has been a mandatory one whereby management decisions, once taken, have to be obeyed by everyone whether they like them or not. While some observers still advocate a mandatory style (e.g. Doran, Low, and Kemp, 1979, p. 45), there is a growing awareness that the general experience so far has been that a mandatory approach is not usually successful. A mandatory system, to be effective, must be backed up by a system of legally valid regulations, inspections, and sanctions whereby permitted and forbidden behaviours are clearly prescribed, and offenders can be detected, identified, halted in their transgression, and punished so that they do not offend again. If such an effective system is not established, those who would prefer to obey will be constantly taken advantage of by those who do not, and either no one will obey the managers' decisions or violent clashes will occur when the obedient try to take the law into their own hands. In pastoral areas the enforcement of private and communal rights to water and grazing, and of regulations for their better utilization, is closely bound up with questions of public security.

We can briefly review the factors which tend to make liberal, contractual, or mandatory styles appropriate in particular circumstances. A liberal style requires that there be some incentive which is attractive enough to persuade people, that is, pastoralists or junior employees, to modify their behaviour in ways which the managers want. Such incentives may be financial, for example higher livestock prices, or they may involve the conferment of status, or the provision of a service. For example, relocating a mobile school or clinic to the particular paddock which managers want to be grazed now may be an effective way of getting pastoralists to leave the paddocks which need to be rested, but only, of course, if the pastoralists actually desire these services. Incentives, whether in the form of money or something else, usually cost money and are therefore only appropriate if government can afford them on a scale large enough to make a significant effect. A liberal style is more appropriate where the managers, either because of an overall lack of knowledge, for example about appropriate technology, or because conditions in the ranges change faster than the managers can monitor, are unable (or ought not to be able) to be certain that their own opinions and prescriptions will be correct, and where pastoralists or junior employees have access to information not available to managers, which means that sometimes they can make better decisions. A liberal management style leads to greater flexibility. It may also lead to a greater diminution in the burden on the government bureaucracy, if providing an incentive induces pastoralists to carry out construction or planting work that would otherwise have to be done by government itself. On the other hand, certain kinds of incentives can create enormous amounts of accounting, inspection, and auditing work where opportunities exist for corruption.

A contractual style probably involves the greatest inflexibility because it requires both partners to agree to changes, and it is only suitable, as already pointed out, when contracting partners with adequate powers can be identified and concurrent rights and obligations be clearly spelt out in a way that prevents subsequent legalistic quibbling. It is more appropriate in a system where the parties to the contract are not so disparate in power and influence that the junior partner can be ignored by the senior. A contract between a government and a major and powerful ethnic group is viable, but between a government and a tiny and uneducated group, in a country whose judiciary is not independent of the government or sympathetic to the rights of the individual, it will simply be swept aside at the government's convenience. A contractual style requires that the penalties for breaking the contract should be proportionate to the offence. If the penalties are too severe, e.g. total loss of title to land in conditions where no alternative livelihood exists, then governments will never enforce these penalties for minor infringements of a land-use agreement. This is pretty clearly demonstrated by the Kenya group ranch experience as well as by experience in enforcing conditions of pastoral leases in Australia.

A mandatory style is likely to be appropriate where the action or compliance which the managers wish to stimulate is simple and routine and does not need the exercise of judgement or initiative. It requires that the action the managers desire is one which both the pastoralists and the junior employees regard as reasonable. It is not necessary that the majority of them agree with it. Taxes, for example, can be collected from unwilling taxpayers. But programmes which seem to be irrational, not only to the victims but also to the perpetrators, will not be enforced. As already pointed out, a mandatory style must be backed by an efficient enforcement system, and the penalties imposed for offences must be seen by those who operate the enforcement system as being proportionate to the offence. A mandatory style will be appropriate where the losses to the community imposed by those few non-compliers who cannot be influenced by an incentive or contractual style are seen as being very large; and it is appropriate where the nature of property rights, e.g. the existence of a communal rather than a private form of land tenure, and the nature of local society, e.g. competition between groups for the same resources, make liberal and contractual styles ineffective.

Enforcement of regulations

The ineffectiveness of a mandatory approach in the past is often ascribed to a failure to explain the purpose of management decisions and a failure to win pastoralists' opinion to the managers' side, as well as to lack of political backing for enforcing the regulations. All these reasons may be partially correct, but a further major reason lies in an inappropriate administrative structure for enforcing the regulations. A good deal of attention is often paid to the question of having proper legislation to back up managers' decisions. But legislation, to be effective, must be accompanied by a large enough corps of inspectors for infringements of regulations to have a high probability of detection. The inspectors must be able to identify offenders when they find them and must be backed by adequate force not to be intimidated by them; and the courts where offenders are to be judged must be close enough to the place where the offender is apprehended, and must sit sufficiently frequently for it to be reasonable, in terms of the cost in time and money, to bring the offender before the court for trial and punishment. Very little attention in the planning and appraising of range-management programmes is generally paid to this aspect. For example, in one country I visited the place of an offence might be 200–300 km from the nearest court and there was no transport system to carry offenders, witnesses, and those who arrested them to the court; and once they arrived there they might spend many days before the court heard the case.

The administrative arrangement which makes the enforcement of regulations most feasible is probably one in which decisions are made by a local community which sets its own rules and has its own inspector and penalties to enforce these rules and a court in which the rules of procedure and evidence are governed by what the community sees as being good sense; and where everyone knows each other well enough for it quickly to become common knowledge who has committed an offence. While rules for regulating grazing pressure through the limitation of stock numbers are not a common feature of pastoral societies, rules to enforce migrations, rotations, and proper use of water supplies are; and in the past offenders have been effectively punished and deterred by traditional institutions and organizations from repeating their offences. Such traditional systems have now often broken down. Sometimes this breakdown has occurred because the enforcement of sanctions depended on a mutual interdependence between pastoralists, which meant that no one dared flout public opinion and risk ostracism. This interdependence may have been destroyed by changes in technology, for example the raising of water from wells by mechanical means rather than by pooling of labour, or by a change in economic and political relations between the pastoral and the surrounding non-pastoral world which has enabled individual pastoralists to draw on the support of non-pastoralists when they get into disputes with their pastoral neighbours. Sometimes the breakdown in the effectiveness of a traditional control system has occurred because government, unintentionally or in ignorance of its usefulness, has destroyed it by abolishing the traditional courts and declaring their judgements invalid. In the latter case the position can be restored simply by government reversing its intervention. But where the traditional system depended on a mutual interdependence between pastoralists which technical, economic, or political change has caused to disappear, then new institutions which reflect the influence of new relationships will be required.

Where competing pastoral groups use the same water and grazing resources, a community-based system of drawing up and enforcing regulations is unlikely to function well, since all infringements of regulations will be regarded in the light of inter-group competition and neither equitable nor enforceable judgements will emerge from a community court. In such cases, if an authoritarian style is necessary on other grounds, a power that is neutral between and superior to competing groups will have to draw up and enforce regulations.

CONCLUDING COMMENTS

This chapter has been able to discuss only a small part from the full scope of what is involved in the organization and management of improving range productivity. For certain kinds of activities, involving strong linkages with the non-pastoral sectors of national economies, the chapter examined the consequences of these linkages for participatory management by pastoralists. For other activities it focused on systems of communication, in both directions, between pastoralists and governments and on the day-to-day management of these activities, examining the consequences of choice of selected forms of organization and management. Even the small part reviewed in this chapter defies brief summary, since the essence of the analytic approach adopted in this study is to avoid blanket solutions applicable to all pastoral situations, and instead to see how certain characteristics, which vary from one situation to another, coupled with concern for particular objectives, should influence choice of the form of organization and management.

NOTES TO CHAPTER 7

1. Some of the studies (e.g. in north Kenya and north-east Iran) related to processes of desertification which have been financed by the UNESCO MAB programme are beginning to rectify this lack of historical perspective.

2. For the reasons set out, for example, by Schultz (1979).

3. To be more precise, the number of adults registered as members of groups was equal to just over half the number of households. However, some households may have had more than one member of some group.

4. For detailed calculations of minimum herd sizes required to follow a pastoral way of life see Dahl and Hjort (1976).

5. I am heavily reliant in this passage on Tapper (1979a).

6. The interests may be competing where two ethnic groups, who herd the same sort of livestock and with the same sort of domestic economy, are both trying to use the same grazing and water resource. The interests may be divergent, even between members of the same ethnic group, where different people herd different kinds of livestock and have different sorts of domestic economy, e.g. more subsistence or more market-oriented.

7. For a fuller description of alternative systems see Stoddart, Smith, and Box (1975, pp. 290–299).

8. Paddocks are defined as the lowest level of land-unit for which management decisions are made by anyone other than the individual animal or its herdsman. Paddocks may range in size from fractions of a hectare to thousands of square kilometres.

9. This and the next paragraph owe a debt to ideas expressed by Goode and Goode (1975).

Chapter eight
Improvements in animal health and husbandry

INTRODUCTION

This chapter is concerned with improvements in animal health and husbandry. After a brief introduction to the scope of this there follows some descriptions of the wide variety of ways in which the same general functions have been managed or organized in different countries. The purpose of this section is to illustrate that options between different forms of organization and management really exist, and that different choices between these options have, in fact, been made. The following section discusses why different choices have been made and the factors which should influence choice. The rest of the chapter then concentrates on a detailed examination of five main sets of options.

The usual objectives of pastoral development were set out at the beginning of Chapter 2. In measures to improve animal health and husbandry the main deliberate focus is on one of these objectives — improving pastoral productivity — although there may be important side-effects in terms of the others. Improving pastoral productivity is often conceived in terms of improving output per head of livestock, with emphasis being put on, for example, calving rates, milk yields, daily weight gains per head, etc. This concentration on improving output per head of livestock is often unjustified, however; what one should be concerned with is total output from all the resources of the pastoral sector, i.e. natural forage, herding labour, and livestock. In the long run, the resources of herding labour and livestock can usually be increased fairly easily and at fairly low cost; in contrast, the supply of natural forage in dry areas is severely constrained by rainfall and is much more difficult to increase, and then only at high cost. Usually, therefore, we should be concerned with maximizing output per unit of natural forage. Measures which increase output per head of livestock may sometimes be identical with measures to increase output per unit of natural forage, but there is no necessary correspondence between them (for further discussion of this see Jones and Sandland, 1974, and Sandford, 1978a).

The subject-matter of this chapter has a very wide scope. Improvements in animal health include measures against the main epizootic diseases and internal and external parasites, the treatment of wounds and injuries, routine operations such as castrations and dehorning, raising the fertility of individual animals, and the control of predators. Improvements in animal husbandry include genetic improvements, i.e. introducing superior breeds or upgrading within existing breeds, supplementing the diet of livestock with feed or mineral supplements not contained in the natural forage, maintaining an appropriate herd structure in terms of species, sex, and age, and other improvements in the management and housing of animals not already covered in the chapters on water and range. The organization and management of these improvements will, explicitly or implicitly, be dealt with in this chapter. It will not deal at all with the control of trypanosomiasis or tsetse flies, nor will it pay any significant attention to certain activities which have traditionally been undertaken by animal health and husbandry services in improving the preparation of milk products or hides and skins, or in meat inspection at abattoirs and butchers' shops.

VARIETY IN ORGANIZATION AND MANAGEMENT

The improvement of animal health and husbandry in pastoral areas involves a wide spread of functions. Some of these functions, e.g. vaccination or treatment of individual animals, can sometimes be carried out by pastoralists in respect of their own animals. Others are best performed by organizations (e.g. central government or community organizations) or private entrepreneurs as services for pastoralists. Research has to be carried out, for example, into the nature of the areas' diseases and how to prevent or treat them or how most effectively to lessen the burden of parasites. Policy decisions have to be made about which diseases or services should receive attention, and in what way, and which should be ignored. Where disease breaks out, a correct diagnosis needs to be made to ensure that appropriate measures are taken; sometimes compulsory regulations need to be made and enforced in respect, for example, of slaughtering or quarantining sick animals or those which may have come in contact with disease. Information needs to be passed in both directions between livestock owners and animal health and husbandry technicians about where disease has broken out or where supplies and services need to be delivered. Supplies of vaccine, acaricides, or semen have to be ordered, delivered in good condition, and paid and accounted for. Structures such as dips and crushes have to be properly sited, constructed, operated, and maintained. Technical advice needs to be given to livestock owners and herdsmen and they need training in some specific skills.

Different countries with large pastoral areas and populations have, at different times, carried out these functions in a variety of different ways. For example, until the mid-1970s, the diagnosis of livestock diseases in Kenya, to the extent that this could not be done by veterinary officers in the field with the simplest of equipment, was extremely centralized, with a single veterinary laboratory near Nairobi receiving all specimens sent in from the field. This laboratory, therefore, served an area of about 600,000 km^2, with a bovine livestock population of about 10 million. In contrast, in India each district in the dry areas will have at least one veterinary laboratory able to do most routine diagnostic work, to serve an area of 10,000–30,000 km^2 with a bovine population of between 250,000 and 1 million. In Tanzania veterinary investigation centres cover one or more provinces (regions) and each serves, on average, an area of about 200,000 km² and a bovine population of about 3 million. These veterinary investigation centres each have not only a fixed laboratory but also (at least in theory) a mobile van equipped to do field investigations and which can go out to the area of disease outbreaks. In Iran, although diagnostic laboratories exist (data as at 1977) at provincial (*Ostan*) level, these are unable to cope with the volume of work and, as one veterinary officer told me, 'The diseases in this province are pretty specific to particular areas, so if a stockowner comes in from an area and describes the symptoms it is usually pretty easy to fix him up with the remedies he needs.'

For vaccinating and treating individual livestock a similar variety of approaches have been tried. In nomadic areas of northern Nigeria for many years the main emphasis was on permanent 'immunization camps' located near seasonal grazing areas or migration routes, at which all the major immunizations and vaccinations were given. At a later stage mobile camps were introduced into the more densely populated and settled areas (Nigeria Veterinary Department, 1929). In nomadic areas of Iran temporary tented vaccination camps are set up on the major migration routes during the weeks of the annual migration between winter and summer pastures (Sandford, 1977b). In dry India there is a hierarchy of animal clinics and hospitals at district levels, with different complexities of treatment available at different levels. For example, a district will have one or two 'district-level hospitals', with residential accommodation for animals and a capacity to do major operations on livestock. There will be 10–15 other 'hospitals' with a slightly lower level of facilities and a capacity for less complex operations. Each of these hospitals will be under the supervision of a senior veterinary officer (veterinary assistant surgeon). Below these in the hierarchy will be up to 60 minor or rural veterinary dispensaries under the control of veterinary officers or more junior officials called 'compounders', able to do vaccinations, castrations, treatment of wounds, and other minor veterinary work. To these fixed centres livestock owners bring their animals and receive treatment free, though the materials used may be charged for. Out of official working hours veterinary staff are permitted to practise privately and to charge fees for visiting livestock at their owners' homes. Alongside this core system of animal health there are a variety of special programmes aimed at particular areas (e.g. 'drought-prone area programmes'), for limited periods (using 'spearhead teams'), at particular products (e.g. wool), at particular social classes ('small farmers') or using particular techniques (e.g. artificial insemination), and these special programmes may be run parallel to, but separate from, the core programme, or be more or less closely integrated into it in terms of joint use of facilities or combined channels of administrative direction. In parts of Iran and Ethiopia a cadre of junior veterinary workers is being formed — whom we can, following the Chinese parallel of 'barefoot doctors', call 'barefoot livestock assistants' (BLAs). These are of minimal educational qualification, but they are drawn from, selected by, and sometimes also remunerated by particular groups of pastoralists, to whom, after a practical training of a few weeks or months, they are attached to serve and with whom they will move during any migrations.

In parts of Tanzania in the mid-1970s, programmes for breed improvement included the distribution of bulls free of charge, or on loan on very favourable terms. The recipient was to use these bulls not only on his own cows but also on those of his neighbours (Moluche, Kuney, and Hatfield, 1975). In Botswana bulls of recommended breeds are purchased by government, performance-tested as to weight gain, and then resold to farmers at a subsidized price that is related to each farmer's income; and artificial insemination (AI) is provided, at heavily subsidized rates, to breeding females belonging to pastoralists, which are brought into and then kept for some time on special AI ranches. There they are examined, inseminated, and subsequently checked for pregnancy before or after being returned to their owners (Bingana, 1977). In parts of dry India AI posts are set up in villages to which semen is brought daily or every other day by motor transport and to which villagers bring their on-heat cows or buffaloes for insemination, taking them home immediately afterwards; in some cases the inseminators at these posts tour the village looking for on-heat animals and inseminating them. In some countries, Pakistan, for example, improved bulls are kept at village-level veterinary posts and village livestock are brought to them to be served. In part of Gujarat State in India cross-bred rams are taken round, in four-wheel-drive vehicles, to visit insemination posts on village grazing areas according to a predetermined timetable. On-heat ewes are brought to these posts and AI (which both reduces the risk of spreading disease and enables one ram to serve more ewes) is then used to inseminate them (DPAP, 1977). All these programmes have tended to suffer from problems of cost, or spread of disease, or of difficulty in detecting oestrus in bovines in the tropics.

At some times and in some areas animal health (veterinary) activities have been integrated with programmes for improving animal husbandry, using the same facilities, staff, and management structure, and in others they have been separated. Throughout India they seem to be most closely integrated. The same staff may be responsible at the same time for animal health, artificial insemination, and extension work; at other times, although particular individuals or organizational units may have specialist functions at subdistrict level, the staff are all drawn from the same cadre with the same basic technical qualifications (e.g. as veterinary assistant surgeons) and come under the same general management structure at district level or just above. (Source: officials in drought-prone areas in Andra Pradesh, Karnataka, Gujarat, and Rajasthan in 1977.) In contrast, in Iran the veterinary service does not see a role for itself outside strict animal health functions; it does not do routine extension work nor in general does it think that training farmers is its proper role, although in some areas it runs short training courses for farmers during seasons when otherwise the staff have rather little else to do. (Source: senior veterinarians in Iran in 1977.) In Kenya in the high potential areas officials of the veterinary department restrict themselves fairly closely to animal health functions and AI, leaving animal husbandry and extension work either (in the more distant past) to the general agricultural service or (more recently) to a specialist animal production service whose staff's basic qualifications are in agricultural and animal rather than in veterinary science. In the dry areas of Kenya, however, the animal production service does not operate and its functions, to the extent that they are carried on at all, are split between the veterinary and range-management services. Much the same division of responsibility occurred in northern Nigeria, at any rate up to the early 1960s.

CHOICE OF FORMS OF ORGANIZATION AND MANAGEMENT

The choices of particular organizational forms which have been made in particular pastoral situations have partly been due to the technical factors of local disease situations and the technology currently available to deal with them. Partly also, the organizational forms chosen have been adaptations to physical, social, and economic characteristics of the situations concerned and the levels of resources, particularly of trained staff but also of money, which the local community or government concerned could afford, and to the objectives being pursued. The choices were also due to the personal idiosyncrasies of the particular officials who initiated or adapted programmes, and to the general cultural and educational background from which these officials were drawn. Decades after many countries regained their freedom from colonial rule their animal health and husbandry services — the livestock services — still bear the stamp of their colonial past. Veterinary services in Anglophone West Africa are more similar to veterinary services in Anglophone East Africa than to those in Francophone West Africa; and both East Africa and India relied heavily in the initial years of their veterinary services on recruiting qualified staff from among veterinarians of cavalry regiments made redundant by new military technology. As a consequence their veterinary organization for some years retained aspects of this military past.

It is easy to be anecdotal about the experiences of particular organizational forms which have been tried in particular situations in the countries of dry Africa and Asia since animal health and husbandry services began about 60 years ago. It is much more difficult to go beyond this and so to structure the way we think about these experiences that we can draw lessons from one set of situations that may be applicable in others. But it is essential to do this, because copying exactly all the features (including sometimes even the name!) of a project in one situation for replication in another seldom leads to happy results. What one needs to do is to identify the key organizational variables or options (i.e. the things which the managers and project designers can choose or change) which are the really important things in determining how effective performance is in different situations. The rest of this chapter will examine several of these key variables and the characteristics with which they most interact.

Two key variables to which we shall not pay much attention are the availability of finance to fund animal health and husbandry improvements, and the relation between the cost of these programmes and their outputs. In fact, availability of finance is often *not* a variable which those associated with pastoral development can control. It is controlled by other parts of central government, often with little interest in pastoral development programmes. The relationship between costs and outputs is also obviously a matter of great importance in determining what should be done. But the economics of pastoral health programmes is a subject of its own which cannot be satisfactorily covered in the present study. The only financial variable which will be discussed here — and that only briefly — is the ratio between expenditure on the non-staff and staff items of livestock services. This is something over which the managers of livestock services do have some control.

There is seldom only one possible way to carry something out, and an important task, as we have seen, is to identify the key options which are available. There is equally seldom only one *best* way to do something, which is applicable as a blanket solution to all situations. As was discussed in Chapter 1, and reiterated at the ends of Chapters 2 and 7, the best way to do something (i.e. the best form of organization and management) in a particular situation will be determined by the objectives of development being pursued, the technology available (i.e. what animal health and husbandry improvements have been devised and tested for use), the physical, social, and other characteristics of the particular situation, and the ways in which these interact with each other and with different forms of organization and management. In the discussion which follows of particular organizational forms, specific universally applicable recommendations in favour of particular forms will not, therefore, be made. Such recommendations can only be made for particular individual situations in the light of the particular objectives being pursued and the particular characteristics of that situation.

In the sections which follow, five organizational variables, which have been identified as key ones, will be discussed. In each case there will be a brief review of actual experience and an analysis of how different factors affect the appropriateness of particular forms. The first variable is staffing density, as exemplified by the ratios between the numbers in different categories of staff, e.g. veterinarians and auxiliaries, or between veterinarians and livestock. The second is the allocation of functions between different sorts of organizations, e.g. central government, parastatals, local governments (e.g. district councils in some countries, government-directed rural development organizations in others), community organizations of pastoralists, and private entrepreneurs. The two functions discussed in this way are the supply of livestock requisites (e.g. vaccines or mineral licks) and the employment of the most junior level of field staff. The third variable discussed is whether livestock services (i.e. animal health and husbandry services) in the field should be concentrated in central locations in pastoral areas or dispersed throughout them, and whether they should be mobile or stationary. The fourth variable is the level of formal technical skill and training which field staff should be required to possess, in contrast to the emphasis that is put on their direct personal knowledge of the local area and their acceptability in the local community. The final variable concerns the degree to which livestock services should be provided by a variety of separate single-purpose specialist staff or organizations or should be combined, even with other components altogether, in a single multi-purpose organization.

THE DENSITY OF STAFF

Much of what scant literature there is on the organization of animal health and husbandry services has concentrated on only one factor — the 'density' of veterinarians, measured by the ratio between the number of veterinarians and the number of domestic livestock to be looked after or the number of livestock owners. Depending on which classes of veterinarians and of livestock are included in the enumerators and denominators, and on what weight is attached to different species and classes of livestock to reduce them to a common unit, one finds a range of ratios from about one veterinarian to between 1000 and 6000 livestock units in Western Europe to about one veterinarian to between 20,000 and 400,000 livestock units in the poor countries of Africa and Asia.[1] In fact, these ratios can sometimes be quite misleading about the level of attention actually available to livestock in the field. For example, in Afghanistan, 14 out of 18 Afghan veterinarians in the government veterinary service in early 1977 were stationed in or very near the capital Kabul, and extra recruits seemed to get swallowed up in this bureaucracy. In Upper Volta in 1975 out of 30 expatriate and national veterinarians only 6 were engaged in the normal veterinary field services (GTZ/SEDES, 1976).

Another point is that the number of fully qualified veterinarians is extremely difficult to do much about; the period of professional training is about five years, it is, even on an annual basis, an extremely expensive form of training, and the supply of recruits to the profession tends to be heavily influenced by the demand for recruits in other occupations into which veterinary trainees may be seduced by better prospects and material rewards. However, in spite of the difficulty in changing the density of indigenous veterinarians, there is scope for recruiting expatriates to swell the ranks of national cadres and to concentrate the veterinarians who are available in the country into particular favoured areas, leaving other areas unstaffed.

The density of veterinarians affects the range of services which they are able to provide, and this in turn is affected by the extent to which the veterinarians (fully qualified at degree level) are supported by cadres of 'lay' (i.e. not fully qualified veterinarian) assistants or 'auxiliary personnel'. These auxiliaries may range from rather well-qualified 'sub-professionals' with two years post-secondary-school specialist training — whom I shall subsequently call 'animal health assistants' to 'veterinary scouts', 'veterinary guards', or 'vaccinators', hereinafter generically 'livestock assistants', with no or only minimal formal education and only a few weeks or months of practical training in animal health and husbandry matters. Where the role of the veterinarian is primarily visual diagnosis in the field, the mass vaccination of livestock against epizootic diseases, and the enforcement of quarantine restrictions, he appears to be able adequately to manage and supervise the work of up to 20–30 auxiliary personnel and with this support to provide a service to up to 200,000 head of (mainly bovine) livestock.[2] By the end of the 1920s the ratio of district-level veterinarians to auxiliary staff in Tanganyika was slightly worse than 1 : 20 (i.e. it was 1 : more than 20). At least monthly supervision of subordinates by veterinarians was felt to be essential, but at ratios worse than 1 : 20 this became difficult; 'to leave veterinary guards for any considerable length of time to their own devices is tantamount to inviting disaster' (Tanganyika Veterinary Department, 1924 and 1929). However, as late as 1977 in the seven mainly pastoral districts of Kenya the average veterinarian : auxiliary ratio was 1 : 27 with a range in individual districts between 1 : 11 and 1 : 66. (Source: Kenya Veterinary Service officials.)

When the range of services is expanded to include some rather more sophisticated diagnosis and preventive veterinary medicine on a herd- or flock- rather than on a mass-vaccination or individual treatment basis, and where this is combined with some simple advisory work to livestock owners, an appropriate ratio of veterinarians to livestock units appears to be in the range 1 : 10,000 to 1 : 30,000. With this range of services it seems to be difficult for one veterinarian to be effectively associated with more than 10 auxiliaries (Robertson, 1978), although at this point, where some activities are being undertaken of an 'animal-husbandry-and-production' nature rather than only those concerned with the prevention of disease, the possible substitution of university graduates in other disciplines for veterinarians and vice versa starts to complicate the significance of the ratios. When a full range of animal husbandry services is provided, including artificial insemination and the treatment of individual sick animals, then a ratio of one graduate to 5000 livestock units or less seems to be necessary, as in parts of India, and the ratio of graduates to auxiliaries comes down to 1 : 5, 1 : 3 or even 1 : 1.

These ratios are further influenced by the species of livestock concerned. Individual sheep and goats do not get as much attention as bovines which in turn get less than equines. They are also affected by herd size. The larger the average size of herd, the more livestock can be dealt with by animal health and husbandry staff at a single visit. This factor tends to obscure the effect of decreasing livestock densities in dry regions. As the livestock population becomes less dense, so, in theory, does it become more difficult for animal health and husbandry staff to visit livestock in a given period of time or for a given distance travelled. We have discussed this in connection with range extension services in Chapter 7. On the other hand, as land productivity falls with a spatial decline in rainfall, so does the extent of human dependence on livestock increase and therefore, usually, average herd size. Moreover, the congregation of animals, especially during the dry season at water points or more temporarily on migration routes, may lead to extremely high local concentrations of livestock in dry regions where the overall average density is very low. Staffing densities, per head of livestock, tend to be lower in dry than in high potential regions, but this is a consequence of an amalgam of a lower range of services being offered, of larger herd sizes and high local concentrations of livestock which enable greater staff productivity, as well as of the low political influence of pastoralists in most countries and therefore of the low priority accorded to providing them with an adequate level of staff and services.

We can come to some tentative conclusions about staff densities. The main factor determining the appropriate density of staff will be the range of different functions or improvements that the staff are to carry out. The wider the range, obviously the less stock can one member of staff deal with. The same is true of the ratio between senior and junior staff; the wider the range of functions and the more complex these are, the fewer the junior staff that a senior official can supervise and the greater the direct role in dealing with livestock that he will have to play. Because of the difficulty and time taken in travelling in sparsely populated areas, the drier the area (and so the more sparsely populated overall) the less livestock will one member of staff, other things being equal, be able to deal with. However, in practice three things in particular are unlikely to 'remain equal'. First, the drier the region, probably the narrower the range of improvements which it will be economic to introduce. Moreover, in drier regions there are usually relatively more camels and shoats — sheep and goats — compared to cattle and fewer 'improvements' are available for these animals. Secondly, the drier the region the greater will probably be the degree of human dependence on livestock and so the greater the average herd size. Thirdly, the drier the region the more likely it is to be subject to a mobile (nomadic) form of land-use which permits high temporary and local densities of livestock, far higher than can be supported over the region and the year as a whole. These three things will tend to work against the general tendency for the drier regions, because of the overall sparseness of their populations and the consequently greater difficulty of contacting them, to require higher densities of staff per head of livestock.

WHO SHOULD DO WHAT?

Another important variable is the division of functions between organizations of different kinds, e.g. central government, local government, parastatal corporations, community organizations or associations of pastoralists, capitalist corporations, private traders, and individual pastoralists. For example, veterinarians are usually employed by central government, but in India they are sometimes employed by farmers' co-operatives or, although employed by state governments during official working hours, are permitted to practise as private entrepreneurs in the afternoons and evenings. The consequence is greatly to increase the attraction, to them, of work in rural areas, to the point where they actually refuse promotion to other more bureaucratic or urban posts because it will lead to a decline in their incomes. However, such profitable private practice is less likely to occur in dry regions of sparse livestock populations.

Who should supply livestock requisites?

We can compare particular functions where different divisions of responsibility between organizations have been tried. One example is the procurement, transportation, storage, and distribution of livestock health and husbandry requisites such as vaccines, drugs, drenches, acaricides, mineral licks, spraying equipment, etc. In much of Anglophone Africa and in India this has usually been seen as properly the task of the central government's veterinary service, although in some cases local government organizations (district councils or native authorities) have also been encouraged to do this under the eye of a veterinarian of the central government. In Francophone Africa the same was true, but in recent years there has been a tendency to establish specialist parastatal corporations to handle this work at national and provincial level but with the central government's veterinary service acting as the retail distribution agent at field level. In imperial Iran the government's veterinary service tended to handle the main vaccines — which were in any case manufactured in a government laboratory — but other livestock requisites were handled both by the veterinary service and also, and more effectively, by pharmacies that also supplied human medical requirements. In north-east Zaire a pastoralists' co-operative at the end of the 1970s was trying to purchase its own livestock requisites direct, without the intervention of any intermediate government organization.

These different mechanisms have all faced problems, some of which are more acute in pastoral regions than in others of higher productivity and denser settlement. Financial procedures of central government (and to a certain extent of local government also) normally handle expenditure on livestock requisites which are to be subsequently resold to livestock owners separately from the revenue from their sale, so that one (gross expenditure) cannot be offset against the other (gross revenue) to indicate a net cost or profit to government. In periods of governmental financial crisis, gross expenditure on requisites (particularly for pastoralists with little political influence) tends to be slashed regardless of the net financial effect, partly out of lack of appreciation of the true net effect, partly because the revenue will not come in early enough to mitigate the immediate crisis. In any case, estimates of future government expenditure have to be prepared for approval sometimes as much as two years in advance of the expected date of actual disbursement; the great climatic unreliability of pastoral areas makes the forecasting of demand far ahead particularly difficult. Further difficulties arise from the fact that veterinary staff are not selected or trained to act as wholesalers or retailers but for other functions, and neither their expertise, their interest, nor their promotion prospects are adequately bound up in their performance in this trading role.

Some governments have tried to overcome some of the bureaucratic problems by establishing 'revolving funds', which are relatively free of normal government financial procedures, or pharmaceutical parastatal corporations,[3] which can both employ specialist staff and use appropriate procurement and financial procedures. However, for the most part both these devices for handling livestock requisites have continued to use the government's veterinary services as their retail agents. Two problems have arisen. Veterinary services are chronically short of money for staff salaries and transportation and have seen these forms of expenditure as having a more important claim on the revenue from selling requisites than reimbursing a revolving fund or parastatal (e.g. in Mauritania and Upper Volta); in any case these 'distribution costs' tend to outweigh the 'material costs' by as much as four times. The second problem is that veterinary services are often not located nor do they operate in a way that is convenient for pastoralists. Veterinary field stations are few, staff are often absent from them for both legitimate and illegitimate reasons, and official opening hours are short and inconvenient.

In imperial Iran many livestock requisites were sold direct by private-sector pharmacies to pastoralists, sometimes on the basis of a prescription from a government veterinarian, and this system seemed to generate little complaint from pastoralists. In other countries the veterinary services of government tend to be suspicious of the activities of private traders and corporations, emphasizing that pastoralists need cheap supplies, not those on which high profits are made, that private traders are often unscrupulous in diluting drugs or acaricides (which may lead to a build-up of drug resistance), and that the private sector will not stock adequate quantities in retail outlets close to the pastoralist. Unfortunately, governments' own records on these points are poor. An official in Afghanistan in 1977 commented that veterinary supplies were available from the private sector and were easier to obtain before a parastatal undertook the task of supplying them. In Tanzania the government was accused by its own officers of selling at higher prices than the pharmaceutical companies (Tanzania Livestock Conference, 1974, p. 10). In Nigeria the veterinary departments' own supplies of trypanocidal drugs were stolen, with 'inside' connivance, diluted and resold to pastoralists on a large scale (Nigeria Veterinary Department, 1959). In most countries, when the veterinary services operate cattle dips they are unable to maintain the concentration of acaricides at an adequate level, and resistance among ticks builds up. In any case resistance by ticks to acaricides frequently also builds up because livestock owners fail to bring their animals sufficiently often to be dipped. Government veterinary clinics never seem to have enough of the requisites that pastoralists want. The correct comparison is not between a malign private sector and a perfect government service but between performances in both which fall a long way short of ideal. The provision of livestock requisites by local government organizations has also often failed to work well, although in many cases (e.g. Tanzania) this may have been largely caused by a general collapse of local government organizations.

In a number of cases governments wish to subsidize the provision of livestock requisites, particularly vaccines and dipping fluids. The arguments for doing so are not only those general arguments about the state using public expenditure as a means of transferring income from rich taxpayers to poor users of government services. There is also the argument that disease prevention in the herd of one individual has greater benefits than will be reaped by him alone, for prevention of disease in his herd will prevent his animals being transmitters of infection to other herds, and that in order to reap these greater benefits it may be necessary to provide the vital inputs at less than full cost. The provision of free vaccines and dips has had a dramatic effect on the extent of their use. In the early 1940s when rinderpest vaccinations in Kenya started to be given free of charge in African areas, the number of cattle vaccinated increased between five- and tenfold in a couple of years at a time when use of other vaccines, for which the charges continued, only doubled (Kenya Veterinary Department, 1937–50). Similarly in Tanzania the abolition of dipping fees for cattle at the end of the 1960s was accompanied by a tenfold increase in the number of animals dipped (source: officials in the Tanzania Livestock Development Division, 1977), whereas the earlier imposition of dipping fees in Iringa District after a period of free dipping led to the total collapse of the dipping scheme there (Lowe and Reid, 1973). The provision of heavily subsidized, or free, livestock requisites through private trade channels would clearly be extremely difficult, given the high ratio between 'distribution' and 'material' costs already referred to, even though distribution costs would tend to be much lower in private trade channels because of the possibility of sharing overheads between livestock requisites and a number of other lines of goods.

There are some circumstances under which, whatever the type of organization responsible for the distribution of livestock requisites, an easy, reliable, and cheap availability of a complete range of such requisites will simply not be possible. These circumstances are where pastoral human and livestock populations are very sparse, communications are difficult, and the prices of livestock products are low. Probably in these circumstances the fact that private traders can spread their overheads over a variety of product lines (grain, tea, sugar, and cattle) may give them a competitive advantage, but they may simply find that the distribution of livestock requisites is not profitable enough at any price. The situation will be aggravated where government provides sporadic competition at subsidized prices. Where the level of pastoralists' basic education is reasonably high, the dangers (from dilution, misprescribing, and consequent growth in drug resistance) that may arise from livestock requisites being handled by unscrupulous private traders can

182

be lessened (but not wholly eradicated) by giving pastoralists adequate training and advice in the dangers of ineffective treatments and in how unscrupulous practices can be identified and checked. Pastoralists also need advice on the choice between products sold under different names but for the same purpose. Unfortunately, government veterinary services are not keen on the growth of pastoralists' skills in this subject area. Although large commercial (and often expatriate) ranchers in Africa have often managed to obtain for themselves permission to administer vaccinations and drugs, this is usually regarded by veterinary services as a regrettable lapse not to be extended further. Senior veterinary officials in both India and Kenya have responded to my queries about training pastoralists in animal health skills by commenting that such skills do not need to be imparted, and should not be, because the government veterinary service is expanding to provide anything necessary. In Iran, in contrast, special courses were sometimes run by the veterinary service to teach pastoralists how to use a syringe. The general tendency among veterinary services, however, is to try to maintain their own monopolistic position as suppliers of both requisites and skills, fearing that if they hand over the supply of requisites to the private sector pastoralists will then ignore the veterinary service altogether.

It is hard, in the case of this option, to draw up general propositions about the relationship between objectives, a particular form of organization and management, and the sort of characteristics that we have discussed in relation to other organizational options. The main conclusion to emerge is that governments' performance in providing livestock requisites, either directly through a department of central government or indirectly through a parastatal, tends to be very disappointing and often to be as bad as that of the private sector in terms of both quality (purity) of product and price. Governments' performance is often actually worse than that of the private sector in terms of reliability and ease of supply. Obviously the balance of relative efficiency between government and private sector is going to be different in different countries and at different times in a way not related to the characteristics of their pastoral situations, and it is this balance which will influence the choice of option. In many cases it seems likely that governments will not be able to supply livestock requisites efficiently and should, instead, concentrate their scarce resources on improving the ability of the pastoralists to make informed use of livestock requisites supplied by the private sector.

Who should employ livestock assistants?

We can look at another example of alternative ways of allocating responsibility for a particular function — namely, the hiring, supervision, and remuneration of the lowest levels of livestock assistants. The tasks of such livestock assistants may include: disease reporting; ensuring adherence to quarantine orders; operation of dipping tanks and sprays; administration of anti-helminthics (drenching); castrations; treatment of wounds and footrot;

some vaccinations or injections either on the livestock assistants' own initiative or under the supervision of better-qualified professionals; the taking of blood slides and other specimens; the sale to pastoralists of livestock requisites; the transmission of government instructions (e.g. on quarantines or vaccination schedules) or extension advice; and other activities of a semi-skilled nature. Such livestock assistants may be employed by central government, as in most countries, or by a local government organization as in northern Nigeria, or be maintained by pastoral communities, as in parts of Ethiopia, or in a way that splits the responsibility. For example, in Madagascar and the range areas of Ethiopia, pastoral communities have a strong say in the selection of livestock assistants, but these are (or have been) paid by central government (Sandford, 1981). In northern Nigeria, at any rate in colonial times, they were selected and paid for by local government (i.e. the native administrations) but supervised by central (i.e. the Northern Region) government (Henderson, 1973). In Sudan for many years tribally appointed veterinary retainers worked with very little supervision (Jack, 1973). In Shiraz province in Iran 'tribal veterinarians' are (1977) selected and trained by the veterinary department of the university, paid for by the local government administration, and rather unwillingly and loosely supervised by the central government's veterinary service. (Source: members of Pahlavi University Veterinary Faculty, 1977.)

If central government has the full responsibility for these livestock assistants, then central government veterinarians are able to exercise much more authoritative supervision over them; this is appropriate where a major part of the livestock assistants' job is to report disease and enforce quarantine orders on a pastoral population that resents these activities. The more 'mobile' the land-use system involved, the more unpopular will such quarantine orders be, for they will not only, as in settled areas, affect people's right to sell or purchase stock but also their ability to feed the stock they already have. Whereas 'quarantine' 50 years ago was almost the only weapon veterinary services had in the fight against disease, the development of efficient vaccines has lessened the relative importance of quarantine restrictions. The more mobile the land-use system the more difficult it also is to give adequate supervision because of the difficulty of communication between supervisor and those he supervises. Where strict authoritative supervision by the central government veterinarian is needed but not given, then this system is wide open to abuse of both negligence and corruption. This charge was raised against livestock assistants in Tanganyika, for example, at the end of the 1920s (Tanganyika Veterinary Department, 1924–1930). However, where community or local government organizations are given full control of livestock assistants, the latter will not, naturally, take actions which are against the interests of the larger stockowners who are leaders in the community.

Where the central or local government pays the salary of livestock assistants but the selection of these is left in the hands of the community, then the posts tend to be seen as valuable prizes to be grabbed by the most powerful families or factions rather than as opportunities to get the most appropriate persons to carry out services efficiently. Once installed by a faction, favourite sons tend to be very difficult to control even for the faction that installed them. This is true of community posts in general. Specific pastoral examples can be found in the case of 'veterinary scouts' in the north-east rangelands of Ethiopia and of 'nomadic teachers' in Mauritania. The more sparse the population, the more mobile the land-use system, the more multi-purpose the job concerned and the more complex the technology involved (providing scope for mystification and for blaming deficiencies on technical break-downs), the more difficult it is for the community as a whole to supervise, to assess and to reward good performance and to penalize poor.

It is, for example, relatively easy to control a water attendant whose job it is to sell water from a single public tap during fixed hours; the job and the criteria for assessment are simple and there are plenty of on-the-spot wit-nesses to the evidence. It is very difficult to assess performance of a livestock assistant who has several different functions (disease-reporting, vaccinations, marketing advice) and who has to travel long distances between sparse nomadic groups who do not understand the technology on offer. It is un-realistic to expect the neighbours of a community's employee to take a harsh line in criticizing or penalizing his incompetence when this cannot be clearly and unshakeably proved. In such circumstances, almost certainly the only way for members of the community to reward good and to penalize poor performance is by a system in which individuals, or small groups such as encampments, pay for specific services at the time these are rendered. Of course, this means that the wealthier stockowners will get more service than the poor; but this is likely to happen in any case even if the livestock assistant is paid a fixed salary, since the wealthy are likely also to have political influence which will enable them largely to capture the livestock assistant's services. When communities pay remuneration on a fixed salary basis there is a particular problem of whether the community that pays is exactly the same as the community that receives the service; we shall return to this point later.

One problem that occurs where communities employ livestock assistants concerns the latter's career structure. Central government animal health and husbandry services may agree to communities employing their own livestock assistants and co-operate with them. Thereby a financial burden will be lifted off central government and communities may use better criteria and know-ledge in selecting livestock assistants than will the recruitment procedures of central government, which tend to select academically well-qualified candi-dates from non-pastoral backgrounds who do not wish to live with pastoralists and are not able to communicate with them. But central government officials do not want such community employees subsequently to obtain promotion into central government's own cadres where their training and experience may not fit in well. On the other hand, the size of pastoral community best able to select and pay a livestock assistant is not one which provides scope for a number of senior supervisory posts to which those who start as junior livestock assistants can aspire for promotion. It seems likely that the post of community livestock assistant will be filled for a period of a few years by competent young men who still have inadequate numbers of livestock to set up as independent pastoralists and who use the post as a way of acquiring additional livestock before they do so. (This is a system I have observed being practised by teachers in Koranic schools among nomads in north Kenya.) Otherwise, posts may be filled by the socially handicapped or less competent who cannot ever aspire to such independence. The training facilities, and the role which livestock assistants are expected to play, should be tailored accordingly.

Most of the arguments set out so far in this subsection review the circumstances in which a local pastoral community may not be an effective employer of livestock assistants, i.e. where the main task is enforcement of quarantine, where the salary is provided by central government, where the job is technically complex or multi-purpose, or where the livestock assistant's remuneration cannot take the form of payment for specific services, etc. On the other hand, central or local governments are also often ineffective in ensuring that their most junior staff levels do their jobs properly. Partly this is because of such government's staff remuneration procedures, whereby livestock assistants receive the same reward whether or not they do a proper job; partly it is because a junior employee of government is in no position to nag at his superiors to provide him with an adequate supply of livestock requisites. In contrast, the employee of a pastoral community, particularly an employee paid for rendering specific services, has both a strong incentive to nag and to acquire such supplies wherever he may, and also a justification for nagging that puts him in quite a strong position to do so. A pastoral community may well be a most effective employer of livestock assistants if their tasks and rewards are properly designed.

THE LOCATION AND MOBILITY OF LIVESTOCK SERVICES

Another important organizational variable in the location of animal health and husbandry services is the extent to which they are stationary or are expected to be mobile and are given adequate resources for this mobility. Many of the arguments involved are the same as those applying to extension workers in range management which have already been reviewed in Chapter 7. In areas, for example, where the land-use system is very mobile, it is likely to be more appropriate for staff to be either centralized at district headquarters, whence they can be despatched to wherever they are needed at any particular time, or for them to be attached as nomads to nomadic groups, rather than for them to be isolated in stationary field stations where they have no clientele for much of the year. Where the nature of the animal health situation is such that the main priority is the containment of sudden unpredictable outbreaks of serious epidemics, rather than a continuing low-intensity struggle against endemic infections, then a concentration of staff at central points whence they can be switched to the scene of outbreaks will be more appropriate than their permanent dispersal throughout the pastoral area.

However, whereas some of the arguments set out in Chapter 7 about competition between groups or classes are of less importance in animal health and husbandry issues than in range management where there is a fixed resource, technical considerations are likely to be of relatively greater importance in animal health and husbandry. For example, many vaccines and semen require deep-freeze facilities for long-term storage and refrigeration for short-term. Such facilities are impossible, or at best very difficult, to provide in isolated stations and they therefore imply rather a high concentration of staff, vehicles, and other facilities at district level, whence they can be sent out with fresh supplies at frequent intervals.

Mass routine vaccination programmes can be run on relatively fixed schedules announced in advance and they mainly require at field level a reliable information service, to report disease outbreaks upwards and the programme of vaccination programmes downwards. Such a reporting system can be operated, at a low level of efficiency, by administrative or law-and-order staff at field level and does not absolutely require permanent interaction between technical staff and pastoralists. Obviously, such a centralized system works best where the natural environment is fairly regular and predictable so that the whereabouts of concentrations of livestock at particular times can be forecast. In South-West Asia, for example in the Zagros mountains of Iran, vaccination posts can be set up at fixed dates on migration routes for quite short periods of time. (Source: local veterinary officials in Shiraz in 1977.) In contrast, an AI service not only requires efficient facilities at district level; it also needs daily contact by technical staff over an extended period with the livestock to whom the service is to be offered, either by sending out the semen daily along fixed routes and at fixed hours or by bringing the cows to be inseminated to stay for a considerable time at a central point.

Field stations as stationary clinics

We can look at the example of some stationary field stations (clinics). In semi-arid areas of India there is quite a dense basic network of veterinary facilities offering prophylactic (preventive) vaccinations, AI services, treatments for wounds and diseases (e.g. haemorrhagic septicaemia), and even some quite technically complex surgical operations. All these are offered at a hierarchy of facilities ranging from a rural veterinary dispensary, usually under a livestock inspector or compounder (equivalent to an animal health assistant), through a minor veterinary dispensary (under a junior veterinarian) to a veterinary hospital under a senior veterinarian. In addition to these 'core' facilities, a number of districts have further facilities related to the operations of special livestock programmes. The range of ratios between the basic facilities and land area, livestock, and human populations found in four districts in dry India are shown in Table 8.1.

Table 8.1 The relationship between facilities, land area and livestock populations in semi-arid India (range of figures for four districts)

Facility	No. per facility		
	Land area (km^2)	Bovines ('000) inc. buffaloes	Shoats ('000)
Veterinary hospital	1400–23,000	62–500	92–1000
Minor veterinary dispensary	300–1700	19–36	19–72
Rural veterinary dispensary (where available)	200–800	9–33	9–50
Combination of the above facilities	180–1600	6–33	6–66

Source: District-level officials in Andra Pradesh and Rajasthan.

In most cases livestock are within 8 km walk of some facility, although even in the best-endowed district they may on average be as much as 21 km away (some will be more) from the facility with the complete range of services. In contrast, in Sahelian Africa the area of land served by a stationary field station of any kind ranges from about 1500 km^2 in the sedentary areas of Senegal to about 13,000–17,000 km^2 in Niger and Chad (GTZ/SEDES, 1977). These Sahelian field stations offer a much narrower range of services than do the Indian ones.

There are few, if any, proper studies of how well, from the livestock owners' point of view, these stationary field stations function. It is clear that in Africa in many cases they perform very badly, for reasons which are not particularly related to their location or mobility but simply arise from a government trying to operate too many of them in relation to the total level of resources it is prepared to make available for animal health and husbandry. The result is that far too high a proportion of total expenditure is earmarked for staff remuneration (salaries and allowances) and too little is then left to finance non-staff costs (e.g. vaccines and other livestock requisites, equipment, vehicle-running, maintenance of structures, etc.). As a consequence vaccines and drugs are not provided; refrigerators have no fuel or are not repaired; supervisory visits are not carried out; and even staff salaries are not regularly paid. Precisely what the ratio between non-staff and staff recurrent expenditure should be will obviously vary from situation to situation depending on the range of services offered, the amount of travel which has to be done to supervise and support field staff, and on relative price levels for staff, transportation, and vaccines/drugs. In dry Francophone West Africa ratios of recurrent non-staff : staff expenditure varying between 1.3 : 1 and 0.03 : 1 have been found (IEMVT, 1980), with an average (over countries and years) of 0.5 : 1. Ratios in (less dry) Anglophone countries of the region tend to be higher with a range from 0.25 : 1 to 17.7 : 1 and an average of 2.3 : 1. It is clear that with ratios of less than 0.2 : 1 almost nothing useful can be done and the Francophone countries' average ratio of 0.5 : 1 reflects an unsatisfactory average performance.

Field stations as residential bases for mobile staff

Many field stations are not supposed to function only or even primarily as stationary clinics to which livestock or their owners come for prophylaxis, treatment, or advice, but rather as residential bases from which staff can travel out. Even in India where the basic network is fairly dense, inseminators may go out from the village centre to try to spot cows (or buffaloes) that are on heat in the village herd, or veterinarians may visit individual homesteads out of working hours to provide treatment to individual animals for a fee. In more sparsely populated and less well-served areas, the field stations are inevitably located at the larger human settlements where staff can live in reasonable comfort. Whatever the alleged policy of using such stations as bases out of which to operate mobile patrols, in practice their staff tend to be monopolized by wealthy livestock owners resident in the same settlement, and the wider the range of services which the station offers, the less will staff be able to meet all the demands on their time and the more their closest and wealthiest (and most insistently demanding) neighbours will monopolize them at the expense of the more distant, poorer, and more nomadic and therefore less closely connected pastoralists.

It is difficult to show this quantitatively, but it is noteworthy that in northern Nigeria in the 1930s, when very few clinics operated, these were attended almost exclusively by equines. Equines may need more individual attention (e.g. for sprains and similar injuries), but they are also almost invariably owned by the better-off, and the work of these clinics took up a high proportion of veterinarians' time. By the 1960s equines accounted for less than 25 per cent of the treatments at a vastly increased number of clinics (Nigeria Veterinary Department, 1934, 1935, 1962/63). In Afghanistan in the 1970s, when there were only about 15 veterinarians in the whole country outside the capital, some veterinarians were so captured by rich peri-urban merchant farmers that they were carrying out Caesarean sections in cases of calving difficulties of dairy cows, leaving other work unattended. In Kenya it has been shown that the rural élite in high potential areas have a five times higher chance of their livestock being visited than have those who are not members of this élite (Leonard, 1977, pp. 184–192), and it is surmised that this is due to their greater willingness and ability to complain if they do not get what they want — the so-called 'squawk factor' (Njooro, 1973). Clearly, residents of settlements containing field stations have much better opportunities to 'squawk' than those out in the bush. The better equipped the station, the better qualified the staff, and the wider, therefore, the range of services available, the higher the probability of their being captured by the élite in this way because they are a more valuable prize.

The use of sparsely scattered field stations in nomadic areas as the bases from which mobile operations can spread out, has been advocated (GTZ/ SEDES, 1977). In Francophone West Africa it has been suggested that the ratio of staff to livestock should be the same, at one livestock assistant (described as *cadre d'exécution*) per 20,000 livestock units, in both sedentary and nomadic ('grand transhumant') zones; however, in the former they should be allocated singly to 'tertiary centres' at a density of about 1 : 3000 km^2 (an approximate radius for operations of 30 km), whereas in nomadic areas they should be kept in groups of four at secondary centres under the direction of an animal health assistant (*cadre moyen*). Such secondary centres in nomadic zones would have an area to be served of about 32,000 km^2, i.e. about 8000 km^2 on average per livestock assistant, with a radius of operations of up to 100 km.[4] Clearly, this kind of centralized mobility requires a good deal of motor transport. With the huge increase in fuel costs over the last 10 years this has become less and less possible for governments to provide. Either the range of services to be provided will have to be severely restricted or alternative forms of transportation will be required, or some other basis of organization sought which requires less transportation.

In Tanganyika in the mid-1920s, under an authoritarian and mandatory, almost military, management style, veterinarians themselves *walked*, on duty, an average of 4000 km per year (Tanganyika Veterinary Department, 1924), and they supervised livestock assistants who also walked as far; it was expected that all cattle should be inspected weekly, with 25,000 head being allocated as the responsibility of each livestock assistant in densely populated and 10,000 in sparsely populated areas. In this system livestock assistants were dispersed and, where appropriate, had to move with their charges, but they offered extremely little in the way of a veterinary service; their prime function was to report disease. With the changes in expectations and in social relations between junior and senior staff that have occurred, especially since the end of colonial rule in Africa, it is improbable that any veterinary staff will now feel obliged to walk so far. Even if they did, to cover with four staff, on foot, an area of 32,000 km^2 (as GTZ/SEDES advocate for nomadic areas), with a maximum radius of 100 km would not, even in theory, permit more than four visits a year to each livestock camp (on certain rather mechanical assumptions about evenness of use of the area and camp locations). In practice far less would be achieved.

Fully nomadic staff

Instead of staff of the livestock service carrying out mobile operations from a few fixed residential bases to which they constantly return over great distances, they can themselves be attached to pastoralist groups with whom they reside and migrate, having contact with other parts of the livestock service, i.e. fixed stations or senior staff on tour, only when they need to replenish supplies, report outbreaks of disease, or to be supervised. Such a system operated 50 years ago in Tanganyika, as we have seen, and in Sudan (Jack, 1973) and more recently in Iran (Sandford, 1977b) and Ethiopia (Sandford, 1981). At the same ratio of one livestock assistant to 20,000 livestock units or head of cattle, as we have already discussed, and with about 60 livestock units being required per household of six people, one livestock assistant will need, on average, to serve a group of about 300–400 households where average herd size is near the minimum permissible if a pastoral way of life is to continue.[5] Where the average size of herd per household is above the minimum the number of households to be served will be less.

In Chapter 7 we already discussed, in connection with extension agents, what sort of groups — principally camping communities, watering communities, or possibly kinship groups — are suitable for the attachment of such staff. Camping units are likely to be the most suitable in terms of closeness of contact, but in very few societies is any one camping unit likely to be of sufficient size, even on a temporary basis, to allow an overall ratio of one livestock assistant : 20,000 lu to be equivalent to one livestock assistant per camp. Whether one livestock assistant can adequately serve more than one camping unit depends partly on what service (interventions) he is supposed to provide, partly on the distance at which neighbouring camps are located from each other (nomadic land-use systems permit higher temporary densities than sedentary), and partly on the extent to which the different camps (or parts of a clan) for which he is responsible remain neighbours to each other through several nomadic or other moves, or tend to split up and go in different directions.

It has already been pointed out that in animal health and husbandry interventions technical considerations tend to play a dominant role in determining the appropriate form of organization. The main technical considerations are the necessity for careful temperature control of drugs, semen, and vaccines if they are to retain their efficacy, the need for a high level of technical skill (e.g. in a surgical operation) in carrying out an intervention, and the degree to which interventions can either be programmed in advance or, in an emergency, require only a single brief contact between the animal concerned and the livestock service, as opposed to requiring continuous or repeated contacts. Disease-reporting and quarantine require continuous and repeated contacts. They used, 50 or 60 years ago, to represent in Africa almost the only weapon in the veterinary armoury. It is not surprising, therefore, to find that in the 1920s and 1930s livestock assistants very closely attached to pastoral groups — a form of organization that provides best for continuous and repeated contacts — were used in several countries, for example, Tanzania, Sudan, and, to a lesser extent, Botswana and Nigeria.

After the Second World War increasingly effective vaccines started to be produced and this coincided with the spread of reliable four-wheel-drive vehicles. Relatively less emphasis was then put on disease-reporting and quarantine and relatively more on centrally directed and supplied mass vaccination campaigns, culminating in the Africa-wide JP15 campaign against rinderpest. Almost all the vaccines now require both careful temperature control (involving bulky, heavy, and fragile equipment for medium or long-term storage) and only a brief single contact to confer an immunity which lasts several months or years. Mass vaccination campaigns can be most economically carried out if a programme is drawn up and announced several weeks in advance[6] and livestock are brought to meet the vaccinators at designated spots of easy access. However, as the danger of epidemics recedes because of successful campaigns in the past, so it becomes increasingly difficult to persuade pastoralists to bring their animals to any rendezvous that involves risk or inconvenience. But where unexpected outbreaks occur successful mass vaccinations can be organized because pastoralists then have a substantial incentive to bring their animals in.

Other interventions are much less suited to such a remote type of approach. Early discovery of disease outbreaks certainly cannot be achieved on the basis of stationary tertiary centres covering 3000 km^2, or by patrols operating out of a base that covers 32,000 km^2, even with substantial help from local administrative or political authorities. Other forms of intervention require much closer, continuous, and frequent contact between livestock service and pastoralist, which in areas of mobile land-use can only be achieved by attaching livestock assistants to groups of pastoralists. In addition to reporting disease outbreaks, such livestock assistants can immediately take blood slides and other specimens from sick animals for diagnosis on the spot or elsewhere and can operate a checklist of symptoms so as to assist diagnosis. They can also initiate or carry out the next round of interventions that follow, in importance, the control of the major epidemic diseases. This next round includes immunization against and treatment of trypanosomiasis and haemorrhagic septicaemia, treatment of wounds and footrot, castrations, control of predators through shooting and poisoning and of internal parasites through drenching, some steps against external parasites (e.g. ticks and mites) through hand-spraying or hand-dressing, and improving the flaying and curing of hides and skins by livestock owners.

In many cases, for example treatment of wounds and footrot, the intervention concerned requires continuous, close, and repeated contact between the person carrying out the intervention and the livestock. In other cases, such as castrations, the advantage gained by using modern techniques in preference to traditional ones is not such as to persuade pastoralists to travel any significant distance to obtain access to them. Most of the interventions do not require highly developed technical skills which can only be acquired by years of specialist training; what they need is simply practical training backed up by conscientious application and reliable access to supplies. In many cases the techniques can easily be learnt by the pastoralists concerned; the role of the livestock assistant is thus to give or to reinforce the necessary specific training to the pastoralists and to be a channel of supplies if private traders will not do this. Livestock assistants attached to groups can also give general extension advice on animal health, nutrition and handling of animals, herding and culling practices, although there is not much evidence that the advice of this kind that is usually given is very useful. It may often be more convincingly transmitted in other ways, for example on the radio.

The general preferability of livestock assistants in nomadic areas themselves being nomadic comes up against two important technical points. Firstly, effective control of ectoparasites requires regular attendance by livestock at either dipping tanks or motorized spray-races, which, while in theory they can be transportable, in practice probably also require substantial fixed facilities. In either case the facilities require permanent properly trained attendants during any season when they are in use. However, in effect these facilities require not only sedentary attendants but also a sedentary livestock population. For unless all livestock throughout an area are regularly dipped, there are dangers of drug resistance building up (Tatchell, 1974) and few advantages over much less frequent hand-spraying or hand-dressing of animals, which is designed not to eradicate tick-borne disease but to reduce the tick burden of individual animals and the mechanical damage to hides and skins and to sensitive parts, e.g. udders. The second point concerns AI. Botswana is using AI in arid regions through the device of permanent insemination ranches to which cows are brought for a period adequate to ensure insemination. Where this cannot be done, an AI service also requires stationary livestock stations at which animals and semen, both in an appropriate condition, can be brought together. No doubt in time technical advances will be made which will allow semen to be preserved at ambient temperatures over a long enough period so as not to require its daily renovation from deep-freeze facilities; but they have not been made so far.

HOW WELL TRAINED AND SKILLED SHOULD FIELD STAFF BE?

A further organizational variable is the level of technical training and skill of the field-level staff — especially at the lowest level, which we have called livestock assistants — and the degree of supervision they receive. This variable is closely related to whether livestock assistants should be employees of central government, of a local government organization, or of their community, and to whether they should be based in urban or large village centres relatively well endowed with social amenities or should be located at a remote station in the bush or attached to a nomadic community. It is also directly related to the type of service they are to provide. For complex surgical operations a proper and full veterinarians' education is clearly required, while for cleaning and cutting sheep's feet in cases of footrot only a minimum of practical demonstration and practice is required. Between these extremes there is considerable scope for choice and manoeuvre.

Partly the choice is simply one between more or less technical skill. On the one hand, longer training will give greater skill; on the other hand, longer training is more expensive, and those who receive this longer training, which often includes long periods of living in well-endowed urban centres, not only subsequently demand high salaries but refuse to live or work in arduous rural, and particularly pastoral, conditions. Partly, and perhaps more importantly, the choice lies between different kinds of expertise — between technical know-how based on formal educational methods and practical knowledge of the pastoral situation, of its language, its social structure, its ecology and geography. In most countries it is now no longer impossible (as it would have been even 20 years ago) greatly to expand the number of people with good training at low or medium level; it is, however, still difficult to obtain potential recruits with a good academic school performance from pastoral backgrounds, and it is very difficult for governments to pay the salaries of people who have had lengthy training.

For the last 60 years the trend has been towards increasing the level of technical know-how in the livestock services — a trend that has run parallel with the move away from dependence on disease-reporting and quarantine towards more reliance on high technology in the form of vaccines, antibiotics, AI, and so on. As the level of technical complexity has increased, so the longer-service field staff who joined with low academic qualifications have often proved something of an embarrassment at a later stage in their lives, and have been unfavourably compared with more recent recruits who seemed better trained to handle the technology. Although various attempts have been made to provide promotion avenues for these technically less qualified but longer-serving staff, they have not been very successful because veterinarians have felt it to be important not to permit the emergence of parallel lines of technical and administrative expertise (GTZ/SEDES, 1977; IEMVT, 1980).

Whereas, however, in the 1920s it was often difficult to recruit people from pastoral backgrounds into the livestock service, because they did not *want* to join (see, e.g. Tanganyika Veterinary Department, 1924), since the 1960s the problem has been that, although pastoralists now want the employment, the recruitment systems, in a variety of ways ranging from emphasis on academic performance at school to straightforward ethnic favouritism and prejudice, have discriminated against people of pastoral backgrounds. The consequence has been, in many areas, a profound distrust and lack of sympathy between the staff of livestock services and the pastoralists they are supposed to serve, and the staff, usually of non-pastoral and often of urban origin, take every opportunity to escape back into urban life. The recruitment of livestock assistants from the ranks of pastoralists tends to be considered by pastoralists as critical evidence of a government's good intentions towards them (Sandford, 1981). It strengthens the position of pastoral communities by making them a little less reliant on other organizations.

With the emphasis now swinging back away from mass vaccination campaigns using relatively high technology, towards a round of interventions using less advanced, more robust technology, but requiring much closer contact with farmers, opinion is moving towards using academically less qualified but locally more expert people recruited from within pastoral society. These have been termed 'paraprofessionals' in the human health and agricultural extension fields or, in the specifically livestock field, 'barefoot animal health assistants' (Halpin, 1981) (BAHAs — the use of the word 'vets' is discouraged by veterinarians, see, for example, FAO/WHO, 1965), 'vet scouts' (Ethiopia), 'tribal retainers' (Sudan), or 'tribal veterinarians' (Iran). Here, as I have already said, we shall call them 'BLAs' (barefoot livestock assistants). They are members of the pastoral community, in some cases employees of central government, in others of local government or of their community. Their use reflects a recognition that, in pastoral areas at any rate, it is likely to be impossible to reconcile the livestock assistant who has passed through an urban-oriented education and training system to the rigours of life in pastoral areas, and that attempting to motivate him through material incentives of special pay and housing is likely to lead to an intolerable inflation of costs with no offsetting increase in efficiency.

While in some cases (e.g. Sudan) the use of these BLAs has been going on for many years, there is exceedingly little published information on their performance (Sandford, 1981, is an exception). There is, however, considerable experience now of the performance of paraprofessionals in other (non-livestock) fields, which has been published and seems very relevant in the livestock field also. In brief the experience is as follows (account based on Taylor and Moore, 1980). Paraprofessionals successfully extend useful services; however, it is advisable initially to limit the scope of activities assigned to them and to expand their role progressively as experience is gained. However, the use of paraprofessionals is neither cheap nor easy, and tacking them on to an existing overburdened programme and expecting them to function without support will not succeed. Support is needed to improve not only their technical performance but also their credibility in the eyes of their own community; they need not only initial training but recurring in-service training sessions; they need supervision, not so much to 'control' them, but to give on-the-job training,[7] to provide visible evidence of outside interest in order to reinforce their credibility, and to sustain their morale; and they need timely and regular deliveries of supplies of the materials required for their job. Literacy is not generally required and older people are more respected. Paraprofessionals should have the same general cultural background as their clientele, but someone who was not previously a member of a particular group may be more effective in it. Communities are seldom able to pay the whole salary cost of a paraprofessional but can make substantial contributions. Local communities play an essential role in selecting paraprofessionals but seldom an active part in managing them, particularly in cases where they perform incompetently; partly this is because the communities have not been adequately briefed or prepared for a management role. The most common response to incompetent para professionals is for their community to cease to use them rather than to engineer their dismissal and replacement.

MULTI-FUNCTION OR SPECIALIST ORGANIZATIONS

The final variable to be looked at is the extent to which, or whether, all the animal health and husbandry services provided to pastoralists, including even range management and water development, should be combined in one integrated multi-function livestock service. This service might be represented at field level at the point of contact with pastoralists by a single multi-purpose 'herd-level worker', with a single chain of command leading up all the way to a 'director of livestock services' in the national capital, possibly even to a Minister of Livestock Development. Or instead, there might be a number of specialist organizations, each with their own field staff, each dealing with a separate activity such as general animal health, tsetse and trypanosomiasis control, artificial insemination, milk production, sheep, ranches, etc.

This issue has, in the past, often been a bitter bone of contention between veterinarians and other professionals. It has been claimed (Provost, 1978) that in Francophone countries the pattern is one of an integrated service, while in Anglophone countries there are several separate and specialist organizations; but the picture is more complex than that. Even in colonial times, Anglophone countries changed their livestock services backwards and forwards at different times between more integrated and more specialist structures (e.g. in Tanganyika between 1930 and 1955), and different structures operated in different areas (e.g. in dry as opposed to high potential areas in Kenya) and for different classes of farmers. A livestock service may be integrated at the very top, then split into specialized sections in the middle, for example at regional or provincial level, and then come together again at district level or below. In some countries a sharp distinction is drawn between animal *health* functions performed by veterinarians and animal *production* (or 'husbandry') functions which are the responsibility of graduates in other animal sciences. In India, however, although responsibility for all livestock activities tends to come together at the top, at the level of state departments of animal husbandry, further down it disintegrates into a multitude of special programmes for different kinds of livestock, for different social classes, for general animal health, for milk production, and so on. Yet in all these specialist units it is professionals with veterinary qualifications who play the leading roles. The distinction, therefore, between specialist and multi-function services is not always one between a system in which other professionals have a significant role to play and one which is dominated by veterinarians; it often is, however.

What are the factors which would cause one to choose a more specialist or a more multi-function service? One problem in the past has been the training and career opportunities of senior officials. Veterinarians have been in such short supply that, once initially qualified, there has then been scant opportunity for them (except in India) to take further training in specialist subjects. Instead, they have been swept into urgent activities to control livestock diseases and then the pressure of this work has prevented them from developing other activities and interests. Their work has tended to be mainly with cattle, partly because of their continuing greater economic importance, but partly also because more technical improvements in animal health are available for cattle than for other livestock; in some countries they have taken considerable interest in equines. In contrast, other kinds of livestock (shoats and camels) and other aspects, for example genetic improvement and livestock nutrition, have been relatively neglected where veterinarians have been responsible for a multi-function service.

Where other professionals who are not veterinarians have been recruited in a unified multi-function livestock service, they have found their promotion prospects blighted. For example, in Tanzania, in a unified 'livestock development' service, non-veterinarian graduates are recruited at a lower salary than veterinarians, whose training is longer, but they are in theory able to achieve parity in salary at a later stage. That sounds very fair. However, in practice, although the senior officials at regional level in a unified service are called 'regional livestock development officers', the requirements of the law (in whose drafting veterinarians played the predominant role) that only qualified veterinarians should prescribe or order drugs, are used to give preference to veterinarians in obtaining these senior posts and the prospects of non-veterinarians are restricted. (Source: senior veterinarians in Tanzania in 1977; Rweyemamu, 1974; Moris, 1981, p. 112.) The same process is repeated at national level, where the requirements of national law are reinforced by international agreements on health requirements for trade in livestock, and where the international solidarity of the veterinary profession again makes it difficult for non-veterinarians to be recognized as the heads of national livestock services. The inability of veterinarians to give much attention to livestock improvements other than animal health measures for cattle, and the reluctance of non-veterinarians to be forever the junior partners, provide permanent impulses for the substitution of several specialist services for unified multi-functional ones, except where, as in India, veterinarians are so numerous as to be able to diversify their interests.

In dry regions where the low overall density of human and livestock populations requires that the livestock services travel relatively further for each herd owner or animal contacted than in high potential areas, there is obviously a case, in order to minimize transport costs, for getting as many as possible different livestock improvement functions carried out at a single contact. In practice, however, the timing, frequency, and method of organizing 'contacts' for one purpose may be ill-adapted for another. On mass vaccination campaigns animals have to be marshalled and handled at vaccination crushes in very large numbers on each day. In Francophone Africa livestock assistants deal with between 200 and 500 animals on each 'touring' day in the field, and the daily number handled is not necessarily lower in dry areas than in those of higher potential. In Chad, for example, the highest number of animals is handled in the driest regions and the lowest in the least dry. In Niger it is the other way round (GTZ/SEDES, 1976). These 'touring' days include time spent travelling, so that neither the atmosphere at the vaccination crushes nor the time available make this a suitable occasion for providing extension advice to pastoralists. Vaccinations require annual or, at most, biannual visits to herds. In contrast, an AI service requires daily visits. Sales of livestock requisites such as mineral blocks or acaricides probably require the potential for contact not less often than once a month.

Mass vaccination campaigns may require only one livestock assistant per 50,000 head of livestock (one occasion per head per year, 400 head per livestock assistant per 'touring' day, 125 touring days per year per livestock assistant[8]). If feasible at all in dry regions, AI programmes would require, at the most optimistic estimate, one inseminator per 2500 head of cattle, and it might be as much as one inseminator for only 250 head.[9] These ratios represent extremes of minimum and maximum need for close contact, but they show clearly that there are considerable limits to the gains to be made by different improvements being delivered by the same resources of staff and transport. In practice in dry regions, as in others, the more complex and the wider the variety of the technical improvements that are on offer, the more likely it is that a single unified service will be of less convenience than a number of specialist ones.

CONCLUDING COMMENT

This chapter has looked at the choice between different forms of organization and management in some selected aspects of the improvement of animal health and husbandry. We have seen that in different regions of different countries at different times quite different forms of organization and management have been adopted to carry out essentially the same basic functions. In this component of pastoral development, the main focus is on the improvement of productivity and thereby increasing output. There are also equity implications in livestock improvement programmes, but neither equity nor the other objectives play as important a role as they do in the water and range components. In livestock improvement the dominating influence on the choice of form of organization and management is technology — what improvements have been developed by research, under what conditions (e.g. of temperature control) the inputs have to be stored, how frequently they have to be delivered to livestock. As technology has changed over the last 50 years, so also have the chosen forms of organization and management. Other important factors are the availability of the most highly skilled staff, i.e. veterinarians, and of finance. These factors tend to be determined outside the pastoral sector. The characteristics internal to pastoral situations which mainly influence choice of form are the density and mobility of the human and livestock populations.

NOTES TO CHAPTER 8

1. The most recent literature on this subject is Braend (1979), Robertson (1978), and Thuraisingham (1978). But the figures quoted also come from other sources.

2. The source of this information is British colonial veterinary department annual reports, especially for Kenya, Northern Nigeria and Tanganyika in the 1930s. Even with the technically inadequate rinderpest vaccines or immunizations then available, the main epizootics were contained if not eliminated.

3. For example Phanavet in Upper Volta and the parastatal Afghan Fertilizer Co. in Afghanistan (1977).

4. Note that this *recommended* density of centres in pastoral areas is lower than the *actual* density at the end of the 1970s. Governments seem unable to finance the actual density adequately.

5. The figure required when the output of a pastoral herd is consumed as the sole source of food for the owner and his family and is not exchanged for a cheaper form of energy is roughly 60 lu. See Dahl and Hjort (1976, p. 266). In economies where much pastoral output is sold lower numbers of livestock are required for the survival of the owner and his family.

6. In Kenyan Maasailand relatively sedentary pastoralists, according to Campbell and Mighot Adhola (1979), find a week, or even less, adequate notice. In more nomadic areas, with more scattered grass and water, longer notice would be needed to allow animals to congregate at a particular place on a particular day.

7. 'On-the-job training' is particularly difficult in pastoral areas and some sort of short in-service residential training will probably need to be substituted. This point is discussed further in Chapter 11.

8. GTZ/SEDES (1977) suggest that livestock assistants can spend as much as 150 days in the year touring. In the mid-1970s the highest average figure actually recorded for any Francophone Sahelian country was 80 (Upper Volta) and the lowest 14 (Senegal). However, these figures were recorded under conditions of financial crisis which restricted touring.

9. In Kenya 260 inseminators cover a herd of between 250,000 and 300,000 breeding females — say 260,000. If breeding females account for 40 per cent of a pastoral herd we get 260,000 ÷ 260 ÷ 0.4 = 2500. Most of Kenya's inseminations are done by inseminators travelling by car whose productivity, at an average of 15 inseminations per day, is four times that of those using motor cycles and ten times that of those on pedal cycles. For source of data see Duncanson (1975).

Chapter nine
Marketing and processing

INTRODUCTION

This chapter is concerned with the marketing and processing (other than processing for subsistence consumption) of pastoral output, i.e. pastoral marketing. After a brief review of the scope of the subject, it will examine two important assumptions — about the responsiveness of pastoralists to changes in the prices of their outputs and about the inefficiency of free marketing systems (these will be defined later) — that frequently lie behind the interventions by governments of Third World countries in pastoral marketing. It will then review some features of pastoral marketing systems which tend to distinguish them from non-pastoral systems and which may, therefore, lead to different solutions being appropriate.

Subsequently it will examine, one by one, four major options which particularly address, or are affected by, these distinguishing characteristics of pastoral marketing. The first of these options is essentially a technical rather than an organizational one; it examines different ways of transporting livestock from producer to consumer. The remaining three options are organizational and concern the role that government can play in improving marketing; and five specific criteria will be suggested for evaluating the appropriateness of particular interventions. A final section of the chapter will deal with a somewhat distinct but nevertheless related subject — the strategy of stratification that allocates to different geographical regions and kinds of organizations specialist functions in the production chain according to their comparative advantage. The reasons for discussing this strategy here rather than in Chapter 2 alongside the other two strategies will be explained.

THE SCOPE OF PASTORAL MARKETING

A number of different aspects fall under the general heading of marketing (and processing) pastoral output. We can classify these under seven general headings. One is the provision of convenient and reliable points of sale to which pastoralists can with ease take what they have to sell, and where they can be sure of obtaining a buyer offering fair terms. Milk or ghee collection posts at or near pastoralist settlements where purchases of milk or ghee take place daily, on cash terms at a fair price, are examples of this aspect. A second aspect is the provision of improved channels of communication through which buyers and sellers can obtain market information of use to them. Daily radio bulletins on which the numbers of livestock traded and the prices paid at terminal, secondary, and primary markets are announced are examples of this aspect. A third is the provision of facilities whereby the quality of the product can be improved, or where different grades can be distinguished and the supply and demand for each better matched. Drying sheds for hides and skins, combined with an inspection, grading, and marking service are examples of this aspect. A fourth is the provision of facilities whereby increased quantities of livestock and products can be handled. The provision of boreholes on stock routes or expanded capacity at abattoirs which can handle not only 'normal' but also 'drought-time' flows of livestock are examples of this aspect. A fifth is the provision of facilities to reduce real marketing costs. An example of this is improvements in transport facilities that reduce the numbers of deaths or the loss of weight in livestock *en route* between producing and consuming areas. A sixth aspect is interventions to change the level and stability of prices which consumers have to pay or producers receive. Price stabilization schemes, or policies and regulations to ensure that livestock are sold under competitive conditions, perhaps only at auctions, or after they have been weighed, or at controlled prices, are examples of this aspect. Finally, there is an aspect concerned to ensure that livestock and livestock products do not cause injury to human health.

Livestock marketing (including processing except where otherwise stated) can be used to promote almost all the objectives of pastoral development already discussed, such as increases in or stabilization of output and incomes or environmental conservation; and most of the aspects mentioned in the previous paragraph can be used to serve each of these objectives. In this chapter we shall deal with some of the aspects in a fair amount of detail and others cursorily or not at all. Partly this is for reasons of space and partly for lack of adequate case studies carried out by other people on which this study could in turn draw. One very obvious defect is that this chapter will almost exclusively deal with the marketing of live cattle in Africa. There are virtually no studies in Asia (at least not in the English or French languages) which match up to the depth and quality of studies undertaken in Africa — except for studies on milk marketing in India which are of doubtful relevance to any other pastoral areas; and the marketing of live sheep and goats, and of animal products generally, has not attracted the same attention as the marketing of live cattle. For Africa some justification for this emphasis on cattle can be drawn from their relatively greater importance in terms of animal biomass, production, and marketed output. Nevertheless, there are surprising and important gaps in our knowledge of the marketing of other kinds of livestock and of other products.

In what follows in this chapter some attention will be given to five out of the seven aspects of pastoral marketing mentioned above. Only the last two, price stabilization and human health, will receive no consideration at all, although the improvement of the quality of marketed output (the third aspect mentioned above) will receive only passing attention.

TWO FREQUENT ASSUMPTIONS

Behind governments' interventions in pastoral marketing there often lie important assumptions about how existing marketing systems work. Before discussing the various options that are available for improving pastoral marketing, we shall discuss in some detail the validity of two such assumptions.

Pastoralists' responses to changes in the price of pastoral products

One important assumption often made concerns the effect of price rises (or falls) on the desire of pastoralists' to sell livestock (and their products). Economists, although they are usually introduced early on in their professional training to the concept of a 'perverse supply response' in which a seller reacts to a price rise by selling less and to a price fall by selling more, tend to *expect* a 'positive' response in which price and the quantity offered vary together and in the same direction. Pastoral development schemes planned by economists, therefore, frequently have as a feature a planned price rise which is expected to evoke further sales, without any consideration or study of whether in the particular case in question the response is likely to be positive or negative.[1] In contrast, social anthropologists, who frequently dislike statistics and rely on pastoralists' own statements, often tend to use the concept of a 'target cash income' which, once achieved, a pastoralist will see no good reason to try to surpass; he will reduce the numbers of animals he sells if higher prices enable fewer animals to achieve his target income for him. There is very little respectable evidence to support either view.

In fact, both conceptually and in terms of measurement, the case of pastoralists, who consume a significant proportion of their own livestock products and who sell live animals, presents the most acute difficulty in both defining and measuring responses to price changes. Their high consumption of their own livestock products means that there is both an important 'price elasticity' and an 'income elasticity' effect. 'Price elasticity' measures the response of supply (or demand) to changes in price; 'income elasticity' measures the response of demand to changes in income; and 'cross elasticity' (mentioned again later) measures the changes in demand for one commodity when there is a change in the relative prices between it and another commodity. A higher price for a pastoral product through a 'price elasticity of supply' effect may tend to make pastoralists want to sell (or produce) more of it, but this may be partially masked by the fact that the higher price gives them a higher 'total income', some of which they want to 'spend' on consuming their own livestock production. On the other hand, the fact that livestock are not only a commodity which can be sold immediately but are also used as 'capital equipment' to generate more of the same commodity in the future — calves in the case of breeding females and bulls, more meat at a later date in the case of castrated males — means that the effect of a price rise which is expected by the pastoralists to endure may be to *reduce* the amount they offer to sell in the short term because of their intention to sell more in the longer term. Similarly, a price fall may induce them to decide to get rid of — i.e. sell more — stock which they had been keeping with a view to higher sales some time in the future.

These cases illustrate difficulties in *defining* 'supply'. Are we talking about the long term or the short? Do we include in 'supply' what the pastoralist allocates to his own investment or consumption requirements or only what he offers for sale in the market? We shall need a different definition depending on whether we are interested in discussing the motivation of pastoralists, estimating future herd numbers, or providing enough cash to finance a parastatal livestock marketing organization's purchases.

There are also acute problems in *measuring* supply response, partly because of the dearth of reliable statistics of any kind in dry areas, partly because statistics for livestock sales usually only record numbers of livestock sold and not their weight (which may fluctuate in sympathy with other variables such as rainfall), partly because, particularly in dry areas, although fluctuations in the numbers sold may be strongly influenced by price changes, the price-induced fluctuations may nevertheless be matched by fluctuations due to other causes. In Swaziland, for example, 40 per cent of inter-annual fluctuations in offtake rates have been attributed to price changes, 25 per cent to rainfall variation, and 35 per cent to other unidentified factors (Doran, Low, and Kemp, 1979). Since prices may change in sympathy with weather conditions, it is obviously very difficult to separate out the impact of the pure 'price-effect' on supply and the influence that the weather has on the abundance of grazing and, therefore, on the ability of pastoralists to retain their livestock. A further complication arises from the fact that the prices expressed simply in money terms may not take into account fluctuations in the prices of cereals — a major item in the expenditure of many pastoralists — which may also vary systematically in relation to rainfall.

It is not surprising, in any case, that no consistent evidence can be found for or against a single universal proposition about the supply response of pastoralists to changes in the prices of their outputs. Equally, 'rational' pastoralists will respond differently depending on their local conditions. In pastoral communities which are isolated from the money economy (the area where Sudan, Ethiopia, Kenya, and Uganda meet is an outstanding example and Tanzanian Maasailand in the mid-1970s is another), once minimal money requirements for taxes and perhaps school fees have been met, a pastoralist may really have no need for further money, not because he does not *want* articles from the money economy, but because no one will supply them. In this case a rise in price will probably divert some animals from market to the pastoralist's own consumption, and, in theory although not I suspect in practice, if the price rise is expected to be permanent could lead to a modest reduction in herd size, since the pastoralist will not need to keep as big a herd as before in order to maintain the reduced level of marketed output needed.

In a more money-oriented economy, where plenty of consumer goods are on sale but where the technical means to increase livestock production are absent, then the effect of an increase in price will depend on whether the pastoralist prefers to sell yet more livestock (at the expense of his own consumption of these) in order to buy cheaper consumer goods (a low income elasticity of demand for pastoral output and a high cross-elasticity between pastoral and non-pastoral goods), or to buy the same or even less amounts of consumer goods and instead to consume more pastoral output (high income elasticity of demand for pastoral output). In contrast, in a cash economy which has the technical means, purchasable for money, to expand output (e.g. veterinary drugs or feed supplements), the most probable response to a price rise for pastoral products may be negative in the short term, as pastoralists retain from market some steers for further fattening before sale or some cull cows in order to try and get another calf out of them. There may be some further substitution between sales and domestic consumption in this case also as a consequence of income and cross-elasticities. In the long run, the response may be positive as the retained animals and any additional offspring come back on to the market. One does not have to call in aid an 'East African cattle complex' or any other 'black box' to explain these differential responses; they are all explicable in terms of differential access to the market provision of means to expand consumption or production. On the other hand, one does not need to rule out other explanations either.

The inefficiency of free marketing systems

Another assumption which often lies behind government interventions is that private marketing systems not substantially regulated by government — we can call these 'free' marketing systems — are inherently inefficient and exploitative. In particular, they are often believed to be incapable of responding to new opportunities (in terms of space, or quality of products), to have unnecessarily high levels of marketing costs, partly because of the presence in the marketing system of too many links and intermediaries, and to allow traders to earn an excessive level of profits through their ability to exploit their monopoly positions and pastoralists' ignorance of the true value of their livestock and products. Often government interventions in the marketing system are proposed without any study of the efficiency of the existing free system, or occasionally even in the face of evidence that the existing system functions quite well.

Whereas little evidence exists either for general or particular propositions about the price responsiveness of pastoralists, there is now an accumulated body of evidence which suggests that free marketing systems are usually quite efficient. This does not rule out the possibility that in a few cases such systems function very badly or that marginal improvements can be made in many systems. Efficiency can be measured in a number of ways. Table 9.1

Table 9.1 A comparison of free marketing systems in live animals in selected African countries (all figures in % of trader's selling price[a])

| Country | Proportion of trader's selling price accruing to: | | | | | | | Method of transport[d] | Distance over which transported[e] | Type of market at which livestock were | | Type of livestock |
	Producer's return	Trader's profit[b]	Sub-total	Taxes	Lorry, ship, rail, costs	Losses and shrinkage[c]	Other			Bought[f]	Sold[f]	
Ivory Coast	90	4	6	1	0	1	4	F	D; long	SE	SE	Cattle
Ivory Coast	79	9	12	1	0	1	10	F	D; short	P	SE	Cattle
Ivory Coast	78	7	15	8	0	1	6	F	I; long	P	SE	Cattle
Ivory Coast	78	4	18	8	3	2	5	F, R	I; long	P	SE	Cattle
Ivory Coast	80	8	12	1	4	2	5	F, L	D; long	SE	T	Cattle
Ivory Coast	70	7	23	8	4	7	4	F, R	I; long	P	T	Cattle
Ivory Coast	60	6	34	12	8	11	3	R	I; long	SE	T	Cattle
Kenya	60	13	27	NA	22	NA	NA	L	D; long	P	T	Sheep
Kenya	93	2	5	NA	3	NA	NA	L	D; short	P	T	Cattle
Madagascar	76	7	17	1	0	7	9	L	D; short	P	SE	Cattle
Madagascar	73	9	18	1	0	11	6	F	D; long	P	T	Cattle
Madagascar	79	6	15	Neg.	5	8	2	F, R	D; long	SE	T	Cattle
Madagascar	83	5	12	Neg.	4	7	1	L	D; short	SE	T	Cattle
Madagascar	76	5	19	2	8	7	2	L	D; long	SE	T	Cattle
Mali	23	16	61	36	8	8	9	F, L	I; long	P	SE	Cattle
Mali	33	6	61	36	8	8	9	F, L	I; long	SE	SE	Cattle
Mali	26	6	68	38	17	NA	13	F, L	I; long	P	SE	Sheep
Mali	94	3	3	NA	NA	NA	NA	F	D; long	P	SE	Cattle
Somalia	63	7	30	3	11	6	10	F, S	I; long	P	T	Sheep
Upper Volta	76	5	14	4	0	2	13	F	D; short	P	SE	Cattle
Upper Volta	53	14	33	11	7	13	2	F, R	I; long	P	T	Cattle

NA = information not available.

[a] 'Trader's selling price' includes not only what he actually received but also what he would have received if there had been no losses or shrinkage en route. In most cases the selling price is for a live animal, but in the first Upper Volta case, and in both Kenya cases, it is for the meat valued at wholesale level.

[b] 'Trader's profit' is what is left to the trader after paying all other expenses as a return to his own entrepreneurship, his own labour, and to all the capital employed (including borrowed capital).

[c] 'Losses and shrinkage' include deaths, strays, and losses of weight en route. In some cases (e.g. Kenya) shrinkage is not adequately measured.

[d] F = on foot; L = lorry; R = rail; S = ship.

[e] D = domestic, i.e. movements within one country; I = international, i.e. movements across one or more international boundaries. Short = less than 300 km; long = more than 300 km.

[f] P = primary market, where sellers are mainly pastoralists; SE = secondary market, where sellers and buyers are mainly traders; T = terminal market, where buyers are mainly butchers.

Sources: Ivory Coast — Staatz (1979); Kenya — McArthur and Smith (1979); Madagascar — SEDES (1979); Mali — Swift (1979); CRED (1980), Vol. 3; Somalia — Reusse and Kassim (1978); Upper Volta — Herman (1979).

reproduces some of the evidence about the proportion of the price which traders receive, at wholesale level,[2] that is, paid by them to producers (producer's return), or consumed in costs of various kinds, and/or retained by the trader as 'trader's profit', i.e. as a return to his own labour, entrepreneurship, and to all the capital he employs.[3] Although there are some problems of comparability in this evidence, which particularly concern the international boundaries and distance (and period of time) over which the livestock were transported between places of purchase and sale, the treatment of 'overhead' expenses, and the extent to which 'shrinkage' (loss of weight) was properly measured, nevertheless in broad terms the results are comparable. The systems compared are described as 'free', because government is not directly concerned in them as a trading partner and because any government price controls or other regulations are largely ineffective.

Some general impressions emerge from Table 9.1. In about two-thirds of the cases cited the producer receives 70 per cent or more of the price that the livestock trader eventually realizes at wholesale level. In about 95 per cent of cases the traders' profit amounts to less than 10 per cent of his selling price. Losses and shrinkage tend, on average, to be *higher* when 'modern' methods of transportation (lorry, rail, ship) are involved (average loss 6 per cent) than when livestock are trekked on foot (average loss 4 per cent). However, losses due to shrinkage are notoriously difficult to estimate since they depend so much on the timing of the watering and feeding of animals in relation to their weighing before and after the shrinkage. Apparent weight losses of up to 15 per cent of the initial weight — the equivalent of six months' or more normal growth — can be reduced by two-thirds by a mere two days of post-loss feeding (Ansell, 1971). Where international boundaries have to be crossed government taxes and similar levies become a significant element in inflating marketing costs and reducing producers' returns. There is a tendency, as one would expect, in those cases where long distances or crossings of international boundaries are involved for traders' profits to be higher because their capital is locked up for longer and at greater risk. Producers' returns tend to be higher when the only means of transport used is foot-trekking but this result is confused by the tendency for such cases also to involve shorter distances. In general, only simple averages have been compiled in arriving at these impressions and not complex cross-correlations.

The figures for 'producer's return' in Table 9.1 which come closest to support the conventional view of the 'exploited producer' are the first three sets of data from Mali, which show a 'producer's return' for cattle of only 23–33 per cent of the trader's final selling price and for sheep of only 26 per cent. These figures, which are right out of line with other figures for producer's returns in the table, are reported by Swift (1979, pp. 321–329), and refer to cattle purchased at pastoralists' camps, primary and secondary markets in East Mali in 1971 and exported to Ghana. In contrast, the fourth set of data for Mali shows a producer's return of 94 per cent and refers to cattle (of the same weight and sex as Swift's) purchased at a primary market in north-west Mali in 1977 and resold at a terminal market also in Mali (CRED, 1980, Vol. 3, p. 372). The differences in trader's profits between the two sources is also quite large, but none of them are greatly out of line with other figures for trader's profit in the table. The purchase price reported by Swift at 15,000–22,000 Mali Francs (FM) per head in 1971 is in marked contrast to the 70,000 FM per head reported by CRED for 1977. A consistent price series for Mali covering the period is not available, but in Ivory Coast, Mali's main export market, cattle prices doubled during this period and there was no change in the official exchange rates between the two countries.

It is not possible, at this distance in time and space, to determine with confidence why Swift's figures are so out of line with the others, but three reasons probably contributed. The lower end of the range of Swift's prices were recorded for purchases nearer the pastoralist's camp than most others and in a particularly remote area. The purchases occurred in the hot dry season during the years of the great Sahelian drought when producers were in a particularly poor bargaining position; CRED's figures were recorded at a time of cattle scarcity. Swift's purchases were for export to Ghana, a market which for a number of reasons was particularly risky. Nevertheless, there are anomalies between Swift's and the other figures in the table which are not satisfactorily explained by these three reasons. In all the figures given in Table 9.1 there is ample scope for their authors to have to make judgements in deciding which data are reliable and which are not. Such judgements inevitably reflect their expectations of what is normal.

Overall the results shown in Table 9.1, apart from those reported by Swift, do not indicate that there are startling improvements (although there are modest ones) to be gained in raising returns to producers simply by improving transportation systems or by reorganizing or regulating the marketing chain between the producer and the point at which sales of live animals are made to butchers or slaughter-houses. These results are in marked contrast to the opinions held during the 1960s, and there is an element of 'fashion' in these changes of opinions. Nevertheless, the studies on which these later opinions are based have tended to be much more thorough than the earlier ones which led to optimism about the scope for marketing improvements, especially in the form of state intervention. Thorough studies are still few, however, and what there are still rely too much on 'synthetic' data drawn from different traders or episodes and not enough on properly selected samples.

The efficiency of a marketing system is not only to be judged by the criterion of the extent to which the real costs of marketing or traders' profits are kept to a minimum but also by several other criteria (to be discussed later), including the extent to which the prices which a producer receives reflect what the consumer wants. One element in this criterion is the extent to which changes in prices at consumer level, due to changes in consumer tastes or in the balance between supply and demand at consumer level, are matched fully and quickly by changes in the price received by the producer so that the producers' production and sales plans adjust to suit consumers' need. We shall not discuss this element further here, although studies in West Africa indicate that non-government systems there are comparatively efficient in this respect (Shapiro, 1979). However, another element in this criterion is the extent to which the price which the producer receives for *each* animals or unit sold reflects consumers' preferences and is not largely composed of a random element reflecting 'luck' or 'bargaining skill'. It is not sufficient that *on average* traders' profits be low and producer prices reflect changes in consumer prices. Producers will change their plans quicker and more fully, the less uncertainty and arbitrariness there is in the determination of prices of particular animals.

Two studies on free marketing systems in Africa throw light on this; on the whole they suggest that the random element in price formation is low. In Upper Volta about 80 per cent of the differences[4] in prices between individual male cattle sold can be explained by differences in the age of the animals, in the season of the year, in the immediate use (i.e. local slaughter or resale far away) for which the animal was intended, and in the market or region where it was sold (Herman, 1979). In Ethiopia, where, in addition to these factors, differences in weight and colour were also taken into consideration, the proportions of the differences in individual prices which can be explained were about 60–80 per cent in the case of cattle, 70–75 per cent in the case of sheep, and 80–90 per cent in the case of goats (Gabre Mariam and Hillmann, 1975).[5] These are very high figures considering that it was not possible in these studies to take into consideration objective but unquantifiable differences between animals, such as differences in their 'fatness' or 'health status' which are clearly very important factors. If these other objective factors could also be quantified, the total proportion of price differences which are random or inexplicable might be extremely small. The results of these two studies in markets where producers confront traders are matched by results in Ivory Coast terminal markets where traders meet butchers; here the distribution of price per kilogram of animals sold is tightly clustered round the mean (Staatz, 1979, p. 455).

One of the complaints most frequently levelled at free marketing systems is that they contain a large number of intermediaries and agents, each of which demands a commission, thereby adding to marketing costs, but who perform no useful service. Where careful analysis has been made of free marketing systems (i.e. Herman, 1979; Staatz, 1979), this charge tends not to be supported. Overall, the total commissions levied by all intermediaries (other than the direct traders whose profits we have aleady discussed) taken together seem to come to less than 3 per cent of the wholesale value of the animals, and these intermediaries play an important role — in guaranteeing ownership of livestock or repayment of credit — in bringing buyers and sellers into early contact with each other, and in providing information on current market prices, in both a particular market and in markets generally, and on other conditions to buyers and sellers. These are valuable services which permit a generally higher level of producers' prices than would otherwise be possible.

THE DISTINCTIVE FEATURES OF PASTORAL MARKETING SYSTEMS

Many features of livestock marketing are common to both pastoral and non-pastoral systems alike. However, in pastoral systems certain features are more frequent or occur to a more marked degree. One of these is that the flow of livestock and livestock products through marketing channels fluctuates more widely between different seasons of the year and between different years. I have not been able to find quantitative evidence to prove this point; either national marketing statistics do not differentiate between output from pastoral and non-pastoral systems or, when they do, the figures have such defects in them, for example some of the output has been intermittently smuggled over national boundaries, that not enough confidence can be put in them. The *relatively* greater fluctuation of marketed flows originating from pastoral than from non-pastoral systems is, therefore, only a probably valid hypothesis at this stage, but it is one which can easily be explained on *a priori* grounds of the greater variability of rainfall in drier than in higher potential areas; this greater variability causes fluctuations both in pastoralists' willingness to sell and in traders' ability to move themselves and livestock in and out of pastoral areas.

In absolute terms, however, we have evidence for some pastoral situations that the fluctuations in market flow are wide. For example, in Kenya the government's Livestock Marketing Division (LMD), which in most years since 1960 purchased between one-half and two-thirds of all cattle sold out of Kenya's northern rangelands (an area of 200,000 km^2), purchased an annual average over 18 years of 30,000 head, with a low annual figure of 1000 and a high of 61,000 (White and Meadows, 1980). The coefficient of variation[6] of annual purchases is 51 per cent. The LMD's throughput was partly governed by its own policies and marketing system, as well as by what pastoralists offered. Rather less reliable figures for total purchases, including those by private traders, from this area during the same period, show an annual average of 51,000, a low of 22,000, a high of 77,000, and a coefficient of variation of 36 per cent. Records for primary markets in northern Upper Volta show a similar pattern in a non-government marketing system; the annual number of cattle offered for sale averaged, over nine years in three markets combined, 31,000, with a low of 15,000, a high of 45,000, and a coefficient of variation of 31 per cent (Herman, 1979). Fluctuations within a year are also very high. In northern Kenya the LMD's month (out of records for eight years) of lowest average numbers of purchases was April, with no purchases ever recorded; its month of highest average was January which had an average of 10,000, a record low of zero, and a record high of 28,000 (Cronin, 1978). In Upper Volta and north-east Uganda (Baker, 1968) variations in throughput from low to high months by a factor of 4–10 have been recorded.

Another feature of marketing in pastoral systems is the difficulty, due to the sparseness of the population, of collecting a sufficiently large mob of cattle, or of other livestock, to transport economically to distant consumption centres; either pastoralists have to walk the one or two animals they want to sell over long distances to the nearest market, or traders have to travel round the pastoral encampments to pick up animals one by one. 'Collecting' a mob of cattle on the dry west coast of Madagascar amounted to two and a half months of work and to 52 per cent of traders' monetary costs, compared to one month and 14 per cent of costs in the more humid north-east (SEDES, 1979, p. 57). The sparseness of the population is also reflected in generally poor communications infrastructure, and hence higher transportation costs. It is also likely to make it more difficult for buyer and seller to obtain up-to-date information, especially on price changes in major livestock markets elsewhere, and to reduce the scope for many buyers and sellers to congregate at one place where keen competition will lead to high price levels. In Upper Volta those livestock sellers who claimed they did not have adequate information about prices in the nearest major market received, on average, only 75 per cent of the average price received by those claiming adequate information. Similarly, there was for male cattle a substantial disadvantage, of the order of 10–15 per cent, in selling cattle away from a market, presumably partly due to the cost to be incurred by the trader in collecting animals from encampments rather than in markets, and partly due to the absence of competition from other buyers in such extra-market sales (Herman, 1979).

Another distinctive feature is the type of animal or product to be marketed and the technical aspects of doing so. For example, in comparison to other systems, in pastoral systems a higher proportion of all cattle sold consists of younger (immature) males and older females. There is far less emphasis on selling males that are ready for slaughter, because in most years there is not enough feed available on the drier rangelands to bring animals rapidly to slaughter weight and because the emphasis in cattle-herd management is on maximizing milk (rather than meat) production and on reproductive potential. However, the composition of marketed offtake is not stable and in years of good grazing the sale of immature males may dry up as they are kept for sale later at a higher weight. The precise proportion that animals from different classes will form of total marketed output will depend on a number of factors, but the figures from one predominantly pastoral and two predominantly non-pastoral systems in Upper Volta given in Table 9.2, illustrate the point.

In northern Kenya in the 1960s, 70 per cent of the LMD's purchases for export to the rest of Kenya were immatures (White and Meadows, 1980); however, since the LMD has a comparative advantage over private traders in the sale of immatures to ranchers (because of quarantine restrictions), this figure is probably not representative of all marketed output from the area.

Table 9.2 The age and sex composition of cattle sales of pastoral and non-pastoral systems in Upper Volta (all figures in % of total numbers sold — male and female combined between May 1976 and February 1977)

Class of animal	A pastoral system		Non-pastoral systems[a]	
	Male	Female	Male	Female
Animals less than two years old	46	6	4	1
Animals more than nine years old	1	18	5	17
Other animals	28	1	65	8
All animals	75	25	74	26

[a] Unweighted average of two non-pastoral systems.
Source: Herman (1979).

Although the physical conditions for moving livestock from producer to final market are tougher for animals from pastoral than from non-pastoral systems, the animals themselves are of a type, either too young or too old, which is unable to withstand the tough conditions well.

The difference between pastoral and non-pastoral systems in respect of live animals sold also applies to other products. Milk yields fluctuate seasonally in all livestock production systems, but they do so to a greater extent in pastoral systems because of the greater inter-seasonal variability in grazing conditions. Coupled with the relatively greater expense of transport in pastoral areas, this seasonal variation in milk supply means that milk is more usually transformed into relatively less bulky and perishable forms, e.g. ghee (clarified butter) and cheese, rather than being sold as fresh milk.

The incidence of disease in pastoral areas can have important effects on marketing; this is particularly true of contagious bovine pleuro-pneumonia (CBPP) which has a relatively long incubation period (up to six months) and the characteristic that apparently healthy animals can be 'carriers' of the disease, able to infect other animals, for up to three years (Hall, 1977). The incidence of infectious disease is probably no worse in pastoral than in non-pastoral areas — it may indeed be better. However, poor communications, low population densities and a mobile system of land-use in which 'contacts' with infected animals are less easy to identify than in settled areas, mean that measures to control disease may be more disruptive. Quarantine areas, within and across the boundaries of which livestock are forbidden to move, imposed as a consequence of a single outbreak, tend to be very large, and if they cover a line of communications for which there is no alternative route (due to a general absence of roads or of water points), they may disrupt the marketing of animals from other very large areas which are not themselves directly affected by the disease outbreak.

Another distinctive feature of pastoral situations with particular relevance to marketing is that frequently mentioned already in this study, namely that pastoralists are usually quite a small minority of the total population of their country and not one which has great political influence. A consequence is that, whatever the original intention with which a government initiated a marketing intervention (e.g. the fixing of retail and producer prices for livestock or meat, or quarantine controls on stock routes), when a clear conflict of interest between pastoralists and influential non-pastoral groups (e.g. urban consumers or rich dairy farmers in high potential areas) arises and when government has to make a deliberate and obvious choice between the two sets of interests, it is unlikely to support those of the pastoralists.

OPTIONS

Many of the aspects of improving marketing mentioned at the beginning of this chapter are applicable to the marketing of output from pastoral and non-pastoral areas alike. A thorough discussion of all of them would require a book of its own. In this chapter we shall discuss only those options for improving pastoral marketing for which a reasonable amount of evidence is available (this proviso excludes most kinds of output except live animals) and which particularly address, or are affected by, the special problems that are raised by the distinguishing features of pastoral areas that have been mentioned in the previous section. Thus, in the section which follows on the movement of livestock from producer to consumer it is the great fluctuations in market flows of pastoral output and the inappropriateness of specialist motorized livestock carriers to move about in and carry backloads to pastoral areas which is stressed; in the case of government abattoirs it is the political impotence of pastoralists, the problems that the physical weakness of cattle (too old and too young) marketed from pastoral areas pose for the location of abattoirs, and, again, the large fluctuations in market flows. In the case of direct government intervention in trading, emphasis is put on the highly fluctuating flows, the sparseness of the population, the types of animals or products, the incidence of disease, and the political impotence of pastoralists; with indirect interventions by governments, it is the sparseness of the pastoral population which is seen as the important factor.

THE MOVEMENT OF LIVESTOCK

One set of technical options which have been tried in a number of countries are improvements in livestock movement and transportation facilities. In some cases (e.g. Kenya, Botswana, Tanzania, Ethiopia) water points, with or without supporting grazing reserves or night security enclosures, have been constructed along routes where livestock move on foot. In other cases (e.g. in Somalia, Botswana, Ivory Coast) private entrepreneurs have adapted lorries to carry livestock, or governments have invested (as in Kenya and Botswana) in specialized livestock-carrying vehicles which can be used either for transporting livestock belonging to parastatal trading agencies or, on contract, the livestock of private traders. In some countries (Sudan, Botswana, Ivory Coast) governments or their parastatals are engaged in improving the facilities for livestock to move by railway.

Experience with these transportation facilities has been mixed. Water points along trek routes have often proved much more difficult and expensive to construct and maintain than had been expected (Ethiopia, Kenya, Somalia). To meet these costs traders have been charged fees for their use and have responded by using them as seldom as possible, instead using alternative routes or 'free' sources of water which are often available, except in the drier seasons or years. In some areas shortage of feed *en route* has prevented proper use of the water facilities provided. Since the facilities have been under-used by traders they have often been taken over, officially or surreptitiously, by private resident herds which have then hindered subsequent use by traders. Nevertheless, although often under-used, such trek-route facilities can provide an important safety valve for handling increased numbers in times of drought, and thus preventing the collapse of the marketing system at a time when pastoralists most need cash to purchase other foods. However, at the worst times of year and in the harshest droughts even these government-equipped stock routes may cease to carry a flow of livestock because of shortage of grazing along them.

In Somalia for many years ordinary lorries, with locally fitted modifications to permit the loading of up to 200 shoats (sheep and/or goats) in several tiers, have been successfully used by private traders to move livestock at times of year when trekking on foot is difficult. In Botswana both small traders and transport firms using ordinary lorries which carry, without substantial modification, between 15 and 50 head of cattle, have transported livestock from the interior to the abattoir as a 'backload' for their normal business of carrying consumer goods in the other direction. In recent years about 10 per cent of cattle destined for the export abattoir (which itself takes 90 per cent of all cattle sold) have arrived by lorry. In Kenya the LMD has introduced large specialist livestock carriers capable of moving up to 100 head of cattle each and has used these to move livestock both on its own account and on contract work for other traders.

There appear, in theory, to be substantial economies of scale in the transportation of livestock by lorry, with costs per head declining by up to 35 per cent as one progresses from small unmodified 7–ton lorries capable of carrying only 15 head of cattle to large specialist livestock-carrying 'road trains' capable of carrying 100 (McGowan *et al.*, 1979, Annex 5). There may be further economies in excess of this figure as a consequence of lower mortality and shrinkage losses in the more specialist facilities. However, in practice these economies of scale do not seem to materialize. The specialist livestock-carriers are not well adapted to moving other goods, both in terms of shape and capacity (much too large for the standard consignment of consumer goods required for typical settlements in pastoral areas). They also require rather better roads than smaller lorries and such roads are least available in pastoral areas. As a consequence, they pick up less easily forward (back-) loads into the interior or obtain other business during slack seasons, which, as we have already seen, are a feature of pastoral marketing.[7] Their greater capacity, in terms of numbers of livestock, implies greater overhead costs, in staff time and interest on capital tied up, in collecting a sufficiently large mob of cattle to transport. Even with full use being made of the time and capacity of motor transport, fixed overhead costs account for 40 per cent of total costs per beast transported; obviously this proportion rises as the equipment is under-utilized.

Detailed costing of alternative ways of transporting livestock have been made in West Africa; they seem to show that where trekking on foot is not rendered impossible by tsetse fly, by the encroachment of cultivation on stock routes, or by a total absence of livestock feed *en route*, it is a cheaper method of transport than either lorries or rail (sometimes half as expensive) even where there is spare capacity in the lorry-transport system and lorry-owners are prepared to charge lower rates than they would when full loads of other cargo are available (Staatz, 1979). For sheep and goats, because of their inability to trek long distances (at any rate in West Africa) and the greater seasonality in market demand for them, lorry transport is already competitive at certain times of year (CRED, 1980, Vol. 1, pp. 9 and 26–33). This detailed empirical work in West Africa is supported by more theoretical work in Botswana which showed that trekking on foot, where possible, is cheaper than by lorry and than the full economic cost of movement by rail, although not than the actual charges made for rail transport which are subsidized (McGowan *et al.*, 1979, Annex 5). There are, however, sometimes advantages in lorry transport, principally the ability quickly to exploit new or temporary situations (see, e.g. Baker, 1971), or to carry livestock through areas where, due to disease or drought, trekking is impossible, that are simply not reflected in these figures for relative cost. Important factors to be borne in mind are the great fluctuations in flows between seasons and be-tween years; in order to cope with these fluctuations one needs to be able to expand one's transporting capacity very rapidly when necessary, but not to be burdened with high overhead costs of idle equipment when the flows are low.

The principal lessons to be drawn then, from the consideration of relative cost and other advantage of different kinds of transportation, is that the advantages of lorries are likely mainly to arise from infrequent opportunistic access to lorry transport at moments of high demand (especially for shoats) or crisis, or of excess capacity in the general lorry-transport business of the sort requiring a highly decentralized decision-making and contractual organ-ization, and not from the provision of permanent services by a specialist and centralized livestock-transporting organization. One needs also to bear in mind that calculations of relative cost advantage are highly unstable over time and space in the light of relative changing prices. The data presented here all come from Africa because no corresponding information is available from Asia; probably this in itself indicates that the relatively high wage rates in South-West Asia (Iran and countries further west), coupled with low fuel prices, rule out, for trade livestock, all forms of transport other than lorries.[8]

FORMS OF GOVERNMENT INTERVENTION AND CRITERIA FOR EVALUATION

Frequently interventions are made by governments in livestock marketing systems in order to secure for pastoralists a higher proportion of the final price for the animal or its product. Such interventions can be made for the sake of the objectives of equity, or improving pastoralists' material welfare, or, on the assumption of a positive price elasticity of supply, in order to increase meat output for consumption outside the pastoral sector, or to reduce livestock populations for the sake of environmental conservation. Usually such interventions are based on misconceptions about how large traders' profits are in a free marketing system and about how inefficient are their operations. As we saw earlier in the chapter, in practice these operations are often not inefficient and the profits represent a relatively small part of the final price. Nevertheless, in spite of the misconceptions[9] on which they are based, we can still examine governments' interventions in marketing systems by various criteria — to see how far they do succeed in providing a convenient service to pastoralists, in reducing real marketing costs and traders' profits, in increasing producers' returns, in reducing the random element in the formation of prices for individual animals, and in providing a marketing channel which can cope with greatly increased flows in times of drought, thereby relieving pressure on the environment as well as providing an income to pastoralists when they need it most.

These interventions have tended to take one or more of three general forms: direct intervention by government or parastatal corporation into trading or processing at some point in the marketing chain; indirect attempts to make the purchasing of livestock more competitive and to increase the amount of information available to pastoralists; and the regulation, by law, of livestock prices so as to ensure that prices do not fall short of, or exceed, certain fixed limits. Price control has been tried in many countries but it does not raise distinctive issues for pastoral marketing systems and will not be discussed here in any detail.

Direct government interventions in abattoirs

Governments frequently intervene in the marketing chain by establishing or taking over abattoirs and meat-processing facilities for domestic and export markets. Such interventions have occurred, for example, in Afghanistan, Ethiopia, Somalia, Kenya, Tanzania, Botswana, Upper Volta, Cameroon, and elsewhere. This kind of intervention can be extremely important, but the experience is too complex to discuss in detail here. The crucial point is that abattoirs represent a point in the marketing chain where control or pressure by government is relatively easy to exercise. In export markets a government-owned, export-oriented abattoir and its output can be introduced more easily than a private one into bilateral intergovernmental trade negotiations between states in an attempt to procure privileged access to overseas markets. In domestic markets an abattoir with some sort of monopoly position presents a point at which price control can be much more effectively exerted than it can over a mass of minor traders and butchers. It can also use its monopoly position to introduce grades and types of product which enable the market to be split up into rather isolated segments, in each of which prices and quantities can be manipulated for various policy ends in the light of that segment of the market's particular characteristics.

In Botswana, where livestock owners are politically powerful, cattle prices have been kept very high and the government-controlled abattoir has played a key role in this. In Tanzania, where urban workers and consumers are powerful relative to livestock owners, the result of government intervention in slaughtering facilities has been to depress livestock prices. In Kenya the situation is very complex. In its earliest days the government-controlled Kenya Meat Commission (KMC) abattoir secured high prices for its politically influential European suppliers; subsequently in the 1960s it depressed livestock prices for the benefit of low-paid urban consumers at the expense of producers (Aldington and Wilson, 1968).[10] In the 1970s, as KMC lost much of its domestic monopoly position in urban markets and the surplus of exportable meat declined, it made large losses but its impact on producer prices has probably been less (McArthur and Smith, 1979; Chemonix International, 1977).

The experience of these government-owned abattoirs does not seem to be of special relevance to pastoral systems in comparison with non-pastoral, except in so far as the abattoirs' monopoly positions will usually end up (whatever the high sentiments with which they started) being used against the interests of politically weak pastoralists, and in so far as the relatively greater fluctuation in output from pastoral areas presents particularly difficult problems in determining the optimum capacity of the facilities. Inadequate slaughter-house capacity led to the collapse of livestock marketing systems in parts of Ethiopia during the 1973 drought, with disastrous effects on the welfare of pastoralists (particularly Afar). The procedures necessary to obtain a 'quota' at the abattoir (i.e. the right to have one's animal slaughtered and paid for at the official price) in Botswana puts owners of small herds at a disadvantage in relation to those of large at times, e.g. of drought, when the supply of livestock exceeds abattoir capacity (Consortium for International Development, 1976). However, the high fixed costs of abattoir facilities act as a force against maintaining spare capacity for periods of drought.

In export-oriented abattoirs with a capacity of 250,000–300,000 head of cattle per year, fixed costs amount to between a half (Botswana; source: McGowan *et al.*, 1979, Annex 6) and three-quarters (Kenya; source: Chemonix International, 1977, Ch. 5) of all processing costs per head when the abattoir runs at 50 per cent of capacity, falling to about a third when the abattoir runs near full capacity. In Botswana the extra fixed costs per head when the abattoir runs at half instead of full capacity only amount to about 10 per cent of the producers' 'doorstep' price. But in Kenya, where livestock prices are much lower, they amount to over 25 per cent of the producers' doorstep prices, and maintaining spare capacity in export abattoirs for use in periods of drought is likely, if the livestock producers have to pay the cost of this, to have a severe adverse effect on pastoralists' incomes and also on livestock output if the price elasticity of supply is significantly positive.

In abattoirs designed to serve, with a reasonable standard of hygiene, local urban markets, fixed costs tend to form a much lower proportion of total slaughtering costs — an estimated 20–25 per cent in Kenya (Chemonix International, 1977, Ch. 5). But unless the output from the pastoral sector forms a small proportion of national output, the price level for livestock is liable to collapse if all the extra output from pastoral areas in times of drought is unloaded on to the domestic market — where consumers' incomes are in any case likely to be adversely affected at that time.

We have seen earlier that cattle marketed from pastoral areas tend to be immature (say less than 30 months old) or very old, and this tendency presents particular problems in the transportation of these animals because they are not strong enough for long hard journeys either on foot or by lorry and rail. In the case of older animals, one response to the difficulty of transporting them over long distances has been to build abattoirs, especially ones with canning facilities for which these animals are more suitable, inside or close to pastoral areas. However, such facilities, when located far from industrial towns, tend to have high costs and frequently they have been sited to serve too small a cattle population, with the consequence that they have functioned at far below optimum levels of throughput with correspondingly high costs. In some cases (e.g. in Ethiopia, but this is not well documented) they seem to have tapped an accumulated reservoir of animals which, once drawn down, thereafter only produced a small annual flow for slaughter. In general, abattoirs located close to production rather than to consumption centres fail to obtain such high prices for offals — although this factor may be of less importance in the case of older animals.[11] Mobile abattoirs have been designed and tested which can move from area to area in order to process accumulated reserves of older livestock or sudden surges in the marketed flow, but the limited experience so far suggests that they are not economically viable (Chemonix International, 1977, Ch. 5). There appears to be no easy technical or organizational solution to marketing difficulties in respect of these older cattle.

Direct government interventions in trading

Governments also sometimes intervene by direct trading at lower levels in the marketing chain. In Kenya the LMD of the Ministry of Agriculture, or its antecedent organizations,[12] have bought cattle in dry regions either directly from pastoralists or from traders who had previously bought in this way over a period of 30 years. In Tanzania a parastatal, the Tanzania Livestock Marketing Corporation (TLMC), has sometimes purchased in competition with private traders and at other times has had a statutory monopoly (monopsony) which excluded private traders from any role at all. In Botswana a parastatal, the Botswana Livestock Development Corporation (BLDC), and in Somalia the Livestock Development Agency (LDA), purchase directly from producers or from traders in parts only of the pastoral areas. Similar examples can be found in several other countries although direct intervention in trading seems to be more common in East and southern Africa than in South-West Asia or West Africa. In Iran in the 1970s the Meat Organization imported meat and livestock or purchased livestock from traders as close as possible to the final consumption market. Its main function was to act as the channel for a government subsidy to consumers in two large cities.

The evidence available does not suggest that, in marketing live animals, governments, by direct intervention in trading, have been able to reduce the real level of marketing costs or the equivalent of traders' profits.[13] There are no well-founded published data contrasting the actual costs and profits of government and private traders operating at the same time and under the same conditions. The evidence consists, therefore, of a few cases where we can calculate the costs of all the elements in a government's direct marketing operation, and of other evidence which throws light on how efficient governments' operations are in selected elements. Such evidence can be unfair to the reputation of managers in government direct trading operations who are often compelled by government policy to trade under conditions, or in classes of stock, which private traders would not attempt because of the risks involved. The evidence should not be used, therefore, to demonstrate the inherent inefficiency of all governmental operations, only the limited point about reducing costs and margins.

Table 9.3 provides for government organizations involved in direct trading the same sort of information about the proportion of the final selling price that goes to different purposes as Table 9.1 provided for non-government trading systems, except that, whereas non-government traders operate at a profit or not at all, government organizations frequently operate at a loss covered by a government subvention, and Table 9.3 therefore has to have an extra column to allow for this. A comparison between the two tables shows that direct government trading does not usually lead to a higher proportion of the final selling price returning to the producer. The relatively high proportion returning to the producer from the operations of the LMD in Kenya is matched by several non-government trading systems in Table

Table 9.3 A comparison of direct government interventions in trading in live animals in selected African countries (all figures in % of trading organization's selling price)

Country	Proportion of organization's selling price[a] accruing to:								Method of transport[c]	Distance over which transported[c]	Type of market[c] at which the livestock were:		Type of livestock
	Trading organizations[b]				Other costs								
						Within which:							
	Producers' return	Profit or (loss)	Over-heads	Sub-total	Taxes	Lorry, ship and rail charges	Losses and shrinkage	Other			bought	sold	
Somalia[d]	67	(12)	NA	45	4	15	13	13	F, L, S	I; long	P	T	Sheep
Tanzania[e]	52	(1)	6	44	5	13	25	1	F, R	D; long	P	T	Cattle
Kenya[f]	83	(20)	37		NA	NA	9	NA	F, R, L	D; long	P/SE	SE/T	Cattle

NA = Information not available; F = on foot; L = by lorry; R = by rail; S = by ship.
[a] The organization's selling price (which in the case of Somalia is c.i.f. Jeddah including hypothetical foreign currency premium) is for a live animal and includes not only the price which was actually received but also what would have been received if there had been no losses or shrinkage *en route.*
[b] See text for different treatments of profits and overheads in government and non-government trading systems.
[c] See notes d–f to Table 9.1 (p. 204).
[d] The organization is the Livestock Development Agency in 1978. Source: Reusse and Kassim (1978).
[e] The organization is the Tanzania Livestock Marketing Corporation in 1975. Source: Texas A. and M. University (1976).
[f] The organization is the LMD in 1968–79. The data come from official sources.

9.1, and in any case is only achieved by a government subsidy equal to 20 per cent of the final selling price. The combination of overheads and other costs incurred by government trading organizations is greater than the corresponding figures for profits and other costs of non-governmental organizations.

The relatively high costs of government trading activities are not surprising. Officials of government trading organizations are paid high wages and field allowances throughout the year whether or not they buy any animals; government organizations have to observe quarantine and other animal health regulations which are extremely costly and which private traders often manage to avoid; government policy often forces government organizations to buy livestock of a kind or at times when serious mortality or losses of condition between point of purchase and point of sale have been inevitable. These factors were particularly important in the cases of Tanzania and Kenya during the mid-1960s. Dishonesty among agents and employees is also a serious problem which affects both government and non-government traders, but whereas a private trader can simply cease to use an agent or employee of whom he is suspicious, a government organization will probably have to obtain a conviction in a court of law before it can dismiss one of its staff. Although direct government intervention in trading is often advocated in order to overcome the problems caused by inadequate competition between private traders, in practice it tends only to substitute a legalized state monopoly over which government has inadequate control and whose monopolistic position is exploited by its employees for their own ends.

We can examine the appropriateness of direct intervention by governments in trading in the light of the distinguishing features of pastoral marketing systems discussed earlier — the highly fluctuating flows, the sparseness of the population with consequences for the costs of collecting mobs of animals and the dissemination of information, the type of animal or product, the incidence of disease, and the political impotence of pastoralists. Highly fluctuating flows militate against the financial viability of government marketing organizations with their high overhead costs and specialist functions; so does sparseness of population where what is required is a trader who can spread the high cost of travel over several enterprises. In many pastoral systems the bottom tier of trading, that is, the collection of a handful of animals from pastoralist camps to take to the nearest market, is most cheaply done by members of the pastoral community who may not yet have accumulated a large enough herd of their own to be self-sufficient fully employed pastoralists, but whose credibility in the local community is high enough for their neighbours to extend them credit for the period necessary to take the animals to market and to bring back the cash. Government trading organizations may more faithfully obey quarantine regulations and price controls; but the weaker the pastoralist community is politically the more likely it is that such controls are biased against pastoralist producers of livestock and in favour of urban consumers or, as in Kenya (Raikes, 1981, p. 190), the owners of dairy or other grade stock in high potential areas who do not want to face either competition in markets or the expense of constant revaccination of their animals against CBPP or foot-and-mouth disease and who, therefore, want to throw the burden of control on to pastoralists.

Most of these arguments suggest that direct government intervention in livestock trading is not usually appropriate in the light of the special features of pastoral livestock marketing. Nevertheless, there is one respect in which such direct intervention does meet a particularly pastoral need; this in in time of drought when very large numbers of livestock are suddenly offloaded into the markets by pastoralists who need cash to buy increasingly expensive food, and who suspect that their livestock are not going to survive much longer and therefore prefer to get even a low price for them rather than to suffer total loss. Both in Tanzania and in Kenya in the mid-1970s government livestock marketing organizations played an important role (and one largely unappreciated by ministries of finance and international donors) in getting livestock out of pastoral areas at a time when private traders no longer felt able to take the risk of heavy mortalities and consequent financial loss. This intervention helped both pastoralists' incomes and environmental conservation. In theory, of course, governments could refrain from direct trading in such circumstances, but still achieve the same result by offering adequate financial incentives to traders to offset their risks; in practice, no one can precisely calculate the risks and the incentives necessary to offset them, and governments are naturally very reluctant in times of drought to appear to be enabling private traders to make large profits from someone else's misfortune.

Indirect government interventions in pastoral marketing

In many countries and pastoral situations, as an alternative or in addition to intervening directly in trading, governments have intervened indirectly by regulating non-government systems. In several countries governments have tried to prevent or discourage private trading in livestock except at recognized markets where an auction system is operated, sometimes in conjunction with the installation of weigh-scales which enable both buyer and seller to know an animal's weight and so to compare, on that basis, the price being offered. In some cases only 'licensed' traders are allowed to purchase animals, and the issue of licences is restricted so as to prevent too many traders trying to make a livelihood out of too few livestock and so, allegedly, inflating unit costs. In some countries attempts have been made to introduce an official grading system for animals (e.g. in South Africa) and meat (e.g. in Kenya) so as to enable higher prices to be paid for superior qualities. In some cases information on market conditions is broadcast on the radio.

Evidence on the efficacy of these measures is patchy and contradictory. In many countries where weigh-scales have been introduced they have not been used or have soon broken and not been repaired. In other countries they have been successfully used for many years but have subsequently been abandoned, while in other cases they were ignored to start with but later became acceptable. They have usually been introduced on the assumption that knowing the weight of his animal will enable a pastoralist to hold out for a better price against an otherwise more experienced trader; but when the scales have not been used it has been assumed that it is the pastoralist who dislikes them. However, both assumptions may be unjustified. Where a system of 'market intermediaries' exists as in Upper Volta, their expertise and knowledge may be available to pastoralists who will not then be in a disadvantaged position *vis-à-vis* the buyer. Where weigh-scales are not used, it may be because traders dislike using them, and spread rumours about their inaccuracy or actively sabotage them. In any case, the inability of pastoralists to judge the value of their animals may have been overestimated and the importance of weight overemphasized relative to other characteristics (e.g. fatness, health) of an animal which determine its value.

In Tanzania a restriction on the number of trading licences in two regions led to such a decline in competition between buyers that livestock owners refused to continue to bring their livestock to market (Texas A. and M. University, 1976, Vol 1, p. 93). In Ethiopia, on the other hand, a detailed statistical analysis found that the number of traders buying at a market did not seem to affect the price level to a significant degree (Gabre Mariam and Hillmann, 1975, pp. 36 and 47–52). This finding, however, is subject to two contradictory interpretations:

(1) that there is such strong collusion between traders, even when there are many of them, that a reduction in their numbers does not affect their ability to fix prices;
(2) that competition is so intense between those consumers buying directly for their own use and traders buying to resell later that, within the range of values observed for the number of traders (between 0 and 51), an increase or decrease does not alter the degree of competition.

Auction systems have a similar chequered history. In ex-British East Africa they were much favoured in the closing years of the colonial regime, but have tended to fall into disuse since then. An expensive attempt to introduce them under a World Bank-financed marketing scheme in Ethiopia totally failed. Governments have tended to assume that only through auction sales could pastoralists obtain adequate information about current levels of prices and adequately competitive conditions be obtained to force traders to pay the full value of the livestock sold. No thorough studies have been carried out which compare the level of prices obtained in an auction ring with prices obtained at a market of similar total throughput, but with sales being concluded on the basis of direct negotiation between buyers and sellers. In Sukumaland in Tanzania a study, whose methodology is not disclosed, reported that 'a comparison of [auction] ring and private sales [in the same market] revealed that generally [prices in] the former are higher' (Hatfield, 1971). However, many comparisons made are between prices at an auction and prices away from a market altogether, in which case one is not comparing marketing systems only but also places (and hence costs) of sale and purchase.

A great deal of attention gets paid in official reports to the prices at which livestock are sold, and rather little to the convenience of the sale to pastoralists. In Sukumaland in Tanzania sellers disliked the lack of privacy involved in an auction sale, which enabled tax-collectors and party and club treasurers as well as importunate relatives to know only too well how much cash was available to be looted (Hatfield, 1971, quoting Jina, 1970). In any case, auction sales require not only buyers and sellers but also auction masters and other officials with a bad record for attendance and punctuality and also for corruption. The more arid the area and the sparser the population, the further will a pastoralist have to drive his animals to get to market and the greater difficulty will he have in feeding and watering them there if he does not obtain a quick sale. The sparser the population, the less frequently (and probably the less reliably) will market days be held near by because the volume of sales will not justify the attendance of traders and officials. Distance to and frequency of markets, together with the orderliness with which business is conducted, all help to determine convenience of marketing to the pastoralist.[14]

Measures which forbid any transactions in cattle except at markets may improve the level of prices at which pastoralists sell their animals: but this may take place at the expense of costs and inconvenience to the pastoralists in taking their livestock over long distances to markets which may be delayed or cancelled — an expense far in excess of the improved prices to be obtained at markets. As we saw earlier, collecting livestock mobs of adequate size to transport to a far-off consumption centre is a time-consuming job which may take a couple of months and a high proportion of a trader's total costs: but these *are* real costs, and forcing the pastoralist to do this part of the job by taking his livestock to a market only transfers the cost from the trader to the pastoralist. All the evidence (see Herman, 1979; Texas A. and M. University 1976, p. 75; Dahl and Sandford, 1978, p. 136) suggests that pastoralists are perfectly aware that they get higher prices for their livestock in markets than at their camps, but nevertheless sometimes choose to save time and to get their money quickly in preference to the higher price. In some cases this is not so much preference as necessity, when, for example, auction markets are held only every six months and their timing can be influenced by traders with an interest in picking up livestock cheaply from pastoralists forced into 'distress' sales by drought and the long interval before the next official auction market takes place (Hjort, 1979, pp. 80–87).

Although detailed studies of existing free marketing systems have usually found that they work rather efficiently, no one would deny that sometimes they do not; on these occasions traders make high profits, pastoralists cannot sell conveniently at fair prices, and the prices paid for individual animals do not reflect these animals' true worth. The real question is under what sorts of circumstances government interventions will improve or worsen the situation. Many of the indirect interventions in regulating markets have involved high costs for the salaries of auctioneers, market clerks, attendants, and their transport. These marketing costs are then usually passed on to buyers and sellers through the levying of market fees, which discourage people from coming to market at all. In Tanzania, for example, in the mid-1970s a market fee of 20 shillings per head of cattle was levied, whether or not the animal was actually sold. This fee usually amounted to between 2 and 8 per cent (Texas A. and M. University, 1976, Vol. 1, p. 94) (average probably 4–5 per cent) of the animal's value. This is higher than the figure for commissions paid to all intermediaries in the free markets referred to earlier in this chapter, and those intermediaries normally provided a wider range of services (including guarantees on debt payment and ownership) than was provided by the Tanzanian Government at its markets. A survey of users of some of these markets in Tanzania's main livestock areas revealed that at half of them (in 1975/76) there was no water supply, that 97 per cent of sellers did not use weigh-scales although 90 per cent claimed to sell in the auction ring, and that nearly two-thirds of the markets took place only once a month (Texas A. and M. University, 1976, Vol. 2, pp. 65–70). In 1976, 28 marketing teams (of four people each) controlled the marketing of about 450,000 head of cattle, an average of less than 70 cattle per team per working day. (Source: officials of the Tanzania Livestock Marketing Corporation in 1977.)

Governments have tended to respond to the abuses found in free trading systems by imposing government control and regulation. Unfortunately, each new step towards greater government control is also an opportunity for a government official to demand a bribe and this is what very frequently happens. For example, on export routes from Mali to the Ivory Coast, cattle traders — both private and parastatals — have to pay 'unofficial' fees (= bribes) in order to get through various official checkpoints on both sides of the borders; these fees amount to 15–20 per cent of total trading costs (excluding the purchase price of animals) or 8 per cent of the traders' final selling price. These bribes are additional to the official fees and taxes which amount to a further 13–17 per cent of the final selling price (CRED, 1980, Vol. 1, p. 180; Vol. 3, pp. 377–385). Bribes may also be levied at earlier stages in the marketing chain, and the sparser the livestock population and the less frequent the market, the greater will be the cost to both buyer and seller of refusing to bribe and so of being unable to make a purchase or sale. It seems probable that in many countries the government's best contribution to improved marketing will be to provide personal security at or near markets to potential buyers and sellers so that all who want to can attend without fear; the next step beyond this might be a radio programme — as has been proposed for Mali (CRED, 1980, Vol. 3, p. 417) — reporting the prices of livestock transactions in major markets on the previous day, but even this limited activity gives an opportunity for manipulation by traders to the disadvantage of the pastoralists.[15]

STRATIFICATION

In Chapter 2 'strategies' were described as occupying in this study an intermediate level between objectives and components, and we there reviewed two strategies — the settlement of nomads and the control of livestock numbers — in some detail. In this section we shall deal with only one aspect of a third strategy which, since it shares common features with what has been said about pastoral marketing, is being dealt with here rather than in Chapter 2.

A strategy for the development of dry pastoral areas that has been put forward for many years is one that allocates to different geographical regions and to different kinds of organization specialist functions according to their comparative advantage. These advantages may be founded on their natural environment, their location in respect to transport facilities and consumption centres, their access to inputs of various kinds, their skills, etc. By such a strategy, which is usually called a policy of 'stratification' and which has important implications for the kinds and locations of marketing and processing facilities, the drier pastoral areas would specialize in a cow–calf operation to produce immatures which would be removed at an early age for further stages in their growth to be conducted elsewhere. The comparative advantage of the dry areas is seen to consist mainly of one positive and one negative factor. The positive factor is that the disease situation is often less serious in drier than in more humid areas; the negative factor is that the overall shortage of feed, and in particular the marked inter-seasonal differences in feed supply, mean that livestock in dry areas take a very long time to reach the best weight for slaughter, reasonable increases in weight during the wet seasons of each year being followed by severe losses of weight during the succeeding dry season. Stratification of the livestock industry has been proposed whereby the immatures from the cow–calf operations in the drier rangeland are channelled into 'growing-out' operations on commercial (or parastatal) ranches or peasant smallholdings, which may in turn be succeeded by final 'fattening' either in large-scale feedlots or in stall-fed operations by peasants.

The flow of immature cattle from pastoral areas on to ranches takes place on a larger scale in Kenya, Botswana, and Tanzania, both as a result of direct transactions between pastoralists and ranchers and through government intervention in marketing or credit channels. Governments also often play a crucial role in determining and regulating the procedures for animal health inspection and quarantine that have to be followed in the movement of livestock from pastoral to other producing areas. The movement of immatures, or recently matured male cattle, from pastoral areas to peasant farms takes place on an unknown but often large scale. Sometimes the animals are used for a period as draught animals before resale, sometimes the operation is purely one of preparing them further before slaughter. In Kenya, and to a more limited extent in West Africa, some cattle, either direct from pastoral areas or after a period of growing out on ranches, enter large-scale feedlots for a period of intensive fattening. Stall-feeding and fattening of animals prior to slaughter on peasant farms also takes place in Ethiopia, elsewhere in East and Southern Africa and in West Africa (e.g. Upper Volta; source: CRED, 1980, Vol. 1, p. 69). The initiative for the establishment of feedlots has usually come from government, although private entrepreneurs have sometimes subsequently taken up the idea.

The reasons for the promotion of feedlots and for the subsequent results of these have more to do with events in overseas markets than with the particular characteristics of pastoral areas; they are therefore only marginally relevant to the present study. In brief, in the early 1970s world prices for meat rose sharply and for a time it looked as though exports of chilled or frozen meat from Africa might obtain access[16] to the European market where prices were above world levels. World meat prices subsequently declined sharply in relation to prices generally, and it became clear that additional African countries would not obtain access to the European market, and even those countries (especially Botswana) which already had access found difficulty in maintaining it. However, the most important feedstuffs (e.g. oil cake and molasses) which would feed animals in African feedlots could be exported and fed to cattle in Europe, and therefore feedlotters in Africa, who could obtain only world prices or below for their products, could not compete successfully in procuring their inputs of feedstuffs with farmers in Europe who received higher than world prices for their products. As a consequence, most of the feedlots initiated in Africa in the early and mid-1970s have now closed down due to economic and financial unviability. In contrast, many of the schemes for enabling the fattening of cattle on smallholdings, especially through the provision of credit to purchase livestock, seem to have been relatively successful.[17] In part the relative success of fattening of cattle by peasants is due to the fact that they have access to low-cost sources of feed which cannot enter into international trade.

However, there is one respect in which the differing performance of fattening activities by feedlots and by peasants is related to the pastoral origin of many of the cattle being fattened. We have already seen that the overall supply of cattle fluctuates widely from year to year, although we do not have any substantial evidence whether or not the supply of immatures for fattening fluctuates more or less than that of other cattle. What is clear is that in regions where the rangelands and the fattening areas are subject to the same general climatic influences, the demand by fattening enterprises for cattle for fattening and the offered supply of these cattle fluctuate out of phase with each other. When drought conditions obtain, pastoralists want to sell more cattle (the supply increases), but fatteners have less feed with which to feed them and so their demand decreases. Conversely, when good rains fall, the demand by fatteners increases but pastoralists now believe that they can fatten the animals profitably themselves under range conditions, so the supply decreases. This problem occurred on a large scale in both Kenya (ranches and feedlots) and Tanzania (ranches) in the mid-1970s. If the demand by fatteners for cattle from pastoral areas accounts for only a small part of the overall supply, then the effects of these divergences in supply and demand need not be very serious; but in that case neither is fattening playing any significant role in a process of stratification and specialization according to comparative advantage. If, however, fatteners collectively form a significant part of overall demand, then there are likely to be very substantial fluctuations in the prices of livestock for fattening or in the supply of feeder animals or both.

In the case of feedlots, fixed costs tend to form quite a high proportion of total costs. In the case of feedlots established in Kenya in the early 1970s the proportion came to about 15–20 per cent of total costs (excluding the cost of the animal itself and of mortality) when the feedlot operated at full capacity.[18] In Mali, at the end of the 1970s, fixed costs amounted to about 33 per cent of total costs at full capacity (CRED, 1980, Vol. 3, p. 289). The operator of a feedlot, who will incur the fixed costs whether he fattens any animals or not, will therefore feel compelled to bid for livestock while the margin between his buying and his selling price is greater than his current (mainly feed) costs; in this way he can make some contribution to fixed costs even if the feedlot operation runs at an overall loss. The consequence is likely to be sharply fluctuating prices for feeder animals, with the upper limits to price fluctuations being set by the point at which feedlots go bankrupt or cease to buy because they are no longer covering operating costs, or by the pastoralist concluding that the high price offered for his feeder animal outweighs the advantage of fattening the same animal himself. The initial instability of the system caused by fluctuations in the weather is augmented by further instability caused by the competition of feedlots for scarce supplies and by bankruptcy.

Peasant fatteners of cattle, however, though they face the same inherent instability of supply, are likely to react by temporarily dropping out of the fattening business, coming back into it again when prices readjust. Because they have virtually no fixed costs, temporary exit and re-entry into fattening operations can be relatively painless. The implications of this analysis are that in areas of relatively high climatic instability peasant fattening, even if it leads to lower daily weight gains than feedlots in the short run, is likely to have greater long-term viability, and that peasant fatteners should not be encouraged to invest in housing or other facilities for their fattening animals which will increase the proportion of their fixed costs.

SUMMARY

This chapter, after briefly reviewing the scope of pastoral marketing, examined two assumptions which frequently lie behind government marketing interventions. One of these, that pastoralists respond positively to price increases by increasing the supply of marketed output, it found to be neither consistently supported nor disproved by the available evidence. In any case, it is improbable that a single generalization about price responsiveness could cover all pastoral situations which differ so much among themselves in their dependence on subsistence consumption, in their technical ability to increase output, and in their access to consumer goods. The other assumption, about the general inefficiency of free marketing systems, it found to be contrary to the available evidence, which is, however, largely confined to Africa and to the marketing of live cattle.

A review of the features which distinguish pastoral from non-pastoral marketing systems highlighted the following: firstly, the very large fluctuations in market flows both within and between years; secondly, the extra costs involved, due to the sparseness of the population, in taking animals to the nearest primary market, or in collecting a sufficiently large mob of animals to transport economically to a consumption centre; thirdly, the particular types of output (e.g. in the case of cattle very young and very old) which are normally marketed from pastoral areas; fourthly, some particular features of disease control; fifthly, the weak political position of pastoralists in most countries.

The chapter then examined a limited number of marketing options particularly relevant to these features of pastoral marketing. One of the options is a technical (rather than organizational) one and concerns choices of different ways to move livestock from producer to consumer. It found that trekking on foot is still, in Africa, normally the cheapest way not only in direct money terms but also (and surprisingly) in terms of mortality and shrinkage; however, in some cases trekking on foot is not feasible. It found that transport by lorry can sometimes be economic, but this is normally when it is done on an *ad hoc* basis to take opportunistic advantage of particular situations rather than when using specialist transport on a regular basis.

The other three options considered were organizational ones and concerned the role that government should play in pastoral marketing. This is a much more limited range of options than has been considered in the other main components of pastoral development, i.e. water development, range management, and improvements in animal health and husbandry, although to a certain extent other options, for example about centralization versus decentralization of decision-making, have been subsumed in the choice between government and non-government organizations. The range of options was also more limited because the choice posed was between government and private trader, and the question of pastoral community involvement in marketing was, for lack of evidence, not examined. The conclusion drawn from the examination of the options was also much more forthright than in the case of other components; it was much less possible to distinguish between one set of circumstances in which government intervention would be more appropriate and another set in which it would be less. Except for the cases where government organizations have been used to buy up livestock in crises caused by drought, government intervention in pastoral marketing, at least in the forms it has taken in Africa, has proved inappropriate when it has reached beyond the simple provision of personal security at or near market-places.

A final section of the chapter looked at the strategy of stratification, and concluded that a fundamental difficulty in the operation of feedlots (or other capital-intensive elements in a stratification strategy) is their dependence on a highly fluctuating flow of feeder animals from pastoral areas. Feedlots, because of their high proportion of fixed costs in relation to total costs, actually further aggravate price fluctuations and then run into acute financial difficulties. In contrast, peasant fattening enterprises of low capital intensity are likely to be more economic and more appropriate elements in a stratification strategy.

NOTES TO CHAPTER 9

1. For a general discussion of supply response by pastoralists see Low (1980). For detailed empirical studies see Khalifa and Simpson (1972), Low (1978), and Doran, Low, and Kemp (1979).

2. 'Wholesale level' in this case means the point at which livestock traders sell animals to butchers, slaughter-houses, or to those who will export them out of Africa alive (except in the Somalia case where the price is c.i.f. Saudi Arabia). Further evidence, for which space was not available in Table 9.1, on Upper Volta can be found in CRED, 1980, Vol. 1, pp. 180–181. However, it may not be independent separate evidence from that already contained in Table 9.1.

3. 'Profit' is an emotive term, but the alternative, 'net margin', conveys too little meaning. The definition of profit used here includes the return to the trader's own labour and to borrowed capital and thereby somewhat exaggerates the benefits a trader derives from involvement in livestock trading.

4. The 'differences' referred to in this case are measured in terms of the square of the 'multiple correlation coefficient' = 'coefficient of determination' = R^2 in multiple regression.

5. The low value of R^2 for cattle in this study may arise from the fact that, whereas the weight of sheep and goats could be measured directly by spring balances, that of cattle could only be estimated on the basis of heart girth, which produced an element of error into an independent variable in the regression.

6. The 'coefficient of variation' is the standard deviation divided by the mean. There is no secular upward trend in the LMD purchases but there is in total purchases, and this means that the coefficient of variation is not an entirely appropriate measure of relative fluctuation.

7. Indirect confirmation of this comes from Cronin (1978).

8. In Iran this seems to have been the case since the early 1960s (Tapper, 1979c, pp. 55–61).

9. These misconceptions do not always arise from innocent ignorance. In at least one African country officials deliberately suppressed a report which provides evidence that the existing free marketing system worked quite well because they wished to have a parastatal organization take over instead.

10. However, Raikes (1981), which was published too recently to have much impact on this study, suggests (pp. 191–203) that in recent years the Kenya Government's control of beef prices and grades has been of more benefit to consumers with high incomes rather than to those with low.

11. For a general discussion on the location of abattoirs in West Africa see Ferguson (1977).

12. For a summary description of LMD's antecedents see Dahl (1979, p. 197) and Raikes (1981, Ch. 4).

13. When a government or parastatal intervenes directly in trading the equivalent of 'trader's profit' are the interest charges on capital employed and the costs of management and overheads.

14. Texas A. and M. University (1976, Vol. 2) reports the results of a survey which analysed the convenience of livestock marketing in different regions in Tanzania.

15. ILO (1976, p. 240) provides an example of how traders manipulate the spread of information for their own advantage. In that case they spread the (false) news of high prices to attract large numbers of animals to a market for sale; the influx of large numbers then, through the operation of the normal laws of supply and demand, drove down prices.

16. The principal overt bars to access are animal disease regulations, especially in respect of rinderpest, foot-and-mouth disease, and CBPP. However, the stringency with which these regulations are applied is largely determined by political and economic factors rather than technical ones.

17. For a description of such schemes in Niger and Mali see Wardle (1978) and CRED (1980, Vol. 3, pp. 292–299).

18. The source is various papers by the UNDP/FAO Beef Industry Development Project in 1971. The assumption is that interest and depreciation on all capital (except the animal) is 'fixed', as are water, labour, and management costs, giving total 'fixed costs' per animal per day of about Ksh (Kenya shillings) 0.30–0.50 compared with 'variable' costs for feed and veterinary services of about Ksh 2.00–2.30 per day per animal.

Chapter ten

Organizations of pastoralists

A CHANGE IN FOCUS

Previous chapters have looked at the organization and management of particular components in pastoral development, such as the provision of water, range management, animal health and husbandry services, and livestock marketing. This chapter, on organizations of pastoralists, and the next, on the organization of government, shift the focus from components to organizations, partly drawing together what has been said previously, partly adding new dimensions to it.

This chapter will start with a review of the general roles that organizations of pastoralists may play in pastoral development. Then, after a brief recapitulation of the main organizational variables within which choices can be made, there will be a more detailed discussion of five main options. The first of these is the choice between making use of existing or establishing new organizations and this option is approached from three angles: the implications for social equity of using existing organizations; whether existing organizations will have as much competence as new ones to undertake new tasks; and the problems involved in the creation of new organizations.

The remaining four options to be discussed are closely related to each other and interact. The issues involved are: how big should pastoral organizations be; how complex in terms of number of different levels and functional specialization within an organization; what should be the basis of membership — should organizations be inclusive or exclusive; should they be single- or multi-purpose (function)? For different roles or functions in pastoral development different sizes of organization may be optimal. These differences in optimum size can be accommodated either by there being a multitude of separate, simple, single-purpose organizations each with its own membership based on appropriate criteria, or by allocating different tasks to different levels or 'specialist units' in a single, complex, multi-purpose organization whose membership should probably be inclusive and even compulsory. Two final sections of the chapter will discuss the involvement of pastoralists in the planning of pastoral development and how to ensure that organizations of pastoralists have the right kind of flexibility to adjust their size and functions in the light of changing circumstances.

The most important new dimension which needs to be brought in is time and the changes which take place over time. Previous chapters have been concerned with optimizing in a static context, i.e. with deciding, given the physical, social, economic, and political characteristics of a pastoral situation, given the objectives of development, given the available technical components, and given the range of organizational options which are open, what is the combination of particular components and particular organizational forms which will lead to the best results in terms of objectives. But objectives in development do not stay constant: the same person's or group's objectives change over time, and different persons and groups change in their relative importance and so in the extent to which their objectives have to be taken into account; social, economic, political, and in some cases even physical characteristics (e.g. the state of degradation of soil and vegetation of pastoral regions) change; the technologies of components change and so do the options for organizational form. We need also to be concerned with how best to manage these changes, and with how particular organizational forms change in their competence over time as, for example, their experience builds up.

During the 1970s there has been much talk of the need for an integrated approach to pastoral development (e.g. Haaland, 1980b; FAO, 1974). Sometimes what is meant is integration in *understanding*; pastoral systems are so complex, and different elements within them interact so strongly that, it is felt, it is dangerous to study or to meddle with just one element without fully taking into account the whole system and all the consequences for the other parts of the system that intervention in one part may create. At other times what is meant is integration of *action*. One should not, it is said, intervene with only one component at a time; advances in veterinary services must be matched by improvements in marketing or else the result will be a catastrophic build-up in livestock populations; new water supplies must be incorporated into an overall scheme of range management that allows for recuperation of vegetation around the water points and limits stock numbers to the carrying capacity of the vegetation rather than to the watering capacity of the water point.

Integration in action may mean no more than that different interventions are planned to coincide *in time* with each other. Or it may mean a strong common guiding mechanism to ensure, for example, that the policies of different organizations are fully compatible with each other, and that the provision of different services is carefully 'co-ordinated', e.g. that the range-management office is located in the same village as the veterinary office. This is a 'weak' definition of integration which is probably best described instead as 'co-ordination'. Co-ordination has been defined as 'various efforts to alter or smooth the relationships of continuing *independent* elements such as organizations, staffs and resources' (emphasis added). In contrast, a 'strong' definition of integration is 'action which brings previously separated and independent functions and organizations (of personnel, or resources, or clientele) into a new unitary structure' (Honadle *et al.*, 1980, pp. 30–32 and 210–211). While here we shall follow these definitions of 'co-ordination' and 'integration', it should be noted that they give perhaps rather more emphasis to formal structures and chains of command than is often appropriate in the Third World where informal behaviour is often a far more important element in achieving unity of purpose and compatibility of action than is formal structure. Integration in this chapter is discussed in the section on interacting options and again in several places in Chapter 11.

ROLES OF ORGANIZATIONS OF PASTORALISTS

In Chapter 1 an organization was defined as any durable grouping of more than one person with a common or definite purpose. By this wide definition an organization of pastoralists can be anything from a nuclear family of man and wife to a confederation of tribes, a multi-purpose livestock co-operative, or a group whose main purpose is the performance of ritual. This section is about roles. There is no sharp distinction between roles and functions; the latter are more specific and concerned with details, the former wider and more general.

Organizations of pastoralists can play a variety of roles in pastoral development. They may be involved in *defining the rights* of access of individuals to certain fixed resources, mainly of grazing and water. By national or traditional law these resources may be open to all members of a particular pastoral society or group, either on equal terms or in differential terms to different classes of members; the society or group then has organizations and procedures of its own (e.g. a meeting of clan or camp elders) to decide which individuals have claims to be members on what terms.

Organizations may take this control of access to fixed resources a stage further and become actively engaged in the day-to-day *management of the fixed resources*. For example, the organization concerned may lay down rules governing the order of watering at wells, and the duties of well-users in the operation, maintenance, and repair of wells. It may lay down dates for opening and closing dry season pastures and organize the planned burning of these pastures. Organizations of pastoralists may also be involved in *the provision and management of other pastoral development services* (i.e. those not related to fixed resources), such as the provision of animal health and husbandry services or livestock marketing. Many of the issues involved in the management of resources and services have been discussed, with examples, in Chapters 4–9; one of the elements involved may be the raising and spending of money or similar variable resources.

Organizations of pastoralists can play an important role in *representing pastoralists* to government and to other outsiders. This role can include that of defending pastoralist interests, of being a persistent lobby in favour of particular kinds of developments and government services, of transmitting information between pastoralists and outsiders, of some involvement in decision-making and planning of pastoral development, that is, in obtaining the commitment of resources (both external and internal) to pastoral development and in designing particular interventions. Governments of many countries have found it convenient to identify representatives of pastoralists to whom they can transmit orders or information and from whom they in turn can seek information and advice, both about pastoral development and about other matters. In British colonial Africa the colonial power, e.g. in Sudan (Haaland, 1980c) and northern Kenya (Dahl, 1979), either established or greatly strengthened the power of chiefs to fill this role; in post-colonial times in Botswana, land boards, composed partly of traditional tribal authorities, partly of representatives selected through the ballot box, have been given an important role in the allocation of water and grazing land rights (Botswana, 1968). These boards are dominated by important cattle owners and have superseded other local institutions in planning pastoral development. In Mongolia *negdels* (pastoral collectives) not only implement the development and management of pastoral activities; they appear to have a major role in planning it. In the USA, subsequent to the passing of the Taylor Grazing Act in 1934, so-called 'advisory boards' elected by those with permits to graze public land succeeded in obtaining quasi-executive control over federal government programmes to manage the rangelands of the western USA (Heady and Bartolome, 1977).

Some organizations of pastoralists can assist in *smoothing the transition*, when circumstances demand it, from a wholly pastoral way of life to one based on crop cultivation or other occupations. They can do so in a variety of ways; for example, by providing a mechanism for supporting the dependants of pastoral migrants (mainly young males) who go off to establish themselves in urban life, until such time as they are able once again to support their dependants either from their new occupation or by a return to their old. Organizations of pastoralists can help in this case by allocating male labour to herd the livestock left behind and by sharing, over the community as a whole, the burden of providing subsistence for the dependants left behind (Dahl, 1979, Ch. 10; Bonte, 1975).[1] They can also provide a mechanism for the specialization of labour within the pastoral region, with some people looking after the livestock of the whole community and thereby releasing others from herding to specialize in crop production or to obtain training in more technical skills which can then be harnessed to new activities of the organization. Of course, at this point it becomes difficult to distinguish between the accepted function of a particular pastoral organization to do this sort of thing and the general institutional background of a pastoral society, including its social values and behavioural norms, which encourage mutual support. We do not need to make a sharp distinction since it is not relevant to discussions in this chapter. This role, of smoothing the transition, seems to have been important in the development firstly of co-operative associations and then of collectives in the pastoral regions of the USSR (ILO, 1967). Finally, as also happens in the USSR, organizations of pastoralists can act as an *investment channel* whereby money and other resources from outside pastoral society can be invested in diversifying the economies of pastoral societies and regions.

ORGANIZATIONAL OPTIONS

We have met the main organizational variables, that is, the options between different forms of organization and management, in earlier chapters on particular components, and they were also listed in the section on organizational forms in Chapter 3. In brief, they are as follows. Organizations can be of different kinds, e.g. government, community, etc. They can be larger or smaller in terms of area of jurisdiction or population (membership). They can be based on residence or use of an area, on kinship, on occupation (*sheep*-keeping in contrast to *cattle*-keeping), on voluntary association, or on some other principle. They may be required to include everyone or may be allowed to exclude those they do not want. They can be single-purpose (function) in scope (e.g. only for water supplies) or multi-purpose (water supplies *and* range management *and* animal health). They can also be more or less complex in terms of the number of different levels in the organization at which functions are carried out, of the specialization of functions (planning committees, audit committees, etc.) and of staff. Management in these organizations can be more or less centralized, more or less authoritarian or participatory, and its style more or less mandatory (relying on rules) or liberal (relying on offers and incentives). In managing pastoral development use can be made of existing ('traditional') organizations,[2] possibly giving these some new tasks and operating procedures, or new organizations can be introduced in various juridical forms such as companies, co-operatives, or other associations. Pastoral organizations may be loaded with several new tasks all at once or they may gradually expand their responsibilities over time as they grow in experience, confidence, and competence.

These seem to be the appropriate ways of categorizing organizational forms rather than in terms of labels such as 'group ranches', 'collectives', or 'commercial ranches'. In the rest of this chapter the consequences of some different choices of organizational variables will be examined, but no attempt will be made to summarize arguments set out in previous chapters. Instead, this chapter will concentrate on those aspects not substantially covered in the chapters on particular components.

NEW OR EXISTING ORGANIZATIONS

The existing social system in and around pastoral society will probably have a number of institutions — both organizations and other features — concerned with the various roles discussed earlier. Often one of these roles, the defence of pastoralists' interests, has been performed so effectively in the past that governments, usually representing non-pastoral interests, place high priority on abolishing the existing system and on replacing it with a new, more amenable one, and this change is often justified on the grounds that the existing system is too conservative and ill-adapted to modern needs and that the leadership of existing organizations is corrupt and exploitative of its followers. Such claims can be heard in both socialist countries, e.g. in the USSR after the 1917 revolution (Tursunbayev and Potapov, 1959), and in Ethiopia after 1975, and in capitalist ones, e.g. in Kenya today. Existing systems vary widely in the extent to which the other roles are performed; of course, most of them have rules, and means of interpreting and enforcing these rules in respect of ownership rights to livestock and water, and to a less obvious extent to grazing, since access to water so often also determines access to grazing. Active management of fixed resources is less frequent, or at least less obvious, and occurs more often in respect of water supplies than other fixed resources. Very few existing organizations of pastoralists are involved in the provision of other pastoral development services.

Existing organizations and equity

We can examine the circumstances under which existing organizations are likely to carry out these roles more or less effectively than new ones,[3] where continuation of an existing organization, or change to a new one, is defined in terms of a combination of formal title, internal procedures for taking and implementing decisions, and the composition of its leadership. In defining rights of access to fixed resources, existing organizations have the advantage that they will have built up a body of precedents and case law which is both relatively well known among society's members and also all-embracing. Even in the face of new regulations about access, the existing organization can apply its past experience, especially in dealing with unforeseen consequences of the new regulations. In contrast, new organizations will be relatively unpredictable since, even if many of the same individuals are involved as in the old organizations, they will be less confident about procedures and functions and less bound by old rules and obligations. On the other hand, existing organizations will reflect, in their leadership and their procedures, the existing balance of power in society which will itself reflect the existing pattern of access to fixed resources. Where the existing balance of power is inequitable between different ethnic or occupational groups, different families within a group, or different sexes or ages within a household, then continuation with an existing organization to manage rights of access to fixed resources is likely to result in continued unequal access even if the overt policy and law change in a more equitable direction. It is precisely in dealing with the unforeseen consequences of new regulations or with areas of uncertainty about rights that a leadership that represents the interests of the already powerful will be able to steer the operations of existing organizations in favour of its backers.

However, merely replacing an existing organization with a new one will not of itself reduce the ability of the already powerful to sabotage measures intended to reduce inequality, for they may be able to continue to use their power to ensure that they gain the leadership positions in the new organizations and that the new procedures also serve their interests; this is what happened with agricultural co-operatives in India (see, e.g. Hunter and Bottrall, 1974, Ch. 8). If government wishes to alter any existing pattern of inequality in pastoral society towards greater equity, it will almost certainly have to do this directly with its own management resources (or those of its political party) in the first place, and not rely on organizations of pastoralists to act as its agents. Once the previous pattern of inequality has been broken, and the previously less powerful have achieved effective control over resources previously controlled by the powerful, it will then be possible to restore the right of managing access to fixed resources to pastoralists' organizations which, whatever their title, will in fact be new ones. Failure to bring about this change in effective control over resources has meant that the policy and regulations provided for group ranches in Kenya, whereby the relatively well-off would have to reduce their livestock herds in order to allow, within a fixed overall livestock ceiling, for the relative expansion of the herds of the less well-off, have never been implemented (Helland, 1980, pp. 190–192).

Existing organizations in societies marked by inequality are unlikely to define access to fixed resources in a fashion that will help the weaker members of the society. The same does not necessarily hold true, however, of their management of these resources, of their management of other pastoral development services, or of their representation of pastoralists' interests; for in these cases the interests of the powerful and wealthy pastoralists may coincide with those of the weak and the poor. In defining access to fixed resources, in contrast, their interests are almost by definition opposed, since one person can have more access only by another having less. In the case of the other roles, however, the wealthy may actually benefit if pastoral organizations act in a way that is of use to the poor as well as to the rich. For example, in the provision of water supplies, if the actual quantity of water is not a limiting factor, then the wealthy pastoralist will benefit if the water point is efficiently managed and maintained and if the poor are provided with a good enough service there to induce them to contribute to the cost of maintenance.

Similarly with the management of a community animal health service, the owner of a large herd will actually benefit if his poor neighbour's animals are provided with an effective prophylactic vaccination service; however, if either the vaccines are in short supply, or if the health worker has not got time to deal with everyone's livestock, then the interests of wealthy and poor are in conflict again. Where non-pastoralists are trespassing on pastoralists' land, then the wealthy pastoralists may need the help of the less wealthy but more numerous poor in beating off the incursions; but where powerful leaders of pastoralist societies can sell off pastoral common land to invading cultivators, and can convert the proceeds to their own private good, then their interests are in conflict with their weaker neighbours. In these cases when the interests of rich and poor coincide, then the poor will probably benefit more if the service is provided by an existing organization whose procedures are better rooted in the pastoralists' own cultures, perceptions, and objectives than by new organizations whose constitutions and procedures are usually tailored to the convenience of central government's legislation and bureaucrats.

Existing organizations and competence for new tasks

The most usual point of argument is whether existing (traditional) organizations are more or less effective or competent than new ones in carrying out new developmental tasks (roles and functions) rather than whether they act fairly in doing so. This argument can be further subdivided into three points — whether existing organizations have the right motivation, that is, whether they will *want* to carry out the new tasks effectively, whether their procedures and the technical skills of their leaders and staff are appropriate for the tasks to be carried out, and whether the experience and authority, as a management team, that they have acquired in carrying out their existing tasks can be usefully transferred to new and wider ones.

No organization, new or old, is likely to be adequately motivated to continue to perform in the long run any task which is not in the interests of its members (or at least of its powerful ones). Where societies are relatively homogeneous, in terms of physical wealth, culture, and education, it may be possible, if existing organizations decline to take up new tasks, nevertheless to get them undertaken, with the aid of intensive propaganda, by establishing a new organization to do them under the leadership of people excluded from leadership in existing organizations, perhaps because they are not yet old enough or because they have been defeated by rivals in competition for that leadership. But unless the new tasks are quickly recognized as being of benefit this initial enthusiasm is likely to die away. Even where the leadership of existing organizations in such societies can be pressurized by government into taking up tasks for which it has little enthusiasm (as, e.g. the leadership of the Samburu tribe of Kenya were in the closing years of the colonial era in Kenya), the tasks will be abandoned when the members object. In contrast, where new tasks bring clear benefits to members, existing organizations, even under what has so far been considered 'conservative' leaderships, are prompt to undertake them. For example, in the mid-1960s the tribal elders (heads of extended families) among Bedouin in the Syrian desert organized, within a period of only two years, a complete change in their mode of transportation from camels to motor transport. While subsequent use of lorries has tended to promote more action and initiative by individuals, their original introduction, because of the high unit cost, required group action in order to generate the investment funds, and consequently a new task for the existing organization — the extended family (Chatty, 1980).

Where societies are not homogeneous, then the reluctance of existing organizations, under the domination of the powerful, to undertake new tasks may spring from a fear that carrying them out may assist the weak to the detriment of the previously powerful. In contrast, the establishment of new organizations with the assistance of a government or other outside agency may give the previously weak the opportunity to break away from the dominance of the powerful. However, if this is to happen successfully, the assisting agency must be aware of the nature of the situation in which it is intervening and create the general belief that it is prepared to give the new organizations and their clientele its continuing political support, or else the weak will not be willing to challenge the powerful by giving the new organization their loyalty.

One reason for preferring to entrust new tasks to new rather than to existing organizations is a belief that the procedures and leadership of the existing organizations are ill-adapted and inadequately skilled to cope with the managerial and technical requirements of the new tasks, and that the establishment of new organizations, endowed from the start with appropriate procedures and skills, is easier than the reform of existing ones. An example can be given of what is meant by procedure: a common form of pastoral organization is a camp, clan, or neighbourhood council at which all adult males can speak and where debate continues until a decision based on consensus emerges. That is probably not an effective procedure for (as examples) selecting a contractor out of several tendering to drill and equip a borehole, or negotiating the details of a bank loan, or checking a community-employed livestock assistant's medicine box and cash to make sure that he is not fiddling. We have already seen, especially in the chapters on water development and on animal health and husbandry services, that some components of pastoral development do have requirements substantially different from previous ways of doing things, and that both technical (e.g. repairing borehole pumps) and administrative skills (e.g. calling for tenders and assessing bids) may be called for.

In some respects this is not so much a matter of procedures and skills as of the division of political power between a traditional, possibly elderly, pastoral leadership, usually without much formal education, and a group who have acquired modern technical and managerial skills, whether this group come from a rising generation within pastoral society or from a completely different tribe or occupational class. There are plenty of instances in which existing pastoral organizations, whether in the form of autocratic individuals or more corporate leadership, have been able to acquire new technical skills without fundamentally, or in a revolutionary manner, altering the nature of the acquiring organization. One can see this with Bedouin kings in western Asia hiring a wide range of outside skills, with the Aussa sultanate in Ethiopia hiring expatriate irrigation and agronomic skills, and with the Maasai pastoralists of Tanzania using Chagga or other non-Maasai to repair or improve their water wells (Jacobs, 1961).

However, increasingly those with modern education and technical skills, especially those from non-pastoral origins, dislike being involved in relations of this kind with traditional organizations headed by traditional pastoralists. They prefer instead new organizations with procedures whereby those with education can play a more confident role, with privileged access, because of their education, to the positions of leadership. In some respects the new procedures and new technical skills *do* perform a necessary part in bringing the fruits of new technology. In other respects, however, they are a smokescreen behind which a large part of these fruits are diverted into the hands of the newly privileged educated class, and new organizations are a useful device whereby unnecessary salaried posts can be created which are only to be filled by people with superior academic qualifications, often selected by government officials. This phenomenon is not restricted to pastoral societies. In India a report (Government of India, 1960, p. 134) notes that:

the rules and regulations for the formation of co-operatives were far too complicated . . . with the result that even where they [tribals] have become members of a co-operative the management is generally in the hands of a non-tribal. In fact the co-operatives have become one more way whereby the non-tribals control the economic and social interests of the tribals.

Elsewhere in India, for example under the Drought-Prone Areas Programme, existing sheep owners were organized into pastoral co-operatives with a unified management system and a total flock size of less than 600. Each co-operative not only had a nine-man (presumably unpaid) governing board, three of them government nominees, but was also required to have as its manager or secretary a 'qualified' stockman (probably 11 years of school education and 9 months of vocational training); in addition it employed at least two shepherds. The annual salary of the stockman alone amounted to nearly as much (85 per cent) as the maximum total amount that the co-operative's regulations *allow* (after a run-in period) to be distributed to members, and stockman and shepherds together received between 25 and 50 per cent of the total annual gross (before deducting any costs except mortality and flock replacements) turnover of the co-operative (Sandford, 1978a; Johnson, 1979a). Given the level of other government support to the co-operatives, it is hard to believe that the additional product occasioned by the stockman's skills can have been so high as to justify this division of proceeds. Plans for hiring 'managers' for many of the group ranches proposed in Africa imply similar disproportions.

It seems, then, that the question of whether new or existing organizations will adapt more flexibly to the need to acquire new procedures and to use new skills has less to do with the willingness of the organizations to use them than with the willingness of the skilled to be employed and with the terms which they can extract for this employment. Partly this will be a matter simply of the existence of a sufficient supply of skilled people; clearly, if there are very few of them, they will be able to extract a high reward. Partly, however, it will be a matter of the extent to which the skilled are able to enlist the support of other parties, e.g. central government, international donors, or commercial banks, to use their leverage over other factors, e.g. money or land, to ensure that pastoral organizations are required to employ the skilled on terms favourable to the latter. This support is likely to be

forthcoming more as a consequence of personal connections and preconceived notions of the necessity for qualified management than from any
objective assessment of this management's real productivity.

Establishing new organizations

Establishing new organizations of pastoralists takes far longer than is usually
foreseen. In Botswana, the Village Area Development Programme expected
to establish 40 group ranches in western Botswana in five years; in fact, not
one was established (Odell and Odell, 1980). In a livestock project in Upper
Volta the formation of nine group ranches over a five-year period was
proposed (Gooch, 1979); in the event, only three were started and these are
very shaky. Where formation of a new organization is a precondition for
pastoralists to acquire or to retain the right to use grazing land, fairly rapid
formal establishment (e.g. demarcation of boundaries, acceptance of new
constitutions, 'election' of management committees) can take place; for example, 64 group ranches were formally established in Rwanda within five
years and 36 pastoral units or associations in east Senegal in three years
(Oxby, 1981). But otherwise, e.g. where pastoralists can continue to enjoy
grazing rights whether or not they form new organizations, or where establishment of new organizations is defined not in terms of formalities but of
actual execution of new tasks, progress tends to be very slow, as experience
with group ranches in Kenya, *Ujamaa* ranches and ranching associations in
Tanzania, and range associations in Ethiopia demonstrates. New organizations not only often fail to carry out new tasks expected of them, but those
within them vested with policy-making and management authority tend to
respond only to outside pressures rather than themselves taking an initiative
(Helland, 1980, p. 192). Although herding collectives were first established
by law in Mongolia in 1928, and the law was at first rigorously enforced by
compulsion, it was not until the 1960s that these collectives really started to
function on a wide scale and in the way intended (Humphrey, 1978; Rosenberg, 1981).

This failure of new organizations, and their leadership, to fulfil the hopes
placed in them is not surprising. In some cases the plans they are expected
to carry out are simply technically unsound, but also, very often, the new
organizations are expected to form effective management units at a quite
unrealistic speed. Established with new constitutions, new tasks, new procedures, new ways of selecting their leaders, they have no successful model
of behaviour to copy. In the Western world even where exact models exist,
for example of fighting units (battalions, divisions, etc.) in the military, and
of limited liability companies in industry, the value of keeping together
management teams used to particular procedures and personalities is recognized — and in industry such 'teams' have market values greater than the
sum of the values of the individuals concerned. Even so, it is recognized that
new tasks are best undertaken one by one, gathering strength by experience.

When new organizations are established for pastoral development not only are relative strangers often expected to co-operate with each other in newly formed groups for the first time, but simultaneously they have to cope with new individual roles (chairman, committee member), new procedures (election of officers, auditing of accounts) and new tasks (planning a fodder bush planting programme). Not only are the pastoralists involved in doubt about the appropriate model of behaviour to follow, having been repeatedly told that their traditional organizations are outmoded, but the government officials sponsoring the new organizations are often themselves in doubt or in dispute about what should be done.

In a number of cases where new pastoral organizations have been formed they have, intentionally or otherwise, reflected in their territories, in their membership, in their leadership, the traditional organizations which preceded them and which they were supposed to replace. Surprisingly, this seems to happen even in places like Mongolia and the USSR. It has both advantages and disadvantages: disadvantages because if the pre-change situation was inequitable the post-change one will tend to copy this; advantages because the continuation of the old order may provide the lubricant by which the new order can be made to work. An anthropologist has written of group ranches in Kenya: 'Rather than being replaced by it, such institutions as clanship, age sets, and territorial organization provide the principles which constitute the actual social order of the Group Ranch'; 'In conclusion the Group Ranch may appear in summation to represent a positive innovation precisely because of its limitations, for in the cracks and crevices of its limitations Maasai may be able to make it work — through their own system' (Galaty, 1980, p. 169).

At the same time, while the new organization can be helped to work by the continuation of elements of the old, it also provides an opportunity for new and growing interests and pressure groups, for whose advancement the old provided no avenue, to acquire a footing and expand their influence without having directly to challenge and overthrow the previous authorities. In Tanzanian Maasailand the traditional organizations for many 'authoritative internal decisions' were the elders' councils. Village councils, established in principle by government, but with a leadership elected by members, in the mid-1970s tended also to be largely composed of elders but with a somewhat greater representation of younger age-groups and educated people. Steering committees (elected by members) of newly formed ranching associations in turn had a much greater representation of the young and better educated (Hatfield, 1977).

SOME INTERACTING OPTIONS

Several organizational variables interact to such a degree that they need to be considered together. These variables are size, basis (of membership), scope (i.e. single- or multi-purpose) and complexity. The variables have already been described earlier in this chapter. Many of the details have already been discussed in chapters on particular components. For some purposes organizations of pastoralists have to be large, in terms of area of jurisdiction or membership; for other purposes a smaller size is required. In regions where the environment is spatially variable and unreliable in time the basic unit of land management has to be large, and if management is to be by pastoralists this implies also a large (in terms of membership) organization. Some examples of size, in terms of membership and land, under government programmes are given in Table 6.1. If pastoralists are to act as effective pressure groups to defend their interests, then they need to be grouped in organizations large enough — possibly tens of thousands of households — that they cannot be ignored, submerging their internal differences in a common front able to speak up against external interests and threats, but not so large that they present such a challenge to the integrity of the nation state that they have to be crushed rather than accommodated. For other purposes, e.g. for the effective allocation of labour to different classes of stock and to different functions, much smaller groupings and organizations, perhaps of only two or three households, may be appropriate. For the management of other services, e.g. water points or community animal health workers, organizations of intermediate size are required.

Given that different sizes of organizations of pastoralists are suitable for different tasks, in a pastoral situation where there is more than one task to be performed then one can opt either for several independent single-purpose organizations each carrying out its own task, or for one multi-purpose organization with an internal structure of some complexity which allocates different tasks to different levels in the organization. An example of this latter sort of option can be seen with *negdels* in Mongolia (Rosenberg, 1974; Humphrey, 1978). The *negdel* as a whole runs (through its 'auxiliary brigade') certain transport, consumer (e.g. baths, hairdressing), production (felt-making) and agricultural (cropping) services. At the next level down, three or four herding brigades within the *negdel* each have their own territory and to a certain extent specialize in different species of livestock — e.g. cows and horses in one brigade, sheep in another. The brigade carries out some services (e.g. veterinary) for its members directly and allocates other specialist tasks (e.g. looking after livestock of a particular age and sex) to its constituent *suurs* — which are roughly equivalent to camping groups in other pastoral societies. *Suurs* do not have their own territory but are allocated migration routes for a particular year by the management of the brigade. Sometimes there is an intermediate level between *suurs* and brigades, a level at which fodder-making and storage is carried out. All these different levels operate within a single overarching organization — the *negdel*; and although in earlier times membership of *negdels*, and by extension, of individual *suurs*, was on a voluntary basis, it appears that in more recent years an individual may only leave a *suur* for a particular authorized reason. On average *negdels* have about 700 member households, brigades perhaps 100–200, and *suurs* 3–10.

In many traditional societies there appears to be a large variety of different organizations, each with a different task or set of tasks and each often appearing to act in relative independence of the others. Control over the sale and slaughter of livestock may be vested in individuals (which are not organizations by the definition set out earlier in this chapter) or in families (which are); control over herding or other husbandry matters may be vested in the same hands or elsewhere, e.g. in camping communities.[4] People who camp together in a camping community may be members of the same watering community or they may belong, in partnership with some people from other camps, to different watering communities; where this happens there may be no effective overarching organization which unites these divided interests again at a superior level vested with the *formal* authority to give orders to inferior levels in a hierarchically organized system. But this apparent anarchy of organizations may be misleading, arising from an unconscious model of Western business or military organization that stresses sharply defined responsibilities and powers independent of particular personalities. In traditional pastoral societies coherence between different activities may be provided in other ways, partly by the influence of individual personalities and by personal power based on individual wealth rather than by formal position in an organization, partly by appeals to group solidarity and social values rather than to explicit laws and regulations. In some traditional societies an individual or household is bound — perhaps by virtue of descent — relatively permanently to particular organizations, e.g. to particular watering, camping, or cultivating communities; in others it is relatively easy to shift membership from one organization to another.

In contrast, in many pastoral development schemes in the non-communist world the tendency has been to allocate several tasks to a single level in a single 'chosen' organization of pastoralists, and provision has not been made in these schemes either for the delegation of some tasks to levels subordinate to the chosen one, or for the creation of superior federations or alliances to perform those (superior) tasks where economies of scale operate which the chosen organization is too small to capture. Such superior tasks, for example operating machinery to construct water points, or the allocation of temporary or permanent grazing rights to the individual chosen organizations, are, instead, allocated to government. In fairness it should be pointed out that where governments have tried to take a key part in establishing such federations in other, i.e. non-pastoral, parts of the agricultural sector, the usual, though not invariable, result has been the creation of a costly, inefficient, bureaucratic monster.

Typical pastoral schemes in which organizations of pastoralists have been planned with only a single level have been projects to establish group ranches (or near equivalents) in Botswana, Kenya, Rwanda, Upper Volta, or pastoral units or associations in east Senegal and Niger. Group ranches in Kenya, for example, have a single level, represented by the ranch committee, which is expected to enforce stock quotas, culling rates, and grazing systems, to supervise the construction and maintenance of physical facilities such as water points and dipping tanks, to provide for the purchase, distribution, and fattening of steers bought on credit, and to organize the collection and repayments of loans (Helland, 1980). In the range of tasks carried out, in the concentration of all tasks into a single organization, and in the *intended* relative permanence of their membership, group ranches are substantially different from that which preceded them. We do not yet know how permanent membership will be or whether, *in practice* and *de facto*, Maasai will shift their membership from one group ranch to another. Previously, shifts from one 'locality' to another, although relatively rare, did take place (Jacobs, 1975). Some recent investigations suggest that some Maasai group ranches now have non-members or members of other ranches more or less permanently residing within their boundaries. It seems that the old habit of shifting is still continuing.

We now turn to considering the basis for membership of pastoral organizations. We have already seen in earlier chapters, especially in Chapter 6 on land allocation, that membership in pastoral organizations can be relatively inclusive, e.g. obligatory or open to all who want to join on the same terms as existing members, or relatively exclusive, e.g. restricted to those resident in an area at a given time, or to members of a kinship group, or to a restricted number on a first-come-first-served basis. We have already discussed in Chapter 6 the relative merits of different bases for membership in respect of land allocation. Where membership is relatively inclusive, this may serve social equity well, but at the possible expense of the environment and the speed of development. Exclusivity may be difficult to apply in practice in an equitable manner because of adjudication problems; the more mobile the land-use system, the less sensible is membership based on residence on a given date and, conversely, the more sensible is one based, for example, on kinship.

However, some of the arguments about different bases for membership do not apply to other tasks to the same extent as they do to land allocation. Land is a fixed resource and what is allocated to one member is then not available for someone else; hence the need to stress equity, because the more exclusive is the membership of the organization — especially when it is based on a 'first-come-first-served' basis — the greater the danger that the already privileged will get a disproportionate share and will exclude those less well-off from subsequent benefit. As an example of this we can quote the case of group ranches in Rwanda. During the process of adjudicating rights to membership of group ranches, a new criterion for membership was suddenly inserted — the possession at the time of adjudication of at least six head of cattle. Those not fulfilling this criterion at the time of initial adjudication were given 'small agricultural holdings', too small ever to support more than two or three cattle.

But when the task involves the provision and management of services other than fixed resources — hence where, in effect, for one pastoralist to get the service he wants involves no diminution in what another pastoralist can also get — the arguments against exclusivity no longer have the same validity. Indeed, if the rich pastoralists club together to hire, for example, their own animal health auxiliary at their own expense, there may be positive benefits for the less well-off in terms of the greater general availability of veterinary supplies elicited by a regular demand for them. In this context, however, fixed resources are not only land and water but any resource, e.g. qualified veterinarians or government funds, whose supply cannot be easily and quickly expanded.

Earlier in this chapter organizational complexity was defined in terms of the number of different levels within an organization at which functions are carried out and of the specialization of functions (e.g. different planning and audit committees) and of staff. Organizational complexity will certainly be influenced by the size of an organization and by the number of different functions it has to carry out. The bigger the organization and the larger the number of functions, the more probable will it be that the organization is more complex. But complexity is not wholly determined by size and number of functions, in that for any given size and number it is still possible to opt for greater or less complexity. Greater complexity should normally permit greater attention and expertise to be brought to bear on particular subjects. On the other hand, for a complex organization to function efficiently there must be good communications between different levels and between different specialist groups within the organization. Communication, however, in many pastoral situations, is particularly difficult, partly because of the great distances over which people and messages have to travel, partly because many pastoral societies are illiterate. As a consequence it may involve considerably less resource cost, and permit much better knowledge by decision-makers about what is going on, if a single group (committee) meets for two days to discuss two subjects rather than for two separate (specialist) groups to meet for one day each. On the other hand, some mechanism has to be found firstly for compensating those who give a lot of their time to directing the affairs of a pastoral organization and, secondly, for ensuring their accountability to the other members of the organization.

In the light of these arguments we can turn to the question of whether organizations of pastoralists should be single- or multi-purpose. Partly the answer will depend on how integrated pastoral development needs to be, in the sense set out at the beginning of this chapter, partly on whether there are economies of scale to be achieved in combining many tasks in one organization, either on the part of the pastoralists, where different development tasks can share the same equipment, staff, and decision-making process, or on the part of government, when it has to maintain contact with only one rather than a number of organizations.

Clearly, some development tasks require much closer integration than others; for example, the location of new water supplies and the dates in the year on which these are opened and closed to use are critical to the success of some range-management components, because controlling the availability of drinking water is the easiest way to control where livestock graze. On the other hand, other routine aspects of operating water supplies, such as the provision of fuel and pumps, the care and maintenance of watering troughs, are not critical. If the responsibilities for managing the vegetation are in different hands from those that control the location of new water supplies and their opening and closing dates, there is quite a high probability that one of these components will cause the failure of the other; but responsibility for the routine operation of the water points does not have to be in the same hands. However, as we have seen in respect of different kinds of animal health work, the way in which staff are required to do one job, even if overall they do not have a heavy work load, may conflict with the way in which they are required to do another. One may require patient, unhurried, friendly, and frequent contact; another close adherence to time schedule; a third a firm and strict adherence to regulations. Different management styles may be required to play different roles or to carry out different functions and there may be severe diseconomies of scale in trying to put them all into the hands of the same staff or decision-makers.

There are other diseconomies of scale that arise when one puts into a single organization people of very divergent interests. Such divergences may arise from disparities in stock wealth, from ethnic or age divisions, or where, for some further reason, some members of the organization want to concentrate on one activity and others on another (e.g. livestock-keeping versus cultivation, cattle versus shoats versus camels, etc.). For some components, e.g. range management, it may be essential to group many divergent interests into a single organization and to insist that people of different interests act together for the good of all. But organizations whose members' interests diverge sharply tend not to be dynamic. On a group ranch in Kenya, for example, although various different opportunities exist for improving aggregate group income, the costs and benefits, not always identifiable solely in economic terms, of different opportunities fall unequally on different groups within the ranch, with the consequence that 'members are reluctant to make decisions for fear that this could upset the delicately balanced status quo' (Doherty, 1979, p. 20). The result is stagnation.

A satisfactory solution in most pastoral situations is not likely to be achieved by forcing people of quite divergent interests into a single, permanent organization responsible for all those components of pastoral development, or for all the roles set out at the beginning of this chapter, which organizations of pastoralists can perform. Nor is it to be found in trying to form groups of people of apparently homogeneous interests into permanent multi-purpose organizations. The ways in which interests may diverge are too numerous (i.e. it is not only a question of relative wealth), and the same individual's interests change over time. Much more dynamism is likely to be found in organizations where membership is voluntary rather than compulsory and where members can shift from one organization to another — even one carrying out the same kind of task — according to where they see their current needs as being most adequately met. On the other hand, voluntary associations will not normally be suitable when the task is to define access to and to manage relatively fixed resources. For some roles and for some functions (e.g. control over water supplies and range management) the need for integration is such that single multi-purpose (to cover these functions) organizations with inclusive, possibly compulsory, membership are required. But the functions of such organizations should be kept to the bare minimum.

A policy of permitting or promoting multiple voluntary organizations, each with only one or a few tasks, might seem to present government services with a major administrative problem of having to deal with a multitude of small organizations, each with a changing membership;[5] for example, within the same clan or geographical area there might be more than one organization sharing an improved bull, several involved in animal health improvements, and others with livestock marketing functions. On the face of it, dealing with so many might seem a very time-consuming affair, leading to low productivity among government staff. On the other hand, low productivity also arises from dealing with one organization in a monopoly position, riven with factions, and whose key leadership positions command such power over resources that they are filled not on the basis of personal merit and efficiency but of factional representation. The more unreliable the natural environment, the more the different human groups will be in competition with each other in times of stress and the more prone larger organizations will be to internal strife.

PASTORALISTS AND PLANNING

A common exhortation is that pastoralists should have a greater say in planning their own developments. To an extent this can be achieved by arrangements whereby the maximum number of tasks and functions are carried out by individual pastoralists for themselves or by organizations of pastoralists in which they genuinely manage operations; to an extent in other cases it can be achieved by allowing pastoralists, as individual consumers of pastoral development services, a choice between alternative sources of these services, with the prosperity of those employed in each source (whether in government agencies or in private enterprise) depending on their attracting enough customers, thereby giving them a direct incentive to pay heed to pastoralists' preferences expressed in their expenditure. But not all pastoral development services (e.g. allocation of scarce grazing land) can be structured in these ways; some decisions cannot be made in, or services rendered through, pastoralists' organizations or the 'market-place', but only through the political and bureaucratic planning process. We need to consider how pastoralists can have an appropriate impact on this.

It is not, in fact, an easy or simple matter to involve pastoralists in bureaucratic planning. Among the difficulties are the following. In some countries governments wish to reduce rather than to increase the political influence of pastoralists. In other countries the existing organizations of pastoralists do not have any legitimate authority, in the eyes of either pastoralists or bureaucrats, to 'represent' pastoralists' points of view or to enter into binding agreements on their behalf. The existing organizations are very numerous and often in conflict with each other and it is very costly, in terms of government staff time and transport, to consult them properly, and each group may (correctly) judge that its own interests are best served by actions which harm its rivals rather than by actions for the common good of both groups. The timetable for planning which governments, especially if they are seeking development funds from overseas aid agencies, need to follow (often requiring four or five years and more between identifying a pastoral development project and taking the first real steps to implement it) is so lengthy that pastoralists become bored by it and do not believe that the government concerned is being serious (Fortmann and Roe, 1981, pp. 143–151). Where more than two parties are involved in planning negotiations, e.g. government, donor *and* pastoralists, so great is the practical difficulty of conducting the negotiations, in terms of getting the parties together in the same room, or getting written statements understood and answered, that the views of the least powerful partner, the pastoralists, tend to be ignored in order that at any rate progress can be maintained in negotiations between the other two.

Pastoralists usually have little experience of bureaucratic procedures and do not know how to operate the system to achieve their ends. Pastoral societies often have within them many competing interests (different ethnic groups, rich and poor, keepers of different species of livestock); outsiders do not recognize this but look for some single 'pastoralists' point of view', which is then supplied by the dominant group within society as though it were the unanimous view of the membership as a whole. Above all, the most frequent problem is that government officials believe that pastoralists do not have anything useful to contribute to the planning process and this belief reinforces the often unconscious desire of the officials to retain power in their own hand.[6]

In some countries government's nervousness about giving power to pastoralists' organizations is such that there is no prospect of these being given a direct participatory role in the planning process; the best that can be hoped for is that the officials concerned become reasonably well informed about the pastoral systems in which they are about to intervene, and that pastoralists' aspirations be interpreted to them through a competent intermediary who may even be able to act as negotiator. By their training, social anthropologists are better equipped than other professions to fulfil this role.[7] However, this is a very second-best solution since if the intermediary is a regular employee of the government it will be difficult for him to mobilize political support against recalcitrant officials, and if the intermediary is a short-term consultant his report can be shelved and he has no mechanism to get it back into consideration.

Where, however, government is willing in principle to support active participation by pastoralists in the planning process, what is required is an effective channel through which the interests of all sections of pastoral society can be identified and considered, so that pastoralists have some effective way of ensuring that their views are not ignored by officials, and that they are able to understand official procedures and can follow the planning process and influence it at the appropriate time.

A great difficulty arises where (as is usually the case) the pastoral society or societies for which development is being planned are heterogeneous, with different groups within the society having different and conflicting interests. There are a large number of cases (e.g. imperial Russia, Iraq in the 1930s, Sudan during British rule, Botswana) in which the leaders of pastoral society have allied themselves with politicians or officials of central government to acquire for themselves as individuals land and other assets which were previously the property of the society as a whole; this can happen quite quickly, even in societies which were previously rather egalitarian. There are, therefore, great dangers (as well as positive features) in building into a planning process some mechanism which enables pastoral leaders to veto or insist upon particular features of pastoral development. An example of such a 'mechanism' has occurred in the last 15 years in Botswana where district land boards, partly indirectly elected, partly appointed, have an important role, established by central government legislation, in the allocation of tribal land. This mechanism, often to the great irritation of central government officials and foreign aid agencies, has ensured that the views of the local (mainly livestock-owning) influential people in the boards have to be taken into account in planning development programmes involving land allocation in tribal areas, and these land boards have, for example, effectively amended the original intentions of the Tribal Grazing Land Policy enunciated by the Botswana Government in 1975. If the land boards' power had been only advisory and not mandatory, and if they had been entrenched not in law but only in administrative regulation, the boards' opinions would probably have been ignored.

A crucial element, however, in the ability of Botswana's land boards to influence events has been that they have been endowed with sufficient funds to employ staff of good education and administrative experience. The boards have not, therefore, been dependent on the goodwill of government officials to explain what is going on; they can find this out for themselves through their own staff and manipulate the procedures for the boards' (and no doubt also for their own individual) ends. Effective participation by pastoralists in planning requires some means whereby they can penetrate the mysteries of government administrative and legal procedure. Paid staff are one such means; another is the co-option of volunteers. In northern Kenya organizations of pastoralists have co-opted into the membership, or as unpaid 'secretaries', of their committees, those educated officials from pastoral backgrounds who are working in government schools and clinics in the area, so that their official contacts and experience can be put to the service of the pastoral communities (Dahl and Sandford, 1978, p. 184).

In matters where the interests of all sections of pastoral society coincide, e.g. in preventing incursion by non-pastoral agriculturalists into pastoralists' rangelands, a permanent organization of pastoralists, with legal powers and representing in a single organization as many pastoralists as possible, is likely to be the most effective way of representing pastoralist interests. It will not, however, be effective in bringing to government's attention the way in which the interests of different pastoral groups conflict, since the leaders of the organization, representing the dominant group, will want to pass off their views as those of all pastoralists. It will, therefore, be important for government officials to have as many contacts as possible with other pastoralists; and the multiple voluntary organizations, each with its own task, mentioned earlier, represent possible channels for such contacts.[8]

FLEXIBILITY

Almost no pastoral development programme turns out in the way that was originally planned; those that do — the Ankole Ranching Scheme in Uganda is one such example — are usually of little replicability or relevance to their countries. This characteristic unpredictability is not unique to pastoral development; it occurs in most projects in the rural sector, although it is probably more pronounced with pastoral projects because of the greater environmental unreliability of dry areas and governments' relatively greater ignorance of them. But as a consequence of this unpredictability, organizations in pastoral development need to be very flexible; they have to cope with initial miscalculations by planners which have to be set right, with short-term fluctuations whether from political, economic, or climatic causes; and with long-term trends. Such trends include changes in the size, composition, and skills of the human population, developments in technology, e.g. the use of boreholes to tap deep groundwater, and changes in people's ambitions and expectations and hence in their willingness to become or remain pastoralists on the same terms as previously. Consequently, flexibility is required in the size of organizations, in their range of functions and tasks, and in their internal structure and procedures.

There is something of a conflict between the need to entrench pastoralists rights in legislation in order to protect their interests in land against non-pastoralists and their influence in the planning process, and this need for flexibility. It is not easy for governments to return at frequent intervals to the legislature in order to amend previous legislation, and they are reluctant to do so, particularly in countries where pastoralists are of low relative political importance. Fresh legislation requires a great deal of political and administrative time and effort on each occasion, and legislators will cause political embarrassment by questioning governments' competence if they have to change course so frequently. In capitalist economic systems investment in the pastoral sector will be discouraged by frequent changes in the law, unless compensation is paid to those disadvantaged by successive changes. In Chapter 6 attention has already been drawn to rapid changes in the size of pastoral collectives in Mongolia and the USSR and of pastoral associations in Tanzania. In New South Wales in Australia the authority administering the rangelands intervened to reduce the maximum size of holding (of leased land) three times between 1930 and 1950, and that policy is now being revised yet again (Young, 1979).

Although traditional pastoral organizations are frequently described as 'conservative', the arguments are more complex than can be comprised within a simple dichotomy between 'inflexible traditional' organizations and 'flexible new ones'. There are two major practical questions: the first is how to adjust the human population to the capacity of the land to support them — which may involve boundary changes between pastoral groups or sloughing off pastoralists into non-pastoral occupations either within or outside the pastoral area; the second is how to incorporate new needs for and supplies of skilled manpower into old management structures. The second we have already discussed. In the case of the first, traditional organizations have always had to cope with population imbalances. Some pastoral societies have well-worn mechanisms for sloughing off surplus populations into other occupations inside or outside the pastoral sector: some characteristics of most traditional societies — their common ownership of grazing rights and the rather diffuse rights to ownership of livestock — make it quite easy to manage the gradual transition, of first the young men, then their wives and families, and finally their remaining capital from pastoral to non-pastoral occupations and sometimes back again (e.g. see Dahl, 1979; Bonte, 1975).[9] Similarly and probably for the same reasons, pastoral collectives — new organizations — in the USSR also seem to have been very successful in managing the release of people from pastoralism into new occupations — either in industry elsewhere or in cropping activities on the collective. In contrast, events in Australia 'have highlighted the disadvantages of establishing small single family stations. These stations, because of their small size, are relatively inflexible. In times of stress pastoralists on small stations are faced with the decision of either buying additional land, or finding off-farm work and neglecting the work which is essential to the long-term survival of their stations' (Young, 1979). Because all the stations in some densely settled areas are the same size, it is very difficult for a pastoralist to sell out, since his neighbours, facing the same adverse conditions, are not in a position to buy him out.

It is not necessarily a mark of failure that pastoral development programmes do not turn out in the way that was initially planned. If one believes that pastoral situations are particularly subject to unpredictable large fluctuations in their physical and social environment and that appropriateness of components of development and organizational forms depends on the objectives pursued and on the characteristics of pastoral situations, then if the latter change so too should the former. One corollary of this could be to be entirely opportunistic in one's approach to organizations of pastoralists, never investing too many resources in their development because by tomorrow they may have become obsolete and redundant in the light of some unexpected turn of events. An alternative corollary is to endow pastoral organizations with the competence to turn their hands to as wide as possible a range of functions that may be thrust upon them and with an ability to change and adapt. In principle that is a sounder approach, but organizations that can turn their hands to anything do not 'spring from nowhere', but emerge as a result both of training and of that confidence that arises from having done other tasks successfully. Most pastoral development programmes invest very little in training pastoralists in how to manage organizations; what training does take place emphasizes technical innovations and principles of range science rather than, for example, simple accounting or how to take minutes. This failure to train in management skills is in marked contrast to what has often happened in the past in respect of agricultural co-operatives and local government institutions — at any rate in ex-British colonies which often invested heavily in co-operative and local government training schools. The training in these was not a sufficient condition for the success of co-operative and local government institutions, but without it they had no prospect of success at all. In Indonesia it was found that 'training in basic management skills such as bookkeeping, planning, and project control gave villagers the confidence to contribute to project planning decisions, to detect financial irregularities, and indirectly to challenge and even remove corrupt leaders' (Honadle *et al.*, 1980, p. 129).

There is also a good deal of experience from other kinds of human activities and development programmes that doing and managing one activity well is of the greatest help in subsequently doing other more numerous and more complex tasks; working procedures are learnt and confidence gained, from overcoming difficulties in one activity, that one can overcome them in others also. This experience suggests that, even if eventually organizations of pastoralists will be required to undertake a wider variety of powers and functions, these need to be taken up in sequence and not too many at once. Development programmes seldom have a long enough time-scale for governments to set out deliberately with the intention of gradually fostering institutional capabilities in this way; where new pastoral organizations do mature and develop in competence it seems to be in spite, rather than because, of plans for their establishment laid by government. *Negdels* in Mongolia now seem to function as effective multi-purpose management units, but in 1928 when they or their precursors were first established no one expected that it would take 30 years before they became effective.

253

SUMMARY OF MAIN POINTS

In this chapter there was a shift away from looking at the organization and management of particular components of development and, instead, the focus turned to organizations of pastoralists seen as a whole over the broad range of their functions in components and of other wider roles such as representing pastoralists' interests generally in relation to other pastoral or non-pastoral groups, including government. There was also some shift away from a static point of view, i.e. from considering what may be the best way of organizing things at a particular moment of time, towards a more dynamic view, i.e. to considering how organizations change over time.

After a brief review of the various broad roles organizations of pastoralists can play, five organizational options were explored. The first option concerned the choice between using existing organizations in preference to establishing new ones for new tasks. The extremely slow rate at which new organizations have been established under some development programmes and the faster rate under others was noted, and it was suggested that the critical factor favouring speed is the extent to which pastoralists see the establishment of new organizations as the only way they can get or retain secure title to use their land. Traditional organizations in a number of cases seem to have adapted fast and well to new tasks, and the critical issue to be considered in regard to establishing new organizations or using existing ones is often one of equity rather than of efficiency.

Four other options were considered together: size, basis for membership, scope, and complexity. There are both economies and diseconomies of scale in organizations of pastoralists. As far as defining access to and managing fixed resources are concerned, the balance of argument will often come down in favour of large size and of inclusive, possibly even compulsory, membership, and in those cases such organizational complexity will be required as is necessary to manage those activities which need to be integrated (e.g. control over water supplies and range management). But as far as the provision and management of other pastoral development services (e.g. animal health or livestock marketing) is concerned, the balance of advantage will often lie in favour of a large number of small, simple organizations with voluntary and exclusive membership. Partly this is because more dynamism will be found in such organizations where there is more homogeneity of interests, partly because the pastoral environment is a particularly difficult one in which to cope with organizational complexity.

The involvement of pastoralists in the planning of development was next considered and the difficulties in this recounted. To a great extent what is needed is a way in which pastoralists' interests *vis-à-vis* the interests of other groups can be vigorously promoted in the planning process. For this large, politically powerful organizations of pastoralists, whose involvement is entrenched in law and cannot be disregarded, are what is required. However, such large organizations will not adequately represent the interests of weaker sections of pastoral society and governments need to develop and maintain other channels for the representation of these interests.

Organizations of pastoralists need to be flexible so as to meet changing circumstances. Confidence and competence are best built up by gradually giving them increased responsibilities rather than by overloading them all at once. More help needs to be given than is usual in development programmes, to enable organizations of pastoralists to develop management skills which will enable them to adapt flexibly to changing circumstances.

NOTES TO CHAPTER 10

1. Bonte (1975), however, stresses the negative impact on pastoral society of this transition rather than the positive role of the society in facilitating it.

2. Many existing — often termed 'traditional' — organizations of pastoralists have grown up in response not only to factors internal to pastoral society but also to deliberate pressures from governments wishing to exercise general political control. The contrast being made here is between 'existing' organizations which have grown up in these ways and 'new' ones introduced specifically to manage some of the kinds of pastoral development discussed in this study.

3. For a summary discussion of this issue see Gow and Morss (1981).

4. For an example of a detailed description of these rights in one society see Dahl (1979).

5. From Botswana Willett (1981) reports that at least 1100 separate voluntary 'groups' in the agricultural sector — mainly livestock-oriented groups — had been formed in a total human population of less than 1 million. Willett's report came out too late to influence this study.

6. For a case study of how government officials (in a non-pastoral context) manipulated allegedly participatory planning procedures to keep their own power intact, see Conlin (1981).

7. For an example of a social anthropologist in this role see Marx (1981).

8. This conclusion about the need for multiple channels of communication is similar to that reached by Uphoff and Esman (1974).

9. But for an opposite viewpoint see Haaland (1977).

Chapter eleven
The organization of government

INTRODUCTION

This chapter will deal with the organization and management of the activities of governments in relation to pastoral development. The chapter falls into three main sections. The first will contain a discussion of some general issues in relation to government's activities. Among them are the role of government, the major problems of government's organization and management which have been experienced in pastoral development programmes, issues of political support and of staff development and motivation, the need for special administrative procedures, and the relative desirability of a project or programme approach to pastoral development. The second main section will deal with central government at the national level. Two issues will be discussed in detail, organizational structure and the formulation of general policies and specific plans. The third main section will deal with government's activities at the levels of districts and below. The focus will be on two main issues, organizational structure and the management of field staff.

GENERAL ISSUES

In this section a number of issues will be discussed which are relevant to the organization and management of government's activities at both the national and local (i.e. district and below) levels.

The role of government

In pastoral development government has five broad roles to play. Firstly, it must ensure an adequate level of security from attacks on persons and property in pastoral areas by forces both internal and external to pastoral society. Such security is a precondition for the success of other components treated in this study. Secondly, government will, in almost all cases, have to carry out the research required to improve the technology of range and livestock management. Thirdly, it will also normally have to act as the channel through which funds from sources outside pastoral society (often foreign aid sources) flow into pastoral development. Fourthly, government usually influences the general institutional background, in terms of land-tenure policies, the price ratios between commodities which pastoralists buy and sell, and the provision of social and physical infrastructure (schools,

255

clinics, roads), against which pastoral development takes place. Fifthly, it usually provides some of the services, e.g. animal health and water supply, involved in specific components of pastoral development. It is this fifth role which has been the main focus of attention in previous chapters. It will continue to receive attention in this chapter also, but the other roles will receive relatively more attention than they have had so far.

A review of recent problems

A review of recent pastoral development projects in Africa reveals that, serious as are the difficulties found in implementing these at field level, many projects are defeated by defects in the organization of government far away from field level. Prominent among the defects are the following: the policies of different parts of government that affect pastoral development are contradictory or non-existent, particularly policies about the prices at which pastoral commodities should be sold; government's financial support to pastoral development is small and unreliable, agreed contributions to pastoral projects not materializing when required; administrative procedures for budgeting, spending, and accounting for development funds and for procuring supplies are inappropriate or not properly adhered to; recruitment and subsequent performance of government staff is unsatisfactory. In part, staff problems arise from there simply not being enough trained people available; however, sometimes the qualifications required to fill specific posts are unnecessarily overstated and, although there are adequately trained people available to fill them, the posts are left unfilled because people with the extra qualifications demanded are either not available at all or, even if recruited for the posts, are soon seduced away into more attractive positions. In part, the staff problems arise from the incompetence of individuals with apparently adequate qualifications or from poor management of staff, for example inadequate definition of tasks or delegation of responsibilities. In part they arise from poor staff motivation.[1]

Only some of the problems can be solved through changes in the organization and management of government services and of staff directly related to pastoral development. Other problems derive from the generally weak political position of pastoralists *vis-v̀-vis* other occupations or ethnic groups in the country, or from the ambitions and incentives of government staff and their relation to other classes. Government services directly related to pastoral development will not operate in fundamentally different ways or with totally different degrees of efficiency from other non-pastoral government services. Some differences may be expected, but pastoral services cannot be isolated completely from the general pattern of government administrative ethics and behaviour; modest improvements, however, can be brought about.

Coalitions of interests

Some of these improvements are outside what would conventionally be described as administrative and organizational reform. In countries where pastoralists, or particular groups of them selected for attention, are politically weak, an important management tool is so to design a pastoral development programme that it simultaneously and indissolubly serves the interests of both weak pastoralists and other politically more powerful groups who can then apply political pressure to reward those promoting the programme and punish those obstructing it. A corollary of this is that one should not design programmes which only favour the politically weak to the detriment of the politically powerful. Coalitions of interests in support of a programme can motivate both the staff directly concerned in it and other bureaucrats and politicians responsible for providing it with finance and other support. Projects for the construction of rural roads benefit from the political support they receive not only from weak and isolated rural inhabitants but from the powerful engineering companies with offices in the national capital that are awarded the contracts for construction; they are a powerful lobby to overcome bureaucratic inertia. In pastoral development programmes some opportunities for similar coalitions of interest arise: international pharmaceutical companies will lobby for programmes for the control of tsetse and internal and external livestock parasites and for some vaccinations; engineering companies will apply pressure for some kinds of water development.[2]

However, programmes to improve livestock marketing or the productivity of rangelands present rather few opportunities for coalitions of powerful interests in their favour. A programme to control livestock markets and stock routes in Ethiopia during the 1970s was intended to favour politically impotent consumers and pastoralists, but seemed likely to injure livestock traders and municipal officials; it was effectively obstructed and was an almost total failure. In a very few cases of range-improvement programmes, all pastoralists may benefit from physical and mechanical work to improve soil and moisture conservation, or from fencing or the application of chemical fertilizers or herbicides, interventions in which commercially and therefore politically powerful companies may become involved. In most cases, however, range development is likely to create or exacerbate conflicts of interests: between pastoralists and cultivators forbidden to intrude into pastoral areas; between poor pastoralists and rich ones who do not wish to abide by stock quotas or who wish to team up with outside financial interests or management companies to develop private ranches for their private benefit. In Botswana the 1975 Tribal Grazing Land Policy was intended to be a two-pronged approach — to assist large herd owners on commercial private ranches and poor herd owners in communal areas. In practice there has been some, albeit slow, progress with commercial ranches but almost none in communal areas; the linkage between the two prongs was not indissoluble and the powerful political forces, which have been promoting the commercial ranches, have not been so anxious to press ahead with changes in the communal areas which might have diminished their own grazing rights there.

A sense of success

Pastoral areas are harsh, and they are not places in which most government staff choose to live and work. Even basic household goods may be difficult to purchase, housing is usually hot and uncomfortable, and facilities for education, health, and recreation are lacking; consequently staff working there are often separated from their families. Their morale in such circumstances *can* be kept high, either because they believe that they are performing well in a successful programme which will earn them honour and promotion in due course, or because they have an almost ideological commitment to their work (e.g. a sense of 'rolling back the desert') that inspires them to slog away in spite of the lack of normal incentives.

In practice, however, in most cases neither the incentive of success nor ideological commitment points in the right direction. There is a pervasive sense of failure about most pastoral development programmes and they ruin far more reputations than they make. Partly this is due to real technical and social problems which even well-planned and well-endowed programmes would face. Partly it is due to unrealistic programmes, where precise targets and timetables have been set which there was never a real hope of meeting in the time and with the resources available; such programmes are afflicted from the outset by a sense of crisis and scramble. Partly it is due to the fact that the ideal model for successful development which we have in our minds is an inappropriate one. It is a model in which careful detailed surveys lead to blueprint plans which are exactly followed during the course of implementation ('blueprint' plans are defined later); in which expert officials impart knowledge to ignorant pastoralists; in which project managers issue orders for managing the ranges which well-disciplined pastoralists obey; in which care for the long-term condition of the natural environment (soil, water resources, vegetation) takes precedence over the convenience of the human population, and where any excess in the human population over the long-term capacity of the natural environment to sustain it can be and is accommodated in other occupations or areas. And to many staff whose training has been in North America or Australia, or who have come under the influence of range experts from those continents, the notion of a proper form of pastoral development is inextricably bound up with the emergence of capitalist forms of ranching; to them anything else seems insincere and a third-rate solution.

This ideal model is far removed from either the practical possibilities or the real requirements in most pastoral situations. Its prime consequence is to generate inappropriate attitudes and ambitions (i.e. to give orders rather than to transmit information and to meet needs) among programme staff engaged in pastoral development. As events diverge from ideal programmes the staff tend to blame unco-operative and conservative pastoralists and lack of support from higher levels in government. Similarly, those higher levels express dissatisfaction with the competence of programme staff, who therefore seek to leave pastoral programmes as soon as they can get a transfer elsewhere. The resulting rapid turnover of staff generates the very incompetences of which they were accused in the first place.

Some pastoral development programmes seem to suffer from a sense of failure and from inappropriate ideology to a somewhat less degree than others. Among the more complex programmes the main examples are the Drought-Prone Areas Programme in India, the Tribal Grazing Land Policy and its associated programmes in Botswana, and perhaps in their earlier, but not in their more recent, stages, the company and group ranching elements of two pastoral development projects in Kenya. Among less complex programmes are some of the vaccination campaigns against major epizootic diseases of cattle in some countries, particularly in the late 1950s and early 1960s. The evidence is too slight to draw firm conclusions, but these programmes display the following characteristics to a greater degree than do others: a coherent policy was largely evolved by government's own institutions (including long-term expatriates but not short-term consultants) and was not imposed from outside by a donor; the programmes are flexible and not tightly scheduled for more than a budget-year ahead, being of a 'process' rather than a 'blueprint' nature; substantial responsibility and power of initiation and self-evaluation are devolved to staff at district level and outside reviews are relatively infrequent. However, while these are characteristic features of programmes which suffer less of a sense of failure, it is difficult to be sure which of the phenomena are causes and which effects.

Responding to needs from below

One of the most striking features of most pastoral development programmes is the extent to which a responsiveness, by government services and staff, to needs expressed from below, i.e. by pastoralists, not only has low priority but is even discouraged. Both in range management and animal health services the roles in which the services are cast are those of regulatory agency and stern instructor rather than of responding to customers. The emphasis is on what is 'good' for the pastoralists, not on what they want. Of course all government services in all countries tend to follow this pattern to some degree; teachers and doctors, for example, refer to professional skills and ethics as standards of performance rather than to satisfaction afforded to clients; but even in schools and clinics a good deal of attention has to be paid in practice to the views of parents and patients. In pastoral development the opinions and desires, i.e. the expressed needs, of pastoralists are reckoned of little account.

This feature presents a problem for the effective management of government services, since it rules out one criterion for assessing the effectiveness of individual services and staff which is both defensible on philosophic grounds and widely used in assessing the value of other goals and services. Not only does 'fulfilment of pastoralists' expressed needs' provide a potential criterion but also in many cases a way of actually measuring effectiveness in terms of this criterion and hence of rewarding it — in material terms or by promotion or status. One simple system in the case of animal health, for example, would be to calculate the quantity of veterinary supplies sold to pastoralists and to reward livestock assistants and provincial veterinary officers on a commission basis. However, such a system, although relatively simple, can have severe drawbacks, both in terms of inappropriate technical packages being pressed on pastoralists not yet familiar with them for the sake of short-term gain by project staff, and in the incentive that this would create for staff to concentrate only on better-off pastoralists most likely to be able to purchase supplies. For other services, e.g. for range management or for water development, where pastoralists' expressed needs are less well measured in cash terms, this system for assessing both performance and reward would be less applicable.

Nevertheless, not only is the concept of fulfilling pastoralists' express needs valid in itself, but paying attention to these needs would also incorporate pastoralists' own knowledge into the planning and monitoring systems. There is a good deal of evidence that the usual bureaucratic procedures fail to do this and, as a consequence, planning mistakes are made and opportunities to learn lessons are missed, which need not have been if pastoralists had been properly consulted and full use made of their knowledge. However, usually in planning systems, although lip-service is paid to consulting pastoralists, there are no real incentives for planners to do so, only costs. The incentives for planners, and the pressures on them, are to produce plans involving major capital expenditures quickly; less attention is paid to how effectively they can be implemented later. Consulting pastoralists and obtaining their agreement is very time-consuming, and if it is to be done thoroughly planners need to be rewarded, not penalized, for doing so. Similarly in implementation and monitoring and evaluation. There may be some modest gain in private satisfaction in obtaining the approval of pastoralists for what one has done or their opinions about a programme, but this modest and private satisfaction needs to be reinforced by more significant and public rewards if it is to become an effective incentive to desirable behaviour. There is a further point about assessing staff performance in terms of their responsiveness to pastoralists' needs. At the moment, staff selection and promotion procedures are excessively weighted in favour of academic qualifications rather than effectiveness. Whether effectiveness were to to be measured in terms of commodities purchased by pastoralists or by their approval expressed in some other way, the criterion of effectiveness in terms of fulfilling pastoralists' needs would provide some kind of fairly objective counterweight to the present emphasis on academic qualifications. We shall return later to the question of devising mechanisms for consulting pastoralists and for structuring services to be responsive to their expressed needs.

Not all government services in pastoral development can realistically be planned or evaluated on the basis of their popularity with pastoralists. While all pastoralists might agree that in the long run quarantine procedures need to be observed in the event of outbreaks of disease, that there must be effective and impartial policing to prevent stock theft, grazing trespass, and outbreaks of violence, and even that stock limitations and quotas need to be enforced to limit overgrazing, in the day-to-day progress of affairs competition between individuals and groups is too intense, especially in the more arid pastoral areas, for popular approval to be consistent enough to guide, evaluate, and motivate the staff of essentially regulatory services. Of course such government services should not be entirely indifferent to popular opinion, but they need to stand off somewhat and pastoral pressure needs to be filtered through several intermediaries if these regulatory agents are not simply to serve private and factional interests.

There are very few examples of government services being so structured that organizations and staff respond sensitively and rapidly to pastoralists' expressed needs. One example comes from the USA. After the passing of the Taylor Grazing Act in 1934 advisory boards elected by pastoralists, at least in some areas, had effective control over the selection and career prospects of range staff. Professional opinion seems to have deplored this and the control to have diminished or ended in about 1960, with favourable results in terms of the better regulation of grazing pressure (Heady and Bartolome, 1977, pp. 25, 64, 74). Twenty years later, however, in the so-called 'Sage Brush Rebellion' (federal) government range agencies are under heavy attack for their alleged uselessness, and while many of the attacks are inspired less by concern for the productivity of range vegetation and more by a desire on the part of commercial interests to exploit non-vegetation resources for their private profit, the range agencies have not built up adequate political support among pastoralists to be able to brush off their attackers with impunity (Shanks, 1978). In some pastoral areas in other countries, e.g. India and Kenya, elected or appointed representatives of pastoralists sit on committees at district level or below; but these committees either have only advisory status or else the pastoralists' representatives are outnumbered by officials and their influence is small. For example, in one Indian district a senior official suggested that these representatives were too illiterate and ignorant to make sensible decisions, but that they are allowed a say as to *where* facilities should be located (i.e. which groups of livestock owners should be favoured) but not in what the facilities should do or how they are run. In Botswana the direct political influence of wealthy livestock owners, through their own positions in central government or through their personal contacts with national politicians, as much as the influence they exert through land boards, makes the services fairly responsive to their needs.

Staff specialization in pastoralism

Some pastoral development services, e.g. range management, mainly consist of staff who by their qualifications are specialized in arid and semi-arid areas and whose entire professional career is therefore likely to be spent on pastoral affairs. Other services, e.g. water development, animal health, livestock marketing, political administration and police, education, and health, are provided in non-pastoral as well as pastoral areas, and the staff of these services may, therefore, in countries with both kinds of areas, be transferred into senior positions in pastoral areas without having had any previous experience of them. This frequently causes serious problems when they either try to make pastoral area facilities conform, inappropriately, to the pattern of non-pastoral areas, or where they propose specifically for pastoral areas new patterns, but ones which are not adequately based on understanding and experience of the special characteristics of these areas.

In some cases governments have defined a corps of 'pastoral area specialists' within services that serve both pastoral and non-pastoral areas. For example, in Kenya under British colonial rule the political administrators of the northern pastoral areas were something of a *corps d'élite* apart (Chenevix-Trench, 1964), who normally served almost all their careers in these areas unless appointed to very senior government positions outside, and it was very difficult for those not members of the corps to obtain a posting to these areas. The sense of 'éliteness' that they built up made these postings much sought after (in contrast to the status of 'punishment postings' that they have sunk into in the post-colonial period). Members of the corps were very able, very experienced in pastoral affairs, physically very tough, but somewhat impervious to new ideas other than their own. In imperial Ethiopia governors of sub-provinces and districts in pastoral areas tended, on transfer, to be rotated only between postings in the same sort of areas, although they did not constitute the same sort of élite as in Kenya in the colonial period. In imperial Iran a special teachers' training college provided teachers only to schools in pastoral areas.

Some mechanism or procedure is highly desirable for ensuring that senior staff without previous experience of pastoral areas are adequately oriented towards their special characteristics. Otherwise, officials of the only service which *is* regionally specialized, the range-management service, are liable both to spend too much of their time trying informally to teach their non-specialist colleagues (and in the process are often overruled by them) and also to be credited with a status as general experts in pastoral affairs which they do not really merit. In most countries the importance of the pastoral sector is not sufficient to justify regular or frequent induction courses for those posted into these areas, or to positions of responsibility for them; hence a regionally specialized corps in which staff learn about these areas by experience in junior posts before taking up senior ones is a more likely solution. It has, however, dangers in that rules of thumb devised at and suitable for one period of time may achieve the status of permanent principles which a small inbred corps may not have the imagination to challenge.

Special administrative procedures

Some government procedures are particularly ill-adapted to the needs of pastoral development; such procedures which occur in budgeting, procurement, recruitment, staff remuneration, tend to be devised in urban areas which are relatively well endowed with contractors and other sources of commercial supply and services, with reasonably good communications to ministerial headquarters, with fair concentrations of government staff and with means for depositing and drawing money. They tend to be somewhat inappropriate for rural areas in general and this rural maladaptation is magnified in pastoral areas. As an extreme example one can quote (an actual case) the problem of obtaining estimates for repairing shallow wells in pastoral areas. Government procurement procedures frequently demand obtaining, say, three competitive bids for carrying out repair work above a certain cost level. The contract is then awarded to the lowest bidder; but the cost of visiting and inspecting a series of shallow wells in livestock areas may amount to 70 or 80 per cent of the total cost of repairing them if the repairs are carried out on the same trip as the inspection. Obviously, contractors will not be prepared to submit bids in such a situation where two out of three bidders will certainly lose US$80, say, for every 100 that the winning bidder receives from the contract.

Government budgetary procedures normally require the ability to forecast financial needs for a year or more ahead. In stable environments this can be difficult — in unstable environments it becomes impossible. One example is the cost of material and transportation for mass vaccination campaigns against unexpected outbreaks of disease. Another example is the cost of fuel for pumping water at boreholes where livestock normally only water for brief periods during a year, but where they may have to water for several months in bad years when inadequate rains have failed to fill the usual stockponds. As we have seen in Chapter 4 and 8 government accounting procedures often require that the revenue received from a service (e.g. from selling veterinary supplies or watering livestock at boreholes) be deposited intact and that other money be then drawn from the bank to meet the recurrent expenditure of providing these supplies. This is a useful administrative device to prevent corruption and involves only modest inconvenience in, say, provincial capitals where there are branches of banks. But government boreholes in pastoral areas may be 300 or 400 km from the nearest branch and a borehole operator may spend a week or so each month travelling to deposit the watering fees he has collected and to draw his salary,even if the fees collected only just cover his salary cost. Government recruitment procedures may require that the candidates be interviewed by selection boards of senior officers, emphasize the academic and professional qualifications of candidates, and require that all appointments be approved by a central government employment agency. These may be sensible procedures in towns; they make little sense in pastoral situations where one needs to recruit people acceptable to remote communities in preference to those with formal qualifications, where senior officials rarely travel in groups into the field, and where suitable job applicants are unlikely to come to administrative headquarters.

Different pastoral situations and programmes will have their own specific procedural requirements. In general, however, the more dissimilar the social and physical characteristics of the pastoral sector in a country are from those of the rest of the economy, the more likely it is that special administrative procedures will be required to facilitate sound pastoral development. In particular, the more remote the areas of pastoral development, the more unstable their natural environment, and the less educationally well-endowed pastoral people are in comparison with other citizens, the more necessary it will be to have flexible and decentralized administrative procedures. In contrast to these requirements, the relatively heavy dependence of pastoral development programmes in most countries on financing from external donors means in practice that they are often particularly afflicted by having two sets of inflexible procedures, of national government and of foreign donor, both of which have to be satisfied simultaneously.

A project or a programme approach

Many government interventions in pastoral development, especially since the mid-1960s, have been termed 'projects' and are often financed mainly by foreign aid donors. Other interventions, particularly in the veterinary field, are called livestock 'services' or 'programmes'. Although sometimes the choice of terms simply depends on the whim of the user, sometimes also the differences in terminology reflect real differences in approach (for further discussion of terminology and real differences see Sandford, 1980b). In contrast to programmes, projects tend to be bounded in both space and time; we talk, for example, of a project area and the life of a project. Projects tend to be planned in advance with a few fairly clearly specified and relatively inflexible objectives and with relatively clearly identified and even quantified outputs and inputs of men and money; they tend to follow the blueprint approach (mentioned earlier) while programmes are more likely to follow a process approach. A 'blueprint' approach is one which is typified by certainty on the part of planners and managers that predetermined technologies and intervention techniques will work in a given local situation. In this approach implementation follows after planning in discrete phases.

In contrast a 'process' approach is a managerial orientation which assumes considerable uncertainty and is characterized by flexibility, by learning by innovation, and by continued openness to redesign and adaptation to changed circumstances. On-the-spot study and solution of problems are relied on rather than remote expertise, and planning is more or less continuous (Honadle *et al.*, 1980, pp. 42–46 and 209–212). The funds to finance projects are not only identified in advance but often to a considerable degree committed by some kind of formal agreement. Projects usually have management and organizational structures which cut across divisions of responsibility in respect of other services and programmes and which often lead to greater independence from central government direction than would be accorded to non-project activities at a similar level, and also to a shorter communications link between projects and ministries, as intermediate levels in the existing hierarchy are bypassed.

In recent years the project approach to agricultural development has come in for a good deal of blanket criticism as not matching the requirements of rural situations (Hunter, 1978, p. 111), although even for the case of pastoral development an influential voice has recently stated 'projects offer a relatively suitable framework for pastoral development' (Ruthenberg, 1980). We need to go beyond such blanket prescriptions and consider the circumstances in which the project approach is more or less appropriate. Such circumstances include the physical, social, and political characteristics of the particular pastoral situation and, where applicable, of the central government of the country.

One important factor will be the quantity and reliability of rainfall. The less plentiful and reliable the rainfall, the more wide-ranging and less predictable will be the nomadic movements of pastoralists. Both among the Borana and Somali people of the Horn of Africa — with substantially different social structures — the unpredictability of these movements has caused serious problems to projects. For example, in the Yabello Pilot Project of Ethiopia and the Grazing Block Projects of north Kenya, which were narrowly defined in space, unexpected movements of people — partly, although not wholly, sparked off by the projects themselves — upset the calculations for grazing capacities and stocking rates and the preconceived administrative arrangements. In contrast, projects on both sides of the Kenya–Tanzania border in Maasailand, where the environment is much less unpredictable, have not suffered this problem to the same degree.

The same applies to the boundedness of projects in time. The more unreliable the rainfall over time, the less meaningful it will be to work out prearranged schedules of timing and quantities for inputs and outputs. The inputs which, at the time of project planning, seem to be of the highest priority (such as an expert to advise on cactus plantations as forage reserves) can look pretty irrelevant in a five-year project which happens to start just after a drought has wiped out 50 per cent of the breeding stock so that animals rather than feed have become the most urgent constraint. The same applies to objectives. It is really very difficult to preach the urgency of resource conservation and the need to prevent overstocking when the previous livestock population has been wiped out by disease or drought; and projects, far more than conventional, long-term, less focused programmes, face great difficulties in readapting themselves to new priorities. The more unreliable the natural environment, the less useful is the project framework, with its built-in inflexibility and need for predictability.

We can turn from the natural to the administrative environment, and start by looking at the administrative circumstances in which the project framework *will* be appropriate. Where no pastoral development, or very little and that unsuccessful, has previously been undertaken in a country, then the project framework provides an opportunity both to show what can be done in the way of technical and organizational innovations, and, by concentrating effort in time and space, to generate adequate bureaucratic and political momentum to overcome inertia. These are the standard arguments for a pilot scheme for which a project framework is appropriate. This framework is also appropriate where, although what should and can be done is well known, the existing organizational structure for carrying it out is hopelessly defective, or where existing resources have become too thinly spread to make an impact and the existing structure is incapable of reconcentrating the resources. In such cases, the project framework is really a way of destroying the old structure by providing a successful rival to which support can be switched.

A project framework can also help where the existing provision of services to pastoralists is organized on narrowly specialized lines, with each department's policies and priorities being handed down separately from the centre through provincial and district officials without adequate opportunity for co-ordination of parallel services or for adjustment to meet local variations. It can even provide for a complete integration (i.e. bringing into a unitary structure) at the local level of personnel and resources from separate organizations which, at the national level possibly for reasons which are mainly appropriate for non-pastoral areas, need to be in separate organizations. Range management and water development may be examples of such a case. In these circumstances, a project framework can be useful, as it has been in the Drought-Prone Areas Programme in India, in imposing local-level co-ordination on departments that otherwise prefer to operate independently. A project framework can also be appropriate where the normal budgetary and financial procedures are too inflexible to allow the rapid expansion of services to cope with unexpected demand (e.g. for vaccinations in the face of an outbreak or epidemic, or for more pumped water supplies in the face of a drought); and where a project, in contrast to normal government services, is allowed to retain and recycle its own revenue rather than being forced to hand it over to the Ministry of Finance.

Projects may also facilitate participation by ordinary people in deciding on and managing the development programmes which affect their lives. In many countries, the relationship between pastoralists and government and its officials is such that the kinds of political and quasi-political pressure which non-pastoral people can bring to bear on ordinary government programmes to better adapt them to their needs in their locations are simply not available in pastoral areas. The physical and cultural gulf between government and pastoralists is often simply too wide, a gulf whose origin often lies in past political history, but which is further accentuated by staff recruitment procedures for government services which, by stressing academic qualifications, systematically discriminate against pastoralists. Pastoral projects can, in circumstances where the 'popular participation' objective is paramount, provide an institutional framework unhindered by precedents and procedures established elsewhere, in which new and special measures can be instituted for involving pastoralists in planning and managing development, and for adjusting staff recruitment procedures to the special needs of the pastoral situation.

The dangers of the project approach are probably well known and require only brief mention. When the central co-ordinating mechanism is relatively weak, different projects become semi-independent empires, competing with each other for scarce resources by offering, for example, special salary scales and conditions for key staff which do not increase the overall supply or efficiency of such staff but cause them to surge to and fro as first one project and then another improves its terms. Where the physical characteristics of the project areas, or decisions about the technicalities of particular components dictated by donor agencies, require specialist equipment involving economies of scale (some borehole drilling rigs and earth-moving machinery spring to mind), the project framework can lead to duplication, over-investment, and hoarding of this equipment.

MANAGEMENT AND ORGANIZATION AT THE NATIONAL LEVEL

In this section we turn to issues of management and organization of government activities at the national level. Two main issues will be discussed. Firstly that of organizational structure, the formal way in which different responsibilities and functions are allocated to different staff or organizational units, and the way in which these staff and units are, or are not, related to each other in terms of a chain of control from top to bottom in an organizational hierarchy. The second main issue relates to the formulation of general policies and specific plans at national level. This issue will be discussed in relation to the need for policies and plans and what their general content or scope should be, the institutional environment and structure in which planning (including policy-making) should take place, the role of monitoring and evaluation, participation by pastoralists in planning (at the national level), and the planning of specific investments.

Organizational structure

One important set of options relate to what we can call organizational *structure*. Should there be a separate ministry for pastoral or livestock development or should, for example, the Ministry of Agriculture be responsible for these subjects? Should responsibility for the *execution* of pastoral development be put in a parastatal which has its own board of directors with some degree of financial, administrative, and even legal independence from government? Where pastoral development is put inside the same umbrella organization (i.e. ministry or parastatal) as non-pastoral affairs, should it be 'in-line', i.e. subject to direct day-to-day control from senior officials who have non-pastoral as well as pastoral responsibilities, or should it be given a substantial degree of day-to-day managerial autonomy, with only broad issues of policy or annual budget allocations subject to control from above? Where (as is usually the case) there are several components in the national pastoral development effort (e.g. water development, range management, veterinary work) what should be the mechanisms at national level for co-ordinating or integrating their activities? Should co-ordination relate only to broad policy issues or also to the execution of programmes? At what level in central government should decision-making or the swapping of information between different components or services take place?

A very wide variety of different organizational structures have been tried in different countries or at different times, each attempting to provide the right answer to these questions. It is extremely difficult to see any overall pattern emerging from the results. This is not to suggest that it does not matter what the structure is; on the contrary, it may matter a great deal. What it does suggest, however, is that, at the national level, there is not a very close relationship between, on the one hand, the fact that one is dealing with pastoral areas or livestock and, on the other hand, organizational structure. Very similar organizational structures in two different countries give quite different 'results' — in terms of administrative and organizational behaviour — whereas 'similar results' may emerge from quite different structures in different countries. For example, a system in which there is a 'co-ordinator' and an interministerial co-ordinating committee at middle levels of seniority, to co-ordinate the activities of different government agencies operating in the pastoral field, seems to work quite well in Botswana but rather badly in Kenya. On the other hand, government's activities in purchasing livestock in pastoral areas seem to operate in much the same way in Kenya, where these activities are run by an 'in-line' unit in a ministry, and in Tanzania where (1977) it is run by an autonomous corporation itself owned by another parastatal agency. Whereas in some cases (e.g. livestock purchasing) the characteristics of the pastoral situation and of the development component seem to dominate results whatever the structure, in other cases it is general political and administrative behaviour, not formal structure, which determines the behaviour of all government organizations in whatever field.

Of course it is always possible to point to some apparently minor differences in *prima facie* similar structures or results and to claim that it is these which are the really important ones: of course, also, I believe that virtually all phenomena must have 'causes' which it should be possible, given enough attention, to trace out. But the effects of different structures at the national level have not proved a very fertile field of investigation in this cross-country study. Partly this is because the very concept of 'structure' carries with it certain implications, for example about the importance of differences in legal personality between ministry, parastatal corporation, or government-owned company, or about the way in which staff, or units, in a position of in-line subordination to senior staff or units will respond to or seek their seniors' opinions. In many countries differences in legal personality do not have much importance, nor are nominal inferiors in practice subordinate to their seniors in the way in which those who stress the importance of organizational structure believe. Structures in these countries then behave quite unexpectedly. Particular organizational structures are often advocated in order either to ensure that adequate political priority is accorded to pastoral development ('the Head of Range Management must have direct access to the Minister') or to avoid political meddling in operational details (especially in staff appointments). Such structural manipulation seldom seems to work, and the thinking behind it confuses cause and effect. If pastoral affairs do not have intrinsic political importance no amount of personal contact between Head of Range Management and Minister will obtain political support (although it will excite bureaucratic jealousy and obstruction from other professionals or departments not given similar ministerial access); and if politicians want, but are not allowed, to interfere with autonomous operational units, they will starve them of funds and of other needed support.

The formulation and co-ordination of policies and plans

In many countries planning, with reference to the pastoral sector, has come to mean no more than planning projects for funding by outside donors. This involves identifying potentially discrete investments in particular areas or sets of activities, and then carrying out studies and writing these up in the amount of detail and in the sort of way which satisfies outside donors' criteria for giving aid. In some countries with little experience in pastoral development such project planning provides almost the only occasion on which different government agencies (i.e. ministries, parastatals, or discrete organizational units within these) involved in the pastoral sector get together to discuss a common subject. It can be a very important first step in fostering the idea of inter-agency co-operation and joint consideration. But meetings to consider particular projects are not good occasions to discuss policy in general. The problem is that the process of project planning (especially as required by some aid donors) is so extravagant of scarce administrative resources that it positively discourages and crowds out further joint consideration of matters of common interest which are not apparently part of the project but which in fact strongly influence the success not only of the project but also of the pastoral sector as a whole. In what follows we shall first discuss policy-making and planning of a broad kind and later planning specific investments or projects.

The need for policies and plans

It is extremely common to find that the policies of different government agencies conflict with each other. This occurs most obviously over pricing policy, e.g. where one agency is promoting commercial or parastatal ranches, comparatively high-cost enterprises (in relation to traditional pastoralism) which need high price levels for their output in order to be viable, while at the same time another agency (e.g. the Price Commission) is trying to control meat prices at a low level for the alleged benefit of urban consumers. But the phenomenon is much more frequent than that. In their role of ensuring public security the political administration, police, and military often act, apparently quite unconscious of the results, for example by restricting nomadic movements, in a way that severely damages the natural environment or the welfare of livestock and people; indeed their actions may provoke the very insecurity they set out to eradicate. Ministries of education promote schools, and ministries of health promote clinics, of a kind that requires too static and spatially concentrated a population for the good of the environment; ministries of water provide water supplies in places, on conditions, and of capacities, that are contrary to the activities of range-management departments; and so on.

Contradictions in policy between different agencies are least likely to be resolved where there are not only clashes of interest between different nationwide economic interests, e.g. between consumers and producers over livestock prices, but where there are also great differences between ecological zones or ethnic groups. In countries of reasonable uniformity — e.g. Botswana or Somalia — one does not have contradictions of policy peculiar to pastoral areas; such contradictions are nationwide and the Cabinet or interministerial working parties of officials provide suitable mechanisms to deal with them. In countries of great environmental and cultural diversity there are several of them, however, it is extremely difficult to get policy contradictions which are peculiar to pastoral areas discussed at all. National unity is too fragile for anyone to want clearly to demarcate pastoral areas for separate treatment; to do so may seem to lend legitimacy to secessionist sentiments ('these areas really are quite different from the rest of the country'); it is better to continue with contradictions that ignore politically weak groups than to jeopardize national integrity. Of course it is not put in that way — what is said is that nothing must be done to create second-class citizens and this means that the 'best facilities', i.e. those provided in the areas of the majority, or politically potent parts, of the country must be made available (even if they are inappropriate) to the minorities as well.[3]

As already pointed out, pastoral planning in most countries has consisted of an extremely centralized system of producing very detailed 'project plans'. Sometimes these plans have been produced by special project planning units in which economics has been the dominant discipline; often the work has been done by expatriate advisers or consultants, with very little input from field officers of the areas where plans are to be implemented, or even from the national headquarters of the technical services (e.g. veterinary) involved. The whole process of project planning has been too specialized — almost a religious ritual — for much part therein to be played by non-specialists — the laity. Planning of this kind has been rather effective in one way, that is, in procuring external funds for pastoral development. Some US$600 million or more of funds, mainly external, have been made available for livestock (for the most part pastoral) development in Africa in the last 15 years (ILCA, 1980a, p. 3) — a sum probably much greater than could have been effectively utilized even if project planning and management had been better than in fact they were. But this kind of planning has been very *un*successful in producing proposals or forecasts which were then actually implemented or even fully endorsed or understood by the field staff responsible for implementation. Symptomatic of this failure is the fact that frequently insufficient copies of the project plan which has been agreed by the external donor and the national government are available for all those implementing staff who need it.

Improving the planning of pastoral development by central government is not easy. One does not get a better, more feasible, plan simply by displacing the economists or by insisting that staff at district or provincial level contribute to the planning process. Without further reform even worse plans usually result, where all that is done is to aggregate district and departmental demands. For improvement two main kinds of change are needed. Firstly, everyone concerned needs to recognize that plans which attempt to forecast in detail the future more than a year ahead, or which contain many distinct elements the success of each of which is dependent on the thorough success of others, are futile. Governments control too few of the factors which determine what will happen in pastoral development, and one of the most important factors, rainfall, is by its very nature not only uncontrollable but unpredictable also.

Secondly, at the national level much more attention needs to be given to matters which can only be dealt with at that level. For example, sensible and compatible departmental policies for pastoral areas must be drawn up. Where national procedures for budgeting (including not only estimating but also releasing funds), procurement, and accounting are not suitable for pastoral areas, special ones must be devised which are. Research priorities must be identified. The forthcoming supply of basic categories of manpower — e.g. veterinary officers, range-management assistants, water engineers — must be estimated, realistic allowance made for natural wastage, and provisional allocations for four to five years ahead made by province, department, and function. Agreement needs to be reached (on a rolling basis reviewed annually) on fairly firm orders of magnitude for two years ahead, and vaguer orders of magnitude for five years ahead, of the amount of domestic government finance (including both recurrent and capital expenditure but excluding foreign aid) which will be available for pastoral development. These things are the framework on which good programmes and projects can be hung. Most countries lack this framework.

The institutional environment and structure of planning

Senior officials in agencies related to pastoral development spend much time in coping with the problems and crises caused by failure to formulate policies and plans of the kind set out in the preceding paragraph. If they are to deal with these matters properly they must spend much more time considering them and must simultaneously be provided with the information, training, time, and place needed to make this consideration fruitful. By way of information they must have an evaluation of the effectiveness of existing operations and they need to know what alternatives are open to them and what are the likely consequences of taking one option rather than another. Without this information, altering procedures and making policies and allocations of staff and money become theoretical exercises and occasions on which to aggrandize personal positions. Busy staff with important executive responsibilities will soon tire of these. At the same time, many senior staff need not only information but also some training in how to use this for policy-making purposes. Usually their basic academic training has been in a single discipline, and their career has similarly often confined them to a narrow range of technical operations and considerations, often in a very hierarchically managed system. When they arrive at the top they are ill-equipped for, and feel ill at ease in, meeting with equals to discuss policy issues over a broad field; and by their consequent failure to attend these meetings they will sabotage them. Often what is needed is some form of (short) management training course, not so much to teach specific management techniques, although some introduction to financial and personnel management skills would greatly increase their authority and self-confidence, as to give them concentrated experience in tackling issues which cut across many different fields and disciplines and in which uncertainty and imperfect knowledge are inevitable ingredients. 'Business games' of the sort used on management courses can be useful in this.

Most senior staff in most countries already work extremely hard and an increase in the amount of time spent considering policy issues will require a cut in the time spent on other work. The usual solution proposed is for more delegation of responsibility from senior to junior levels; that this does not take place, however, is an indication not only of power-grabbing (probably reflecting insecurity) by those at the top, but also that the system is overloaded and ill-designed. Senior staff have to spend time in supervising details because they have learnt, to their cost, that they suffer if they do not. Particularly if more monitoring and evaluation of existing policies are to be undertaken, other things will have to be jettisoned completely or hived off to other organizations (e.g. the private sector), where performance is less dependent on the quality and intensity of supervision and more on self-interest on the part of junior staff. Some activities (often those advocated by foreign aid donors) have extremely small utility, for example detailed surveys of vegetation, mapping, and the estimation of carrying capacity, forecasting expenditure on a quarterly basis, herd projections (forecasting herd size and composition); yet much time is spent on doing these things and in their administration and supervision.

As far as possible operational interdependence[4] should be avoided to prevent the domino effect when the collapse of one ruins all. Nevertheless, policies, procedures, and outline allocations of staff and money cannot be decided department by department or ministry by ministry because not only do the policies and programmes of one department, through their results in the field, affect the operations of others, but they also compete for some categories of staff and money. A forum is required where collective consideration of the issues can take place. In a number of countries high-level (e.g. at the level of permanent secretary, or head of veterinary services, etc.) interdepartmental or interministerial permanent committees have been established in the livestock field, usually in connection with particular livestock projects financed by foreign donors. The record of these committees is not impressive.

There seem to be three reasons for this. Firstly, where co-ordinating committees are set up in connection with specific projects, heads of services fear that if they sit on such committees with their equals they will lose operational control of the services for which they are responsible. When such committees are set up at a more junior level they function quite well as places where information can be exchanged and problems discussed, because a head of service is in no way threatened by the views of a committee of officials junior to him. Experiences with livestock projects in Kenya and Mauritania and with the Tribal Grazing Land Policy in Botswana confirm this. A second reason for the poor record of committees at senior level is that a secretariat is essential to programme meetings and to ensure a flow of items and papers for consideration; often such a secretariat is not laid on and the committees languish and expire for lack of the guidance and impetus that a secretariat can provide.

The third reason why interdepartmental committees at senior level often fail to work properly is structural. Part of the structural problem is internal to departments or ministries and is related to the way they organize responsibility by function rather than by area. For example, the Ministry of Education may be organized on functional lines (tertiary, secondary, primary, education departments), not by geographic areas, and as a consequence it may be difficult to find anyone at senior level with adequate interest or experience in pastoral affairs.

Part of the structural problem concerns relations between departments or ministries and the difficulty of finding an acceptable 'lead agency' to take the initiative in identifying specifically pastoral problems and obtaining the co-operation of other agencies in solving them. Ministries with responsibilities for particular services (e.g. education, health, agriculture) are extremely jealous of their own sovereignty and suspicious of acts of aggrandizement by other ministries. This is a universal phenomenon not restricted to the pastoral scene or to Third World countries. The Ministry of Health may accept an initiative from the Ministry of Education that concerns the health of pastoral schoolchildren, but it would probably be extremely resentful of Agriculture taking an initiative in reconciling policies on a multilateral (e.g. three or four ministries) rather than on a purely bilateral basis. 'Neutral' ministries, for example of finance, development planning, rural development, may try to play a leading role in this field. However, such neutral ministries tend to suffer from a lack of expertise in the pastoral development field, because they lack field offices in which junior officials can pick up practical experience in pastoral areas. In too few cases have post-colonial states succeeded in integrating the officers of the political provincial administrations (i.e. district governors or commissioners) into the central government rural planning bureaucracy (India, of course, is an exception); that bureaucracy then lacks the authority and credibility that field experience confers. The problem of lack of expertise is least severe in those countries where pastoralists are well represented in government — but it is these countries that suffer least from contradictory policies.

The lead agency needs to be of sufficient political standing to be able to ensure that other ministries or departments do not ignore it, and it probably needs, as already pointed out, to have within it a small unit (or a small part of a large unit) to act as secretariat and to provide one person or team with an overall view. This unit needs to call meetings, draw up agendas, take minutes, draw attention to decisions made but not yet carried out, and ensure that papers are circulated in good time before meetings. An important task is to identify subjects which need discussion and decision and to designate an appropriate forum for this. It may need to service a *number* of interministerial or inter-agency groups, most of them of an *ad hoc* rather than a permanent nature, staffed at different levels of seniority — very rarely at the most senior — and set up to investigate and determine policy and procedures in particular subject areas. Certain agencies should feature in almost all such groups, for example the political administration, the range-management agency, the veterinary services; others such as the health service much more rarely; the Ministry of Finance (and the finance departments of particular ministries) should feature frequently — not often in their role as investment appraisers but much more often in their roles as day-to-day controllers of financial flows and regulators of budgeting, accounting, and procurement procedures. Foreign aid agencies should also be co-opted in those roles, although few countries — now that the pressures of the McNamara era on World Bank staff to increase the flow of funds to agriculture in developing countries has ended — are in a strong enough position *vis-à-vis* aid donors to get them to come to such meetings where the impact of their activities as well as those of other organizations can be reviewed.

The most successful example of a lead agency in pastoral development in Africa is the Rural Development Unit in Botswana. It has few or no executive functions and partly for this reason it does not threaten other agencies with a 'take-over bid'. It is located in the Ministry of Finance (and Development Planning) and, although the Unit does not itself control budget allocations or releases, this gives it some authority because of its organizational closeness to financial power, and some reason for other ministries to pay attention to it.[5] Equally important, however, is the fact that the Unit has acted with restraint and has neither tried to aggrandize its own position nor forced its view on other departments. However, there are other factors, the relative homogeneity of the rural economy, the dominant political position of pastoralists, and the small size of the bureaucracy and of the total population concerned, which also assist matters.

Participation by pastoralists in planning

I know of no case in Africa or Asia in which pastoralists or organizations of pastoralists have a formal role or representation in the planning of pastoral development at the national level (or state level in the case of a federation). In contrast, in Australia and the USA representatives of pastoralists are frequently allocated positions on (state-level) planning or regulatory organizations. Nevertheless, in many Asian and African countries pastoralists have exercised decisive influence on particular issues or policies through the application of political pressure. In Botswana many, possibly most, senior civil servants and politicians are also the owners of large herds of cattle in pastoral areas, and the interest of the owners of large herds is pervasive in national decision-making. In Kenya also, a number of civil servants and politicians have ranches of their own or are shareholders in company ranches; livestock traders have also been able to obtain specific decisions about the operations of the Government's Livestocking Marketing Division made in their favour. In imperial Ethiopia a handful of politically important individual pastoralists could also obtain favourable decisions from the Emperor. No doubt the same is true of most pastoral countries. The distinguishing feature of such informal influence is that it is exerted by individuals behind closed doors and the arguments used are not subjected to examination in the light of evidence. Some decisions reached in this way are beneficial from almost all points of view; others merely advance private or sectional interests under the guise of the general welfare of all pastoralists. There are some quite persuasive arguments which can be marshalled against formal incorporation of pastoralists' representatives into the national pastoral planning process; but these are seriously weakened where the consequence of excluding them is not well-thought-out decisions reached from a careful review of the evidence but snap decisions based simply on personal and secret influence. Formal incorporation of pastoralists could also help to break up cosy interdepartmental arrangements not to raise awkward issues. On the other hand, in some countries the only pastoral representatives likely to be chosen would simply champion their own private interests, and official recognition of their position would reinforce rather than moderate their greed.

Monitoring and evaluation

Sound reforms in policies and procedures cannot be made unless what is happening under the existing system is known and understood. Often descriptions given by senior officials of agencies concerned in pastoral development about what the agencies are doing bear very little resemblance to what is happening on the ground, sometimes because the officials are dissembling, sometimes because they actually do not know the true state of affairs. In particular, the longer-running domestically financed permanent programmes, such as the veterinary services, are seldom subject to review, certainly not in any formal or quantitative way, and usually not in any way at all. Even the limited internal monitoring required in order to write an annual departmental report for publication has lapsed in most African countries since independence.

There is little sign that the formal monitoring and evaluation exercises which have been carried out have affected policies and programmes.[6] Some programmes have been modified before the evaluation results were available; sometimes the evaluation has been ignored and the policies and programmes have continued unchanged. A number of factors are to blame; monitoring and evaluation have often been too late, too slow, too bulky in presentation and too academic in format. The main problem seems to have been that they have been too little related to identifying the changes which those in charge of programmes (the managers) can bring about. They have, in fact, so far not been useful tools for management, although they have had more effect on those (e.g. ministries of finance and foreign donors) who determine the pattern of investment. Probably precisely because of this, and because of the consequent threat posed to their programmes, managers have little enthusiasm for these formal exercises. (For further discussion of evaluation see Chambers, 1974, pp. 118–129.)

If monitoring and evaluation are to become more effective in improving performance they need to be seen by managers as likely to be useful tools to them. This means that their scope must be broadened to include the constraints (e.g. staff recruitment) and procedures (financial, procurement) which managers see as their main problems; it also means that managers must have a greater say (at the expense of monitoring specialists) on the content (what is monitored or evaluated and how), they must be seen as the main audience to which reports are addressed, and they must have an opportunity to comment and refute the reports. Giving managers more say on the content may initially lead to the collection of some rather trivial information by doubtful methods. Managers also need to be involved in reviewing the usefulness of monitoring and evaluation from time to time, so that they can themselves see why different information and techniques are needed; in this review they may need specialist assistance.

Provided that senior staff managing programmes have a sufficient control over their content and opportunity to comment on their results, it is not particularly important who carries out evaluation and monitoring. There are actually advantages in the 'secretariat' not itself being responsible for this function. Some monitoring is of a sufficiently routine statistical nature, re- quiring a repeated collection of the same information year after year, that it can really only be done by the government statistical services. Other kinds of monitoring are done once or twice only, are of a much more subjective nature, and may require very specialist expertise. These are probably best done by organizations which are not part of government, e.g. by international organizations, by academics, or consultants. If their reports are embarrass- ingly critical, government is not caught in the position of having either to admit that the critical reports are true or that it has carried out an incom- petent evaluation; it can disown the report while at the same time quietly rectifying the weaknesses which have been highlighted (for further discussion see Sandford, 1980a).

Planning specific investments

One part of planning pastoral development is drawing up specific proposals for innovations or investments in development programmes and projects. The record of such plans drawn up at national level is a poor one; most of them were technically, socially, and organizationally unsound and they have not been successfully implemented. It is fashionable now to deride them as the inevitable results of top-down bureaucratic centralization. In fact, at the time many of them were conceived the option was not between centralized top-down bureaucratic planning and decentralized bottom-up participatory planning, but between the former and no new initiatives at all. The level of staffing at district and provincial level, and the level of institutional devel- opment, were such that more sensible proposals did not come from the bottom; this remains the case in many countries. A few of the big projects in fact involved a great deal of consultation between the national and district levels and with the pastoralists. The first World Bank-financed Kenyan Live- stock Project is such an example.

Some part of planning specific investments must, in the circumstances of most poor countries in the 1980s, take place at national level; this is because a large part of the investment funds involved come through national budgets and probably from foreign aid donors, and the latter negotiate with recipient governments at national level and require that applications for their money conform to certain conventions in presentation and analysis. There is a technique involved in preparing such applications (misleadingly called 'pro- ject preparation') which has not much utility at sub-national level for other purposes. This technique can be acquired and exercised by a permanent 'project preparation unit' of a ministry of agriculture or development; or it can be borrowed from the foreign aid donor concerned or from FAO; or it can be hired from a consultancy firm for the preparation of applications for particular projects. Where the finance required comes from the country's own central government funds rather than from foreign donors, rather less cumbersome procedures usually apply and the work requiring expertise at the national level is correspondingly reduced.

A distinction must be drawn between the techniques of preparing applications for finance and the real preparation of pastoral development, that is, the work required to identify potentially useful investments or innovations (components) and to acquire the information, to raise the political and public support, and to identify and assemble the local resources of land and people which, together with finance, are required to start and carry out the new development. Successful financial applications usually follow the blueprint approach already described and deal in large sums of money earmarked for big categories of expenditure; they have relatively long time horizons; they imply that data once gathered remain valid and can usefully be aggregated, and that information gathering, obtaining agreements, decision-making, and implementation follow sequentially one after another. They also imply that constraints and solutions are fairly uniform throughout a project area and that, even if they cannot be precisely controlled, inputs, outputs, and activities can at least be forecast with certainty and accuracy. These characteristics of successful financial applications derive from the internal requirements of the financing agencies; these requirements are as much facts of the situation as the production parameters of livestock or the educational level of pastoralists, not totally immutable (and certainly not ideal), but they cannot just be wished or laughed away.

In the real world, however, every little part of the whole area selected for development has its own problems and potential; information which is important for one area is irrelevant for another; the data change rapidly over time; socio-economic data are at least as important as technical; community support and agreement has to be carefully nurtured and rapidly built upon once obtained — too much delay and it will melt away; agreements and decisions often follow on successful implementation, as people are convinced by example and by a persuasive and respected personality; success by a group in one activity tempts it to try something new which only a short while before seemed far beyond its capacity. No one can forecast precisely that an agreement will be forthcoming, and pastoralists are unlikely to be impressed by threats that a foreign donor's financial support to a project will come to an end on a precise date. Time horizons are, therefore, very short and space horizons parochial. Realistic preparation for development with these features has to be done at a very local level, with even district plans being simply a collection of local requirements fitted into the framework of annual budget requests and of the work plans of district-level branches of government agencies (and also, as we saw earlier, into conformity with national policies).

Only in a few cases, e.g. plans for abattoirs, irrigation of land in conjunction with feedlots, or the drilling of boreholes along stock routes, does the real preparation of investment plans bear a resemblance to the technique of preparing financial applications.

Although realistic preparation for pastoral development requires to be done at a very local level by staff with detailed local knowledge in close contact with pastoralists, very few countries have been able to do this, partly for external reasons because donors have been too certain of what needed to be done and too inflexible, partly for internal reasons because district-level staff have not existed or have not been adequately briefed or trained. As a consequence, project preparation has been carried out by units located at national level or by consultants; the results in physical terms have been poor, although it may have been an inevitable part of building up a cadre of staff who could subsequently man district-level institutions, and of a learning process, the principal (and very expensive) lesson being that projects cannot be successfully prepared in this way. But if district-level staff are to prepare pastoral development they need much more training and recurrent briefing than they get. District-level staff usually have inadequate knowledge either of the real constraints on the development of their areas or of the technical innovations or components available to overcome them; their own proposals tend to be either unimaginative or technically or economically unrealistic. Often they have little understanding of the social structure in which they are working or of the social consequences of their proposals. They are sometimes unaware of governments' policies (where these exist) or of what precisely to do in applying them. They do not know what external (both to the district and to the nation) financial resources might be available for pastoral development or what procedures or conditions (e.g. as to sources of procurement) limit their use.

One country in Africa, Botswana, seems to have had greater success than others in getting feasible pastoral development plans drawn up at district level. Such plans have included zoning land for different uses and modest investment proposals, e.g. for building fences between cultivated and communal grazing areas. This greater success can be directly attributed to two main sets of causes. Firstly, Botswana's strategic position in southern Africa makes it much courted diplomatically, and consequently it receives more offers (in the 1970s) of aid than it can take up; donors have to compete with each other to get this aid spent, and consequently have attached much less onerous procedures than is normal in other countries for the approval of projects and the disbursement of funds. Secondly, not only are policies well worked out at the national level but great effort is put into ensuring that officials and community leaders at the district level, as well as the general public, are made aware of them. Physical distances in Botswana are huge but the human population is small, which in some ways eases problems of communication. Frequent national seminars, attended by officials and community leaders from each district, are held to consider policy issues in development; officials from districts are encouraged, when in the national capital, to attend meetings of standing committees of (middle-to-senior level) officials; above all ministries issue 'guidelines' to district-level officials and local leaders which not only explain policies but set out in very considerable detail advice on how organizations at district level should implement the policies.

Botswana has also been much more open to social science research than other countries; not only have permits to carry out social research been relatively easy to obtain, but government has taken positive steps to get the results of such research disseminated to its technical and implementation agencies. Naturally there are time-lags during which government officials continue to believe myths which have been shown to be unfounded. Nevertheless, politically inconvenient findings are published at government-sponsored meetings and in government's own official publications, and policies are, in time, adjusted accordingly. This is in marked contrast to many other countries where social studies have been discouraged, suppressed, and ignored. Botswana's relative success in making use of social science and in preparing feasible development plans at district level is partly due to much greater emphasis being put on improving flows of information within the country than on acquiring technical information abroad. It probably also arises from the hitherto considerable political cohesion of the country's important interest groups which makes politically inconvenient research findings less of a threat. In contrast, several other countries make no use of the social science research which has been done and discourage further work.

MANAGEMENT AND ORGANIZATION AT THE DISTRICT LEVEL

Previous sections have discussed organization of central government at the national level, including the steps central government needs to take in order to be able to make planning and implementation at district level more effective. The following sections will look at organization and management at the 'district' level. By 'district' is meant a geographical division of the nation state. It may be an 'administrative' district, with an administrative centre (village, town) at which are located offices and supervisory staff from a number of different government services and ministries. These offices and staff normally represent the lowest tier in the administrative hierarchy to which substantial autonomy in day-to-day personnel and financial management are decentralized from the national ministries or other organizations of the nation state. In the pastoral regions of most countries administrative districts have human populations of between 25,000 and 250,000 people; usually there is a resident representative (district governor or commissioner) of the political authority of the central government. Alternatively, in this section a 'district' may mean the 'project area' of a multi-component pastoral development project, where this area includes a substantial part of a normal large administrative district or cuts across the boundaries of several. Two issues will be discussed in respect of organization and management at district level so defined; the organizational structure in which different government services relate to each other at this level; and the management of government staff. Another important topic — the participation of pastoralists in organizing government activities at district level — has already been touched on in Chapter 10 in the section on pastoralists and planning. Although there are more functions involved than just planning, what has already been said in Chapter 10 mainly applies *mutatis mutandis* to these other functions and will not be repeated here.

Organizational structure

In some countries pastoral development is implemented through district-level branches of the regular agencies (animal health, water development, range management, etc.) and there is little attempt at district level either to co-ordinate the activities of these independent branches, that is, to ensure they are compatible in time, in space, and in general intention and effect, or to integrate them in the sense of uniting their resources such as staff and vehicles into a single unitary structure (for definitions of co-ordination and integration see beginning of Chapter 10). In other countries or on other occasions, although implementation is the task of formally independent branches of separate agencies, mechanisms are established at district level for co-ordinating activity. Such mechanisms can be informal, e.g. monthly meetings of district heads of branches at which information is exchanged and group decisions reached for which the only pressure and sanction on individual branches to comply with group decisions is the moral authority of a chairman (often the district governor or commissioner) or the disinclination to go against the majority view. In some cases the mechanisms are more formal and, although execution is the responsibility of the individual branch, the money with which to pay for the execution is provided by a district-level authority with formal legal status which enters into a contract with the branch to carry out a particular piece of work in a particular way. District heads of branches may form a board of directors for this authority (with every head being of equal formal status in this board) as happens in some districts covered by the Drought-Prone Areas Programme in India, although often central government's political representative (the Collector in India, the district governor or commissioner elsewhere) achieves a pre-eminent status.

In other countries or on other occasions project development units or authorities have been established to implement pastoral development at district level. This has most frequently happened where a pastoral development project has been heavily dependent on foreign aid for funding. Such project development units usually have a semi-autonomous status with a 'director' or 'manager' responsible to a minister in the national capital or occasionally to a board of governors. The manager then has executive authority (at least in theory) over all the components of the project. One such development unit in north-east Ethiopia had a territory of 75,000 km² and was intended to serve about 45,000 pastoral families (225,000 people). The boundaries of the project's territory cut across the boundaries of seven administrative districts in two separate provinces. In only one of the districts concerned were pastoralists a majority of the population, and in no case was the administrative centre of the district located in a pastoral area (i.e. one where pastoralism was the main form of land-use). Those parts of the districts not inhabited by pastoralists were excluded from the project's territory. The project's task was to provide animal health and husbandry, range management, marketing, road making, water spreading, and a few other services but not, for example, security, education, or (except to a minor extent) human health services. The administrative centres of the two districts furthest away from each other were more than a day's hard travelling by vehicle apart.

Part of the reason for establishing project development units at district level is the belief that pastoral development, even more than other forms of rural development, must involve the planned and interlocking provision of several different components and services, and that the piecemeal provision of single services or components may do more harm than good. Coupled with this is the feeling that only by putting the different interdependent components under the clear executive authority of a single manager at district level can the necessary degree of integration be achieved, because mere co-ordinating mechanisms at district level between otherwise independent branches of government agencies will not be able to overcome inter-agency rivalry or the problems caused by priorities being determined at national level by national agencies and then handed down to agency branches for implementation at district level regardless of local needs.

It is true that branches of different agencies at district level often act in contradiction to each other. However, the project development units have rarely (probably never) done better. The plain truth is that almost nothing in pastoral development gets done at the time or in the way that was originally intended; the idea that a skilful project manager can bring in the different components of a project when needed, like the conductor of an orchestra bringing in musical instruments, is a myth. In practice what happens in many multi-component projects is that project managers are given direct executive responsibility over too wide a range of different technical services. Too many people report directly to them and no one individual can have the necessary technical expertise (in range science, in animal health, in water engineering) to supervise all those reporting to him adequately; but because the project management unit is outside the normal agency structure technical supervision is not available in the same way as it would be to an in-line branch.

There are a number of other problems with project management units with executive responsibility at district level. Usually they are funded more liberally than are the services run by the conventional in-line branches of agencies operating in the same geographic area; this causes jealousy, resentment, and a consequent lack of co-operation. In most cases projects with semi-autonomous project management units cannot provide a proper career structure for technical staff, both because they often have a limited expected period of life (say 5–10 years), and because in the context of a project (because of limited numbers of posts) it is difficult to provide a smooth transition to senior posts for staff who perform well. Projects have difficulty, therefore, in establishing a self-replacing cadre of qualified technical staff (e.g. veterinary officers, range assistants, water engineers) and have to rely on 'secondment' or similar arrangements for recruiting staff from the regular technical agencies of government. However, staff so recruited may be those regular agencies wish to get rid of or, if competent, they may prejudice their future promotion in the regular service by choosing 'secondment' rather than loyally serving in the conventional way. They therefore demand high salaries and often leave early out of a sense of insecurity. Project management units fill vacancies for senior posts more slowly than the regular agencies fill equivalent positions, because it is seldom possible to recruit internally by cross-posting or promotion within the project — the field for selection is too narrow. They have to rely, therefore, on the good will of regular agencies (often themselves short of staff) spontaneously to provide seconded officers, or on public advertisement and consequent slow selection procedures. These defects of project management units in pastoral development are not of a totally different nature from those of similar units in other forms of rural development; possibly the defects are more serious because such a wide range of different technical skills are involved.

In spite of these problems, semi-autonomous project management units are frequently, and sensibly, chosen as the organizational instrument at district level. In such cases the existing branches of regular government agencies are simply too weak to form even the foundation for expanded pastoral development; and to build on them would simply be to incorporate their weaknesses in staff, procedures, and ambitions. The establishment of a pastoral project management unit is a necessary precursor to the dismantling of the existing branch structure and its replacement with something radically different. In other cases, as in the Ethiopian one mentioned earlier, the boundaries of existing administrative districts enclose pastoral minorities alongside non-pastoral majorities. Where pastoralism and agriculture are closely integrated in land-use, in mutual exchange, or in use of products and by-products, this binding together of pastoralists and non-pastoralists in one administrative framework may be desirable; but where this close integration does not exist, the inevitable result of leaving pastoral development in the hands of agency branches in existing administrative districts will be that too little managerial attention and too few other resources will be given to pastoralism, with a consequent neglect of pastoralists and their development. In some cases the problem is not so much weak branches of regular technical agencies but one of overall political direction at the district level. Where the cadre of district governors or commissioners cannot be trained to provide adequate overall guidance and co-ordination, then a project manager may be brought in as a substitute. In all these cases, however, the semi-autonomous project management unit is a second-best alternative rather than desirable in itself.

Where money for pastoral development is channelled down from the separate budgets of different central government agencies (veterinary, range management, water development) through provincial offices to district branches (the 'conventional system'), it is inevitable that the heads of these branches, in order to ensure a fair and regular flow of their agency's funds to their district, have to pay more attention to their superiors' views of what should be done than to the views of their colleagues from the branches of other agencies in their district. Consequently, where funds are channelled in this way there is a tendency for development activities to reflect the centrally determined priorities of individual agencies rather than an overall view of what is needed in the circumstances of a particular district.

Instead, funds for pastoral development can be channelled direct from ministries of finance as 'block grants' to each district, to be spent according to a plan agreed at district level — by heads of branches, or by representatives of pastoralists or by a combination of these. The actual work financed by the block grant can then be carried out by agency branches in accordance with this agreed plan. Such a block grant system will not necessarily work any better. If the Ministry of Finance, in turn, applies too many conditions and requires district plans to be referred back to it for approval, less may be spent, and less sensibly, than under the conventional system. If too much discretion is given to districts with too little guidance it is difficult to prevent the block grant being split up, on the basis of 'fair shares' to finance each branch head's pet scheme or on the basis of short-term political priorities.[7] For the block-grant system to work well it needs to be backed by firm policy guidance, reiterated staff training, and programme evaluation, and for the size of the grant to be adjusted in accordance with experience. In pastoral development it seems to work well in the Drought-Prone Areas Programme (DPAP) in India (as at 1977). Although other activities carried out by district-level branches of Indian agencies tend to reflect heavily priorities laid down by central agencies (in this case at state level), in the DPAP case, where in some but not all districts the development funds are channelled direct, in block, from Government of India to district level, a satisfactory degree of collaborative planning between branch heads has been obtained, although in some cases the 'consensus' view that emerges bears very strongly the stamp of the District Collector's (i.e. governor or commissioner in other countries) preferences. Strong and experienced chairmanship, as is provided by Indian Collectors, is probably an indispensable condition for the block-grant system to work well.

The management of field staff

This subsection will deal with the management of government staff involved in pastoral development at district level and below, i.e. 'field' staff. Management of staff at these levels includes a number of elements. The jobs which are to be performed have to be specified and responsibility for taking different kinds of decisions located. The 'management style' ('authoritarian', 'participatory', etc.) which is to govern relations between different levels has to be defined. Within the procedures and policies laid down by central government, staff need to be provided with a package of material incentives (annual increments, opportunities to earn legitimate professional fees or *per-diem* field allowances, well-located housing, etc.) and non-material ones (praise, status, self-respect) that is conducive to their carrying out their tasks effectively. In particular, it needs to be in the interests of field staff to solicit and pay attention to the views of pastoralists rather than merely to dictate to them. Appropriately qualified junior staff have to be recruited into ranks for which there is not a nationally recruited cadre, and daily, monthly, and annual work programmes for all staff have to be planned, then monitored as to the extent to which they are carried out, and finally evaluated for effectiveness. The technical work of field staff has to be supervised to ensure it reaches adequate professional standards. On-the-job and in-service training has to be provided for staff. Within budgetary limits set by central government, staff have to be provided with the accommodation, transport, equipment, and supplies that they need. Meetings and other forms of communication have to be arranged which enable information not only to travel from top to bottom but also from bottom to top in the amount, timing, frequency, and accuracy that each task requires. Different kinds of management solutions, in terms of incentives, programming, and supervision for example, are likely to be required for regulatory staff (or tasks) compared to extension or service-providing ones.

As has been pointed out in previous chapters (and will be reviewed again below) pastoral development has distinctive features from other kinds of rural development which pose particular management problems. There is a still small but growing number of field studies, and consequent publications, on managing staff in other forms of rural management (for example, Chambers, 1974; Leonard, 1977). There is virtually nothing on pastoral development, no systematic studies which tell us, for example, how livestock assistants or their supervisors plan their time, how they actually spend it and why actuality deviates from plan. There is no systematic evidence on how often or at what expense in their time and money, individual pastoralists make contact with the livestock services, what help or information they actually get from them, or what alternative sources for this there are. We do not know which kinds of 'extension', e.g. by radio, public meeting, demonstration farm or individual visit, are most persuasive for particular kinds of information. Of course, heads of agency branches *do* manage their staff and carry out all the elements of this management listed in the previous paragraph. But they do so without benefit of real information on the effectiveness of different management methods, relying on personal hunch, on anecdote, and on rules of thumb, often drawn up under different circumstances, which have achieved the status of conventional wisdom. Often, for example, in defining management style, they are unaware that they are faced with a management option at all.

In the absence of systematically collected evidence, what follows can only be described as 'impressions' based on a rather wider look (geographically, historically, and in terms of different government services) at past and present practice and a rather longer or more intensive period of reflection than most other people have been able to achieve. The main distinguishing characteristics of pastoral development that raise particular management problems are the relative sparseness of the population and the unpredictability of its whereabouts, the generally low reliability of the environment and consequent unpredictability of crises and opportunities, the low endowment of pastoral areas with infrastructure such as roads or with social services such as schools and hospitals, and the usually low level of formal education of pastoralists and the consequent tendency for technically well-qualified government staff to be recruited from other ethnic groups.

In what follows we shall focus on tasks of work planning, supervision, monitoring, and evaluation, and their associated management style and systems of incentives. Chambers, in trying to draw up a management system for district level staff and below in Kenya in the early 1970s, found that for livestock staff 'the work was more routine, more planned in advance and less liable to change' (Chambers, 1974, p. 71) than for crop staff; the same is probably true for staff in India engaged in dairy development in dry regions with irrigation facilities. Chambers was working in an area of reasonably high potential. Even in dry areas with nomadic populations, work programmes for junior staff can probably be fixed by district heads of branches quite far in advance, where routine vaccinations are to be carried out by centrally based district teams or where staff are mainly concerned in operating fixed facilities such as water points or dips. Even when staff are involved in less routine work, or not at fixed points, if they work in large teams, e.g. in mass vaccination teams dealing with unexpected outbreaks of disease, decisions on the work programmes of junior staff can still be made 'centrally', i.e. by the head of the district branch of the agency concerned who is travelling with the team, even if such decisions have to be short-term and opportunistic. In such cases, where work planning can realistically be done in a centralized fashion, it may also be appropriate to apply an authoritarian style of management coupled with frequent close supervision in order to elicit high productivity and quality of work. However, an authoritarian style of management, to be effective, requires that managers (e.g. district branch heads) can swiftly apply sanctions and rewards to poor and good performers. In many countries, especially in Africa, this is not realistic. The political and administrative system is such that branch heads in practice (whatever the theory) cannot apply sanctions or rewards. Good performance has to be elicted in some other way.

Where junior staff have to be in continuous or frequent repeated contact with particular livestock or pastoralists in drier areas, a different system will, in any case, be required. Unpredictable variations in time and space, and poor physical communications, require that work programmes be drawn up on a much more short-term basis and with individual junior staff being given a great deal of discretion in deciding what they shall do. In sparsely populated areas with poor communications, close supervision by senior staff of junior staff's work on the job will also not take place. The cost of transport will simply not allow it (and the trend in costs is deteriorating). Not only will work programming have to be decentralized and supervision be infrequent, but these will require a different management style; more emphasis will have to be put on training and retraining in formal in-service courses (i.e. not 'on the job'), and meetings between senior and junior staff will have to be more supportive and advisory, involving a great deal of interchange to discover problems in the field, rather than authoritarian. An effective management system will have to be one which does *not* rely on close supervision by senior staff but on some other means of obtaining good performance. Tasks which can only be done effectively if closely supervised will probably have to be abandoned altogether.

In some cases the work of field staff can, in effect, be both programmed and evaluated by pastoralists themselves. For example, where the main task of junior animal health workers (livestock assistants) employed by government is to sell to pastoralists a narrow range of veterinary requisites (e.g. treatments for internal and external parasites), and where the whole or a significant part of the livestock assistant's income is derived from a commission on the requisites sold, then giving the livestock assistant the power to determine his own work programme is tantamount to allowing it to be determined by the whereabouts of his main customers and by the timing and nature of their demand. That is the simplest system; it will favour rich pastoralists and is open to abuse if, for example, a livestock assistant is able to overprescribe or dilute the treatment. It is a system which will work much better if pastoralists have a relatively good general education so that they can read pamphlets and newspapers, or if they have been given adequate specific training, on special courses or on the radio, that enables them to know what to ask for and how to detect malpractice by the livestock assistant. In such cases the senior staff are, in effect, enabling the pastoralists to do the programming, supervision, and evaluation of junior staff instead of having to do it themselves.

In only a few cases, for example in the supply of veterinary requisites and not always even then, is it possible for this market mechanism to take over the tasks of work programming and evaluation. Where the technical package to be delivered is complex, or where the task to be performed is not one where levying a fee on recipients of the service is feasible, e.g. in the case of much extension and demonstration work, work-programmes will have to be determined between supervisory and junior staff in a more structured, premeditated, and less opportunistic way with, as already stated and as will be reiterated, considerable decentralization of decision-making to individual junior staff in the drier areas. However, it may still be possible to get pastoralists to do the job of monitoring and evaluation through 'institutional' rather than 'market' mechanisms. As the recipients of services pastoralists are in rather a good position to know how effective they are, and this knowledge needs to be put to good account. What is needed is an institutional mechanism through which pastoralists' views on the performance of particular development components and of individual staff can be fed back to more senior levels. The precise mechanism can vary from situation to situation. In some cases a single select committee of pastoralists can effectively represent the views of all pastoralists on a wide range of subjects; in other cases such select committees will be captured by an élite serving only their own interests. In some cases the best mechanism will be an open meeting of all the pastoralists using a particular facility such as a water point or dip, who will, at that meeting, present their views only on the performance of that particular facility.

Whatever the precise mechanism used to present pastoralists' views, such an evaluation system will work effectively only if a number of conditions are fulfilled. Firstly, the views of government and pastoralists must roughly coincide about what constitutes good performance; if government wants a reduction in stock numbers and pastoralists do not, it is no good asking pastoralists to evaluate the performance of 'stock-reduction inspectors'. Secondly, pastoralists must be taught what services to expect and demand so that they can protest vigorously if they are not available. However, this requires greater realism by governments than is usually shown about the speed with which new developments can be introduced. It is no good teaching pastoralists to demand, for example, foot-and-mouth vaccination from their livestock assistant, if central government has not yet succeeded in procuring the vaccines and cold storage equipment. Pastoralists also need to be taught enough about the details and technicalities of what field staff should do so that they can complain if, for example, anti-helminthics are overprescribed, containers of acaricide are tampered with to permit dilution, or pastoralists are overcharged for particular services. Good channels of communication need to be established if pastoralists are to be taught what they need to know in order to evaluate effectively.

A third condition that must be fulfilled, if pastoralists are to monitor and evaluate effectively, is that there must be an immediate connection between the evaluation made by pastoralists and the rewards and sanctions received by the staff concerned. Pastoralists will not continue to criticize junior staff if the result is not sanctions against the staff by their superiors but sanctions by the staff against the pastoralists who complained; it is not enough that the staff should receive a black mark in a confidential report that mars their long-term career prospects; something immediate and obvious is needed. This will require a change in normal government procedures and a firm commitment by senior officials to the principle that pastoralists' opinions should be listened to, which will overcome the protests of district-level staff and below. Paradoxically, it also requires that field staff be given more control over their own activities; for only if they can control their own activities, and the resources necessary to make those activities effective (transport, supplies), will field staff be able to tolerate a system in which their present rewards and future prospects are dependent on an evaluation of their performance. No one can afford to be the scapegoat for someone else's inefficiency. An evaluation system such as that discussed here has been initiated in an integrated rural development programme in the Philippines (Honadle *et al.*, 1980, pp. 145 and 153), although staff pay was not, in that case, tied to the evaluation result. The conditions for evaluation by pastoralists to be effective set out here are a long way from fulfilment in most countries with pastoral sectors. Perhaps Botswana comes nearest to satisfying them, although in that case such evaluation would provide yet further incentives for government staff to concentrate their attention on the wealthy and powerful.

Inducing staff to work in the field

A recurring theme in the management of pastoral development is the difficulty of getting government staff to go out from their bases in district centres into the field and to work with pastoralists and their livestock; or, if such staff are already located (i.e. have staff housing) in the field, to get them to stay there rather than drifting back on various excuses to district headquarters. The problem is partly a question of the cost and difficulty of transport in pastoral areas, partly a question of human reluctance. This human reluctance is not absolute; it varies with age, ethnic origin, and standard of education, and it varies over time as expectations change about what hardships and amenities staff *ought* to put up with. Whereas qualified veterinarians in Tanzania in the 1920s were expected to (and did) walk 2500 miles per year on duty, to suggest to a veterinarian in the 1980s that he do the same would provoke a sense of outrage not based so much on the physical discomfort of walking as on the low status implied. This trend over time may not necessarily continue in the same direction in the future, since part of the past change in expectations (this applies mainly to Africa) resulted from the extremely rapid rate of promotion available to indigenous professional staff after the end of the colonial era, which led to exaggerated expectations of what those of similar age, qualifications, and experience could expect in the future. Already the expectations of the next generation who missed that opportunity have been cut back and the growth in supply of qualified manpower is likely to further reduce prospects and eventually expectations in the future.

In an attempt to allay the reluctance to work or live in pastoral areas, governments have sometimes tried to improve the material conditions of living, by providing relatively high-quality housing or 'hardship area' allowances. These seem to have done little to alleviate the problem. High-quality housing has been extremely difficult to maintain in good condition in remote areas, and a house with electric stove, shower, and water-borne toilet system which do not work is more depressing than one which did not have these facilities in the first place. Obviously some accommodation must be provided if staff are to live in pastoral areas, and when other needs are met, high-quality housing may be a powerful attraction; but the evidence is that in most countries at the present it is transport which is the critical issue. Hardship allowances have often been paid to staff both in administrative centres and in remote stations, and while it may have been 'fair' that staff in pastoral development should be compensated for the rigour of their work in this way, the payment of the allowance has not been sufficiently tied to the actual performance and length of stay of individual staff in the places where they are needed.

Transport is required to take staff resident in a district's administrative centre to work in the field. In pastoral areas, especially in the drier less densely populated ones where commercial bus and freight transport hardly exists, it is also required to carry official supplies and equipment for their work to staff resident inside pastoral areas as well as to service them and their families; that is an aspect often forgotten. In discussing transport to get staff into the field it is possible to talk of the relative merits of travel by foot, on horse or camel, by bicycle, motor cycle, or four-wheel vehicle. After a long period during which relative costs moved in favour of the four-wheel vehicle, the recent trend, especially due to rises in the price of petrol and diesel since 1973, is probably in the other direction. In many African countries now the capital cost of vehicles for pastoral development is entirely derived from aid funds and even then governments seem unable to meet the running costs, of fuel, repairs, and tyres, from the national domestic budget. In areas of sandy soil a shift back in favour of animal transport and in other areas towards more use of bicycles and motor cycles seems imminent. But none of these forms of transport are suitable for shifting supplies in bulk, nor, particularly, for transporting the families of staff.

The main problem with getting staff to live in pastoral areas concerns their families. Even in countries with relatively efficient economies (e.g. Kenya) it is extremely difficult in many pastoral areas to purchase the household necessities (flour, cooking oil, sugar, tea) which the families of all except completely subsistence pastoralists need, and those who live in these areas need to spend considerable time and energy in procuring these supplies. Moreover, all staff, except for young unmarried men, will be very concerned about the provision of social services; for young families medical facilities are the first priority, later primary and then secondary schools. Some junior staff with minimal educational qualifications and drawn from pastoral groups may be prepared to live with their families in remote areas. The less they come from a pastoral origin and the more educated and older they are, the more reluctant they will be to live far from health and education services, and much of the housing provided by governments in remote areas lies empty or is occupied by staff who have left their families elsewhere and who escape to them at the slightest opportunity. In north Kenya, for example, primary schoolteachers abandon their schools on the day term ends, not returning till the day the next term opens. With other services monthly visits to the district administrative centres for salary and supplies are stretched to last a week or more. While all rural areas present problems of lack of amenities for government staff and their families, these problems in the drier pastoral areas are far more acute.

Sound management will seek to alleviate these special problems for staff. Other things being equal, staff should be stationed in places where they have access to social services. An ordering and delivery system should be arranged whereby what staff need not only for their work but also for their homes will be supplied to them on a regular basis. A reliable procedure needs to be established whereby if staff or members of their families fall ill in remote areas information can be sent to this effect, and an emergency transport service laid on to evacuate them. These things are likely to be more important in improving the efficiency of staff in post than the payment of hardship allowances for postings to remote areas. Preference must be given — for this as well as for other reasons — to recruiting people from a pastoral background for posts requiring residence in pastoral areas, and it should be recognized that the less educated staff (and their consequently less well-educated wives) will be happier than the more educated in remote postings. It should be a feature of the system of posting all grades of staff that the young, with fewer family obligations, go to more remote areas, while those of longer service can expect to be posted to positions with better access to social services that older children need. Some of these arrangements will lead to higher costs. One which would not, would be a system that discouraged or forbade junior staff from marrying; that would find an echo, albeit largely for other reasons, in the age-grade systems of several East African pastoral societies and in the regulations for professional staff of the former colonial powers, both of which sought to delay the age of marriage. Some of the increased costs of providing reliable regular and emergency transportation can be lessened where several government agencies co-operate in servicing their remote staff.

SUMMARY OF MAIN POINTS

This chapter has been concerned with the organization and management of government activities. It looked, in its first main section, at some general issues. After reviewing the main roles of government in pastoral development it identified the major problems in organization and management which have occurred in the past: overall policies concerning pastoral development have either not existed or have been contradictory; the financial support for pastoral development provided by governments has been small and unreliable; the administrative procedures which have been applied have been inappropriate to the special characteristics of pastoral development; and staff performance has been poor.

Three major devices were then identified to enable future programmes to be more successful than past. First, pastoral programmes must be designed in such a way that the interests of the politically weak pastoralists whom one wishes to help are in some way indissolubly linked with the interests of politically more powerful groups who can ensure adequate government support for the programme. Such linkage is possible with some components of pastoral development, but much more difficult in the case of marketing and range management. Secondly, if they are to perform well, staff must either have strong ideological motivation or be inspired by a sense of the success of what they are doing. In contrast, most pastoral development is imbued with a sense of failure, largely because staff often have a quite inappropriate model in their minds of what good pastoral development is like. A major difficulty has frequently arisen because it was felt that good pastoral development may conflict with, rather than conform to, what pastoralists want, and so the opinions of pastoralists have not been used as a means of monitoring or eliciting good staff performance. Thirdly, special administrative procedures, e.g. in the field of procurement, accounting, and staff recruitment, are required which are appropriate to the needs of pastoral development. Finally, this first main section looked at the appropriateness of a project rather than a programme approach to pastoral development. A project approach often suffers from inflexibility as well as other problems. On the other hand, projects may be useful ways of testing new ideas on a pilot basis, of starting the process of disbanding old and useless government services, of getting an integrated approach where this is necessary, and, in some cases, of getting a higher degree of participation by pastoralists in planning and management than would otherwise be possible.

The second main section of the chapter looked at the organization and management of central government at the national level. Although in particular circumstances an organizational structure can be appropriate or inappropriate, this study did not find comparisons of different organizational structures of central government in different countries a fruitful field of enquiry. This is partly because in many pastoral countries the way in which bureaucracies actually behave is quite different from the way in which the formal relationships of control between different organizations suggest they ought to behave. This section then proceeded to look at planning and policy-making. At national level in the past the attention devoted to planning specific projects has displaced consideration of policy issues; at the same time project planning at this level, although successful in securing external funds, has not been successful in getting projects successfully implemented. Policy formulation can only be done successfully at national level, and for this to happen senior staff must have time to consider policy issues and be trained to do so, they must be supplied with information on the effectiveness of present policies and their alternatives, and there must be a proper forum in which discussions can take place. *Ad hoc* rather than permanent committees to discuss specific subjects may be appropriate, and interdepartmental or interministerial committees staffed at levels below the most senior may be less threatening to departments' cherished operational independence. A secretariat is essential if interministerial committees are to function effectively. It is also desirable for there to be a 'lead agency' to take the initiative in getting interministerial discussions going. A 'neutral' lead agency may be more effective than one with executive functions in the pastoral field which may arouse jealousy and fears of a take-over from rival executive ministries. Although formally incorporating representatives of pastoralists in central government's policy-making structure and procedures may cause trouble, it may nevertheless be preferable if the alternative is for pressure to be applied by politically important individual pastoralists in secret behind closed doors. The planning of projects and specific investments is best done at district level or below, although staff at these levels need special training as well as guidance about national policy.

The final main section of this chapter concerned organization and management at district level, and two issues were discussed, organizational structure and the management of field staff. Different ways of co-ordinating and integrating district-level government services, and in particular the use of project management units, were examined. Project management units can be useful, for example as substitutes where the overall political direction normally exercised by central government's provincial governors is weak, or as precursors to the complete dismantling of existing field services and their replacement by others in a new mould, or where a number of adjacent administrative districts, whose boundaries cannot be altered, each contain both non-pastoral and pastoral areas and the latter get neglected by the normal government services in favour of the non-pastoralists. But project management units suffer a number of difficulties and where they are, nevertheless, the preferred solution it is because of serious defects in the alternatives rather than because of their own intrinsic merit.

In a few cases field staff of pastoral development agencies can be effectively managed in an authoritarian way. But in most cases, especially where close and continuous contact between staff and pastoralists is required, the kind of supervision necessary for an authoritarian style to be effective is not possible, and a different style of management will be required. In inducing staff to remain in the field in close contact with pastoralists a key element is the provision of an acceptable level of welfare services and transport for staff families.

NOTES TO CHAPTER 11

1. This review of problems is based on a study of unpublished documents on more than 30 livestock projects in dry areas, mainly in Africa.

2. I am indebted to Judith Tendler's published and unpublished work for many of the ideas presented in this paragraph.

3. For a discussion of the problems created for pastoral areas by nationwide education policies see Gorham (1980; especially I. 43).

4. An example of operational interdependence is where a new programme to buy young stock from pastoral areas and to quarantine them is the sole supplier to a single new ranch which grows them out and alone sells them to a single new irrigated feedlot which alone sells them to a single new abattoir for slaughter. If one element in this chain fails or lags behind in time the whole package collapses. This is an extreme example, but it is quite like planned (but unsuccessful) parts of livestock programmes in Ethiopia and Somalia.

5. The Rural Development Unit reports direct to the Minister who may also be the Vice-President. It is revealing that the Botswana Government's veterinary service, which has direct personal contact with the most senior political figures whose private livestock it (quite legitimately) treats, pays little attention to the Rural Development Unit and participates little in interministerial discussions.

6. In pastoral development such exercises have been carried out, or commissioned, by the International Livestock Centre for Africa (ILCA), the World Bank, US-AID, Swedish SIDA, and by academic individuals or bodies, sometimes in conjunction with the governments concerned, sometimes independently of them.

7. For a summary account of East African experience with block grants see Chambers (1974, pp. 94–100).

Bibliography

AGROTEC-CRG-SEDES (1974). 'Southern Rangelands Livestock Development Project — Sociology and Pastoral Economy', unpublished report.

Aldington, T. J., and Wilson, F. C. (1968). *The Marketing of Beef in Kenya*, Institute of Development Studies (Occasional Paper No. 3), Nairobi.

Almagur, Uri (1978). *Pastoral Partners: Affinity and Bond Partnership among the Dassenech of South West Ethiopia*, Manchester University Press, Manchester.

Al-Saleh, Nasser O. (1976). 'Some problems and development possibilities of the livestock sector in Saudi Arabia: a case study in livestock development in arid areas', University of Durham Ph.D. Thesis (unpublished).

Anderson, Terry L., and Hill, P. J. (1977). 'From free grass to fences: transforming the commons of the American West', in Hardin and Baden (eds.), 1977, pp. 200–216.

Ansell, D. J. (1971). *Cattle Marketing in Botswana*, Department of Agricultural Economics and Management (Development Study No. 8), University of Reading.

Asad, T. (1970). *The Kababish Arabs. Power, Authority and Consent in a Nomadic Tribe*, Hurst, London.

Australian Rangelands Society (1977). *The Impact of Herbivores on Arid and Semi Arid Rangelands*, Perth, Western Australia.

Axin, G. H., Birkhead, James W., and Sudholt, Allan W. (1979). 'Evaluation of the Kenya National Range and Ranch Development Project', unpublished report.

Baker, Randall (1968). 'Problems of the cattle trade in Karamoja: an environmental analysis', *Ostafrikanische Studien*, Wirtschafts-und Sozialgeographisches Institut, Nürnberg, pp. 211–223.

Baker, Randall (1971). 'The supply of cattle to the Kampala-Mukono area, Uganda', *Zeitschrift für Ausländische Landwirtschaft*, **10**, 1.

Baker, Randall (1975). 'Development and the pastoral people of Karamoja, north-eastern Uganda. An example of the treatment of symptoms', in Monod (ed.), 1975, pp. 187–205.

Barth, F. (1960). 'The land use pattern of migrating tribes of South Persia', *Norsk Geografisk Tidsskrift*, **17** (164), 1–11.

Barth, F. (1962). 'Nomadism in the mountains and plains of South West Asia', in UNESCO (1962), *The Problems of the Arid Zone*, Paris, pp. 341–355.

Bates, Daniel (1973). *Nomads and Farmers. A Study of the Yoruk of South Eastern Turkey*, University of Michigan, Ann Arbor.

Bernus, Edmond (1974). 'Possibilité et limites de la politique d'hydraulique pastorale dans le Sahel Nigérien', *Cahiers ORSTOM*, Ser. Sci. Hum., **XI** (2), 119–126.

Bernus Edmond (1977). *Case Study on Desertification: The Eghazer and Azwak Region, Niger*, United Nations Conference on Desertification, Document A Conf. 74/14.

Bernus, Edmond (1979). 'Le contrôle du milieu naturel et du troupeau par les éleveurs Touaregs Sahéliens', in EEASP (eds.), 1979, pp. 67–74.

Bernus, Edmond (1981). *Touareg Nigériennes: Unité Culturelle et Diversité Régionale d'un Peuple Pasteur*, ORSTOM, Paris.

Bingana, K. S. (1977). 'Livestock breeding and artifical insemination in Botswana', unpublished paper.

Blaisdell, James P., and Sharp, Lee A. (1979). 'History of rangeland use and administration in the Western United States', in Howes (ed.), 1979, pp. 1–24.

Bonte, Pierre (1975). 'Conditions et effets de l'implantation d'industries minières en milieu pastoral: l'exemple de Mauritanie', in Monod (ed.), 1975, pp. 245–262.

Bonte, Pierre (1976). 'Pasteurs et nomads, l'exemple de la Mauritanie', in Copans, J. (ed.), (1976). Sécheresses et Famines du Sahel, François Maspero, Paris, Vol. II, pp. 62–86.

Botswana, Republic of (1968). The Tribal Land Act (as amended subsequently).

Botswana, Ministry of Local Government and Lands (1977). The Report on the Botswana Government's Public Consultation of its Proposals on Tribal Grazing Land, Gaborone.

Bourgeot, André (1975). 'Analyse des rapports de production chez les pasteures et les agriculteurs de l'Ahaggar', in Monod (ed.), 1975, pp. 263–283.

Bourgeot, André (1978). 'Etude de l'évolution d'un système d'exploitation Sahélien au Mali', unpublished paper.

Bourgeot, André (1981). 'Pasture in the Malian Gourma: habitation by humans and animals' in Galaty et al. (eds.), 1981, pp. 165–181.

Box, Thadis W., and Peterson, Dean F. (1978). 'Carrying capacity of renewable resources related to desertification', in Reining, Priscilla (ed.) (1978). Desertification Papers, American Association for the Advancement of Science, Washington, pp. 37–43.

Braend, M. (1979). 'World veterinary manpower', The Veterinary Record, 1979 (28 July), 77–79.

Breman, H., Cissé, A. M., Djiteye, M. A., and Elberse, W. Th. (1979/80). 'Pasture dynamics and forage availability in the Sahel', Israel Journal of Botany, 28, 227–251.

Brown, Leslie H. (1971). 'The biology of pastoral man as a factor in conservation', Biological Conservation, 3 (2), 93–100.

Burnham, Philip (1979). 'Spatial mobility and political centralisation in pastoral societies', in EEASP (eds.) 1979, pp. 349–360.

Campbell, D. J., and Mighot Adhola, Shem (1979). Mid term Evaluation of Aspects of the Foot and Mouth Disease Control Programme in Kajiado and Narok Districts, Kenya, Institute of Development Studies, Nairobi.

Caroe, Olaf (1953). Soviet Empire, Macmillan, London.

Carruthers, Ian, and Clark, Colin (1981). The Economics of Irrigation, Liverpool University Press, Liverpool.

Chambers, Robert (1974). Managing Rural Development: Ideas and Experience from East Africa, Scandinavian Institute of African Studies, Uppsala.

Chatty, Dawn (1980). 'The pastoral family and the truck', in Salzman (ed.), 1980, pp. 50–94.

Chemonix International (1977). 'Kenya livestock and meat industry development study', unpublished report.

Chevenix-Trench, Charles P. (1964). The Desert's Dusty Face, Blackwood, Edinburgh and London.

Cole, Donald P. (1979). 'Pastoral nomads in a rapidly changing economy. The case of Saudi Arabia', ODI Pastoral Network Paper, 7e.

Coleman, Terry (1965). The Railway Navvies, Hutchinson, London.

Conant, F. P. (1982). 'Thorns paired, sharply recurved: cultural controls and range-land quality in East Africa', in Spooner, Brian, and Mann, H. S. (eds.) (1982). Desertification and Development; Dry Land Ecology in Social Perspective, Academic Press, London.

Conlin, Sean (1981). 'Peasant participation in agricultural planning in Peru: the impediment of expertise', *Rural Development and Participation Review*, **2** (3), 10–12.

Consortium for International Development (1976). 'Livestock ownership and marketing in Botswana', unpublished report (Utah State University).

Cossins, Noel (1971). 'Pastoralism under pressure: a study of Somali clans of the Jijigga area of Ethiopia', unpublished report.

Cossins, Noel (1972). 'No way to live: a study of the Afar clans of the north-east rangelands' (Ethiopia), unpublished report.

Cossins, Noel, and Ymrou, Bekele (1974). 'Still sleep the Highlands' (Ethiopia), unpublished report.

Coudere, Raymond (1975). 'De la tribu à la coopérative: aperçu de l'évolution des hautes plaines oranaises', *Options Méditerranéennes*, **28**, 65–73.

CRED (Centre for Research on Economic Development) (1980). *Livestock and Meat Marketing in West Africa*, University of Michigan, Ann Arbor (5 vols.).

Cronin, A. J. (1978). 'An interim study of the Livestock Marketing Division' (Kenya), unpublished report.

Cruz de Carvalho, Eduardo (1974). 'Traditional and modern patterns of cattle raising in south-western Angola: a critical evaluation of change from pastoralism to ranching', *Journal of Developing Areas*, **8**, 199–226.

Dahl, Gudrun (1979). *Suffering Grass: Subsistence and Society of Waso Borana*, Department of Social Anthropology, University of Stockholm.

Dahl, Gudrun, and Hjort, Anders (1976). *Having Herds: Pastoral Herd Growth and Household Economy*, Department of Social Anthropology, Stockholm.

Dahl, Gudrun, and Hjort, Anders (1979). *Pastoral Change and the Role of Drought*, SAREC (Report R2: 1979), Stockholm.

Dahl, Gudrun, and Sandford, Stephen (1978). 'Which way to go; a study of people and pastoralism in the Isiolo District of Kenya', unpublished report.

Davis, Robert K. (1971). 'Some issues in the evolution, organisation and operation of group ranches in Kenya', *East African Journal of Rural Development*, **4**, (1) 22–33.

De Leeuw, P. N. (1979). 'A review of the ecology and fodder resources of the subhumid zone', unpublished paper for ILCA.

Devitt, Paul (1979). 'Drought and poverty' in Hinchey (ed.), 1979, pp. 121–127.

Digard, Jean Pierre (1979). 'De la nécessité et des inconvénients, pour un Baxtyâri, d'être Baxtyâri', in EEASP (eds.) 1979, pp. 127–139.

Doherty, Deborah (1979). 'Factors inhibiting economic development at Rotian Olmakongo Group Ranch', *Working Paper* 365, Institute of Development Studies, Nairobi.

Doran, M. H., Low, A. R. C., Kemp, A. L. (1979). 'Cattle as a store of wealth in Swaziland: implications for livestock development and overgrazing in Eastern and Southern Africa', *American Journal of Agricultural Economics*, **61** (1), 41–47.

DPAP (1977). 'Note on sheep development and animal husbandry activities in the drought prone areas of Jasdan taluka', unpublished paper of Drought Prone Areas Project Agency, Rajkot.

Draz, Omar (1978). 'Revival of the Hema system of range reserves as a basis for the Syrian range development programme', in Hyder (ed.), 1978, pp. 100–103.

Duncanson, G. R. (1975). 'The Kenya National Artificial Insemination Service', *World Animal Review*, **16**, 37–41.

EEASP (Equipe Ecologie et Anthropologie des Sociétés Pastorales) (eds.) (1979). *Pastoral Production and Society*, Cambridge University Press, London.

Eddy, E. D. (1979). *Labor and Land Use on Mixed Farms in the Pastoral Zone of Niger*. Centre for Research on Economic Development, University of Michigan, Ann Arbor.

Ellis, James E., Jennings, Calvin H., Swift, David M. (1979). 'A comparison of energy flow among the grazing animals of different societies', *Human Ecology*, 7 (2), 135–149.

Evenari, Michael (1975). 'Ancient desert agriculture and civilisations: do they point to the future?', in Mundlak and Singer (eds.), 1975, pp. 83–97.

FAO (1970). *FAO Group Fellowship Study Tour on Settlement in Agriculture of Nomadic, Semi-nomadic and Other Pastoral People*, FAO (TA 2810), Rome.

FAO (1974). *The Ecological Management of Arid and Semi-arid Rangelands in Africa and the Near East*, FAO (AGPC Misc. 26), Rome.

FAO/WHO (1965/1971). *Reports of the Second/Third Meetings of the FAO/WHO Expert Panel on Veterinary Education*, FAO and WHO.

Felton, M. R., and Ellis, P. R. (1978). *Studies on the Control of Rinderpest in Nigeria*, Department of Agriculture and Horticulture (Study No. 23), University of Reading.

Ferguson, Donald S. (1977). *A Conceptual Framework for Evaluating Livestock Development Programs and Projects in Sub-Saharan West Africa*, Centre for Research on Economic Development (working paper), University of Michigan, Ann Arbor.

Field, C. R. (1979). *Preliminary Report on Ecology and Management of Camels, Sheep and Goats in Northern Kenya*, UNESCO/UNEP (IPAL Technical Report No. E-1a).

Fortmann, L. and Roe, E. (1981). *The Water Points Survey*, Ministry of Agriculture, Gaborone.

Frantz, Charles (1975). 'Contraction and expansion in Nigerian bovine pastoralism', in Monod (ed.), 1975, pp. 338–353.

Fraser-Darling, F. (1955). *West Highland Survey: An Essay in Human Ecology*, Oxford University Press, London

Fukuda, Sakiko (1976). 'Effects of risk and uncertainty on decisions regarding herd size and composition in arid areas', M.A. Thesis, University of Sussex.

Gabre Mariam, Ayele, and Hillmann, Miles (1975). 'A report on the Central Highlands Livestock Markets Survey' (Ethiopia), unpublished report.

Galaty, John G. (1980). 'The Maasai group ranch: politics and development in an African pastoral society' in Salzman (ed.), 1980, pp. 157–172.

Galaty, John G., Aaranson, Dan, Salzman, Philip C., and Chouinard, Amy (eds.) (1981). *The Future of Pastoral Peoples: Proceedings of a Conference held in Nairobi, Kenya, 4th–8th August 1981*, International Development Research Centre, Ottawa.

Gallais, Jean (1975). 'Traditions pastorales et développement: problèmes actuels dans la région de Mopti (Mali)', in Monod (ed.), 1975, pp. 354–368.

Goetz, Harold, Nyren, Paul E., and Williams, Dean (1978). 'Implications of fertilisers in plant community dynamics of Northern Great Plains rangelands', in Hyder (ed.), 1978, pp. 671–674.

Gooch, Toby (1979). 'An experiment with group ranches in Upper Volta', *ODI Pastoral Network Paper*, 9b.

Goode, B., and Goode, M. J. (1975). 'Health Services Development Research Project, West Azerbaijan, Iran', unpublished report, WHO (EM/IRA/SHS/003/DP).

Gorham, Alex (1980). *Education and Social Change in a Pastoral Society: Government Initiatives and Local Responses to Primary School Provision in Kenya Maasailand*, Institute of International Education, University of Stockholm.

Government of India (1960). *The Report of the Committee on Special Multipurpose Tribal Blocks*.

Gow, David C., Morss, Elliott R., Jackson, Donald R., Humpal, Donald S., Sweet, Charles F., Barclay, Albert H., Mickelwait, Donald R., Hagan, Ross E., Zanger, Robin (1979). *Local Organisations and Rural Development: A Comparative Reappraisal*, Development Alternatives Inc., Washington.

Gow, David C., and Morss, Elliott R. (1981). 'Local organisation, participation and rural development: results from a seven-country study', *Rural Development Participation Review*, **II** (2), 1, 12–17.

GTZ/SEDES (1976). 'La Santé Animale en ——', unpublished reports covering Chad, Mali, Mauritania, Niger, Senegal, Upper Volta.

GTZ/SEDES (1977). 'La Santé Animale dans les états Sahéliens au Sud du Sahara: définition d'une politique d'action et élaboration des normes d'intervention et de financement', unpublished report.

Haaland, Gunnar (1977). 'Pastoral systems of production: the socio-cultural context and some economical and ecological implications', in O'Keefe, P., and Wisner, B. (eds.) (1977). *Land Use and Development*, International African Institute, London, pp. 179–193.

Haaland, Gunnar (ed.) (1980a). *Problems of Savannah Development: the Sudan Case*, Department of Social Anthropology (Occasional Paper No. 19), University of Bergen.

Haaland, Gunnar (1980b]. 'Problems in savannah development', in Haaland (ed.), 1980a, pp. 1–37.

Haaland, Gunnar (1980c). 'Social organisation and ecological pressure in southern Darfur', in Haaland (ed.), 1980a, pp. 55–105.

Hadley, R. F. (1977). 'Evaluation of land-use and land-treatment practices in semi arid western United States', *Philosophical Transactions of the Royal Society of London*, Series B, **278** (962), 543–554.

Halderman, J. M. (1972). 'The Kaputiei group ranch development programme', unpublished paper.

Hall, H. T. B. (1977). *Diseases and Parasites of Livestock in the Tropics*, Longman, London.

Halpin, Brendan (1981). 'Vets — barefoot and otherwise', *ODI Pastoral Network Paper*, 11c.

Hardin, Garret (1977a). 'The Tragedy of the Commons', in Hardin and Baden (eds.) 1977, pp. 16–30. (Originally published in *Science* (1968), **162**, 1243–1248.)

Hardin, Garrett (1977b). 'Living on a lifeboat', in Hardin and Baden (eds.), 1977, pp. 261–279.

Hardin, Garrett, and Baden, John (eds.) (1977). *Managing the Commons*, W. H. Freeman, San Francisco.

Hatfield, C. R. (1971). 'Cattle transactions in the Sukumaland range development area' (Part Two), unpublished report.

Hatfield, C. R. (1977). 'The impact of social and political change in Maasailand and its implications for future development', unpublished report.

Hatfield, C. R., and Kuney, Reuben ole (1976). 'Current trends in Maasai development', unpublished report.

Heady, Harold F., and Bartolome, J. (1977). *The Vale Rangeland Rehabilitation Programme: The Desert Repaired in South East Oregon*, USDA Forest Resources Bulletin PNW-70.

Heathcote, R. L. (1969). 'The pastoral ethic', in McGinnies, W. G. and Goldman, B. J. (eds.) (1969). *Arid Lands in Perspective*, American Society for the Advancement of Science and Arizona University Press, Washington and Tucson, pp. 311–324.

Hedlund, Hans G. B. (1971). 'The impact of group ranches on a pastoral society', *Staff Paper* 100, Institute of Development Studies, Nairobi.

Helland, Johan (1980). *Five Essays on the Study of Pastoralists and the Development of Pastoralism*, Department of Social Anthropology (Occasional Paper No. 20), University of Bergen.

Henderson, W. W. (1973). 'Nigeria' in West (ed.), 1973.

Herman, L. (1979). *The Livestock and Meat Marketing System in Upper Volta: An*

300

Evaluation of Economic Efficiency, monograph, Centre for Research on Economic Development, University of Michigan, Ann Arbor.

Herskovits, M. J. (1926). 'The cattle complex in East Africa', *American Anthropologist*, **1926**.

Hinchey, Madeline, T. (ed.) (1979). *Proceedings of the Symposium on Drought in Botswana*, Botswana Society in collaboration with Clark University Press, Gaborone.

Hitchcock, Robert K. (1978). *Kalahari Cattle Posts*, Ministry of Local Government and Lands, Gaborone.

Hitchcock, Robert K. (1980). 'Tradition, social justice and land reform in central Botswana', *Journal of African Law*, **24** (1), 1–34.

Hjort, Anders (1979). *Savannah Town: Rural Ties and Urban Opportunities in Northern Kenya*, Department of Social Anthropology, University of Stockholm.

Ho Chi (1977). 'A Tachai on the grasslands', *China Reconstructs*, **1977** (May).

Hodder, R. W., and Low, W. A. (1978). 'Grazing distribution of free ranging cattle at three sites in the Alice Springs District, central Australia', *The Australian Rangeland Journal*, **1** (2), 95–105.

Holy, L. (1974). *Neighbours and Kinsmen: A Study of the Berti people of Darfur*, Hurst, London.

Honadle, George, Morse, Elliott R., Van Sant, Jerry, and Gow, David D. (1980). *Integrated Rural Development: Making it Work?*, Development Alternatives Inc., Washington.

Horowitz, Michael M. (1979). *The Sociology of Pastoralism and African Livestock Projects*, AID (Program Evaluation Discussion Paper No. 6), Washington.

Howes, K. M. W. (ed.) (1979). *Rangeland Ecosystem Evaluation and Management*, Australian Rangeland Society, Perth, Western Australia.

Huang Zhaohua (1982). 'A pastoral commune on the Ordos plateau — the Sumitu Commune', *ODI Pastoral Network Paper*, 14b.

Humphrey, Caroline (1978). 'Pastoral nomadism in Mongolia: the role of herdsmen's cooperatives in the national economy', *Development and Change*, **9** (1), 133–160.

Hunter, Guy (1978). *Agricultural Development and the Rural Poor*, Overseas Development Institute, London.

Hunter, Guy, and Bottrall, Anthony (eds.) (1974). *Serving the Small Farmer: Policy Choices in Indian Agriculture*, Croom Helm in association with the Overseas Development Institute, London.

Hunting Technical Services, and Macdonald, Sir M. and Partners (1976). 'Savannah Development Project. Phase II Development Plan', unpublished report.

Hyder, D. N., and Bement, R. E. (1977). 'The status of grazing and rest in grazing management' in Australian Rangelands Society, 1977.

Hyder, Donald N. (ed.) (1978). *Proceedings of the First International Rangelands Congress*, Society for Range Management, Denver, Colorado.

Ibrahim, Fouad N. (1978). *The Problem of Desertification in the Republic of the Sudan with Special Reference to Northern Darfur Province*, Development Studies and Research Centre (Monograph No. 8), Khartoum.

Ibrahim, Saad E., and Cole, Donald P. (1978), *Saudi Arabian Bedouin*, Cairo Papers in Social Science 1.5., The American University in Cairo.

IEMVT (1980). *Intensified control of epizootic diseases in West and Central Africa*, unpublished report in 2 main volumes and 19 country studies.

ILCA (International Livestock Centre for Africa) (1975). *Evolution and Mapping of Tropical African Rangelands*, proceedings of Seminar held at Bamako in March 1975.

ILCA (1979a). *District Ranch Development Briefs*, ILCA Kenya Working Document No. 13.

ILCA (1979b). *Livestock Production in the Subhumid Zone of West Africa*, ILCA System Study No. 2.

ILCA (1980a). *Pastoral Development Projects*, ILCA Bulletin No. 8.

ILCA (1980b). *The Design and Implementation of Pastoral Development Projects for Tropical Africa*, ILCA Working Document No. 4.

ILO (International Labour Organization) (1967). *Report on the Interregional Study Tour and Seminar on the Sedentarisation of Nomadic Populations in the Soviet Socialist Republics of Kazakhstan and Kirghizia*, ILO, Geneva.

ILO (1976). *Growth Employment and Equity — A Comprehensive Strategy for the Sudan*, ILO, Geneva.

Ionesco, T. (1975). 'Suggestions pour une stratégie de développement des zones pastorales arides et desertiques de Tunisie', *Options Méditerranéennes*, **28**, 82–88.

Irons, William (1971). 'Variations in political stratification among the Yomuk Turkmen', *Anthropological Quarterly*, **44** (3), 143–156.

Irons, William (1975). *The Yomuk Turkmen: A Study of Social Organisation among a Central Asian Yomuk-speaking Population*, Museum of Anthropology (Anthropological Paper No. 8), University of Michigan, Ann Arbor.

Irons, William (1979). 'Political stratification among pastoral nomads', in EEASP (eds.) 1979, pp. 361–374.

Jack, J. D. M. (1973). 'The Sudan', in West (ed.), 1973, pp. 130–139.

Jacobs, Alan H. (1961). 'Memorandum on the political and economic development of the Maasai', unpublished paper.

Jacobs, Alan H. (1975). 'Maasai pastoralism in historical perspective', in Monod (ed.), 1975, pp. 406–425.

Jacobs, Alan H. (1977). 'Development in Tanzania Maasailand: the perspective over twenty years', unpublished paper.

Jacobs, Alan H. (1980). 'Pastoral development in Tanzania Maasailand', *Rural Africana*, **7** (1) (New Series, spring 1980) 1–14.

Jina, M. (1970). 'Livestock marketing in Maswa District', unpublished paper quoted in Hatfield, 1971.

Jodha, N. S. (1979). *The Processes of Desertification and the Choice of Interventions*, ICRISAT (Progress Report No. 2 Economics Program), Hyderabad.

Jodha, N. S., and Vyas, V. S. (1969). *Conditions of Stability and Growth in Arid Agriculture*, Agro-Economic Research Centre, Sardar Patel University, Vallabh Vidyanagar.

Johnson, Douglas L. (1979a). 'Pastoral cooperatives in Rajasthan', *ODI Pastoral Network Paper*, 9c.

Johnson, Douglas L. (1979b). 'Management strategies for drylands: available options and unanswered questions', in Mabbott, J. A. (ed.) (1979). *Proceedings of the Khartoum Workshop on Arid Lands Management*, the United Nations University, Tokyo, pp. 26–35.

Jones, R. L., and Sandland, R. L. (1974). 'The relation between animal gain and stocking rate', *Journal of Agricultural Science*, **83**, 335–342.

Kenya Veterinary Department. *Annual Reports of the Veterinary Department*, for 1937–1950. Government Printer, Nairobi.

Khalifa, A. H., and Simpson, Morag C. (1972). 'Perverse supply in nomadic societies', *Oxford Agrarian Studies*, pp. 47–56.

Krader, L. (1955). 'Ecology of central Asian pastoralism', *South Western Journal of Anthropology*, **11** (4), 301–325.

Lambton, A. K. S. (1969). *Landlord and Peasant in Persia*, Oxford University Press, London.

Lattimore, Owen (1962). *Nomad and Commissar — Mongolia Revisited*, Oxford University Press, New York.

302

Ledger, H. P. (1977). 'The comparative energy requirements of penned and exercised steers for long-term maintenance at constant liveweight', *Journal of Agricultural Science*, **88**, 27–33.

Leonard, David K. (1977). *Reaching the Peasant Farmer: Organisation Theory and Practice in Kenya*, University of Chicago Press, Chicago and London.

Lewis, I. M. (1961). *A Pastoral Democracy. A Study of Pastoralism and Politics among the Northern Somali of the Horn of Africa*, Oxford University Press, London.

Lewis, I. M. (1975). 'The dynamics of nomadism: prospects for sedentarisation and social change' in Monod (ed.), 1975, pp. 426–442.

Lewis, J. G. (1977). *Report of a Short Term Consultancy on the Grazing Ecosystem in the Mt. Kulal region, Northern Kenya*, UNESCO/UNEP (IPAL Technical Report — E.3).

Livingstone, I. (1977). 'Economic irrationality among pastoral peoples: myth or reality?', *Development and Change*, **8** (2), 209–230.

Livestock and Meat Board (1974). 'Jijigga Livestock Project', unpublished report of the Ethiopian Government's Livestock and Meat Board.

Long, Norman (1977). *An Introduction to the Sociology of Development*, Tavistock, London.

Low, A. R. C. (1978). 'Cattle supply responses in Sudan and Swaziland; motivational inferences and organizational implications', *Oxford Agrarian Studies*, **7**, 62–74.

Low, Allan (1980). 'The estimation and interpretation of pastoralists' price responsiveness', *ODI Pastoral Network Paper*, 10c.

Lowe, H. J., and Reid, N. R. (1973). 'Tanganyika', in West (ed.), 1973.

Marx, Emmanuel (1978). 'Ecology and politics of Middle East pastoralists', in Weissleden (ed.), 1978, pp. 41–74.

Marx, Emmanuel (1981). 'The anthropologist as a mediator between the people and the authorities' in Galaty *et al.* (eds.), 1981, pp. 119–126.

Maasai Range Project (1975). 'Proposed grazing management plan for Kolmonik Ranching Association', unpublished paper.

May, Robert M. (1976). *Theoretical Ecology: Principles and Applications*, Blackwell Scientific, Oxford.

McArthur, I. D., and Smith, C. (1979). 'Price and marketing policies on meat and eggs', in Mukui (ed.), 1979, pp. 205–223.

McGowan, G. P. *et al.* (1979). 'Botswana — a study of drought relief and contingency measures to the livestock sector', unpublished report.

Meadows, S., and White, J. (1979). 'Structure of the herd and determinants of offtake rates in Kajiado District in Kenya, 1962–1977', *ODI Pastoral Network Paper*, 7d.

Mirreh, Abdi G. (1978). 'Nomads and markets in the North of Somalia', unpublished paper.

Moluche, F. C., Kuney, Reuben ole, and Hatfield, C. R. (1975). 'The introduction of improved stock into Maasailand; an initial assessment', unpublished paper.

Monod, Theodore (ed.) (1975). *Pastoralism in Tropical Africa*, Oxford University Press for the International African Institute, London.

Monogarova, L. F. (1978). 'Changes in the family structures of the Pamir nationalities in the years of socialist reconstruction' in Weissleden (ed.), 1978, pp. 297–304.

Moore, Barrington Jr., (1966). *Social Origins of Dictatorship and Democracy. Lord and Peasant in the Making of the Modern world*, Penguin Edition (1974), Harmondsworth.

Moris, Jon R. (1981). *Managing Induced Rural Development*, International Development Institute, Bloomington, Indiana.

Mortimore, Michael (1978). 'Changes in agrarian structure in Dagacheri village, Kano State, Nigeria', unpublished paper.

Mukui, J. T. (ed.) (1979). *Price and Marketing Controls in Kenya*, Institute of Development Studies (Occasional Paper 30), Nairobi.

Mundlak, Yair, and Singer, Fred S. (eds.) (1975). *Arid Zone Development. Potentialities and Problems*, Ballinger, Cambridge, Mass.

Nemati, Nasser (1978). 'Range improvement practices in Iran', in Hyder (ed.), 1978, pp. 631–632.

Newsome, A. E. (1971). 'The research and practical experience gained in the development of semi arid areas of Australia', *Botswana Notes and Records* (Special Edition No. 1), pp. 202–218.

Nigeria Veterinary Department. *Annual Report, Northern Province*, for 1929, 1934, 1935, 1959, 1962, 1963.

Njooro, Solomon (1973). 'Distribution of veterinary services in Mathira Division of Nyeri District (Kenya)', unpublished paper quoted in Leonard, 1977.

Noy-Meir, Immanuel (1975). 'Stability of grazing systems: an application of predator : prey graphs', *Journal of Ecology*, **63**, 459–481.

Nyerges, A Endré (1979). 'The ecology of domesticated animals under traditional management in Iran: preliminary results from the Turan Biosphere Reserve', *ODI Pastoral Network Paper*, 9d.

Odell, Marcia L., and Odell, Malcolm J. (1980). 'The evolution of a strategy for livestock development in the communal areas of Botswana', *ODI Pastoral Network Paper*, 10b.

Odell, Marcia L. (1980). 'Botswana's First Livestock Development Project', unpublished report.

Ormerod, W. E. (1977). Comment in *Philosophical Transactions of the Royal Society*, Series B, **278**, 962.

Overseas Development Institute (1977). *The United Nations Conference on Desertification*, ODI Briefing Paper, London.

Oxby, Clare (1975). *Pastoral Nomads and Development*, International African Institute, London.

Oxby, Clare (1981). *Group Ranches in Africa*, report for FAO, Rome.

Parkipuny, M. L. S. ole (1972). 'Maasai predicament', *Daily News*, 29 Nov.–2 Dec. 1977, Dar-es-Salaam.

Parkipuny, M. L. S. ole (1977). 'The alienation of pastoralists in post-Arusha Declaration Tanzania', unpublished paper.

Payne, Gene F. (1979). 'Rangeland administration in the United States', in Howes (ed.), 1979, pp. 50–59.

Pendleton, Donald T. (1978). 'Non-federal rangelands of the United States — a decade of change 1967–1977', in Hyder (ed.), 1978, pp. 485–487.

Perry, R. A. (1978). 'Rangeland resources: worldwide opportunities and challenges', in Hyder (ed.), 1978, pp. 7–9.

Peyre de Fabregues, B. (1971). *Evolutions des pâturages naturels Sahéliens du Sud Tamesna*, IEMVT, Étude Agrostologique, 32, Maison Alforts.

Phillipson, John (1975). 'Rainfall, primary production and "carrying capacity" of Tsavo National Park (East) Kenya', *East African Wildlife Journal*, **13**, 171–201.

Pratt, D. J. (1968). 'Rangeland Development in Kenya', *Annals of the Arid Zone*, 7, 177–208.

Pratt, D. J., and Gwynne, M. D. (eds.) (1977). *Rangeland Management and Ecology in East Africa*, Hodder and Stoughton, London.

Provost, A. (1978). 'Le role du vetérinaire dans la société future: implications pour la formation', working paper for 4th FAO/WHO Consultation on Veterinary Education.

Raikes, Philip L. (1981). *Livestock Development and Policy in East Africa*, Scandinavian Institute of African Studies, Uppsala.

304

Reusse, Eberhard, and Kassim, Mohamoud (1978). 'Livestock marketing performance', unpublished paper.
Ribeiro, J. M. de C. R., Brockway, J. M., and Webster, A. J. F. (1977). 'A note on the energy cost of walking in cattle', *Animal Production*, **25**, 107–110.
Richmond, Amos E. (1977). 'Research priorities and arid zone development', in Mundlak and Singer (eds.) 1975, pp. 263–288.
Robertson, Alexander (1978). 'Planning of veterinary manpower and veterinary education', working paper for 4th FAO/WHO Consultation on Veterinary Education.
Rosenberg, Daniel (1974). 'Negdel development: a socio-cultural perspective', *Mongolian Studies* **1**, 62–75.
Rosenberg, Daniel (1981). 'The collectivisation of Mongolia's pastoral production', *Nomadic Peoples* **9**, 23–39.
Ruthenberg, Hans (1980). 'Economic objectives in pastoral development' in ILCA, 1980b, pp. 15–35.
Rweyemamu, B. T. (1974). 'Drugs and vaccination orders', in Tanzania Livestock Conference, 1974.
Salzman, Philip C. (1972). 'Multi Resource Nomadism in Iranian Baluchistan', in Irons, William and Dyson-Hudson, Neville (eds.) (1972). *Perspectives on Nomadism*, E. J. Brill, Leiden, pp. 60–68.
Salzman, Philip C. (1978). 'Does complementary opposition exist?', *American Anthropologist*, **80** (1), 53–70.
Salzman, Philip C. (ed.) (1980). *When Nomads Settle: Processes of Sedentarisation as Adaptation and Response*, Praeger, New York.
Sandford, Dick (1981). 'Pastoralists as their own animal health workers', *ODI Pastoral Network Paper*, 12c.
Sandford, Stephen (1976a). 'Size and importance of pastoral populations', *ODI Pastoral Network Paper*, 1c.
Sandford, Stephen (1976b). 'Pastoral human populations', *ODI Pastoral Network Paper*, 2c.
Sandford, Stephen (1977a). 'Dealing with drought and livestock in Botswana', unpublished report.
Sandford, Stephen (1977b). 'Pastoralism and development in Iran', *ODI Pastoral Network Paper*, 3c.
Sandford, Stephen (1978a). 'Some aspects of livestock development in India', *ODI Pastoral Network Paper*, 5c.
Sandford, Stephen (1978b). 'Welfare and wanderers', *ODI Review*, **1**, 70–87.
Sandford, Stephen (1980a). *Keeping an Eye on TGLP*, National Institute of Development and Cultural Research (Working Paper No. 31), Gaborone.
Sandford, Stephen (1980b). 'Learning from the experience of pastoral development', ILCA, 1980b, pp. 1–14.
Sandford, Stephen (1982). 'Pastoral strategies and desertification; opportunism and conservatism in dry lands', in Spooner, Brian, and Mann, H. S. (eds.) (1982), *Desertification and Development; Dry Land Ecology in Social Perspective*, Academic Press, London.
Schultz, Theodore (1979). 'The economics of research and agricultural productivity', *International Agricultural Development Service Occasional Paper*.
Scitovsky, Tibor (1952). *Welfare and Competition*, Allen and Unwin, London.
SEDES (1979). 'Étude de la commercialisation due bétail et des prix de la viande à Madagascar', unpublished report.
Shaedaee, G., and Niknam, F. (1975). *Management of Natural Resources in the Arid and Semi-arid Regions of Iran*, Forestry and Range Organisation, Tehran.
Shanks, Bernard (1978). 'Social and institutional barriers to rangeland management innovations', in Hyder (ed.), 1978, pp. 92–94.
Shapiro, Kenneth H. (1979). *The Livestock Economies of Central West Africa: An*

Overview, Centre for Research on Economic Development, University of Michigan, Ann Arbor.

Shen-Chang-jiang (1982). 'Pastoral systems in arid and semi-arid zones of China', *ODI Pastoral Network Paper*, 13b.

Shepherd, Andrew (1981). 'Government policy in the Sudan and popular participation in rural water supply planning', unpublished paper to IAAS International Conference in Khartoum.

Shepherd, Andrew, and El Neima, Asha Mustapha (1981). 'Popular participation in decentralised water supply planning. A case study in the Western District of Northern Khordofan Province, Sudan', unpublished paper.

Singh, N. P., More, T., and Sahni, K. L. (1977). 'Effects of water deprivation on feed intake, nutrient digestibility and nitrogen retention in sheep', *Journal of Agricultural Sciences*, **86**, 431–434.

Spencer, Paul (1973). *Nomads in Alliance: Symbiosis and Growth among the Rendille and Samburu of Kenya*, Oxford University Press, London.

Spooner, Brian (1972). 'The status of nomadism as a cultural phenomenon in the Middle East' in Irons, William, and Dyson-Hudson, Neville (eds.) (1972). *Perspective on Nomadism*, E. J. Brill, Leiden, pp. 122–131.

Squires, V. R. (1976). 'Walking, watering and grazing behaviour of Merino sheep in two-semi-arid rangelands in south west New South Wales', *The Australian Rangeland Journal*, **1** (1), 19–23.

Staatz, J. (1979). *The Economics of Cattle and Meat Marketing in Ivory Coast*, monograph, Centre for Research on Economic Development, University of Michigan, Ann Arbor.

Stoddart, L. A., Smith, A. D., and Box, T. W. (1975). *Range Management* (3rd edn.), McGraw-Hill, New York.

Sudan, Ministry of Agriculture and National Council for Research (1976). *Sudan's Desert Encroachment Control Rehabilitation Programme*.

Swift, Jeremy (1975). 'Pastoral nomadism as a form of land use: the Twareg of the Adrar n Iforas', in Monod (ed.), 1975, pp. 443–454.

Swift, Jeremy (1979). 'The economics of traditional pastoralism: the Twareg of the Adrar n Iforas (Mali)', Ph.D. Thesis, University of Sussex.

Tanaka, J. and Sato, S. (1976). 'The Rendille and the ecology of camels', in Lewis, J. (ed.), 'Man and the environment in Marsabit District', proceedings of a meeting at Mt. Kulal, December 1976. Mimeo.

Tanganyika Veterinary Department. *Annual Reports of the Department of Veterinary Science and Animal Husbandry* (and of successor organizations), for 1924, 1929, 1930. Government Printer, Dar-es-Salaam.

Tanzania Livestock Conference (1974). 'Proceedings of the Senior Livestock Development Officers' Conference', unpublished report.

Tapper, Richard (1979a). 'The organisation of nomadic communities in pastoral societies of the Middle East', in EEASP (eds.) 1979, pp. 43–65.

Tapper, Richard (1979b). 'Individuated grazing rights and social organisation among the Shahsevan nomads of Azerbaijan', in EEASP (eds.) 1977, pp. 95–114.

Tapper, Richard (1979c). *Pasture and Politics: Economics, Conflict and Ritual among the Shahsevan Nomads of North-Western Iran*, Academic Press, London.

Tatchell, R. J. (1974). 'Acaricide resistant ticks', in Tanzania Society of Animal Production (1974). *Proceedings of the First Scientific Conference*, p. 91.

Taylor, Ellen, and Moore, Cynthia (1980). 'Paraprofessionals in rural development: reality and potential', *Rural Development Participation Review*, **11** (1), Cornell University, Ithaca, New York.

Tendler, Judith (1976). *Inter Country Evaluation of Small Farmer Organisation*, US-AID, Washington.

Texas, A. and M. University (1976). 'Tanzania — livestock meat subsector', unpublished report.

Theron, E. P., and Venter, A. D. (1978). 'Methods and techniques for the replacement of native grasslands in South Africa by low cost techniques', in Hyder (ed.), 1978, pp. 620–622.

Thornton, R. F., and Yates, N. G. (1968). 'Some effects of water restriction on apparent digestability and water excretion of cattle', *Australian Journal of Agricultural Research*, **19**, 665–672.

Thuraisingham, S. (1978). 'Planning of veterinary manpower and education with special reference to developing countries', working paper for 4th FAO/WHO Consultation on Veterinary Education.

Torry, William I. (1974). 'Life in the camel's shadow', *Natural History Magazine*, **1974** (May), 60–68.

Torry, William I. (1977). 'Labour requirements among the Gabbra', unpublished paper.

Tursunbayev, A. and Potapov, A. (1959). 'Some aspects of the socio-economic and cultural development of nomads in the USSR', *International Social Science Journal*, **XI** (4), Part I, 511–524.

UNCOD (United Nations Conference on Desertification) (1977a). *Desertification — an Overview*, Conference Document A/Conf. 74/1.

UNCOD (1977b). *Plan of Action to Combat Desertification*, Conference Document A/Conf. 74/3.

UNCOD (1977c). *Ecological Change and Desertification*, Conference Document A/Conf. 74/7.

UNCOD (1977d). *Population, Society and Desertification*, Conference Document A/Conf. 74/8.

UNCOD (1977e). *Tame the Wind, Harness the Sand and Transform the Gobi*, conference document A/Conf. 74/16.

UNCOD (1977f). *Control the Desert and Create Pastures*, conference document A/Conf. 74/17.

UNCOD (1977g). *Combating Desertification in China*, conference document A/Conf. 74/18.

UNCOD (1977h). *USSR: Integrated Desert Development and Desertification Control in the Turkmenian SSR*, conference document A/Conf. 7/22.

UNDP/FAO (1971). 'Range development in Marsabit District', UN/FAO AGP SF/ KEN 11. Working Paper 9. Mimeo.

UNESCO/UNEP/FAO (1979). *Tropical Grazing Land Ecosystems: A State of Knowledge Report*, UNESCO, Paris.

Unger, Jonathan (1978). 'Collective incentives in the Chinese countryside: lessons from Chen village', *World Development*, **6**, 583–601.

Uphoff, Norman T., and Esman, Milton J. (1974). *Local Organisation for Rural Development: Analysis of Asian Experience*, Cornell University (Rural Development Committee — RLG 19), Ithaca, New York.

US-AID (Agency for International Development) (1976), 'Report of the Second Maasai Livestock and Range Management Project evaluation', unpublished report.

Valenza, Jean (1973). 'The natural pasturelands of the sylvopastoral zone of the Senegal Sahel twenty years after their development', in ILCA (1975), pp. 191–193.

Van Raay, H. G. T. (1975). *Rural Planning in a Savannah Region*, University Press, Rotterdam.

Ward, K. W. (1979). 'Livestock marketing and supplementary feeding in time of drought', in Hinchey (ed.), 1979, pp. 240–247.

Wardle, Christopher (1978). 'Promoting cattle fattening among peasants in Niger', *ODI Pastoral Network Paper*, 8c.

Watson, R. M., Tippett, C. I., and Tippett, M. J. (1973). 'Aerial livestock and land use surveys of the Giggiga area of Ethiopia, IV, January 1973 and final report', unpublished report.

Watson, R. M., Tippett, C. I., Allan, T., Tippett, M. J. and Watts, T. A. D. (1974). 'Aerial livestock and land-use surveys of the north east rangelands of Ethiopia: IV: August 1974: an extended survey area', unpublished report.

Weissleden, Wolfgang (ed.) (1978). *The Nomadic Alternative*, Mouton, The Hague.

West, G. P. (ed.) (1973). *A History of the Overseas Veterinary Service* (Part Two), British Veterinary Association, London.

Western, David (1973). 'The structure, dynamics and changes of the Amboseli ecosystem', Ph.D. Thesis, University of Nairobi.

Western, David (1974). 'The environment and ecology of pastoralists in arid savannahs', unpublished paper.

White, J. M., and Meadows, S. J. (1980). 'The potential supply of immatures over the nineteen-eighties from Kenya's northern rangelands', unpublished report.

White, J. M., and Meadows, S. J. (1981). 'Evaluation of the contribution of group and individual ranches in Kajiado District to economic and social development', unpublished report.

Whyte, Robert Orr (1974). *Tropical Grazing Lands: Communities and Constituent Species*, Dr. W. Junk, The Hague.

Willett, A. B. J. (1981). *Agricultural Group Development in Botswana*, Ministry of Agriculture, Gaborone.

Williams, O. B., Suijdendorp, H., and Wilcox, D. G. (1977). *Gascoyne Basin* (a case study presented by the Australian Government to the United Nations Conference on Desertification).

Wilson, A. D. (1970). 'Water economy and feed intake of sheep when watered intermittently', *Australian Journal of Agricultural Research*, **21**, 273–281.

Wilson, A. D. (1977). 'Grazing management in the arid areas of Australia', in Australian Rangelands Society, 1977.

WMO (World Meteorological Organization) (1975). *Drought*, Special Environmental Report No. 5, Geneva.

Wright, Henry A. (1978). 'Use of fire to manage grasslands of the central and southern Great Plains', in Hyder (ed.), 1978, pp. 694–696.

Young, M. D. (1979). 'Influencing land use in pastoral Australia', *Journal of Arid Environments*, **2**, 279–288.

Zghal, Abdelkader (1967). *Modernisation de l'Agriculture et Populations Semi-Nomades*, Mouton, The Hague.

Index

312